Thomas Merton, OCSO

In the Valley of Wormwood

Cistercian Blessed and Saints of the Golden Age

D1595616

CISTERCIAN STUDIES SERIES: NUMBER TWO HUNDRED THIRTY-THREE

Thomas Merton, OCSO

In the Valley of Wormwood

Cistercian Blessed and
Saints of the Golden Age

Edited with an Introduction by
Patrick Hart, OCSO

Foreword by
Brian Patrick McGuire

Cistercian Publications
www.cistercianpublications.org

LITURGICAL PRESS
Collegeville, Minnesota
www.litpress.org

A Cistercian Publications title published by Liturgical Press

BX
3455
.M47
2013

Cistercian Publications
Editorial Offices
Abbey of Gethsemani
3642 Monks Road
Trappist, Kentucky 40051
www.cistercianpublications.org

1   2   3   4   5   6   7   8   9

Library of Congress Cataloging-in-Publication Data

Merton, Thomas, 1915–1968
    In the Valley of Wormwood : Cistercian blessed and saints of the golden age / by Thomas Merton, OCSO ; edited with an introduction by Patrick Hart, OCSO.
        pages   cm. — (Cistercian studies series ; no. 233)
    ISBN 978-0-87907-133-2 — ISBN 978-0-87907-758-7 (ebook)
    1. Cistercians—Biography. 2. Trappists—Biography. 3. Christian saints—Biography. 4. Blessed—Biography. I. Hart, Patrick. II. Title.

BX3455.M47   2013
271'.12022—dc23
[B]
                                                                    2013015121

Contents

February

March

April

May

June

July

August

September

October

November

December

Foreword

For anyone interested in Thomas Merton's inner life as monk of Gethsemani in the 1940s, this collection of biographies of Cistercian holy men and women is a welcome publication. In 1986, when I first visited Gethsemani, I noticed a number of typescript collections of Merton's unpublished works. I wondered what their fate would be, and it is good to know that most of them by now have become available to the world outside of Gethsemani.

In the Valley of Wormwood, however, provides more than insight into Merton. These brief biographies, in the tradition of hagiography or saints' lives, are a welcome alternative to the oft-told institutional history of the Cistercians. Merton wanted to get to know the people who had created what he called "the golden age" of Cistercian life, and so he dug carefully through the difficult and confusing tomes of the *Patrologia Latina* and the *Acta Sanctorum*, together with the supplementary information that he could find within the Order itself. His bibliography shows that he read everything he could get his hands on, and certainly the quiet atmosphere of an old-fashioned Trappist monastery must have been conducive to such intellectual labor. Provided, of course, that the abbot was interested in allotting time to such a pursuit. Merton was fortunate to have such an abbot, Frederic Dunne.

What do I, as a medieval historian, discover when I read through these lives? I find Merton's attention to describing and defining the Cistercian way of life not something that one would expect from a Trappist in the pre–Vatican II world of the 1940s. Merton was attracted to asceticism of Gethsemani, but he wanted to add his own appreciation of literature and to make his own literature. In finding his way into the early Cistercian sources, he contributed to the return to the sources that came to characterize the Trappist-Cistercian renewal of the 1960s and 1970s. As in so much else in his all-too-brief life, Merton was prescient: he saw that his monastery and its Order needed to know more about the people who had preceded the seventeenth-century La Trappe. Merton wanted to return to the great beginning, the *Exordium*, of the Cistercians before they became Trappists.

It was not easy. In his own preface to this collection, Merton claims that the *Exordium Magnum* of the Order "deals only with the monks of two of our old monasteries." The *Exordium*'s stories, collected around 1200 by Conrad of Eberbach, in fact, deal with many Cistercian monasteries, but Merton was handicapped by the incomplete text he found in the *Patrologia Latina*. He would have had to wait for the 1962 critical edition by Bruno Griesser, but by then he had other concerns. It is only recently that Cistercian Publications has issued a superb English translation of *The Great Beginning of Cîteaux*, which makes available to a broader public what Merton could find only in Latin.

The fact that this collection of Merton's biographies of the Cistercian blessed and saints contains small faults and imperfections does not diminish its validity as a witness to Merton's perception of Cistercian life and spirituality in its beginnings and early development. Merton shares with his sources a Cistercian love of story: for example, his telling of blessed Amadeus "the Elder" who used to clean the monastery sewer even in summer when in the heat of noonday he "armed himself with a shovel and attacked this grim task under the burning sun and clouds of flies"—one can imagine the stench; and of Saint Guerin leaving the monastery of Aulps behind, but then hearing its bells "begin to ring of their own accord." Merton is skeptical, for Saint Guerin was several miles from the monastery, but the modern author believe in miracles, just as his saints did.

Merton's sketches will initiate discussion on the question of what Cistercian sainthood involves. He conceded that the Order had not been particularly interested in its holy people, and today one might ask if Merton himself, who is probably the best-known Cistercian of the twentieth century, was a saint. Or the brothers of Atlas in Algeria: Can they be called martyrs? Would they have wanted such a title?

Fortunately, one can read these sketches without answering such questions. Merton opened the door for a new understanding of Cistercian life and spirituality. We can follow him into an attractive but difficult world, a world where few persevere but that inspires many of us watching from the outside and moves us to prayer.

Brian Patrick McGuire
Kalundborg, Denmark
First Sunday of Advent, 2012

Introduction

These monastic sketches of the Cistercian Blessed and Saints were written by a relatively unknown Trappist monk, Frater Louis, in the mid-1940s at the Abbey of Gethsemani, situated in the knob country of Kentucky. Although first published anonymously, they can now safely be attributed to a youthful Thomas Merton.

Shortly after Merton's entrance into the monastery in December 1941, Abbot Frederic Dunne, the first American monk to persevere at the Abbey of Gethsemani, encouraged Frater Louis to make the Cistercians better known in the new world. With his considerable literary gifts, Frater M. Louis Merton set out to do so by writing his own Cistercian Menology of the blessed and the saints of the twelfth and early thirteenth centuries. The text reflects the enthusiasm and fervor of early Cîteaux, then a new charism of the church which would quickly spread throughout the world, east and west, north and south.

It should be remembered that Abbot Frederic Dunne came from a family of book printers and binders in Ohio and was predisposed to appreciate the linguistic abilities and literary gifts that Frater Louis brought with him from his studies at Cambridge in England and Columbia in New York. Once Merton's master's thesis, titled *Nature and Art in William Blake*, was completed, he embarked on the research for his doctoral dissertation about the poetry of Gerard Manley Hopkins. His notebooks are still a part of the Merton Collection at Saint Bonaventure's University, Olean, New York, where Merton taught English literature before entering the Abbey of Gethsemani on December 10, 1941, beginning his novitiate a few days later on the Feast of Saint Lucy.

Merton supplemented his primary source, Migne's *Patrologia Latina*, with the biographies collected in the *Acta Sanctorum*. In a few instances there was a pamphlet or short book in French, Italian, or Spanish written by a contemporary of the blessed or saint in question. Looking back on this early monastic work, one can see that his writing of the saints' lives using the best available sources was something of an exercise to prepare Merton for reaching out to a much wider audience with the publication in 1948 of his autobiography *The Seven Storey Mountain*, which became an unexpected national bestseller.

I would like to mention that Frater Francis de Sales Fischer, OCSO, who had typed the manuscript in 1954, left Gethsemani for the diocesan priesthood in various US dioceses prior to his death a few years ago. I wrote to him about this particular manuscript asking if he had actually edited the work; he responded modestly that he had only been a typist of the sketches which were based on Thomas Merton's own research. In any case, we should acknowledge our gratitude to Fr. Francis de Sales for the countless hours he spent in typing these early monastic sketches on ditto-graph stencils and arranging for their inexpensive printing and binding at Gethsemani. Copies were circulated to the various English-speaking Cistercian monasteries, but at this date there are only two or three extant copies.

As I was editing this work for current publication, my confrere Chrysogonus Waddell, OCSO, confided to me that Thomas Merton had originally titled this work *In the Valley of Wormwood*. We have decided to use this title because it reflected something of the bitter and unpleasant character of the lives of these early Cistercian blessed and saints of the twelfth and thirteenth centuries.

It has taken several years to complete this project for book publication. We began publishing some of the better-known blessed and saints serially in the monastic journal *Cistercian Studies Quarterly* during the past decade, ending with Blessed Eugenius III, Abbot of Tre Fontane and later Pope.[1]

---

[1] Thomas Merton, "Blessed Eugenius III, Abbot of Tre Fontane, Pope," ed. Patrick Hart CSQ 44 (2009): 173–80.

We want to express our thanks to the Merton Legacy Trust for allowing the serial publication of many of these blessed and saints and now for permission to publish the work in book form. Since it is of historical interest to the monastic world, it is being published in the Cistercian Studies Series by Cistercian Publications, formerly of Western Michigan University, Kalamazoo, Michigan, but currently an imprint of Liturgical Press of Saint John's Abbey, Collegeville, Minnesota. We are grateful to all who have cooperated in the long-awaited publication of this manuscript written by the very young monk Thomas Merton less than a decade before his phenomenal autobiography would see the light of day.[2]

Patrick Hart, OCSO
Abbey of Gethsemani

---

[2] ["Thanks are due, not least, to Br. Patrick Hart himself, assisted by Br. Gabriel Lumpkin, for transcribing these lives into electronic form from Fr. Francis de Sales's dittograph originals. It was a time-consuming and eye-straining act of dedication to Thomas Merton and his legacy for which all readers can be grateful."—Exec. ed., Cistercian Publications.]

Preface

Far be it from a Trappist to waste words! But perhaps a word of explanation is required, both as to the aim of this work and of its limitations. First of all, it may surprise many readers to know that, with the exception of one very inadequate collection, long out of print, there exists no modern book, either in English or any other language, about so important a subject as the saints of the Cistercian Order. Indeed, apart from Saint Bernard of Clairvaux and his family, the saints of our Order—one of the strictest contemplative Orders in the Church—have rarely even found individual biographers. As a result, neither the Cistercian monks and nuns of our own day, nor the Catholic student, nor the general reader (whether in England, Ireland, America, France, Spain, Germany, or anywhere else) has any means of entering into contact with the rich traditions of the Cistercian past, unless he or she cares to plough through the rare and almost inaccessible volumes of the seventeenth-century historians Manrique and Henriquez, with their flowery Latin and somewhat sanguine exaggerations. True, those familiar with German may find a dozen or more good biographies in the *Cistercian Chronik*, and, of course, the old *Exordium Magnum*—which is, to our Order, what the *Fioretti* is to that of the Friars Minor—has been translated into French. But even then, the *Exordium* deals only with the monks of two of our old monasteries. As for the Bollandists, there indeed we have an admirable and complete collection of biographies of great Cistercians, often written in the most beautiful medieval Latin, and it is from this source that the present book is mostly drawn. But it is quite obvious that the average Christian, and even the average monk, would not find much facility in reading these originals, even assuming he had access to so expensive a work as the *Acta Sanctorum*, which is far beyond the budgets of most of our monastic libraries.

And yet, consider who the Cistercians are and what they stand for and have always stood for in the Church, and it will be easy to see how necessary it is that the lives of the saints who have embodied and actually lived the Cistercian ideal to its full extent should be added to the chronicles of Christian sanctity.

The name Cistercian naturally suggests, to the mind of the English-speaking reader, the great old abbeys of Yorkshire and Scotland and Ireland, whose ruins speak even today of the past glory of an Order given entirely to penance, prayer, silence, and contemplation, together with manual labor in the fields and forests, and, above all, to the chanting of the praises of God, day and night, without ceasing, through the slow and majestic procession of all the canonical hours and all the liturgical seasons of the Catholic Church.

Protestants and pagans have been unable to resist the appeal made by these ancient ruins to their minds and imaginations and wills, and it was the Cistercian Abbey of Tintern, in its lonely wooded valley, that awakened strange, unidentifiable religious longings in the soul of William Wordsworth, which resulted in a famous, half-mystical, semipantheistic poem: a poem that, whatever its failings, proves how strongly even the long-abandoned ruins of our ancient abbeys have had power to raise the minds of men—if not actually to the God of Christians then at least to beyond the natural order and to some principle of being and goodness and love, transcending our littleness and imperfection. (Its full title is "Lines above Tintern Abbey.")

In the modern world, the name Cistercian may be more of a mystery to us. How many people know that there are Cistercian monks in the Church today? The answer is easy: everybody does. Everybody knows the Cistercians, and yet they do not realize they know them because they have heard of them under another name. The largest and most representative modern family of Cistercians is that Order commonly known as the Trappists—the very name of which sends a cold shiver down the spine of unregenerate nature's self-love. It stands for everything our comfort and pleasure-loving nature shrinks from. It suggests perpetual silence, perpetual abstinence, long and very black fasts, a hard bed of boards, chanting office at two o'clock in the morning, taking the discipline, and breaking one's back in the long hours of rough manual labor. In fact, together with the Carthusians and the Camaldolese, the Trappists are the only religious family of men, of any size and extent in the modern Church, devoted exclusively and uncompromisingly to the contemplative life of prayer and penance.

This has always been the Cistercian ideal. "If you want to enter Clairvaux," Saint Bernard told the postulants who presented themselves there, "only your soul can come in: you must leave your body at the door." The Cistercian lives for God alone. He has given up, or rather he professes to give up, and sincerely strives to give up, all attachments to anything that is not God. He renounces every joy in creatures, not because he hates creatures, or has a grudge against them, or hates life itself, but precisely because he sees how good all these things are, because he really loves life and wants it more abundantly, as Christ has promised it to all who follow him. For the Cistercian knows, by faith, that by giving up all things he gets them all back most perfectly in God. For by renouncing all the things that we cannot really possess, and possessing God, who alone is the life of our souls and the goodness of all that is good, we regain all that we seem to have lost and possess all things most perfectly in him who made them.

Ultimately, of course, this has been the ideal of all the saints. But there is a particular character to the sanctity of every religious family and that of the Cistercians is too great a treasure to be kept in hiding any longer.

In this book, then, we shall attempt to introduce the modern English reader to a group of saints who are most remarkable for their simplicity, their joy, and their childlike love of God and of one another. All these things inevitably follow from the Cistercian ideal of absolute renunciation of all for God; for it is only in this renunciation that we become like little children. The Rule of Saint Benedict, as interpreted by the fathers of Cîteaux, carries out a most thorough stripping of all self-love and self-will, thereby liberating us, chiefly through obedience, from all of our passions and rebellious appetites that imprison us in the darkness and misery of our own pride. And when the soul of a person emerges from this prison of self-love (which the misguided world conceives to be the only true freedom!), it necessarily begins to taste a totally new and most perfect joy: the joy of simple and childlike dependence on God, through his representatives—that is, our superiors and even our brethren—a dependence that puts us and keeps us in contact with the very source of all joy, the Incarnate Word, *Jesus.*

There is rarely a Cistercian saint, then, who is not characterized by a deep and childlike joyousness, although that may often occur in startling and paradoxical contrast with the most frightful bodily austerities, as we see in the case of Blessed Arnulph, the holy laybrother of Villers, who was indeed a fierce champion of asceticism! Yet on the whole, extraordinary austerities are not typical of Cistercian sanctity. They all followed the regular Rule, and most fervently; they even added a little to it here and there, with the blessing of obedience, but on the whole we find that the great Cistercians were all sanctified precisely by their submission to the Rule and their glad immersion of themselves in the deepest depths of obscurity and the common life of the monastery. Indeed, it is this complete immersion into the common life, this abandonment of self to the Rule and the common way of all the brethren, that is most characteristic of Cistercian sanctity: for of all cenobites, Cistercians are always together and always do everything in common. And it is necessary, then, that one of the firstfruits of such a life should be a deep and warm and strong fraternal charity—either that or the life becomes intolerable. Fortunately, God's grace is there to overcome our churlish natures, and the Cistercian monasteries have always been what Saint Bernard desired them to be: schools of charity—they have always been so, that is, as long as they kept the Rule.

The present volume, then, is an introduction to this vast field of sanctity. It is only an introduction, however, only a beginning. These are not, by any means, all the Cistercian saints and blessed. There are many others. But the most important ones are here, and the most interesting. For others, like Saint Robert of Mataplan, about whom practically nothing is known, together with some who are not strictly of our Order (such as Saint Boniface of Lausanne and

Saint Famian), we refer readers to the Cistercian Menology, of which a new edition has been printed.

One thing, however, about our saints. A few, such as Saint Bernard, Saint Gertrude the Great, and Saint Hedwig, are on the Roman calendar for the whole Church. But the great majority are by no means so well known. Indeed, many of them have even been forgotten in our own Order. And it may be said that all of our saints, as a whole, are grossly neglected even in the Cistercian Breviary. Most of them who do have feasts suffered drastic curtailments when the Breviary was revised in the nineteenth century. All this is one more reason for a book like this one. But why have so many and such great saints been apparently forgotten? The chief reason is this: the Cistercian Order as a whole never showed much interest in promoting canonizations or extending the cults of its saintly members. It is even believed, though falsely, that the general chapter once forbade canonizations altogether because there were "too many." It was always left to the individual monasteries to promote the cult of their holy members, and almost everywhere, as soon as they found that the concourse of pilgrims disturbed the monastic peace, the various abbots did everything they could to discourage the cult of the saints. *Ama nesciri* ("love to be unknown") has always been one of the chief Cistercian ideals, and that applies to both life and death. It is one of the instruments of good works in the Rule of Saint Benedict that one should not want to be called a saint. He adds, of course, *antequam sit*, "before he is one." But after all, by the time one is confirmed in sanctity, he is in heaven and no longer affected by whether or not people call him a saint or a sinner.

Consequently, most of our saints were strictly local to a region or nation, and their cult depended on the monastery church that was their shrine. With the destruction of so many of our abbeys by the reformation in England, Germany, and elsewhere, and by the French Revolution later on, the cults of many of our saints and blessed dwindled and were even forgotten. But in many places they survive in villages or parishes that remain where the monastery once was, like Saint Aymon in the village of Savigny, or Blessed Alexander of Scotland, or Saint Asceline. Others, while having a more important regional cult, are still unknown outside their own nation, such as Blessed Ida of Louvain, who is one of the patrons of Belgium but is not widely known in the United States, along with Saint Malachy in Ireland, Saint Peter of Tarentaise in the Alps, Saint Amadeus in Switzerland, and so on. Not all the saints of the Order are included in this volume—a fact that should be clear enough. The "golden age" can be said to cover the first century of Cistercian history. There have been others since then, a few of whom have had their sanctity officially recognized by Rome in one way or another. But nevertheless the golden age was the time of our greatest saints.

Yet not even all of these are included in the present volume. We have certainly striven to present the reader with the lives of those saints who were most truly saints and most characteristically Cistercian. And for that reason we have omitted one or two about whom nothing is known or who, even if they do happen to be known to us, spent most of their lives as hermits and only came into the Order temporarily, like Saint Famian, or on their deathbeds like Saint Galgan. These are certainly holy men, but their biographies teach us little or nothing about the Cistercian life, the Order, or its spirituality. And the same applies to Saint Boniface, the retired bishop of Lausanne, who became the confessor to our nuns at La Cambre, and may or may not have taken the habit of the Order.

If, on the other hand, we have included Saint Malachy, who was no more a member of the Order than Saint Edmund of Canterbury, or Saint Thomas a Becket, it is because of his part in the foundation of the first Cistercian abbey in Ireland and because of his relations with Clairvaux and Saint Bernard as well as out of deference to our Irish and other English-speaking readers.

As may be seen from the list of sources printed with the notes to each individual life, we have tried as much as possible to go back to the fountainhead of information—to the twelfth- and thirteenth-century biographies reprinted in the *Acta Sanctorum*. Most of these lives were written by monks of our Order, and some (though not all by any means) are of a rather high literary quality. The best of them breathe all the simple and delightful fragrance of medieval Cistercian spirituality, and even those that are mere rough sketches, a few garbled notes and a miracle or two, have a kind of ingenuous charm. Not all the sources are of equally reliable authority. Nevertheless, the best of them—Thomas of Cantimpre; William of Saint Thierry; Saint Bernard's secretary, Geoffrey, who wrote on his master and later on Saint Peter of Tarentaise—these are unimpeachable. Nor is there much reason to doubt the authenticity of most of the details on our mystics of the Low Countries, most of which were furnished by their spiritual directors. One of them, indeed, Beatrice of Nazareth, wrote her autobiography, which is our source. Saint Ailred, too, had an exceptionally good biographer in his disciple Walter Daniel—who was careful to substantiate most of his facts and, for the most part, was setting down only what he had seen with his own eyes.

It is when the sole sources are available years after their subject lived that we have reason to be a little reserved in our acceptance of the stories. The first real wave of enthusiasm over the Cistercian saints did not sweep through the Order until the seventeenth century, when there was a kind of a general revival of vitality in the Order at large, besides those special centers like La Trappe and Clairvaux where genuine reforms were instituted.

Among the Cistercians of the Common Observance, this revival of life took the form of an intensified interest in the past of the Order and its history and traditions and sanctity. The Cistercians of Spain, who belonged to a reform of their own rather than to the Common Observance properly so called, were most active in this work of research and produced several monumental works, the greatest of which is Manrique's *Annales Cistercienses*. There is no question that this is a truly great work and that it is generally accepted as thoroughly reliable, except that no modern historian will accept every detail without reserve. However, Chrysostom Henriques, the greatest Cistercian hagiographer and the compiler of the old Cistercian Menology, was altogether too uncritical in his acceptance of any story that redounded to the credit of the Order or its saints. And he was certainly too sanguine in his generous wholesale distribution of the titles of saints and blessed. This has been sufficiently proven by the careful and erudite research of the present commission for the revision of the Menology, headed by Fr. M. Seraphin Lenssen, OCR. Instead of the hosts of saints and blessed who appear on every page of the old Menology—even though some of them have nothing to show for their sanctity except the dubious distinction of never having touched a drop of beer—the new Menology has sifted them down to the point of ruthlessness. But at last we can be satisfied that the results are somewhat nearer to the truth.

The new Menology lists thirty-eight who have a right to the title of saint, but since that number includes several who did not belong to our Order, like Thomas a Becket and Edmund of Canterbury, it would be safer to say that there are thirty-three members of our Order who are entitled to the name of saint in the eyes of the Church. Added to these are twenty official blessed, of whom one is Blessed Humbeline, Saint Bernard's sister, who was a Benedictine nun. Two of these, the Justamont Sisters, were Cistercian nuns of the Common Observance, martyred at Orange in the French Revolution. Finally, there are 124 others who, by virtue of an immemorial cult, can claim to be called blessed in a sense permitted by the Church, although without any official guarantee of their sanctity formally pronounced by her. If we add to this number the Venerable Veronica Laparelli, a nun of the Common Observance whose cause was introduced in the eighteenth century but subsequently abandoned, we arrive at the grand total of 177 publically recognized saints or blessed in the Cistercian Order. One more still may be added to this number from the fact that the diocesan process of the Trappist monk Fr. M. Joseph Cassant, who died in our own century, was completed in 1935 and the documents were forwarded to Rome.[1]

This, then, is the family of saints, and a truly great family it is, that we here present to readers for their study and imitation. Saints have been distributed throughout the volume according to the date on which their names are commemorated, either on the Cistercian liturgical calendar or at least in the Menology. As far as feasts are concerned, most of them seem to have fared better with

---

[1] Joseph Cassant was beatified by Pope John Paul II on October 3, 2004.

the various congregations of the Common Observance than with the Trappist or Cistercians of the Strict Observations; we still fail to include in our breviary any office for Saint Gertrude, although she is on the calendar of the universal Church for November 16. However, this change has already been voted by the General Chapter and only awaits a new edition of the Breviary—one that, it is hoped, will also include the long-delayed feast of the King of All Saints on the last Sunday of October. It is to him, then to Christ the King, *Christo vero Regi*, under whose banner all these holy Cistercians fought in their mortal lives, that this book is offered. They belonged to him, his love, his mercy shone forth in lives. He worked, lived, and praised his Father in them and made their light shine before humanity that we might glorify the Name of his Father and ours, who is in heaven. He lived and breathed and praised God in them, in order to show us that he also desires to do the same in us, if we will surrender our souls completely to the reign of his wisdom and love, if we, moved by the example of such simple generosity on the part of his Cistercian sons and daughters, will also, like them, give him our hearts.

It has not been one of the aims of this book to enter into the detail of immemorial cult, local canonization, canonization *per modum favoris*, and all the hagiological technicalities underlying the titles of saint or blessed applied to those whose biographies are here presented. Suffice it to say that we have followed the new Cistercian Menology, or other reliable authorities in this matter. Henriquez and the old Menology give the title of blessed to almost everyone in their pages, but we have been cautious enough not to follow their example.

It is our prayer to God, through the Queen of Heaven and glorious protectress and advocate of the Cistercian Order, the first religious Order to be dedicated to her, that this book may do something to nourish and foster that holy and fervent spirit in all our monasteries and in the hearts of the faithful all over the world.

T. M.
Abbey of Our Lady of Gethsemani
August 21, 1954

Abbreviations

Ann Cist	Ángel Manrique, *Cisterciensium seu verius Ecclesis-ticorum Annalium a condito Cistercio* (Lyon, 1642–59)
AASS	*Acta Sanctorum* (Antwerp, Paris, Brussels, 1643–)
Butler-Thurston	Alban Butler, *Butler's Lives of the Saints*, ed. Herbert J. Thurston (New York: Kennedy, 1956)
Chron Vill	*Chronicle of Villers*
Cist Chronik	*Cistercienser Chronik*
Coll	*Collectanea O.C.R. / Collectanea cisterciensia*
CSQ	*Cistercian Studies Quarterly*
DM	Caesar of Heisterbach, *Dialogus Miracolorum*
EM	Conrad of Eberbach, *Exordium magnum cisterciense*
Ep/Epp	Letter/s
EP	*Exordium Parvum*
Menologium	Crisóstomo Henríquez [Merton spells it *Henriques*], *Menologium Cisterciense* (Antwerp, 1630; Westmalle, 1952)
PL	J.-P. Migne, *Patrologia Latina*
SC	Bernard of Clairvaux, *Sermons on the Song of Songs*
V Mal	Bernard of Clairvaux, *Vita sancti Malachiae episcopi*
Vita Bern	William of Saint Thierry, *Sancti Bernardi vita prima*

January

January 10

Blessed William, first Abbot of Aiguebelle, near Valence, France

(Source: Hugues, 42–115.)

In the Collect of the Mass for Saint Benedict's Feast, the monks of his monastic family pray to God with these words, "Awaken, O Lord, in Thy Church, the Spirit which Blessed Benedict, Abbot, once served that we, being filled with the same Spirit, may study how to love what he loved, and carry out in our works, what he taught."

The life of Blessed William of Aiguebelle, and of all the holy monks and brothers and nuns in this book, is an expression of the many forms taken by God's answer to this prayer in the old days when the Cistercian Order was at the height of its fervor. And yet, of Blessed William's inner life we know nothing. His personality has come down to us only in the visible product of his energy and vigorous spirituality, the Abbey of Aiguebelle, in Provence, which celebrated its eighteenth centennial in 1937. For the Cistercian life is just as vigorous at Aiguebelle today as it was in the twelfth century.

Aiguebelle, as it stands today, is a monument to Blessed William, and in a sense his portrait. The simple and austere church, chapter, cloisters, refectory all date from his time and were built by his monks under his direction. They are bare, undecorated, severe, firm, strong; but they are the abode of peace and joy. The sunny arches and the stones of the cloister are saturated with eight centuries of monastic peace and happiness. By them we know that a community of fervent monks is an image of Paradise.

3

How did this monastery come into being? From AD 1130 to 1138 the Church was torn by the schism of Peter de Leone, and order and peace and unity were restored, largely through the efforts of the great Cistercian abbot, Saint Bernard of Clairvaux. He traveled tirelessly from one end of Europe to the other, preaching, treating with princes and bishops, working miracles, converting souls. But there was one weapon against the enemies of God in society that did more than the influence of one great man, ever so great a saint, could ever hope to accomplish. In those eight years, one hundred thirty-eight new monasteries of the Cistercian Order were founded in different parts of Europe, but especially in the countries where Bernard had traveled.

Yet the monks in these monasteries did not go out to preach. They did not conduct schools, or write books—except for an occasional volume of mystical sermons or the life of some saintly abbot. They did not even talk. They fled from the habitations of men and built their monasteries in wild valleys or marshes or deep forests where no one else cared to go. They devoted their lives to chanting the praises of God, working with their hands to wrest a living from the hard earth, and meditating on the Holy Scriptures and the Fathers of the Church.

And these poor, obscure monks, who had fled from human society, exercised so powerful a spiritual and social influence over the Europe of their time that they practically dominated the twelfth century. It was a Cistercian age, and the number of souls that were brought back to a true Christian sense to a life of faith, of holiness and even high sanctity by their influence and example, is beyond our estimation.

But let us see what part Blessed William had in all of this. In the year 1137 Saint Bernard told the abbot of Morimond, Blessed Otto of Freisinger, that a new foundation had been asked for in Provence, and that Clairvaux could not afford to send any more monks, being practically exhausted by her many foundations in those years.[1] Otto therefore consented to send a colony from

---

[1] Clairvaux had founded twenty-five monasteries in twenty years, and eighteen had been founded between 1130 and 1137.

Morimond (the fourth daughter-house of Cîteaux, and the mother-house of the whole Order) which had been less severely taxed.

In all this an obscure and humble and zealous monk called William was probably not consulted at all. But one morning in 1137 at Morimond, William and twelve other monks found themselves exchanging blessings and the kiss of fraternal peace, not without a few tears, perhaps, with the brethren whom they would never see again until they met in heaven before the throne of their King, Christ, in whose vineyard there was now work to be done. And before the sun was well above the horizon they were on their way south through the fields of Burgundy.

Their destination was in the far south, Provence, near Avignon. They were to occupy an ancient Benedictine house that was now falling into ruins, or ready to do so. It was a beautiful place for contemplation. High on a hill, it commanded a wonderful view in all directions, sweeping from the snowy peak of Mount Ventoux, to the east, and then over the plain of Grignan, with the old cathedral town of Saint Paul in the distance, and finally, in the west, to the silver ribbon of the Rhone. And yet, this beautiful site was not for White Monks. There is a verse which runs:

> *Bernardus valles, colles Benedictus amabat:*
> *Franciscus vicos, magnas Dominicus urbes.*

Bernard loved valleys, Benedict the hills, Francis loved towns, and Dominic populated the cities. And Saint Bernard had often been very insistent that his monks, occupying some old Benedictine monastery on a hill, should speedily find a humbler situation in some valley. Witness his suggestions at Hautecombe.[2] The Cistercians usually looked for valleys and marshy, uncultivated places for their monasteries, to ensure solitude, and also in order that there might be plenty of water to run the mills and supply all the necessary shops which, according to the Rule, ought to be within the enclosure.

---

[2] See article on Saint Amadeus below (January 28).

William did not have far to look. The nearby valley of Derzas, with its three mountain torrents, and its steep rocky sides covered with thorns and brambles, was just the site to attract a Cistercian founder. It was not long before Derzas became Val-Honnets, and it is hard to express all that the new name implies of comeliness, order and peace.

Blessed William saw to it that everything was done strictly according to the Rule and Cistercian customs. He carried out to the letter Saint Stephen Harding's injunctions about strict simplicity and plainness in the church. No decorations, no paintings, no statues, no fancy woodcarving, no mosaics or designs on the floor or ceiling: nothing to attract the eye and arrest the attention or arouse the imagination to distract the mind from prayer. Curiously enough, however, the one trace of decoration that there is to be found is evidence of the holy abbot's zealous regularity. A delicately graceful acanthus leaf motif on the capital of one of the pillars in the sanctuary is only half finished. It is easy to guess what happened and to imagine the gentle, serious firmness with which Abbot William reminded some forgotten monkish sculptor to restrain his exuberance in the church. There was plenty of scope for it in the cloister, for there the ban was not so strict.

They soon built all the so-called "regular" places, which included everything from the church to the calefactory—a square stone chamber with a huge fireplace to thaw out the monks after a cold night in church. There four times a year, the monks were all bled for the sake of their health. Besides these buildings and apartments, the monks also erected a mill, tannery, and other shops along one of the streams and diverted another stream through the monastery to carry off the sewage. Meanwhile, the thorns and brambles gave place to orchards and gardens and pleasant pastures. Back in the hills they quarried lime and mined gypsum.

The old Bernard Abbey on the hill became a grange, occupied by lay brothers, but they were able to farm all the lands attached to it. Soon secular workers came in to help them, and the fields were thrown open to poor farmers and liberated serfs, all glad to escape the hard regime of their feudal landlords.

Far from having to pay rent to the monks, they even received every spiritual and material benefit over and above the privilege of farming the land. The monks saw to the health of their souls with the sacraments and all the advantages offered by a large monastery and gave them skilled medical treatment. They were probably admitted to the guesthouse of the abbey or one of the granges in time of sickness, for a Cistercian guesthouse was also a hospital.

Blessed William appointed procurators to govern the villages that grew up to accommodate these secular workers and often sat in judgment on their disputes himself. He was tireless in administering to all the needs of these people, whom he considered part of his own monastic family. Not only that, but he fought, all his life, for the rights of the tenants of the neighboring noblemen, and even in his old age he was frequently seen laboriously climbing the hills to one or other of their castles to ask justice for a tenant or mercy for some repentant criminal who had sought sanctuary in Aiguebelle. Other religious communities soon came under the influence of Aiguebelle. One Benedictine monastery, as well as a community of hermits, put themselves under the direction of Blessed William and instituted reforms. Meanwhile there was a great influx of vocations from all classes, nobles as well as peasants and serfs, and the local nobility was greatly influenced by the holy abbot and his monks.

They began to show a new concern for the rights of their subjects and to introduce legislation to prevent debauchery, immorality, violence and usury in the towns and villages under their control.

A great day in the early history of Aiguebelle was that on which Saint Bernard arrived to visit the abbey, founded at his instigation. During this visit, says an old legend, the saint himself miraculously contributed to the welfare of the region by ridding it of magpies. It appears that he was hearing Mass one day, and just at the elevation of the Sacred Host, lo, a magpie flew in the window and took the Host in its beak and flew out again. Bernard laid a curse on the magpie and all its brothers and sisters and even to this day there is not one to be seen anywhere near Aiguebelle, although they abound in neighboring districts. This dubious tale offers, in addition to its general incredibility, the added difficulty that in the time of Saint Bernard the Host was never elevated at the Consecration, at least in the Cistercian Order.

At this time, however, the saint set Blessed William to preach in Languedoc the Albigensian heresy and we know that the holy abbot was at the Abbey of Calers, in the diocese of Toulouse, in 1149. However, preaching against heresy was not the Cistercian vocation, and Blessed William soon returned to the peace of Aiguebelle and to the direction and sanctification of his monks. He lived until 1160 when, having died in the odor of sanctity, he was venerated by his monks as a saint. His name was invoked in the litany of saints in use at Aiguebelle down to the time of the French Revolution.

January 14

Saint Guerin, Bishop of Sion, Switzerland

(Sources: Saint Bernard, Epp 142 and 254; AASS, Jan. 1:347.)

Saint Guerin only receives a commemoration in the Cistercian Breviary, and little is known about his life except for the services he rendered to the Church as defender of her rights when he became bishop of the Swiss diocese of Sion, in the valley of the upper Rhone. History has left us no details of his achievements, although we have reliable information concerning the fact of his zeal and energy and sanctity. For the rest, legend lends a few embellishments to the picture, but the sanctity of Saint Guerin is of the kind that is attested more by a long and flourishing cult than by contemporary historical evidence. For centuries in the Alps of Chablais he has been invoked especially for the projection of the herds of cattle upon which the inhabitants of these mountain valleys depend for their livelihood.

Guerin was born at Pont a Mousson in Lorraine. One might place the date of his birth around 1075. He entered Molesme under Saint Robert but apparently after the exodus to Cîteaux. He seems to have had no connection with the initiators of the Cistercian reform. Yet he numbers among the many souls who were attracted to Molesme by the fame of Saint Robert and who were nevertheless not content with the state of the religious life as it was led there by the community at large.

Accordingly, Saint Guerin left Molesme and took the road to the high Alps of the Chablais, south of the lake of Geneva and in the diocese of that cathedral city. There he found, at Aulps, a few hermits living together in an Alpine valley, or else, having settled there himself, as a hermit, gathered them about him. The usual version of his story suggests that he found the hermits already there. It used to be maintained that he entered an already established semi-eremitical community at Aulps, of which he became the second abbot, but now it is generally agreed that he founded and was the first abbot of the monastery under the patronage of Hubert II of Savoy.[3]

In any case, it must be noticed that in leaving Molesme, he had not entirely severed his connection with that house, and the community of the hermits of Aulps was in some sense dependent upon Molesme. Since it was a monastery of the type of Colan, which had attracted Saint Robert from Saint Michel-de-Tonnerre—in other words since it was the type of community for which Saint Robert may be assumed to have had a special liking, since he twice retired to one—it is probable that the connection with Molesme was essentially spiritual, at least during the lifetime of Saint Robert.

The monks of Aulps professed to keep the Rule of Saint Benedict, but in spite of their austerity, mortification and spirit of prayer, to which Saint Bernard testifies (Ep. 142), they were even further from the Rule in many respects than the monks of Molesme. In common with their brethren at Molesme, they received ecclesiastical benefices and parishes, which meant not only that some of them occupied themselves, at least partially, with the external ministry, but what is more important, they had to be concerned

---

[3] These cells were one of the abuses of the Cluniac system. They housed one or two monks far from the abbey from which they were isolated not for the purpose of contemplation but in order to administer lands or parishes.

with affairs of a more or less temporal and economic character, and the spirit of poverty was bound to suffer.

Another defect of the community was that enclosure was not strictly observed. This evidently arose from the fact that the community had grown up in a somewhat haphazard fashion, and outside the central group of monks living around the abbot, there were various cells scattered through the woods, where two or three brethren lived together, more or less in obedience to the abbot, but without any really close connection with the rest of the community so that they escaped the close control necessary for the maintenance of regular discipline and inevitably tended to formulate rules and usages to suit themselves. Saint Bernard did not like this system at all, and he called these isolated cells "synagogues of Satan."

Another failure in the observance of enclosure arose from the fact that women were allowed more or less unhindered access to some of the regular places in the little monastery. This too probably arose from the fact that the community had been formed by a random grouping of separate cells and resembled a little village more than a monastery of the Cistercian or Benedictine type.

Saint Guerin, realizing the inherent dangers of his unsystematic grouping of monks into what was only a vague and fluctuating kind of community, finally resolved to remedy matters by associating his hermits with an established Order, with a set of clearly defined usages which would allow his monks not only to preserve their austere and contemplative life but even to progress further in the ways of contemplation. His first step was to apply to Pope Innocent II for dissolution of the ties that bound him to Molesme. After that it was natural that he turn his eyes towards the Cistercians, because he had been enabled by his connection with Molesme, to follow with interest the genesis and progress of the Cistercian reform, although from a distance.

Saint Guerin made application, in 1136, for affiliation to the Cistercians through Clairvaux. Bernard was to become the Father Immediate of Aulps and to sponsor the admission of the monks into the Order of Cîteaux.

The two letters of Saint Bernard (142 and 254) which refer to this affair are our chief sources of evidence for the holiness of Saint

Guerin and of his monks. They are, also, among the most interesting of the saint's letters. The one numbered first in Mabillon's edition (which was written two years after the letter which Mabillon
places later in the series) contains the famous passage which sum-
marizes the whole of Cistercian asceticism: *Ordo noster abjectio est,
humilitas est, voluntaria paupertas est, obedientia, pax et gaudium in
Spiritu Sancto*, etc. (Our Order, that is to say, our Rule, our way of
life, is abjection, it is humility, voluntary poverty, obedience, peace
and joy in the Holy Spirit.) Both of them are fine concise treatises
on the virtue and importance of conversion of manners.

Saint Bernard praises Abbot Guerin as a model of this constant
striving for ever greater perfection, the stubborn refusal to be
content with any degree of virtue in this life, to say "It is enough."
Of course, most of these reflections arise, as it were, quite sponta-
neously from the very fact of the abbot's application for affiliation
to the strict Cistercian Order, and therefore they do not necessarily
prove that Saint Bernard had an intimate personal knowledge of
Guerin and his monks. On the other hand, Saint Bernard, though
often enthusiastic in his praise, was never careless in dealing out
compliments at random to persons who had never given him any
evidence that they deserved it.

And as a matter of fact we know that Saint Bernard was basing
his remarks on observations made on the occasion of a visit to
Aulps, probably in 1135, before the application was made by Saint
Guerin. At that time Saint Bernard was returning from a journey
to Italy in the service of the Pope.

It was in 1138 that Saint Bernard wrote his second letter (number
142) to the monks of Aulps, and this time he is advising them to
proceed at once to the election of a new abbot to replace Saint
Guerin, who had just been elevated to the episcopal see of Sion.
The holy abbot of Aulps, now far advanced in years, according to
Saint Bernard's letter, had tried to refuse this appointment but
finally entered upon his new task under obedience to the Holy See.
Sion is a small city in the Canton of Valais and lies in the valley of
the upper Rhone, between two towering mountain ridges, on one
of the principal roads in Italy. At that time, this isolated diocese,
in a wild mountain country, had much to contend with, and although we are not well informed as to the details, Saint Guerin

had no sinecure as bishop there. In 1141, or thereabouts, there is record of an assembly of bishops at Conflans, among whom were Saint Peter of Tarentaise and Saint John of Valence, to decide a dispute between Saint Guerin and Count Amadeus of Savoy, who had claimed possession of two villages of the Valais which had been given by Emperor Henry IV of the Church of Sion.

Finally, around 1150, Saint Guerin ended his long career. The legends tell us that after a visit to his beloved monastery, Saint Guerin had climbed on his mule and sadly taken the road back to Sion. As they were about to leave the valley, passing over the ridge of Mont de Tey, and the saint turned to take a last look at Aulps, the mule's feet suddenly sank into the rock as though it were wax, and the animal could not progress a step further. At precisely the same moment, the bells of the monastery began to ring of their own accord, a fact which so astonished Saint Guerin that he re-solved to return there. The legend does not explain the even more astonishing thing in the incident, which is that Saint Guerin, sev-eral miles from the monastery, knew that the bells were ringing of their own accord, instead of in the ordinary manner.

In any case, warned by some supernatural sign or intuition, Saint Guerin returned to Aulps and there fell sick and died. It was the 27th of August, 1150.

After his death, his body was found to be clad in a coarse hair-shirt, and moreover there was a large iron key bound so tightly to his back that in the course of years the flesh had grown over and around and partly covered it. This was afterwards enshrined in a silver reliquary, and the splendidly entombed relics of Saint Guerin made the abbey a place of pilgrimage for centuries.

In 1689 the Calvinist Vaudois sacked the abbey and desecrated the altars. They had proceeded to the tomb of Saint Guerin and were banging on it with sledge hammers when, once again, says the legend, the bells began to ring of their own accord. The here-tics, however, were right on the scene, and having searched the tower and found no one to explain the ringing, grew frightened and left the abbey. On their way out, they threw Saint Guerin's mitre into a fire, but it did not burn.

Saint Guerin's sanctity was officially recognized by the Holy See, by so-called equivalent beatification, in 1701.

January 15

Blessed Amadeus of Hauterive, "the Elder,"
Monk of Bonnevaux, France

(Sources: Lenain, 2:11; Manrique, vol. 1 *passim* [both these accounts are based on the twelfth-century manuscript life of Blessed Amadeus, from which lengthy quotations are given]; Chuzel, 47ff.)

Of the two Cistercian saints called Amadeus (they were father and son), it is the younger that had the official title of saint and enjoys the greater liturgical cult, while his father is only accorded the title of Blessed on the grounds of his immemorial veneration: but still, we know much more about the father than we do about the son, because his life was written by a monk of Bonnevaux Abbey, preserving in some detail the portrait and history of this man who was so typical of the early Cistercians in his sincerity, his simplicity, his faith and spirit of penance, his love of God, and his inexhaustible desire of sacrifice.

The silent, remote monasteries of the Cistercian reform, lost in their forests and valleys, attracted many noble converts but few who could boast of a more exalted rank than this Prince of Clermont and Hauterive, the close relative of Emperor Henry V. We must not, however, think of him as a German just because he was related to the head of the Holy Roman Empire. His home was in Daughiny, and his domains extended mostly along the foothills of the Alps. His family is still illustrious in a Europe where nobility has either disappeared or tended to waste itself in corruption. Not so the family of Clermont-Tonnerre. But Prince Amadeus belonged, also, to a line which had produced many saints. No doubt the names of Saint Guerry, Saint Elbon, Saint Theodoric, Saint Lecteria, Saint Honulfus mean little to modern Catholics, but at least two of his relatives are well known to Cistercians: Saint Robert of Molesme and Saint William of Bourges.

This powerful lord, having heard of the new foundation of Bonnevaux, in the mountains between the Grande Chartreuse and the

Rhone Valley, conceived the desire of consecrating his life to God as a Cistercian, but it was not enough for him to do so alone. Like Saint Bernard, he spent some time recruiting a band of noble friends and relations to accompany him. Of the sixteen who followed him to the new monastery, one was his ten-year-old son Amadeus.

Although Saint John, the Abbot of Bonnevaux, must have been glad in his heart to see so many fervent postulants arriving at once, he did not show his enthusiasm by any means. On the contrary, he received them with all the reserve that Saint Benedict prescribed. He gave them to understand that he did not believe men of their class would be able to support the difficulties and humiliations of a life of such poverty and obedience as this, and he assured them that in the monastery, noble and serf were treated alike. All would have to wear the ungainly cowls, too warm in summer and not warm enough in winter; there were the long, hard fasts and vigils and the arduous, humiliating work; there was the obligation of submitting without question to the slightest wish of the superior, whether or not he was wise and prudent and considerate in his command. There were heavy penances imposed for the slightest faults. Surely he thought they would do better to go somewhere else: they were mistaken in coming to Bonnevaux.

"We have all sinned much," was Amadeus's reply, "And we all need penance very badly. We beg you on our knees to permit us to expiate our debts here in your community."

The holy abbot gave them an evasive promise that he would see about it and left them to talk it over. The prince's noble companions did not have his faith and intensity of purpose, and they were somewhat shaken by the abbot's apparent coolness to their offer of themselves, but Blessed Amadeus revived their courage, and finally they were all received as novices except the little Amadeus who was too young and had to remain in the guest quarters. The Cistercians, although they had set out to follow the Rule of Saint Benedict to the letter, had immediately discarded at least one item in the Rule: the admission of children to the monastery. Of course, Saint Benedict never prescribed the reception of children: he only tolerated it, or at best accepted it as a matter of course in his own time. The Cistercians felt themselves free to dispense themselves from taking on this burden which did so much to complicate the life of a Cluniac monastery, and in so doing, they insured that the monks would have sufficient time to carry out the essential duties of their state, without spending their days in the labors of education, so foreign to our contemplative life, except insofar as it is absolutely necessary for the training of our priests. Saint John must have felt a little uneasy about the compromise by which he allowed the boy to stay in the guesthouse and receive lessons in Latin there from one of the monks, and if he did, his misgivings were well founded. The child's presence proved to be a stone of stumbling in the path of his father. Amadeus senior continued to be preoccupied with the child's education, and in spite of the vows which now bound him to a life of complete separation from the world, he was worrying about the fact that his son was not receiving the complete training in classical literature, and in the trivium and quadrivium, that ordinarily prepared a cultured young man or a cleric in the world for his career. And when Saint John pointed out that there was no place for Cicero in the cloister, Amadeus's indignation gained such control over him that he finally apostatized from the monastery and headed north with his young son in the direction of Cluny. To leave the monastery and seek an easier observance was regarded as an apostasy by Saint Bernard.[4] But Abbot Pontius of Cluny received the noble Amadeus with open arms and gave him the seat next to the abbatial stall in choir and next to the prior who presided in the refectory. Even then, young Amadeus did not stay at Cluny. For some reason or other he was soon sent on to the court of the Emperor in Germany. Five or six months went by, and the futility of this change of life began to dawn upon the contrite Amadeus as he looked about him and compared this huge, busy, noisy abbey, these lavish decorations and elaborate ceremonial, this atmosphere of preoccupation and ambition, and these innumerable mitigations with the peaceful, forest retreat in the Alps: silent Bonnevaux, with its austerity, its simplicity, and its joy.

[4] See EP 1, to Robert of Châtillon, who left Clairvaux for Cluny.

Finally, one day—it was a great feast—after Tierce, the monks left the choir and went to vest in the magnificent red silk copes in which they were to sing the High Mass of the day. Among them was Amadeus. But instead of being filled with joy by all this splendor, he tasted nothing but bitterness, remembering all at once not only the poverty and simplicity of Bonnevaux but also the plain food, the fasting and abstinence there. His companions whom he had deserted were giving glory to God by their fasts, while he was dressed magnificently and nourished with elaborately cooked foods and spiced wines. It was more than a matter of regretting the joy and the peace he had forfeited by his apostasy: he began to reflect within himself upon the judgment he had merited by such a sin.

He was unable to conceal his state of mind; indeed, those around him noticed the tears in his eyes and spoke of it to the abbot, who summoned him, and in an effort to remove whatever might be the cause of his disquietude, offered him anything that was in his power to give if he would remain at Cluny: he only had to ask, and he could have any priory he wanted, in any country, and there were many to choose from! But Amadeus had now made up his mind that there was only one thing to do: to go back to Bonnevaux and do penance and hope for readmission among his brethren.

When he at last arrived in the "Good Valley of Our Lady" he did not even knock at the monastery gate but took up his post before the door, like a beggar, and began asking the prayers of all those who came and went. Presently someone told the holy abbot John that Amadeus had returned, and he went at once to the gate. The poor old monk seeing his abbot fell at his feet confessing his fault with tears of broken hearted contrition which could not help but touch Saint John's heart. He raised the man gently to his feet, rebuking him without harshness for the great dangers to which he had exposed himself by his sin, and prescribed as a penance that he should spend that day and the next where he was, and the third he would be readmitted to the community under the usual conditions for apostates. But Amadeus could not be satisfied with so light and easy a reparation: he asked to remain there as a beggar until he had fully satisfied for what he had done. Abbot John consented to this, and so for several days Amadeus remained day and night before the monastery gate, accusing himself of being a traitor to his vocation and begging for prayers. The portions of food that were sent to him from the community kitchen he distributed to the poor, and he lived on a few scraps that were left over after the daily distribution of the leftovers from the refectory to all who came to the gate. After a week Abbot John tried to get him to come in to the monastery, but when he once again refused, the abbot had the door where he was locked, and all who went out of the enclosure and returned to it used another gate, far away on the other wide of the abbey. Amadeus soon discovered the trick and moved to the other gate. Another week went by, and again Dom John came out and insisted that the penance should end. He told Amadeus that if he felt that he could not satisfy adequately for his fault by two weeks of public penance, he should trust in the merits of Christ and offer them up in reparation for what he had done, and for the rest, in all humility, he should come and rejoin the community or else incur a greater penalty before God by his disobedience. When Amadeus still showed signs of not being convinced, Saint John finally said to him:

"Very well, then: if you will not come into the monastery now, I will stay here with you until you do." And he meant what he said.

The penitent finally gave in and was readmitted to the society of his brethren.

But from that day on he made it his ambition to be in every way the lowest in the community; he became a genius at self-annihilation. He seized upon everything that was mean and vile and humiliating with a kind of holy greed.

For instance, the monks of Bonnevaux used to blacken their shoes with a vile homemade concoction made of goats' milk and grease and soot. The chief characteristic of this abominable mixture was its nauseating smell. Amadeus presented himself to the abbot with the argument that it was altogether improper that the priests of the monastery, who handled the most pure and holy Body of Christ in the Sacrifice of the Mass, should have their hands contaminated by such filth. He accordingly offered himself for the office of boot-black for the whole monastery, and his request was granted.

The place prescribed for oiling the shoes was the calefactory, or the furnace room. And it was there that one day a noble relative of the former prince found him at work in the semi-darkness and the intense heat, with his face black with grime and his clothes soaked with sweat, toiling over the boots with his evil-smelling grease, and yet at the same time so deeply immersed in prayer that he did not notice that anyone was standing by. The visitor softly stole away without making his presence known and waited until his noble nephew was finally sent to him in the guest quarters.

Another task which Amadeus aspired to and obtained was that of cleaning the monastery sewer. To be exact, it was a small stream which carried away the refuse from the building. In the summer heat, the water fell so low that it could not do the work appointed to it, and the accumulated filth endangered the health of the community. During the meridienne, when the other monks took their noonday siesta, Amadeus armed himself with a shovel and attacked this grim task under the burning sun and clouds of flies. Such was the humility of this great prince.

But all his prayers and penances were not without their fruit, for soon the glad news came to him that his son, the younger Amadeus, had also returned from the world and entered the Cistercian Order at Clairvaux under Saint Bernard. Amadeus senior would one day have the consolation of seeing his son established as abbot in the precarious Alpine foundation of Hautecombe, where he proved himself to be his father's equal in courage and faith.

Amadeus senior was able to do far more for his abbot than these picturesque and difficult penances at Bonnevaux. He soon had an opportunity to make up for his disloyalty in a more material and practical way. In 1122, or thereabouts, when Bonnevaux was making her first foundation, Dom John was able to send Amadeus out to find a suitable site—a wild valley in what is now the Ardeche in the diocese of Viviers in central France—and to superintend the erection of the first buildings to house the monks when they arrived. This became the monastery of Mazan, or "Mansus Adae" (Adam's Farm). In 1132 Saint Peter of Tarentaise left Bonnevaux with a colony of monks to found Tamie in the high Alps of Savoy. But Blessed Amadeus had gone before them and found a site and provided buildings for their reception. It was the same with Mont-peyroux in Auvergne (1134) and with Leoncel in the mountains thirty-six kilometers from Valence. After each one of these founda-tions, others received the credit and glory and became abbots of the various houses, while Amadeus returned to the obscurity of Bonnevaux cloister where he lived always as a simple monk, not even raised to holy Orders.

His great penitential humility and devotion continued for thirty years, in which he had ample opportunity to prove his love for Christ in the true Cistercian way, by self-effacing simplicity and prayer and hard work, without any of the externals of sanctity that so often catch the eye in the lives of other saints.

Amadeus of Bonnevaux has always been a popular saint in the order, and perhaps it is because he is so truly a type of the early Cistercian—a humble, silent patriarch whose heart is purified and cleansed into absolute limpidity by faith and self-forgetfulness born of what is called the fear of God. But fear, in this sense, is nothing else but love: the loyal and perfect filial love which de-taches the soul from the smallest blemish of deliberate imperfec-tion—a love which does not aspire to ornament itself with spectacular virtues for the sake of its own glorification but only to annihilate itself in the sight of God, that he alone may reign and be glorified.

January 19

Saint William, Archbishop of Bourges, France

(Sources: AASS, Jan. 1:627 [three contemporary lives by thirteenth-century authors]; P. Stepan Steffen, "Der Blessed Wilhelm, Ersbischof von Bourges," Cist Chronik 19 [1907]:1; *Petite Bolandister*, 1:258.)

Inquire pacem, says the Psalmist, *et persequere eam* (Ps 33). Seek peace and follow after her. The search for interior and exterior peace, for himself and for others, is more or less the dominating theme of the three lives of Saint William of Bourges, all written by contemporaries of his (although the main one was rewritten by Surius.) Indeed, all the great Cistercian prelates of the Middle Ages—all, that is, who distinguished themselves by the sanctity of their lives—were great peacemakers. But Saint William was not merely delegated to settle quarrels between princes: he had many opportunities to manifest the meekness and forgiveness and charity which are the truest strength, the greatest courage; for by them we give up our own passions and let God work in us for our own good and for the good of others.

William de Donjean[5] came from the family of the Counts of Nevers and was born at the castle of Arthel near Nevers, probably about 1140. His education was entrusted to an uncle who was archdeacon at Soissons, and William became a canon of that Cathedral at an early age, according to the medieval abuse of canonical privileges. Going on to Paris where he completed his studies for the priesthood, he became a canon there also, but he renounced all that a brilliant career in the Church held out to him and retired to the strictest Order he could find: the Order of Grandmont. He entered the mother-house of that Order, Grandmont itself, near Limoges.

We say that this was the strictest Order he could find: that requires some qualification. Grandmont was stricter than Cîteaux in some respects, and in others it was not. Like the Chartreuse, Grandmont was a semi-eremitical community. The monks were never allowed to leave their enclosure; their poverty was stricter than anything that had yet been known in the church and, except for the fact that the monks owned their own monastery, was as strict as the poverty of the first Franciscans. The Rule of Grandmont,[6] though not written by Saint Stephen, the founder of the Order, reflects the fierce idealism of that old hermit, but it is a document full of glaring inherent weaknesses. Saint Stephen of Muret had

---

[5] Also called by some authors William Berruyer. He is also sometimes referred to as William "the Hermit" although there is no evidence that he ever led an eremitical life.

[6] *Regula Sancti Stephani Grandimontensis*, PL 204:1157. This document was really written by Etienne de Licie, fourth Prior of Grandmont.

always said that he had no Rule and that the Gospel of Jesus Christ was enough of a Rule for him and his monks. The jealous insistence with which the compiler of the Rule of Grandmont tried to guarantee the purest perfection of evangelical poverty seems to have so absorbed his mind that he forgot to lay any religious rule. He went into great detail in everything that concerned poverty and separation from the world, even providing that seculars should not take home Holy Water blessed at Grandmontine Churches or adore the Holy Cross there on Good Fridays. The monks were not only not allowed to possess anything—not even cattle—or to cut down trees, they could not even buy or sell anything or borrow or even beg from seculars. If anything was to be bought, they would have to ask "some friend" to do it for them. The vagueness of this provision is characteristic of the Rule. If they were absolutely destitute, they could ask permission of the bishop to beg for some food, but as soon as they had enough food for one day they should go home again. In all things, they should beg rather from God than from men, and the ideal of the Grandmontines was to depend entirely and directly on God for everything.

The other articles of the Rule, for instance those concerned with obedience, seem to have a legislative force and character, but the ascetic life and on a religious psychology. The first words on obedience are that the monks promise obedience *not only to their superiors but to one another.* But instead of going on to explain precisely in what consists this obligation, the writer of the Rule completely ignores that important detail and goes on to talk about some of the interior dispositions of the mind that should accompany perfect obedience of the judgment, particularly in the case where a superior might issue an order in which he had greater regard for the subject's desires than for his own. Such a question manifestly belongs in an ascetic treatise rather than in a piece of legislation.

The Rule of Grandmont is a beautiful example of a spiritual idealism which works well for a few individuals but which tends to defeat itself as soon as it attempts to include large numbers of men in its sphere of influence. No doubt Saint Stephen of Muret never envisaged the possibility of a large Order springing up to follow his example. But when the time came, those whose duty it was to provide a sound Rule for the protection of their own ideal lacked the simple intellectual humility to busy themselves with common and fundamental matters of legislation. The idealism which made them despise such material things as the administrative machinery of a religious Order was shot through and through with human weaknesses which soon spelled the ruin of the Order.

After a short golden age, during which their poverty made them abandon without argument or contestation the original site of their monastery, Muret, when someone else laid claim to it (the Rule forbade all lawsuits), the Order of Grandmont fell into a decline, and from then on until the French Revolution when it finally disappeared from the scene altogether, it was notorious in the Church for its incessant internal quarrels, dissensions, rebellions and scenes of violence. It was constantly being investigated and reformed by the Holy See.

What happened was very simple. The monks were not allowed to own anything, borrow anything, buy anything, or even beg. They were not agricultural workers like the Cistercians: these material considerations were too distracting for them. Their manual labor consisted in a few menial occupations about the house. How were they to live? In order to safeguard their purity of soul from all contact with temporal concerns, the entire business of material administration was put into the hands of lay-brothers. Now in the case of these *conversi*, the Rule made none of the strict provisions it had made for the monks in the matter of poverty. Indeed, it made practically no provisions at all. Besides, there was a great affluence of vocations to the lay-brotherhood of Grandmont. As a result, the Order, in spite of all the ideals of its founders, acquired immense wealth and possessions within fifty years of its foundation!

About the time Saint William became a member of the Order, matters had already reached a crisis. The lay-brothers included a few violent and trouble-making spirits who had been ill affected by the great power that had suddenly come into their hands by reason of the wealth under their complete control. They began to lay down laws for the choir monks, not only in material things, but even in spiritual matters as well: for example, they tried to enforce some of their own ideas on the rendering of the Divine Office, in which of course they took no part. In short, their aim was to gain control of the whole Order in all its departments and run it according to their own lights.

In 1185 the lay brothers of Grandmont were to rise in open revolt, imprison the prior, expel two hundred monks, and leave them wandering around in search of food and shelter in the world which they thought they had done everything possible to leave behind.

Saint William, however, did not wait for matters to reach this pass. Having entered the Order about 1164, and made his profession, he left it again about 1170. The peace he had sought, and which the Rule of Grandmont had seemed to promise, was not to be found here. He made his way to the Cistercian abbey of Pontigny[7] and entered an Order where the monks and lay-brothers lived and worked side by side, sharing their material responsibilities as well as their spiritual advantages and graces.

Having begun over again as a novice, and made his profession, probably together with several other ex-Grandmontines, Saint William so impressed all with his virtues and talents that he was soon chosen as Prior of Pontigny. Some years later, about 1184, he became abbot of Fountains-Jean, a thriving community of over two hundred monks with many lay brothers, but he did not remain there long. In 1188 he was abbot of Chalis, and once again his biographers tell us that he was the admiration of all for his sanctity which made itself evident by the extraordinary interior peace and spiritual joy which he radiated and which affected all who came in contact with them.

---

[7] Pontigny was the abbey where Saint Thomas a Becket had taken refuge for two years (1165–1166) and where Saint Edmund Rich also spent two years. The latter was buried in the basilica of the abbey, which became a place of pilgrimage on his account. Both these great archbishops took the Cistercian habit and shared in some measure the austerities of the monks, without however making profession or even living in the community. *Blessed Hugh of Macon*, the first abbot, one of Saint Bernard's thirty companions on entering Cîteaux, was also venerated there (Old Cistercian Menology, October 10 or 12).

The fame of his virtues and sanctity made it impossible for him to remain longer in the cloister which he loved. He was granted some ten years more of the monastic life. After that he found himself, according to the celebrated comparison of Saint Gregory, torn from the arms of Rachel and left to content himself with bleary-eyed Lia, or the active life.

In 1199 the Cathedral Chapter of Bourges, having come to a deadlock in their efforts to select a new archbishop, drew up a list that included several Cistercian abbots and submitted it to Odo of Sully, Bishop of Paris, with the intention of accepting his choice as final. The archbishop prayed long over the matter, and finally on the feast of Saint Clement, the day he intended to announce his decision, he placed three of the best names on slips of paper under the altar cloth while he said Mass, and then afterwards in the presence of two other bishops, he took one of the papers. The name on it was William of Chalis, who was in any case a close friend of Odo, whom we cannot therefore accuse of acting blindly. The extraordinary character of his selection was emphasized by the fact that the cathedral chapter, while awaiting the decision of Odo of Sully, and discussing the candidates, all suddenly found themselves agreeing that the obvious choice was William of Chalis.

William himself received the news of his election as Primate of Aquitaine with great sorrow, but he was forced to accept by the Abbot of Cîteaux and the Legate of the Holy See.

The new archbishop entered upon his office in a time of grave crisis. Philip Augustus, having illegally repudiated his Danish wife, Ingelburga, and imprisoned her, had married, in 1196, Agnes of Marania. Innocent III had warned him, under pain of interdict, to dissolve this adulterous union and take back his true wife. Philip Augustus made a futile attempt to evade the orders of the Legate, Philip of Capua. But the papal machinery, under Innocent III, worked with inexorable smoothness and efficacy. On December 12, at midnight, the bishops assembled at Dijon filed into the cathedral by the lurid glare of torches. As the deep bell of Saint Benigne tolled slowly in the night the flaring pitch cast fantastic shadows along the bare walls of the great cold church that had been emptied of the sacramental Christ. All the crosses and statues were covered with purple veils. The relics of the saints had been hidden in the crypts. The sacred hosts had been consumed and the last fragments and particles had been burned. In the terrible, torch-lit silence that fell upon the grim assembly, Philip of Capua thundered the papal order that closed the churches of France and drove Christ from the domains of an adulterer, leaving the people to famish for the sacraments and for the life-giving sacrifice. The people of the Middle Ages had a keen sense of certain spiritual realities, and they realized that the emptying of the tabernacles and the closing of the church doors meant that they were being handed over, as Saint Paul said, to the devil, unto the death of their flesh, that their spirit might be chastened and live.

As the last words of the Legate echoed along the stones, the hundreds of torches were all instantaneously thrown to the ground and the fire was trampled out of them. Then in the sudden and terrible darkness, the blackness as it were of hell, the city was filled with the wailing and shrieking of women and children. Thus the interdict descended upon France.

Now the immensely dramatic display at Dijon, powerful as it was, with all the power of liturgy, would itself have meant little unless the bishop of France had carried out the Papal order and enforced the interdict in their several dioceses. Most of them did so, but Philip Augustus saw to it that every possible motive was given them for not enforcing the interdict, and those who resisted him, like Odo of Sully, had to flee for their lives. However, there were many members of the hierarchy and of the clergy in France who put their national loyalty to Philip above the unity of Christ's Church, or who had reasons which made them think it expedient to take the king's side. These were numerous in the Archdiocese of Bourges. William had his own cathedral chapter practically unanimously against him, as well as several bishops in his primacy, and many priests. Consequently when he set out to enforce the interdict, he had a complicated and dangerous task ahead of him.

How he acquitted himself of it is an obscure question. The text of the *Vita Prima*, which mentions William's conflict with Philip Augustus, does so in such guarded terms, and with so many precautions to safeguard the reputation of the king, that the unpleasant affair of the interdict is not openly referred to. The king is pictured as deceived by the advice of evil men, who incite him for some unknown reason, against the archbishop, while William, on his side, is threatened by equally dishonest characters with a trial for high treason if he does not give in.

The vagueness of this account has led some writers to assert that William never came into conflict with the king over the interdict at all and that it was some other unknown matter that caused their disagreement. The writer in the *Cistercienser Chronik* is of this opinion and believes that because William himself was consecrated during the interdict, that it was not enforced at all in his diocese. This does not necessarily follow, but the one fact we do know is that in a conflict over the rights of the Church (and probably the interdict), William withstood the royal party in spite of grave personal danger.

Indeed, if William of Bourges was to prove himself a man of peace, it was only to be in the middle of many conflicts. In all of them his patience and charity and forbearance and quiet firmness won him the respect and even the love of his adversaries. Philip Augustus was reconciled to him, and another of his enemies was finally forced to admit: "For all my hostility and ill will I have received from him (the archbishop) nothing but favors and tokens of kindness: and never have I been able to detect in his eyes or in his expression the slightest hint of resentment at my way of acting."

Saint William made himself remarkable from the very outset as a prelate who refused to maintain a private army and resort to force in order to keep order in his diocese. In those days a sincere and energetic prelate was too often deceived by the belief that he could best serve God and the Church by being a powerful temporal lord, ready to enforce the canons of the Church by force of arms if need be. But William relied first on the example of a life of uncompromising abnegation and ceaseless prayer and then on preaching of the word of God and showing mercy and pardon to his enemies.

He was a contemplative by temperament and by vocation, and if he was called to hand on to others the fruits of his contemplation, that only reminded him all the more of the necessity of keeping in close union with God. Hence the strictness of his life, his continuation of the Cistercian fasts and abstinence (he never ate meat, even when he was ill), and his rigorous self-custody.

His cathedral chapter who, as we have seen, had first chosen him with unanimous favor then resisted him as unanimously in the affair of the interdict, had long viewed with skeptical eyes his nonviolent methods, but to their surprise Saint William was better obeyed and soon restored a more lasting and widespread peace and order in his archdiocese than any of his recent predecessors had been able to maintain.

It is not surprising, then, that in 1201 he was chosen with two other bishops to restore peace in his one-time Order, that of Grandmont, and to impose correction upon the perennially rebelling *conversi*.

In his charity, the holy archbishop refused to indulge in acrimonious criticism even of those who were manifestly guilty of material crimes. He was always mindful of his own ignorance of the intimate motives and of the mitigating factors behind the external act. "Would you forbid a man in the grip of a high fever to tremble?" he once said. "Perhaps these poor men cannot help themselves."

Another abuse which William never tolerated was the imposition of fines upon the excommunicated as a condition for their readmission to the Church. This had become quite common in France, and the money went into the bishop's own private treasury. When someone suggested that William might use this as a legitimate source to provide for the poor, he also refused, just as firmly. He had his own very lucid ideas about ends and means.

It might not seem to be a very great accomplishment on the part of an archbishop that he made sure that canonries that fell vacant in his chapter were given to Masters of Theology, in order that his priests might be well instructed in that Sacred Science. Only when we realize the terrible lack of the theological schools in the great majority of dioceses in the twelfth and early thirteenth centuries does this take on importance. Indeed, two Ecumenical Councils (the third and fourth Lateran, in 1179 and 1215) legislated in vain precisely to this effect, that vacant canonries be given to Masters of Theology, who were to instruct the secular clergy. This provision, first made at the Third Lateran Council, was practically nowhere observed. It was confirmed and made more specific at the Fourth Council, with the same results. What was the cause? On one hand the inertia of the bishops, then the fact that Masters of Theology preferred to remain at the few great centers of teaching where they had some chance of making a name for themselves, and finally the fact that so many canonries were already earmarked, as it were, for preferred candidates. So grave was the situation that the learned Fr. Mandonnet, OP, says,[8] "I have found record of only one case in which a benefice was granted in favor of a master as required by the Lateran councils." The case he refers to is the appointment at Valancionnes, by Baldwin Count of Flanders. Saint William's response to the Lateran Council is all the more significant in that he was prompt enough to obey the third council—he was dead before the fourth.

In 1208, after the murder of Saint Peter of Castelnau,[9] Innocent III sent out a command to raise a spiritual and military crusade against the Albigensians, and William of Bourges was among the first to respond, although he was now seventy years old and broken in health. The great peacemaker was not offering his services as a military leader, and the fact that he "took the cross" must not be construed as "he took up arms." But he did mean to preach against the heresy, and bring the Gospel if he could to the heretics themselves.

Unfortunately he was not to enjoy this privilege. God required no more of him than the desire, and no doubt the saint would have been saddened by implication in a crusade which, for all its good intentions, had its sordid side.

On the feast of the Epiphany, 1209, Saint William must have had a presentiment that his end was near. His people had gathered to assist at the Sacred Mysteries on this great feast and to hear the archbishop preach. It was in the huge, half-finished cathedral of

---

[8] Pierre Mandonnet, *Saint Dominic and His Work*, trans. Mary Benedicta Larkin (Herer, 1944), 183.
[9] See February 16.

Saint Stephen at Bourges, now famous as having one of the most beautiful gothic naves ever built. As Saint William climbed to the pulpit under the soaring arches that were then white and new, not darkened by old age, the icy wind of the plains of Berri came through the scaffolding and boards and flapping canvas where the great structure gaped, almost wide open to the winter weather.

The saint already had a fever. The text of his sermon was: "Now is the time for us to rise from sleep, for our salvation is nearer at hand than when we believed."[10] The whole address was simply a farewell. He had to be helped home and put to bed. It was clear that he could not live more than a week. On the 9th of January he received the Body of Christ, not lying in bed, but kneeling on the floor with his arms out in the form of a cross. After that, however, he could no longer speak. Meanwhile three monks from Chalis hastened to his beside, as well as many other members of the clergy. At midnight he made a sign to those who were by his bed-side to begin the night office, which he had always said at that time in order to be united with his Cistercian brethren at Chalis. The archbishop made the sign of the cross and feebly intoned the *Deus in adjutorium* but could not continue; he sank back exhausted and followed the Office in spirit until finally he entered into his agony. He was then taken from his bed and placed on a haircloth and heap of ashes in the middle of the floor, according to the Cistercian usages, and there he gave up his soul to God.

He had desired to be buried among his monks at Chalis, but the citizens of Bourges set up an armed guard over his body as it lay in state in the unfinished Cathedral, and finally the chapter gave permission for his burial there before the altar of the protomartyr.

Meanwhile, as the archbishop lay in state, a mother brought her crippled ten-year-old boy through the crowd to his body. The child was so helpless that he practically had to be carried. He was lifted up and aided to kiss Saint William's hands and feet. Then they started back through the crowd. Before they got to the door of the cathedral, the child began to walk unaided.

[10] Rom 13:2.

William had worked many miracles in his life, for instance, the healing of a child with a shaking head and a priest with a hand so crippled that he was unable to say Mass. Favors were multiplied after his death.

His process was introduced, strangely enough, not at the suggestion of the Cistercians but of the Grandmontines. The Prior of Grandmont, speaking of his own memory of Saint William as a member of that Order, praised his holiness of life to Innocent III at the Fourth Lateran Council. His successor as Archbishop of Bourges also asked for the introduction of his cause. It was begun under Honorius III, and finished in record time for a Cistercian: Saint William's canonization took only nine years, much less time than that of the great Saint Bernard. It was completed in 1218.

His feast was celebrated at Bourges with an octave, and in the Cisterican Order as a Feast of Two Masses; that is, as a holy day, according to the *Consuetudines*. On such a day there was no work for the choir monks. His feast received the rank of semi-double in the Order of Grandmont and was also kept in many churches of France and in Germany. In the diocese of Rouen his Mass even included a proper sequence.[11]

At the present day his feast in the Cistercian Order has been reduced to the rank of three lessons and a Mass, and his life is practically unknown. Yet he is one of our greatest saints, and we have much to reflect upon and imitate in his perfection of Christ-like charity and apostolic love of souls, which seeks to win men to the kingdom of God by love and mercy and purity of life and prayer. We cannot argue that we, unlike Saint William, will never be called to the episcopate: prayer must always be the basis of our life as it was of his, and charity and forgiveness must characterize our relations with those around us in the cloister as they characterized his apostolic life in the world. But if we, like Saint William, keep ourselves united with God and with our brethren, we can be sure of sharing his glory in heaven, even though our obscure lives on earth may never be enlightened by his miracles or his external heroism.

---

[11] Reprinted in *Cistercienser Chronik*, loc. cit.

January 22

Blessed Walter of Bierbeck, Monk of Hemmerod, near Trier, Germany

(Source: DM, *passim*; this thirteenth-century writer was a contemporary of Walter of Bierbeck, and prior of a daughterhouse of Himmerod. AASS, Jan. 3:60, prints a later ms. which simply pieced together the different passages in Caesar of Heisterbach to make a biography of this saint.)

Bierbeck is the name of the little town near Louvain where this knight and crusader was born about 1155. Walter, like most young noblemen of his age, was bred to a life of fighting, hunting, and jousting, and even though tournaments were looked upon by many as a serious sin, he was completely attached to that bloody and violent form of recreation. But like his contemporary, Saint Theobald, this knight who was to become abbot of Vaux-de-Cernay near Paris, Walter had an intense and faithful devotion to the Mother of God. And as in the case of Theobald, it was she who drew the young knight away from the world, into the cloister and the "militia Christi," to become, as Saint Paul says, a "good soldier of Christ Jesus," fighting under a Rule and an abbot, not with sword and lance and mace, but with the arms of humility and obedience, the "armor of light," the "sword of the spirit."

All through his youth he had daily heard Mass in Mary's honor, had fasted to please her, and given alms to the poor in whom he saw her Son. Finally, in an access of enthusiastic love for the Queen of Heaven, he presented himself one day at the altar of a little church dedicated to her, with a rope around his neck, as her slave. This example was later cited by Saint Louis de Montfort.

She did not despise the simplicity of such love. Indeed, she returned it with an equally direct and ingenuous simplicity typical of her immaculate perfection.

Walter was at Mass: the priest came to the Consecration, and when he raised the chalice, he suddenly perceived that there was a little golden cross lying on the floor next to his feet. Picking it up after Mass he found a note affixed to it which read as follows: "Give this as a token from me, Mary, the Mother of God, to my friend Walter, of Bierbeck, Knight."

The priest got up in the pulpit and asked if a knight called Walter of Bierbeck was present. Walter presented himself and received the cross to his great astonishment and that of everyone else. And this was the beginning of his vocation. The cross became quite famous, and it was later obtained from him by the Countess of Holland by a kind of accident. She sent to Hemmerod and asked for the cross. The monks did not want to give it up, but they were equally unwilling to offend the countess. So they said she could have it if Walter would consent, expecting him to refuse. He, however, immediately spoiled all their plans by saying: "I have made a vow of poverty, and have no property. The cross belongs to the monastery. . . ." But the monastery had already implicitly given it up. And so it joined the collection of relics in the possession of that noble lady.

Walter did not enter religion alone when, in 1183, he became a Cistercian novice at Hemmerod. He had a servant in the world, who was converted by a miracle. The servant, who was to become in religion Brother Arnold, had light work of it at meal times when his master was fasting: he only had to serve bread and water. One day he brought the water as usual, but Walter complained: "Why do you bring me wine today?" He looked, and sure enough the cup was full of wine. He took it back, emptied it, refilled it with water, and tasted the water himself, making sure that it was indeed water. Yet as soon as the young knight tasted it, it again turned into wine. That was enough for the future Brother Arnold. And so he entered religion with his master.

At Hemmerod, which he had chosen because it was a Cistercian monastery and the Cistercian Order was dedicated to the Blessed Virgin, Walter showed such fervent love and interest for the Divine Office that in his year of probation he learned by heart the Psalter and all the hymns and Canticles, together with many other prayers and antiphons of Our Lady. And he had such faith in the value of the inspired word of God, even in the material, written book of

Psalms, that he delivered a possessed man by holding the Psalter over his head. However, he never arrived at any proficiency in Latin, for we are told that he could not understand the reading in the refectory. He made up for this by meditating on the mysteries of Our Lord's life—a "reading" from which he derived such profit that he was often moved to tears.

After his profession he became guest master. And then, although he desired nothing but obscurity and solitude, he was condemned, by the fact of his noble birth and fame among the feudal aristocracy of the Rhineland and Low Countries, to take charge of much of the exterior business of the monastery as an assistant to the cellarer. He was even sent on such long journeys as one, for instance, when he had to captain a river boat belonging to the monastery and sail down the Moselle and Rhine with a cargo of wine to Holland. On this voyage they were far down the Rhine. It was winter, night had fallen, a storm came up. It was the vigil of the feast of Saint Nicholas. The boat was badly tossed by the storm, and they were having a hard time keeping her from being driven ashore when, to add to their troubles, a gang of river pirates saw their predicament and decided to take advantage of it. Walter had recourse to prayer, and brought out a little ivory statuette of Our Lady which he always carried with him. The pirates came to grief on some rocks and sank, and the storm presently cleared, permitting the barge to continue down the river in peace. It was revealed to Walter in a dream that he had been much helped in this danger by the monks at home, who were chanting the night office at that time.

Perhaps it was because Walter had once given away the shoes off his feet to a poor scholar that it occurred, after his death, to a paralytic knight to ask for a pair of his shoes from Hemmerod. At first the monastery, assuming that the request was not to be taken literally, sent him a new pair. They were useless to him, he returned them, and repeated his specific demand. When Walter's shoes arrived, he put them on, and his paralysis left him. The same thing happened over again with another paralytic, wrought by the same pair of shoes. These were only two of many curious and interesting incidents that went to form a *cultus* for this holy man.

January 24

Blessed Felix O'Dulany, Bishop of Ossory, Ireland

Of all the great Cistercian bishops of the twelfth century, raised up by God to save the Church in a Europe torn by wars and schisms and every kind of national and sectional rivalry, not the least was saintly and energetic bishop of Ossory, a worthy successor to Saint Kieran and Saint Cartach. In him we see the energy and devotion of a Saint Peter of Tarentaise or of another Bernard of Clairvaux; and in him too we find the same deep and all-embracing charity, born of close union with God in the Cistercian cloister.

Felix was a member of the O'Duibhshlaine sect in upper Ossory, and was born in troubled days. Ireland, ravaged by the Danes, had seen her ancient civilization put to fire and sword, and in the lifetime of Blessed Felix the Anglo-Normans were to ravage and plunder what remained. And in those years, when the plains of Leinster were to run with blood, the O'Dulanys were to fall before the superior might of the invaders and hand over to them their lands and ruined castles. But there was one force that outlasted all wars and bore in itself the rich seeds of an irrepressible revival of life, and that was the Cistercian Order introduced by Saint Malachy (November 3) and Blessed Christian O'Conarchy (March 18) into Ireland.

While still in his early youth Felix O'Dulany took the white habit of a Cistercian monk, either at Mellifont or at Baltinglass Abbey. We cannot be sure of the place of his profession, as he may have entered the mother-house and passed from there to Baltinglass: but in any event, we know he was a monk of Baltinglass because it was there that having made a great reputation for sanctity and regularity and ability, he was chosen to lead a colony of monks to a new foundation at Jerpoint. This foundation is supposed by some historians to have taken place in 1180, but that is not the case, as by that time Blessed Felix was already bishop, and he was not elected to that office until he had spent many years as abbot of Jerpoint, one of the greatest of our Irish abbeys endowed by two kings of Ossory.

In spite of trials and great hardships the new monastery soon began to prosper, and six years after the foundation it became possible for Felix, by virtue of the concourse of postulants to his novitiate, to send out a new colony to the county of O'Ryan, there to found the abbey of Kilkenny, later known as Barrowmount.

In 1178 he was elected bishop of Ossory; bishop of a territory ravaged by invasion in which the invaders settled on the lands of those they had conquered, gradually to be assimilated into their society. But the assimilation was not easy, and it had hardly even begun. Celts and Normans lived side by side in a state of open hostility. Furthermore, if Blessed Felix had not been a man of deep and truly Christian faith and charity, it would have been easy for him to use his position and power as bishop, as so many others had done, to try to raise an armed force to take revenge on those who had violently taken the lands and heritage of his clan.

But the treasure of this holy bishop was in heaven and not on this earth. It was not for him to endanger his soul for a few acres of land or for a ruined castle, when he had been chosen and separated from the world to do the work of Jesus Christ, to represent him among men, and to transmit His life to their souls. And Felix O'Dulany was a true shepherd to all the sheep of his pasture whether Celt or Norman, acting as a spiritual Father to all alike, as Christ his Lord had done before him. And thus he strove after that perfection which we are all told to fight for: the perfection that makes us perfect as our Father in Heaven, who sends His rain upon the just and the unjust alike.[12]

But such charitable tolerance might be interpreted as weakness. That it was not is easy to see from the firmness and energy with which Blessed Felix defended the rights of God and the Church. When Theobald Fitzwalter, founder of the Ormond family, and a powerful Norman noble, usurped some lands of the Church, Felix

---

[12] Matt 5:4.

was swift and uncompromising in his reprisals, excommunicating him without delay or apology.

The city of Kilkenny and its cathedral of Saint Canice are monuments to the energy of Blessed Felix O'Dulany, who moved here from another part of the diocese because it was a safer and more peaceful place, easier to defend and to control. Thus we see in him a true Cistercian, a lover and promoter of peace, and a builder and stabilizer of society, establishing all upon the rock of the Gospel and the faith of Christ. His energy was rewarded by the coming of many new religious families to his diocese, like the Augustinian canons, who arrived in 1193, but his greatest consolation was the consecration of his own abbey church at Jerpoint, the crowning, in a sense, of all his labors.

He was twenty-four years Bishop of Ossory, until in the year 1202 we read in the annals of Loch Ce:

> *Felix O'Dublhain, Bishop of Osraighe, mortuus est.*

He was buried in an altar tomb in the north aisle of the great abbey church of Jerpoint, near the high altar; and the fact of his burial in such a manner means that he was venerated as a saint. The tomb is still to be seen, and on it lies the stone effigy of the great bishop in his pontificals. Many miracles were wrought at this place, which was the object of pilgrimages for many centuries even down to the nineteenth.[13] In 1850, however, the abbey ruins were put under lock and key, but that did not prevent a pair of the holy bishop's clients from traveling a great distance to his tomb as late as 1892.

---

[13] The remains of Jerpoint Abbey are considerable: they include the roofless nave and transepts of the church in the lancet style, surmounted by a great square central tower battlemented in the north Italian style. In wealth and importance Jerpoint ranked fourth among the mitred abbeys of Ireland.

January 26

Saint Alberic, Second Abbot of Cîteaux, France

(Sources: AASS, Jan. 3:368 [based on *Exordium* (sic), Henriques (sic), etc.; EP; EM; Manrique, vol. 1, *passim*; Seraphin Lenssen, "Saint Robert, Fondateur de Cîteaux," Coll 4 (1937): 2–16, 81–96, 161–177].)

Of the three first Fathers of Cîteaux, Saint Alberic is the one about whom the least is known, both to the world at large and to his own Order. We have no reliable knowledge of where he came from or who he was. We only possess half a dozen really solid facts about his life, but what we do possess is enough to show us a character of remarkable energy and holiness and administrative ability.

We see a tireless and self-sacrificing worker: a man of sure, swift, uncompromising decisions and an exceptionally clear thinker. Above all, we see a man burning with love of God and of the monastic life according to the Rule of Saint Benedict and one who was not afraid to suffer for his ideal. In a word, the Cistercian Order is founded upon Saint Alberic as upon a rock. The first initiative towards a break with the old traditional Cluniac usages came from Saint Robert and the vast, powerful structure of the Order as a whole sprang from the saintly genius of Stephen Harding. But Saint Alberic is nevertheless the rock upon which Cîteaux was built.

Saint Stephen himself describes Alberic, in the *Exordium Cisterciensis Coenobii* (or *Exordium parvum*) as "a man well versed in sacred and secular sciences, a lover of the Rule and of the brethren."[14]

A lover of the Rule: that is, a lover of God. For the Rule of Saint Benedict was to the founders of our Order the sure, swift way to God—provided it was kept to the letter. And then he is called a

---

[14] EP 9.

lover of the brethren. The *Exordium parvum* is one of the most concise documents in the history of monasticism. It was prepared by Saint Stephen Harding at the request of Pope Callistus II, and not a word in it is wasted or out of place. Therefore the reader is entitled, indeed he is compelled, to exhaust all the volumes that are implied in this one phrase: "a lover of the Rule and of the brethren." The student of Cistercian asceticism will soon discover what an immense importance fraternal charity has in the Cistercian scheme of contemplation, and therefore it is not surprising to find this virtue as one of the sources of the inspiration of our Order's early fathers.

But what of his life? He first appears on the scene as a hermit at Colan—the little community which humbly sought and obtained through papal intervention Saint Robert as their abbot and director when he was still superior at Saint Michel de Tonnerre. Colan was an isolated, wooded spot in Champagne, and some hermits had recently formed themselves into a community there (as is described more fully in the life of Saint Robert, April 29). It is not certain whether or not Saint Alberic had joined their number before the arrival of Saint Robert. It is usually thought that he came a short time after. In any case, he had joined the group before their removal to a more spacious site at nearby Molesme.

There the little community passed several years in complete and abject poverty, eking out a desperate living from the newly cleared forest land, and dwelling in huts made from the branches of the trees. But their life was a life of intense happiness and peace, because they possessed God. Indeed, Alberic was never to forget the joy of those days, in which he learned one thing he was never to forget: the blessedness of those who give up everything and take up their cross to follow Christ, without compromise, without bargaining, without the smallest refusal.

This happiness did not last. But the fault was not to be imputed to the monks or to their superior. It just happened that none of them were quite prepared for the sudden prosperity that descended upon them within a few years of their first foundation in 1075. Barely five years had elapsed before Molesme was a wealthy and powerful monastery, with dependent priories in all the nearby

provinces, governing parishes, collecting tithes, exploring manorial mills and bakeries and farms, which had been given them by
the friendly local nobility. But in return, the monastery found not
only that it had recruited a large number of these noblemen as its
members but also that those who remained outside frequently
came and held their court within the monastery walls.

In short, within a few years the life had totally changed from
the austere semi-eremitical vocation which Alberic had embraced
in the solitude of Colan to the busy, elaborate and mitigated routine
of a big community. It is hard to give an adequate idea of the
contrast without going into all the manifold details of the Cluniac
usages: suffice it to say that these were extraordinarily complex
and that no religious life, as we know it today, offers any basis for
comparison with the Cluniac regime. One thing is certain: a good
way to get an idea of what the Cluniac life was *not* is to read the
Rule of Saint Benedict. In that document all is simplicity and charity. The life is extremely plain, divided between the Divine Office,
manual labor and *lectio divina* or meditative reading. The diet is
very spare, the monks' articles of clothing can be counted on the
fingers of one hand, and their daily timetable is simplicity itself.
In a Cluniac monastery, on the contrary, was led a life of extreme
complexity, in which persons of many different groups and cate-
gories were all fitting in, more or less harmoniously, with the main
trend and with one another as the elaborate daily routine progressed. Instead of beginning the day with the *Deus in Adjutorium*
of canonical Matins, around one in the morning, the monks started
out with a procession in which all were aspersed with holy water;
then they proceeded in procession to the altars of various saints,
after which they went to choir for what was called the *trina oratio*
consisting of groups of psalms interlaced with prayers—sometimes totaling thirty psalms altogether. Then there were prayers
for the king, and other special devotions, and finally the *Opus Dei*
properly so called began, followed by the Office of the Dead. Often
enough, after a long night office—all sung, of course, every day—
there would be various litanies and perhaps another procession,
and then the monks, if it was any kind of a feast, returned to bed.
On rising, and returning to choir for Prime, the same routine of

processions, holy water and *trina oratio* began all over again. Every day there were two Masses and the office of the Dead, as well as one or more votive offices, like that of the Blessed Virgin, of the Holy Trinity, All Saints, and so on. In addition to this already incredible burden, some monasteries took on the occasional obligation of having all their monks recite a *daily psalter* for a month, or even a year, for some wealthy benefactor.

At the same time, however, there were in the monastery a certain number of children who took part in some but not all of the offices, and who required the attention of certain monks deputed to supervise their education. Besides these, there was always a large group of monks charged with the task of administering the vast estates of the monastery, and these were too busy to come to choir at all, at least during the day hours. They were, therefore, permanently dispensed. Since so much time was devoted to liturgical prayer, manual labor was impossible, and as a matter of fact even at Molesme it was unnecessary. The monastery was more than supported by its revenues. So, out of choir, the monks who did not have to occupy themselves in manorial business devoted their time to intellectual labor. Here again, the meditative and prayerful reading prescribed by Saint Benedict gave place to labors of scholarship and research for which he had made no provision, although of course the *lectio divina* was by no means neglected. Indeed, we read of one monastery where the abbot had four deacons simultaneously read aloud the four Gospels in the four sides of the cloister on Ember days, but this was not what Saint Benedict had in mind either!

Although they kept the strict hours of Benedictine fasting considered beyond the strength even of the strictest Orders today, the Cluniac monks could always rely on an appetizing variety of fish and egg dishes, and even in some really relaxed monasteries, on meat to compensate for the long delay.

It must not be imagined, however, that all this implied an easy life. It was certainly strenuous enough in its own way. But could it be called contemplative? Was this the life of solitude in whose peace the noise of the world became silent so that God could be heard speaking to the soul? Sometimes it was so. But too often it was not. And because of the intimate connection between the monastery and feudal society, and the frequent irruptions of the world into the cloister, contemplation was an extremely precarious thing.

It is small wonder, then, that when the influx of postulants who were accustomed to the Cluniac usages, and had never imagined anything else, transformed Molesme into a second Cluny, the fervent minority, led by Saint Alberic and Saint Stephen, soon began to protest. Their protestations were not the querulous complaints of souls whose plans had been thwarted but the voice of God's grace, moving them to act in defense of the contemplative ideal which they had formed under the guidance of His Holy Spirit. But, although they approached the problem in the mildness and moderation of charity, they were firm in recognizing the abuse for what it was.

All the documents and early testimony of the event are unanimous in agreeing that the reformers considered not merely that the Cluniac usages were not good enough for them but openly denied that they were in accord with either the letter or the spirit of Saint Benedict. "Often among themselves," says the *Exordium parvum*, which all the chief authorities agree was written by Saint Stephen Harding, "these monks under the inspiration of God's grace talked about the *transgression* of the Rule of Saint Benedict,"[15] that obtained at Molesme. Without stopping to argue whether they actually believed that the Cluniac life implied a condition of permanent prevarication against the vows of obedience "according to the Rule of Saint Benedict," we are compelled to admit that they all believed that these usages were completely alien to the simple and austere life of prayer for which the great legislator had written his Rule.

Alberic and Stephen, accordingly, approached Saint Robert, their abbot, who listened to them willingly, not only out of respect for Alberic, who was his prior and trusted friend since the days of Colan, but because of his own wholehearted agreement with what

[15] EP 3.

they had to say. And as a result of this conversation he convoked the community in chapter and placed the issue before them. There followed a more or less amicable discussion from which, however, it transpired that the conventional element was in the majority and that they were not to be shaken in their specious arguments in favor of the mitigated life. It was the only form of monasticism they knew, and they sincerely believed that anything more austere was simply a piece of eccentric exaggeration. They accused their abbot of trying to demand the impossible of men of their time and to impose on them the fantastic austerities of the old Desert Fathers. All that was out of date was not for them. The prudent thing to do was to keep these usages framed by wise directors of souls—indeed, canonized saints—and approached by the Church. Anything else was presumption.[16]

We cannot be certain whether all this took place as of 1093 or 1094 when Saint Robert left Molesme for the hermitage of Aux. Did the situation become difficult, and did Saint Robert, realizing the futility of trying to carry out a reform at Molesme, decide to abandon the project and attend to the needs of his own soul by retiring to a hermitage? It is certain that his departure indicates that there was some trouble with his monks, and the most likely hypothesis is that it had something to do with the beginnings of the time that Saint Alberic, who remained in charge of Molesme as its Prior, suffered the physical violence and imprisonment of which the *Exordium parvum* speaks.[17]

We do know, however, that several years later, when the reform was well under way, Saint Robert led his delegation, which included Saint Alberic and Saint Stephen, to Hugh, the papal legate, and put their case before them. The legate agreed with their case before them. The legate agreed with their contention that they were not keeping the Rule as it ought to be kept *quae tepide ac negligenter in eodem monasterio tenueratis*[18] and also agreed that if they wanted to do so, they would have to leave Molesme and

---

[16] Oderic Vital, *Hist. Ecclesiastica*, PL 188:638.
[17] EP 9.
[18] EP 2.

establish themselves somewhere else. For this he not only gave his permission but, more actively, his command: *ut in hoc perseveretis praecipimus.*[19]

From now on it was quite clear that the desires of the fervent minority at Molesme were indeed inspired by the Spirit of God and that it was clearly God's will that they should found a new monastery in which the Rule of Saint Benedict might be kept, in all simplicity, to the very letter.

Returning to Molesme, the monks began to canvass the other members of the community, recruiting likely candidates for the new monastery. And this was when trouble began in earnest. The most zealous of them all, in trying to stir up enthusiasm for the new foundation, was Saint Alberic, and the *Exordium parvum* tells us what was the result.[20] That Alberic was beaten and imprisoned seems to imply that the abbot was absent at the time, but in any case, the tempers of the recently converted knights, many of whom were probably none too intelligent and who were insulted and a little frightened by what they considered eccentricity and fanaticism, finally exploded and vented themselves on the one they evidently considered to be at the root of the whole affair. The fact that they did resort to this entirely illegitimate outburst of violence goes far to prove the truth of the accusation that their spirit of regularity and of prayer was only skin-deep. These were serious and sincere men, no doubt, and they meant to live up to their obligations as they understood them, but their zeal had in it too much of human nature and of their social prejudices which they had never given up, in spite of the habit which they wore.

The last thing in the world that would change the mind of a man like Alberic was injustice and violence! Confirmed in his convictions, he was probably the most determined and uncompromising of all those who left Molesme for the swampy woods of Cîteaux towards the end of Lent, 1098.

[19] EP 2.
[20] EP 2.

Legend says that they found the place by wandering more or less aimlessly around until suddenly a voice was heard from heaven, saying either *Ciestavus* (the local patois for "Stop Here!") or *Siste hic*. From the letter some think the word Cîteaux was taken. But it is more probable that they had a more or less definite place in mind before they started; besides, the most reasonable etymology for the name Cîteaux is that it was taken from the reeds or "cistels" that grew there. After all, the name Cîteaux was of local origin and was a Burgundian name, not a Latin one, and therefore should be traced to something in the patois of the place. This therefore militates strongly against the ingenious explanation that Cistertium came from the Latin Cis- tertium, meaning "this side of the third milestone." Besides being vague and complicated, and much too abstract for an ordinary place name, we must remember that Cîteaux is the original name and it is French. *Cistertium* is merely a latinization of Cîteaux, and nothing is gained by trying to work out a special Latin etymology for it. Besides, William of Malmesbury, writing in the lifetime of Saint Stephen Harding, referred to the monks of the new monastery as "Cistellenses" which he certainly would never have done if the accepted name of the place had been Cistertium at that time.[21]

Cîteaux was on the lands of Viscount Reynard of Beaune, and it was a flat, unlovely tract of wooded land bordered by cultivated fields and intersected by three small streams. There was a small chapel to the Blessed Virgin on the property, but it was still a wild and desolate spot. That was exactly what the monks were looking for. All the official documents, the correspondence with the Legate, and later with the Pope, indicate that their greatest concern was to get as far away from feudal society and conventional monasticism and all that is called the "world" as they possibly could. It is often thought that the early Cistercians chose wild remote places for their monasteries because they were lovers of nature: but it was quite the contrary. The men of the Middle Ages were almost unanimous in their hatred for such sites and avoided them not

---

[21] William of Malmesbury, *De Gestis Reg. Angl.*, PO 179.

only because of the danger of brigands and wild beasts but also because they chose these locations because they were rightly convinced that people would leave them to themselves in the forest.

When Walter, Bishop of Châlons, the ordinary of the place, gave Saint Robert his abbatial blessing, Saint Alberic was also installed as prior, and Saint Stephen Harding was under him as sub-prior, but within sixteen months Saint Robert was forced by obedience to return to Molesme, and a second election resulted in the elevation of Saint Alberic to the position of first superior—which he was very unwilling to assume.

However, he shouldered the difficult task of governing his small community with great courage. There was not only the hard physical toil of clearing the ground for cultivation—and also of draining it, no doubt, in many places—but the much more important and difficult responsibility of placing the new monastery on a firm legal footing.

The machinations of Molesme against them would clearly not end with the recall of Saint Robert. The monks of their former monastery were doing their best to rouse antipathy against the reformers by criticism and misrepresentations of their ideal and aims, and no one knew quite what the next step would be. It was certainly no new thing for violence to be employed against an isolated group of defenseless monks, and Saint Alberic would have felt no great surprise to have the little wooden monastery burned down over his head by the relatives of his former brethren in religion.

Consequently, Alberic made haste to procure letters of recommendation from Walter, Bishop of Chalons, from the Apostolic Delegate, Hugh, and from two Cardinals. With these documents he armed two monks, John and Idbold, and sent them off to Rome. Paschal II replied by Apostolic Letter of April 18, 1100, confirming the desire of his predecessor that they should lead their strict Benedictine life apart from Molesme and offering them the full protection of Rome in no uncertain terms. Anyone who molested the Cistercians would fall under excommunication. The Holy Father ended by congratulating them on their reform and giving them his encouragement in the strongest language, urging them to persevere in their resolve to empty their minds of all worldly things and live lives "absolutely dedicated to God without compromise."[22]

Saint Alberic now found himself free to turn his mind to the most important work of all: that of laying down the foundation of the new usages according to which they were to live. He had been perhaps the loudest of all in criticizing the Usages of Cluny: but one could not simply discard all usages and live by the Rule alone. There were so many interpretations of Saint Benedict's Rule that it was also necessary to make quite clear at the outset what they understood by its literal observance. A simple body of statutes would be absolutely necessary in order to make their position and their aims unmistakable both to themselves and their successors.

In many minor details of ceremonial which the Rule does not cover, the Cistercians simply preserved what they had always known at Molesme and which had always been more or less uniform in all Benedictine monasteries for several centuries. But the essence of the Cluniac usages was completely rejected, so that the *Consuetudines* of Cîteaux, afterwards drawn up by Saint Stephen, give us a picture of a widely different form of monastic life from that led in a Cluniac monastery. Saint Alberic made it his business to cut the very heart out of the Cluniac observance by his *Instituta*.

The first thing he attacked was the problem of clothing. Although Saint Benedict did indeed allow for differences of climate, the Cistercians did not mean to avail themselves of this permission. The saint only normally permitted underclothing to be worn by the monks going on a journey. Therefore the Cistercians faced the hardships of the northern winter with the wardrobe prescribed by the Patriarch for Italy—although the mountains of Italy are by no means warm in winter. They would simply have a robe, scapular and cowl, stockings and shoes. That was all. But what a contrast to the Cluniacs, bundled up in their extra capes lined with sheepskin, wearing their mufflers and coats, linen shirts and drawers, with their day shoes and their night shoes, and their plentiful

[22] EP 14.

supply of blankets and quilts on their beds! Saint Alberic did not forget either to forbid the use of combs. To the modern reader this might appear to be a piece of gratuitous barbarism: but Saint Alberic knew what he was doing. For combing the hair and beard had assumed the status of a piece of minor ritual in the Cluniac usages: there was a special time of the day when all the monks went and combed their beards and hair, and another when all the children of the monastery combed their hair likewise. The Cistercians had their heads shaved often enough to make all this combing unnecessary.

The next thing on the list was the monks' diet, which was drastically simplified, all lard and dripping being forbidden in the cooking, as well as the great variety of extra dishes and pittances, and *a fortiori* flesh meat. Some monasteries had taken to feasting on chickens, pigeons, and so on, on the grounds that the Rule only prohibited the flesh of four-footed animals, but most Cluniac houses did not serve meat in the common refectory. Cluny was, after all, itself a reform.

The most significant and important article of the *Instituta* was that which struck out against the tremendous economic abuses which had crept into the monastic system especially since the time of Charlemagne. Saint Robert had accused the monks of Molesme of "living on the blood of other men"[23] and he was right. Saint Alberic absolutely forbade the possession and administration of parish churches, the collection of altar and burial dues, the exploitation of serfs, manorial bakeries, mills, fairs, the acceptance of tithes, and so on. The monks might receive presents of land and cattle and even buildings suitable for their own use in farming, but they were to live by the work of their own hand. Indeed, this was the keystone of the whole reform, on which everything else depended.

The dependence on manual labor was what characterized the Benedictine concept of evangelical poverty. The necessity to work meant the abandonment of all the extra liturgical services in use

---

[23] Orderic Vital, *Hist. Ecclesiastica*, PL 188:637a.

at Cluny. It also meant that the monks could never accept on a large scale gifts and emoluments to be repaid by long community prayers for the benefactor. Prayer, for them, was purely and simply the Divine Office and a few adjuncts like the Office of the Dead, and later on, that of Our Lady. Long intervals for meditative reading and private prayer were also safeguarded. Furthermore, the monk not only supported himself by the labor of his hands but also devoted his surplus, if any, to the aid of the poor, of the bishop of his own diocese, and the parish priests there, as well as to the upkeep of their own monastery church.

However, although it was necessary to live by manual labor, manual labor was not an end in itself. It was an end only insofar as it was an integral part of the Rule. But the other two main divisions of the Benedictine life had to be safeguarded: prayer and *lectio divina.* Work must not ordinarily be allowed to usurp the time devoted to these essential duties of the contemplative monk, although the harvest and other special reasons would sometimes make the sacrifice of contemplation necessary. But in order to help the monks live up to their obligation to pray and meditate upon the Holy Scriptures, Saint Alberic instituted lay-brothers. He was not the first to have done so: the Order of Vallombrosa had preceded him in this respect, and others among the numerous reforms of the twelfth century were doing so. These lay-brethren were to become associated in life and in death in all the privileges of the monks without the monastic quality itself, that is, without the obligations of the choir. The greater part of their day was to be devoted to work, but they were, and still are, on a more equal footing with the choir religious than are the lay-brethren of any other Order. The Cistercian lay-brother is never the servant of the choir monk: he is his fellow-worker. And, often in the field and on the farm, it is the choir monk who takes orders from the lay-brother, since the latter usually have a monopoly on the skilled occupations and excel in the management of the farm.

Another important consideration for Saint Alberic was to provide for a proper test of vocations. The monks of Cluny were proud of the fact that they made applicants for their life spend at least a month as novices before being received to solemn profession, and this was indeed some improvement over the old abuse of receiving the profession of strangers after two or three days. However, the Cistercians returned to Saint Benedict's prescription in this extremely important matter and ensured that postulants should only be admitted with difficulty even to the novitiate and that they should there spend a full year in their secular dress before taking their vows. This afforded some protection both for the novice and for the community, although as time went on, the Cistercians were almost universal in their extreme benevolence in receiving practically everyone who presented himself: so long as he was willing and able to survive the hardships of the first year.

One of the Cistercian innovations that caused the most criticism of the new monastery was something quite accidental to the reform itself: the change in the color of the habit from black to white. The black Benedictines threw up their hands in horror when they saw these monks wearing, as they said, the color of joy in the region of penance. Their horror at this presumption was only equaled by their horror at the eccentricity with which these fanatics were fasting and abstaining from flesh meat and devoting so much of their days to hard penitential labor in the fields.

The Cistercians rightly retorted that theirs was indeed a life of joy, for since they had left everything else behind them for the love of God, they were already receiving the hundredfold promised by Christ; but it is hard to see the reason for the change unless we admit the old tradition that the Blessed Virgin herself appeared to Saint Alberic and asked him that the monks of the new monastery dedicated to her should wear white in her honor. The only other explanation is perhaps that unbleached wool would be grey, and their poverty suggested that they use no dyes, but the usual explanation offered by the Cistercians is that Our Lady intervened in the affair. Unfortunately the origin of this tradition is extremely obscure. We are by no means entitled, with Henriques,[24] to name a definite year, month and even day on which Our Blessed Lady is supposed to have appeared not only to Saint Alberic but to the

---

[24] *Menologium*, Aug. 5 (1101).

whole community as well. Not only did she appear to them, but she instantaneously changed the color of all their habits from black to white with a wave of her hand. If this had been the case, surely there would have been some reference to it in the documents of the twelfth and thirteenth century. Imagine the author of the *Exordium magnum* or Caesar of Heisterbach letting such an item slip through their fingers. We can only conclude that all these details sprang from the fancy of Henriquez himself, but that does not alter the fact that the tradition of Our Lady's appearance does exist and did exist before Henriques. However, the first documentary evidence of it is not to be found before the fifteenth century when the forty-third Abbot of Cîteaux, Jean de Cirey, appealed to it in an exhortation to his brethren, referring to it as something with which they were very well acquainted and which went back to the early days of the Order.

It was largely due to Saint Alberic's great devotion to the Mother of God that the Cistercians were the first Order dedicated to her. To be strictly exact, they were the first Order dedicated exclusively to our Lady. But the Carthusians a dozen or more years before had already consecrated themselves to Our Lady and Saint John the Baptist.

Vincent of Beauvais[25] relates that at this time there was a young cleric at Lyons who had a dream in which he beheld a mountain with a beautiful city standing on the top of it. This city attracted him mightily so that he longed to get there. But between him and the mountain was a river, and in the river he saw twelve men washing their garments. With them was another, different from them, in a shining white robe who was helping them in their task. The cleric asked the stranger who they all were, and He replied that He was Jesus Christ and that those were men doing penance with His aid, and as soon as their robes were clean, they would be able to go on to the city which they all desired, that is, to heaven. Some time later the cleric told his dream to the Bishop of Châlons, who advised him on the strength of it to enter Cîteaux. He accord-

[25] Helinand, *Chronicon*, PL 212:1000.

ingly made his way to the woods where the monks were dwelling, and finally found the enclosure of the little monastery.

The gate was made of wattles, and there was an iron hammer hanging there for a knocker. When the porter responded to his summons, what was the astonishment of the cleric to recognize him as one of the men in his dream. He also recognized all the other members of the community too, and he was not long in becoming one of them. However, he must have been practically the only one who did so in those years, together with the son of the Duke of Burgundy, if we are to believe Manrique.[26] But the *Exordium parvum* assures us[27] that at this time, instead of coming to Cîteaux, all the likely candidates for the monastic life were staying as far away from it as they could get, so discouraging was the reputation the monks had acquired by their austerities.

If, during his nine and a half years as abbot, Saint Alberic did not have the consolation of seeing his monastery grow, at least it is true that as soon as Cîteaux was definitely separated from Molesme by the brief of Paschal II, the animosity of their former confreres died down, and peace between the two houses was established and even grew as the years went on into an association of close friendship.

However, Alberic was called to his reward even before the aged Saint Robert, who lingered two years beyond him at Molesme. It was on January 26, 1109, that the second abbot of Cîteaux went to heaven. Henriques, with his usual voluble wealth of detail, gives us a vivid account of that holy death,[28] but as usual we have no idea of his authority for all the statements he makes. The early Cistercians had resolved to bury no one in their church—a custom that was soon abandoned—so Saint Alberic was laid to rest near the church door, which was at least a sign of a somewhat special respect. The liturgical veneration of this great Father of the Order, like that of his companions, Robert and Stephen, was more or less in abeyance for a time. The only Cistercian whose canonization

[26] Ann Cist, vol. 1, ann. 1104.
[27] EP 14.
[28] *Fasciculus Sanctorum Cisterciensium*, Dist. II.

was enthusiastically backed by the whole Order in those days was Bernard of Clairvaux. Saint Alberic had to bide his time until the eighteenth century, when he was finally beatified *per modum favoris* with the title of saint. All this means that, in the Middle Ages, the Cistercians were more concerned with being saints than with getting themselves or one another canonized. But it may be said of our own day that Saint Alberic and his work for the Order is receiving greater and greater appreciation as his part in the foundation of Cîteaux becomes better and better known. It is high time then for us to pay him his due by our trust in his intercession and our practical love and imitation of his example.

January 28

Saint Amadeus, Bishop of Lausanne, Switzerland

(Sources: PL 188:1299; Lenain, 2:59; Ann Cist, vols. 1 and 2, *passim*; Nicholas of Clairvaux, Ep 34; PL 196:1625.)

When the great Prince Amadeus of Clermont entered Bonnevaux with his sixteen companions (as we read in his own story, January 14), he brought with him his ten-year-old son, Amadeus, too young to enter the novitiate with his father and the other knights. The child, remaining in the guest quarters, was committed to the care of the monks, who began to teach him Latin—enough to be able to understand the Psalms and Holy Scripture, to sing the Divine Office intelligently, *Psallere sapienter*. But this was not what his father desired. For the father, having neglected to discard at the door, along with his other possessions, his worldly ideas of education, was unable to see the value of an education that did not include the pagan poets and philosophers, Cicero and Ovid and Vergil. It must be remembered that Amadeus had all the views and opinions of a cultured knight and courtier in the time of what has been called the "twelfth-century renaissance."

So attached, indeed, was Prince Amadeus to his opinions that they struck at the very roots of his vocation. He left Bonnevaux for Cluny and sent his son on to the court of his near relative, the Emperor Conrad in Germany.

The young nobleman remained there until he was sixteen, and then, perhaps because of the prayers of his converted and repentant father, who had returned to do penance at Bonnevaux, he also received the grace to see that he could not be perfectly happy in the world. And so he fled to Clairvaux and was received there into the novitiate of Saint Bernard.

Now in the Alps, on the banks of the long and narrow Lake Bourget, was the Cistercian monastery of Hautecombe, previously a Benedictine house[29] which had come over into our Order on the advice of Saint Bernard, taking the Abbot of Clairvaux as Father Immediate. And on their entrance into the Order, in 1134, a symbolic change had been made in the location of the house. From the high peak (*haute combe*) on which it had been previously situated, the house was moved to a site picked out by Saint Bernard on the shore of the lake. The reason for the change was that the Abbot of Clairvaux found the abbey's site and its buildings too ambitious and prominent for a Cistercian monastery.

Now in its humbler situation Hautecombe had indeed been brought low in more ways than one. The soil was poor (a factor that had not been of much importance in the previous site), and worse still, the inhabitants of the countryside were hostile and half barbarous thieves who pillaged their crops and decimated their flocks at night, so that the situation at Hautecombe was as desperate as anywhere in the Order. So desperate was it that the abbot asked Saint Bernard to accept his resignation and allow him to return to Clairvaux.

Amadeus must have been an energetic and fervent monk if Saint Bernard selected him in preference to all others to go to Hautecombe as the new abbot to try and save the situation. It was

[29] To be exact it was a community of hermits from Aulps, who followed the Rule of Saint Benedict in a way suited to the semi-eremitical life (Janauscheck, 34).

thirteen years after the young man's profession. Soon after his installation in his new home, he was visited by his father Amadeus of Bonnevaux, who, although by no means one who feared difficulties or work (since he had supervised four new foundations for his abbot, John), advised his son to abandon Hautecombe as a hopeless enterprise and go back to Clairvaux. To this advice, which in the natural order was probably extremely intelligent, the son replied with a supernatural prudence of blind faith which greatly edified and rejoiced the heart of his father. He simply answered that no one was able to steal their heavenly goods, and there was much merit and sanctification to be found here at Hautecombe and consequently they would stay.

However, Amadeus was not to remain there himself for more than five years. In 1144 the people and clergy of the Swiss diocese of Lausanne elected him bishop. Against his will he was forced to go north to the city that was to be his new home, and there he was consecrated bishop on the Feast of Saint Agnes: a day significant in his life, for on it he had also been born, had left Bonnevaux, had made his profession at Clairvaux, and had been elected abbot.

Haunted by the words of Saint Paul, "*oportet episcopum irreprehensibilem esse*," [30] a bishop ought to be above reproach, he entered with great diffidence upon his new task. And indeed, he proceeded with the greatest discretion in all that he did, in all things purifying his intention of all self-seeking, all ambition, all selfish anger and pride, keeping himself always in the presence of God, and judging all things by the light, not of private interest or selfish appetite, but by the light of God's infinite truth.

In this he remained a true Benedictine, and this humility and self-mistrust was the foundation of all the other virtues which endeared him to the hearts of his people. He was a tireless shepherd, tramping like Saint Peter of Tarentaise into the highest and most remote mountain villages to tend his spiritual sheep. His bearing had that simplicity and charity which is only poorly described by the word "democratic." He was all things to all men,

[30] 1 Tim 3.

dignified without being proud, learned but not pedantic, firm but not harsh, prayerful and devout but not eccentric because his devotion was in his heart, and not a thing for the street corners and the high places at official banquets. He was serious and yet not owlishly solemn, and pleasant without the cheap, forced gaiety of a campaigning politician.

One of his greatest services to Lausanne was to preserve the city by peaceful negotiation from the threatening regiments of the Count of Geneva, who built a fort right over the city's walls in preparation for a siege. His influence with Bl. Eugene III, the Cistercian Pope, and with the emperor, procured many favors for Hautecombe and for his diocese.

In 1145 he composed eight homilies in honor of the Blessed Virgin, which are full of unction and love and may be read in Migne's Latin Patrology. He died, after fourteen years as Bishop in 1158, being only 49 years old. He became the patron saint of French-speaking Switzerland, where his feast is celebrated on the day of his death, August 27.

The Cistercians of the Strict Observance commemorate him with a feast of Three Lessons on January 28. He was beatified twice—first in 1701 and by formal procession in 1903.

January 29

Blessed Alan of Lille, The Universal Doctor, Lay-brother of Cîteaux, France

(Source: Writings PL 210, prepared by Notitia Historica Litteraria.)

One entire volume of Migne's Latin Patrology is given to the works of this famous Doctor of Philosophy, once one of the most popular figures of the schools in thirteenth-century Paris. He was famous for his immense learning, and indeed, his epitaph at Cîteaux says with a rather sweeping optimism: *Totum scribile scribit.*

"He knew everything that could possibly be known." With all due allowances for the sanguine generosity with which the fraternal charity of monks tends to exaggerate even the most mediocre and insignificant intellectual achievements attributed to one of their brethren, and for the fact that the limitations of sign language inevitably transform any poor drudge from the graduate school into a great doctor, Alan's works are there to prove that he was an erudite man and a teacher of considerable versatility, well calculated to create a wide popular reputation for himself. The most typical of his works is an immense allegorical poem called the *Anticlaudianum*, concerning the functions of the "good and perfect man" and which reads pretty much like a verse Encyclopedia. He also composed a popular manual for preachers (*De arte praedicatoria*) and a *long* attack on the heretics of the time.

His character as a popularizer of learning is clearly enough brought out by the story of his conversion from the world to the cloister. For it is said he was one day walking along the Seine, turning over in his mind a project he had long been cherishing of a work that would reduce the Mystery of the Holy Trinity to terms that would be clearly understood by every reader. And as he was busy with these thoughts, he observed a little boy, playing on the river bank, who was industriously scooping up the waters of the river in a toy bucket and pouring them into a ditch that he had dug in the earth. Considering the blissful confidence with which this child was working as if to empty the whole river into his little ditch, Alan reflected upon himself, and his own presumption, and gave up not only his great work on the Trinity but his chair in the university as well. He simply disappeared from Paris: no one knew where he had gone.

So it was that he concealed his identity and entered the monastery of Cîteaux, not as a monk but as a lay-brother, and he was given the humble office of shepherd. How many years he enjoyed his peaceful and obscure life of contemplation we do not know; but eventually a fortunate accident led to the discovery of his identity and talents.

Many abbots and bishops had been summoned to Rome to consult with the Pope concerning heresies, and Alan was sent along with the Abbot of Cîteaux, not in his capacity as scholar and theologian, but simply to look after the horses. However, he was frequently at his abbot's side in his encounters with great dignitaries and also in his controversies, and one day, hearing the sophisms of a heretic, Alan was unable to contain himself any longer. Asking permission of his abbot, he began to demolish the arguments of the stranger one by one, with such rapidity and force that the latter finally cried out in astonishment:

"Either you are the devil, or you are Alan."

Without stopping to consider in what sense this disjunction could be taken as complete, and whether such a sense could ultimately be complimentary to himself, Alan quietly admitted that he was not the devil but was indeed Alan of Lille.

After his return to Cîteaux, although he still remained a poor and humble lay-brother, Alan was charged with writing books to instruct the brethren in Christian Doctrine, and it is probably to this period that his greatest work, a commentary on the "Canticle of Canticles," belongs.

This work is particularly devoted to showing how the great mystical poem of the Old Testament applies to the Virgin Mother of God, and as such it was quoted by Pius IX at the time of the definition of the dogma of the Immaculate Conception as one of the many thirteenth-century documents in favor of it.

For the rest, the life of Alan of Lille is shrouded in uncertainty. Henriquez rather blandly reconciles the date on his tombstone (1294) with other dates in his life in such a way as to conclude that the good brother lived to be one hundred and sixteen years old. Wise scholars have preferred to call at least some of these varying dates into question. But in any case, it is evident that Alan lived to be a great age and died some time in the thirteenth century, being buried with considerable circumstance and veneration in the abbey Church of Cîteaux.

He was venerated as a saint, but the cult was never confirmed by ecclesiastical authority.

January 30

Blessed Gerard, Brother of Saint Bernard, Cellarer of Clairvaux, France

(Sources: Saint Bernard, SC 26; EM 3.1–3; Vita Bern 1.3; AASS, June 3:192, based on EM, etc.; Vacandard, *passim*.)

The second son of Tescelin of Fontaines was endowed, by God's providence, with a nature that was quite a contrast to that of his brother, and it was to become evident in the course of their lives that the Lord had special designs by which this contrast was to serve as a material and spiritual aid to the sanctification of both.

Bernard was a man of an ardent and enthusiastic nature, predisposed by his very temperament to receive the highest mystical graces. He was gifted with a brilliant intellect, was a born theologian and poet. Gerard, on the other hand, was born a knight and a fighter and an administrator of practical things. His hard-headed sobriety at first opposed his brother's notions of the religious life, and Gerard, like Guy, the eldest brother, answered Bernard's appeal to leave the world with him with a blunt and curt refusal.

This was in the summer of 1111 when Saint Bernard approached his brothers and uncle who were encamped with the Duke of Burgundy before the town of Grancey in one of the innumerable local wars that were almost continually being fought all over Europe in the Middle Ages. Gerard's soldierly common sense found only offense in the notion that he should leave the only existence that had any meaning to him, to engage in what most of the reputable minds and sane heads of Burgundy still regarded as a dangerous experiment: the life of extreme mortification as it was being practiced under Saint Stephen Harding at Cîteaux.

It took a miracle to operate the conversion of this thick-skinned soldier. When he had finished his indignant expostulations with his younger brother, the latter simply put his finger to Gerard's side and told him that this was the spot where he would be wounded in battle for refusing to obey the voice of God.

The prediction was not long in being fulfilled. Not many days later, in the heat of battle, Gerard was surrounded by the enemy and fell, pierced by a lance. The men of Grancey picked him up and unceremoniously carried him off as a prisoner. He came to himself surrounded by hostile faces, and the first thing he uttered by way of comment on the situation was the inarticulate and, to his captors, unintelligible cry: "I am a monk! I am a Cistercian monk!" The sign had its effect.

Unfortunately, now that he had the desire to be a monk he had lost all power to put it into execution, since he was locked up in a prison in Grancey. There the Lord left him to meditate for some time upon his refusal of the grace of a vocation. After a few days, Saint Bernard, as a neutral in the war, entered Grancey as freely as any other private citizen, and standing some distance from his brother's prison, cried out the news that he and the rest of them were now leaving for Cîteaux.

"Be a monk in your prison," he cried, "if it is impossible for you to come with us."

In due time, however, Gerard's imprisonment expiated his refusal of grace, and God miraculously set him free. First, in a dream, at night he heard a voice assure him: "Today you will escape." The day dawned. He waited. It was almost evening when his chains suddenly fell from his wrists and ankles. The doors of the jail opened by themselves. He passed out among guards as if he were invisible and went his way as the sun was going down.[31]

After his profession at Cîteaux Gerard was sent by Saint Stephen to assist his brother in the labors of the new foundation in the "valley of bitterness" that was to become the "valley of light." Saint Bernard gave him the position of cellarer, in which he remained all his life. This was the work for which God had destined him, and how important a work it was may be seen from the debt Saint Bernard owed his brother by the time that obscure and fruitful life had ended.

[31] Vita Bern 3.12.

Saint Bernard paid off that debt in some measure in the famous funeral sermon on Gerard, which interrupts his exposition of the Canticle of Canticles and is the chief basis for his beatification.

Without Gerard many of the invaluable works of Saint Bernard, many of those sermons so full of unction and of light, would never have been written and never preached. Without Gerard, the hours of contemplation that slowly and imperceptibly filled the mind of the great saint with grace, as a reservoir upon which his charity was to draw for such treasures of fructifying wisdom, would never have been possible. For the prudent and devoted Gerard took upon himself quite unobtrusively the task of interviewing most of the visitors who came to see the saint and diverting them and sending them away with the "kind words" recommended by Saint Benedict to the cellarer. And so, in a sense, Gerard was a kind of coauthor of his brother's great sermons.

"Thanks to thee," says the saint, "thanks to thee, my dear brother, my soul enjoyed greater recollection and sweet repose; my sermons were more effective, my prayer more fruitful, my time for reading long, my prayers more fervent."[32]

Nor was his assistance to his brother and abbot merely negative: Gerard was a prudent and wise counselor to whom Saint Bernard frequently turned in difficulties; and not merely by way of a sort of condescending precaution against the possibility of too much self-assurance. The extent of his reliance upon Gerard's experience and tact is set forth with a striking simplicity in the funeral oration. Gerard too was able to supply an ever-greater practical experience than his brother could command in the direction of work in the construction of the monastery. Whether it was a matter of instructing and directing the monks in the work of carpenters, masons, farmers, smiths, farriers, cooks, tailors, millers—anything inside or outside the house—the practical genius of Gerard was always there to see that everything was expedited in the most perfect and economical manner. Yet he was a most humble man: humble as he was self-sacrificing in his generosity towards the whole community.

[32] SC 26.7.

"He worked more than the others," says Saint Bernard, "and received less, and often after he had provided for the needs of others, he had to go without many things himself, in the matter of clothes, for instance, and food."[33]

Finally, however, there was one thing that was greater than all of these. For it can often happen that an efficient and devoted cellarer, while admirably serving the needs of the community, and doing so with generosity and self-sacrifice, can lose all the fruit of his work by doing it merely for the love of work, or merely out of natural and human motives. This was not the case with Gerard. We must not imagine that his conversion had been any less complete than it was sudden. He had entered Cîteaux to become a contemplative, and he often humbly asked his brother to relieve him of a charge which took so much time and threatened his recollection with such numerous and distracting cares. But he was never discharged, and if he continued to exercise his functions so successfully, he also did so for the only motive pleasing to God. He accepted the charge through obedience, out of loving faith, and he persisted in it also for one reason alone: charity.

He accompanied Saint Bernard when the latter traveled to Italy in 1137, at the command of the Pope, to fight the schism of Peter de Leone. And when they were at the papal court in Viterbo, Gerard suddenly fell ill, so ill that it was apparent to all that he must soon die. Stricken with grief, Bernard prayed God to spare his brother. It was not many months since Guy had died outside of the monastery. Gerard was spared. Bernard forgot, however, that he had asked only for him to be spared until he returned to Clairvaux.

There, once again, Gerard was struck down. This time it was the end. But what a beautiful death! It was a death that confessed the glory of Christ by the depth and simplicity of the peace and joy and confidence with which the saintly cellarer entered into the arms of his heavenly Father. Suddenly in the middle of the night he had begun to sing a psalm filled with the exultation of his approaching dissolution to be with Christ. And when the psalm

[33] SC 26.6.

was ended, he exclaimed: "Father, into Thy hands I commend my spirit." He knew what he was saying. Indeed, now for the first time the full truth and significance of what he was saying must have dawned upon him as it never had before. For he looked up with a transfigured face and kept repeating: "Father . . . Father . . . ." And then, as if to explain his inexplicable depth of joy in that word, he said: "How good God is, how good, to be the Father of men! And what glory for them to be the children and heirs of God! For they are His heirs because they are His children."

And with these words he passed quietly into the immense radiance of the truth which had begun already in the last moments of his mortal life to pour into the chambers of his finite mind.

He died on June 13, 1138, and was beatified in 1702. The Cistercian Order keeps his feast on January 30.

February

February 4

Blessed Helinand, Monk of Froidmont, Picardy, France

(Sources: PL 212:477; Hans Hublecher, *Helinand von Froidmont und sein Verhaltmis su Johann von Salisbury* [Regensburg, 1913].)

The romantic revival in literature attached a certain amount of glamour to the same Troubadour, and the Troubadours were extraordinary men, although perhaps not quite in the comic-opera style in which the nineteenth century liked to picture them. These poets were men of great brilliance, talent and versatility, who flourished at a time when there was growing up a new and powerful literary movement. Helinand himself, who was one of them, appears at a crucial point in literary and social history: he flourished in the midst of the years when so-called courtly love was a fashion that was transforming the face of society and when literature was developing out of the old grandiose *chasons de geste*, those monumental and heroic romances of the great medieval men of war, into the more subtle and flowery and sophisticated romances of the Arthurian cycle.

Helinand was one of the greatest men at the court of Philip Augustus (1165–1223), not because he was a great soldier, or a great diplomat or prelate, but because he was a good poet. Yet a troubadour had to be more than a poet. He had to be an accomplished singer and actor as well. Helinand was all these things and had one talent besides: a genius for impromptu wit which, as far as the king was concerned, was his most valuable gift. He was a genius, a virtuoso, and he was also funny. Everybody admired him. He was a prodigious success. The world, as they say, was at his feet.

Nor are we ever allowed to forget that it was a brilliant world for all its underlying crudity: a world in many ways more polished and attractive in its intellectual and social fashions than many later cultures have proved themselves to be.

"Yet what doth it profit a man to gain the whole world and suffer the loss of his soul?" And we can see how Helinand was a man lost and wandering in the exterior darkness, a man whose soul had lost its center, a man whose spirit was emptied and hollow and could find no rest in anything on earth.

He had been born under circumstances that portended a life without peace: his father had been forced to flee from his native Belgium after partaking in an unsuccessful conspiracy against Count Charles of Flanders. Helinand had been born of a French mother whom his father met and married in Picardy, and growing up was educated by one Master Ralph of Beauvais, an Englishman, and pupil of the great, unhappy Peter Abelard. Having abandoned his studies after developing a thorough knowledge of classical and pagan poetry, Helinand found his way to the King's court and continued a wandering life that carried him from one end of Europe to the other, going to war with his monarch, visiting the courts of other princes, never able to satiate his thirst for praise and power and pleasure.

"You used to know Helinand," he writes of himself, to his brother, from his monastery, "as well as anyone ever knew any man—if, indeed, Helinand could be called a man. For he had been born not so much for labor, as befits a man, as for flight, like a bird, going about the earth, and prowling up and down seeking whom he might devour, either by his flattery or by his contentions!"

But suddenly, perhaps as some writers think as the result of a grave sickness, he received the signal grace to become totally disgusted with the futility of that hopeless search for rest where there is no rest to be found. He suddenly realized the full bitterness of the poisoned cup he had taken up to drink. And to taste this bitterness is one of the greatest graces God can give a soul. There is no sinner who does not spend all his time and efforts in trying to forget or deny the emptiness of a life without God, and the children of the world congratulate themselves when they find an anesthetic that helps them to forget their own futility for a little while. Happy the ones whom God does not allow to forget! Happy the ones He pursues with sickness and failure, until they suddenly come to themselves and begin to fight for life, with confession and penance and prayer.

Helinand's conversion was so complete that he sought the strictest cloistered order of monks that could be found and entered the Cistercian monastery of Froidmont in the plains of Picardy. The very name of the monastery has something forbidding to the flesh about it: It means *cold mount*. In addition to the normal burden of the Rule, Helinand had to suffer from a constitution greatly weakened by his former life. Yet he sought no relief or mitigation of the austerities of the Order. He had come to realize the truth pointed out in the *Spiritual Directory* of the present-day Cistercians of the Strict Observance, or Trappists, that the only good we are capable of doing on earth is to fulfill the will of God; and God's will, for us monks, is that we should carry out all the prescriptions of the Rule with generous self-sacrifice and not seek any alleviations dictated by our own natural desires.

Helinand was devoted to every detail of the Rule in all its strictness and to the spirit of the ancient usages of Saint Stephen. He even vigorously opposed the tendency towards a more elaborate and ornate style of architecture which was beginning to creep into the order in the thirteenth century. For the rest, he lost none of his natural buoyancy and joyfulness in the cloister; indeed, his writings bear definite traces of the successful troubadour who had seemed so funny to Philip Augustus and the lords and ladies of Paris. Nor did he lose any of his familiarity with the poets of pagan Rome. He is just as likely to quote Juvenal as the Book of Job.

His principal ascetic work has a typically Cistercian theme: it is the *De cognitione sui*—"on the knowledge of one's self." Now everyone knows that this question of self-knowledge was fundamental to many pagan philosophers, and Helinand was well aware of the inscription *gnothe seauton* that was to be seen on the temple of Apollo at Delphi. But, like all the other Cistercians, particularly Saint Bernard, with whom this was a favorite subject, he teaches us that self-knowledge does not really begin until we have reached the point where the pagan philosophers left off. For how can we know ourselves if we ignore that our very essence is that we are constituted in the image of God? For God created us in His image and likeness. The likeness has been lost but the image inheres in human nature itself, and since that nature is immortal, the image is itself undying. Indeed, its immortality is precisely one of the notes by which human nature is constituted in the image of the divine. But another of these notes, and the most important of all, is our freedom. And it is by free will, also, in cooperation with grace, that we can recover the lost likeness to our Creator and Exemplar and End. But if God is our Exemplar, how can we be said to know ourselves, His image, if we do not know him? Ultimately, then, the whole program of Christian asceticism has to be followed out to its logical conclusions before we know either God or ourselves. For our nature does not recover its beauty and perfection until our will is in perfect harmony with God. For our will was made to be free by virtue of its likeness to God, Who is infinitely free. And our perfection is to participate in His infinite freedom, which we know, by another name, as Love. But we can only do this, para-doxically, by obedience and absolute renunciation of our apparent freedom, which is not freedom at all, because it is independence of Him on Whom we must either depend or die the death.

His *Letter to Walter*, defending the strictness of the Cistercian regime, is also of the greatest interest. In it he answers all the fool-ish arguments that asceticism and mortification, as practiced by so strict an Order, are against nature and harmful to it. Drawing upon his own experience, Helinand points out several things about this fallacy. First, that it proceeds almost entirely from a cowardice that shrinks even from the slightest difficulty or mortification. Second, that our austerities, which seem so difficult to those who have never practiced them, as much easier to get used to than we imagine. For, as we read in Saint Ælred, it is not the Rule that makes us suffer so much as our self-love kicking against the goad. And as soon as we cease to rebel, we truly find that the Lord's yoke is sweet and his burden light. To quote Saint Ælred: "If our coarse fare still causes me to suffer, my difficulty in bearing it is merely an indication of the power of concupiscence in my flesh: nor does the hardship come from the fact that I have taken up the yoke of Christ, but from the fact that I have not yet totally cast off the yoke of my self-love."

So much for those who cannot fast because they get a headache. Many a headache disappears as soon as generosity has obtained for us the acquisition of a good habit, although without question, it may take a month or two for us to make the adjustment.

Without delaying to consider his numerous sermons or the tract on government called the *De regimine principum*, his famous history, The Chronicon, let us add one more of his arguments to his brother Walter's, to cure the latter's cowardly hesitation at the threshold of the religious life. To his complaint that, after all, there were other ways of being saved besides this one, so hard and so unpleasant to the flesh, Helinand replied drily: *Est plane, sed not tibi!* Yes, there may be another way, but not for you!

Helinand's final and most convincing argument that the Cistercian life was not only not against nature but even profitable to it was the fact that he lived, himself, to be a great age. The exact year of his death is not known: it is put variously at 1223, 1227, 1229 and 1239. In all these cases, he would have reached an age between eighty and a hundred. His feast was kept on February 3 in the Diocese of Beauvais until the revision of the Roman Breviary.

February 6

Saint Raymond, Abbot of Fitero, Spain, Founder of the Order of Calatrava

(Source: AASS, Feb. 1:254 [not a contemporary life but an article by the Bollandists].)

There is some doubt about the birthplace and early life of this saint whose feast is celebrated by the Cistercian Order on the sixth of February. But whether he was born at Barcelona or Tarragona, it is certain that he was a Catalan. And whether he was a secular canon or a hermit (the latter seems less likely), before he entered our Order, we know that he eventually became a Cistercian. At that time, there were as yet no Cistercian monasteries in Spain, and he crossed the Pyrenees into France, to the land of Navarre, the country of the Basques. There he was received at the monastery of Scala Dei, a daughter house of Morimond, and there he made his profession.

It was from Scala Dei that the Cistercian Order first crossed the mountains into Spain. The colony was headed by one Durando, and the Catalan, Raymond, was his prior. They first settled in the wildest and highest part of the mountains of Spanish Navarre, but the place was too inaccessible and rough for an agricultural life. So they moved down into the plain, settling near the ruins of a town called Nienzava, which had been destroyed by the Saracens. From there they made another move, crossing the borders of Castilla la Vieja, where, near the village of Cervera, the monastery of Fitero was founded. It was the year 1141. This monastery was to become a famous shrine of the Mother of God, and its first abbot was Saint Raymond.

Now the ancient Castilian city of Calatrava had been recaptured from the Moors by Alphonso V. But it still lay open to the threat of attack from the Saracens in the south. Consequently, Alphonso had turned it over to the Knights Templars for defense. The garrison of the Templars was small, and there was not much prospect of their being able to defend the place against a real threat. And so, when it became known that a large army of infidels was preparing to march north, the Templars resigned their charge and retired from the threatened city. It did not seem likely that Alphonso could replace them from his own troops, and the place appeared to be doomed, when Saint Raymond, and another monk, Diego Velasques, applied to the King and received permission to recruit an army of volunteers to garrison Calatrava. From the Archbishop of Toledo they quickly received faculties to preach and offer indulgences to those who would join them to fight the invaders, so that in a short time a large and enthusiastic force of fighting men was raised.

However, for some reason, the Saracens did not attack. And so the new army was left in Calatrava with nothing to do. Rather than disband them, or leave them to vegetate in the city, Saint

Raymond organized them into a religious and military order following the Cistercian usages. It is perhaps hard for us to realize that these military orders were not something produced by a bellicose age for the glorification of war. On the contrary, they must be looked at as the praiseworthy and generally successful attempt of Christianity to sanctify fighting men in a troubled and warlike age when wars were everywhere and when there was inevitably a large class of men in society whose permanent office it was to fight. The application of a religious and penitential discipline to the life of the camp made many saints and saved many thousands of souls from among men that would otherwise have become brutalized and depraved by their way of life. But because war is what it is, it was also inevitable that these Orders, for all their good intentions, should fall victim to great abuses.

The Knights of Calatrava followed an adaptation of the Cistercian usages. They sang the Divine Office and were, in general, dedicated first of all to a life of prayer and penance. They had manual labor, kept silence and fasted. They were vowed to poverty. However, they had one outstanding obligation, which was to be ever ready to fight against the Moors. Their martial character meant that their habit needed certain modifications, since the cowl of a Cistercian was not designed to permit him to spring out of bed and into the saddle and gallop into the night to meet the Saracens, with lance, sword and buckler! Also, the use of flesh meat was soon permitted them, for the same reason. Not only that, but they were allowed to supply themselves with this meat by hunting when they were campaigning in wild territory. Obviously, for all their good intentions, these Knights were far from being Cistercians after the heart of Saint Stephen or Saint Alberic. But Saint Bernard had wisely realized the value of applying our Rule to the life of a knight: and Calatrava saved and sanctified many a tough fight. In the material order, these knights did much valuable work for Castille and Christian Europe, recapturing many towns and much territory from the Saracens and serving as a firm bulwark against any further northward incursions.

Saint Raymond was Grand Master of this Order, but he also remained Abbot of Fitero until his retirement shortly before his death. He then withdrew to the monastery of Bonval, which had been founded by our Order in the diocese of Toledo, and there he died in 1163, with great fame for sanctity. He was beatified in 1486 with the title of Saint. His relics, celebrated for their miraculous powers, were translated in 1488 to the abbey of Mount Sion in Toledo.

February 7

Blessed Nivard, Monk of Clairvaux, Brother of Saint Bernard

(Sources: Vita Bern; Gregory Mueller, "Der Selige Nivard," Cist Chronik 83 [1896]: 43-51.)

Because of the fact that Saint Bernard is the only Cistercian saint who has had any widely read lives of himself written in the present day, his brothers are all much better known than many other Cistercians who achieved a far greater reputation than they and left far more of a record even during Bernard's lifetime. Really, of Blessed Nivard we know comparatively little, only a few bare facts and dates.

Yet he is one of the best known of the Cistercian saints in the sense that the one detailed story that has come down to us about him is familiar to everyone who has ever read a life of Saint Bernard. Who will forget how, on that April day in the year 1112, Saint Bernard and his brothers stopped at the Castle of Fontaines on their way from Châtillon to Cîteaux to bid farewell to their father and their ancestral home. On that day little Nivard was playing under the castle walls on the hill overlooking Dijon, and he was seized with apprehension, seeing what was going on. Were his big brothers leaving home for good?

"Where are you going?" he asked them. "To Cîteaux," was their answer. They probably did not have to explain at great length what Cîteaux was; in the past few months everybody at Fontaines had heard not a little about this most severe of monasteries.

"And will you leave me behind?" said the boy.

Guy, the soldier brother, tried to console him. "All this, the castle, the lands, everything, will belong to you some day, my little brother." But that was no consolation to Nivard. "So you take heaven," he said, "and leave me with the earth: the division is not fair!" But the older brothers rode off southward, and Nivard was left for a time at least with his sister, Humbeline, and their father at the Castle.

He was at that time only twelve years old. But he already desired to follow after them. His visits to Cîteaux were frequent during the next three years, and finally he was admitted by Saint Stephen when he was fifteen. By this time, Bernard and the rest had gone on to found Clairvaux, so it was evident enough that Nivard did not merely come to Cîteaux looking for the company of his brothers. However, after his profession he was sent on after them by Saint Stephen, and thus he entered into the thick of the difficulties of the new foundation with its bitter struggle for life in the forest glen that had once been the repair of bandits. He shared with Bernard and all the other heroic pioneers of that great monastery their hunger, poverty, cold, and back-breaking labor, the temptations to despair that so often nearly made them give up and go back. But with them he came through the trial and entered upon the glory of Clairvaux's prosperity. The next we hear of him is in 1129, when he accompanied Saint Bernard to Montbard Castle (The ancestral home of their mother, Aleth of Montbard) on business concerning the affairs of a novice at Clairvaux, who was Lord of Montbard and left his property to Molesme. Nivard and Bernard were there in the interests of the Benedictine Abbey—an illuminating fact. We see how little rancor there was in their hearts against Molesme, or even against the usages of Cluny, which favored the acquisition of large properties. We clearly see what the Cistercian attitude was in its reality: the fathers of our Order did not despise Molesme as dissolute and scandalous. They did feel that the usages of Cluny were open to great dangers and abuses and did not want any such dangers for themselves, but otherwise their relations with Molesme were always cordial. They would have also been the same with Cluny, had not certain hotheads in the Cistercian

Order launched an exaggerated and pharisaical attack on Cluny which involved Saint Bernard in a discussion with Peter the Venerable—a discussion which made clear Saint Bernard's refusal to compromise with nature but in which Peter the Venerable appears in no unfavorable light either.

In 1132 Saint Bernard sent his youngest brother to the new foundation of Vauxcelles on the river Scheldt, less than a mile out of Cambrai. Blessed Nivard was thus concerned in the foundation of what was to become one of the most important of the Cistercian "Schools of Charity" in northern France. He spent three years there as novice master and was then called back by his Father Immediate to be sent on a much more difficult expedition, one which must have been a singularly arduous and purifying trial.

In 1135 Saint Bernard answered what seemed to be a generous offer on the part of Conan, Duke of Brittany, who wanted a new Cistercian foundation in his duchy and held out an attractive prospect with a gift of land and a promise of support at Buzay on the left bank of the Loire, below the city and port of Nantes. Nivard was sent as prior of this foundation, but his most generous and self-sacrificing efforts were doomed to failure, since Conan went back on his specious promises, and the struggling foundation was left helpless and without support. We do not know the details of what must have been a heartbreaking failure, but Nivard came back to Clairvaux, and we find him in 1148 engaged in the foundation of Val-Richer in the woods of Souleuvre, near Thorigny in Normandy, a house of which we do not hear much in the history of the Order.

Finally, it seems that Blessed Nivard was sent as far afield as Spain, although it is hard to confirm this part of the story. The abbey of Saint Pedro de Espina in the diocese of Palencia was founded as the gift of the Princess Sancha in a place belonging to her. Yepes, in his manuscript "Chronicle of the Order of Saint Benedict," says that Nivard came and helped establish this foundation and returned to Clairvaux, leaving it in the hands of Abbot Baldwin. As for the story that he was called back to France by an angel, summoning him to the deathbed of Blessed Humbeline, this is hardly credible, in view of the fact that the probable year of Humbeline's death is 1141 or 1142—long before Nivard ever thought of going to Spain, if he went at all. At any event, he certainly did not die there but probably at Clairvaux, sometime after 1150.

His feast is still celebrated by the Spanish Cistercians, and Fr. Gregor Muller says that Our Lady of Stams, in the Tyrol, used to give him a feast of two Masses.

February 11

Saint Adolph, Monk of Camp, and Bishop of Canabruck, Germany

(Source: AASS, Feb. 2:571.)

When Caesar of Heisterbach made his famous collection of edifying stories for the instruction of his novices, he included that of the conversion of Saint Adolph from the life of a secular canon to that of prayer and penance;[1] and this is one of the few things we know about that saint.

He was a canon at the Church of Saint Peter, second only in importance to the great Cathedral in the city of Cologne, and one day he traveled out into the flat and fertile lands of Westphalia to the Cistercian monastery of Camp, intending only to make a brief visit there. However, something happened that so impressed him that he never returned to Cologne. After Mass (the usages, in this respect, seem to have been very different in those days), he beheld the extraordinary spectacle of all the monks, young and old, hastening with great compunction to the various side altars around the church, where each one rapidly stripped to the waist and began to beat himself, with equal vigor and dispatch, with a discipline. So edified was he with this sight, and so profoundly moved with

[1] DM 122. Caesar was writing in the lifetime of Saint Adolph, while the latter was still bishop.

the sense of his own failure thus far to punish his rebellious flesh or to make up, in his own body, for what was wanting in the sufferings of Christ, that he immediately felt an irresistible conviction that this was where he belonged.

He became a monk of the greatest humility and modesty, distinguished for his love of Sacred Scripture and the fervent zeal with which he meditated upon the inspired words of the Bible.

In the year 1204, however, he was called forth from the peace and obscurity of the cloister to become bishop of the ancient Westphalian See of Osnabruck, founded by Charlemagne, and dedicated to Saint Peter and Saints Crispin and Crispinian. In this office he distinguished himself, like many other Cistercian Bishops with his work in carrying from the cloister to the world the liturgical perfection that characterized the performance of the "Work of God" in Cistercian monasteries. Saint Peter of Tarentaise, for instance, had seen to it that many collegiate churches in the Alpine cities and towns under his influence were occupied by regular canons, to replace the secular canons who had been, for the most part, noblemen occupying such positions only as a lucrative sinecure and demonstrating no skill in chant or sense of the meaning or function of the liturgy. Such men in many cases had so little of the spirit of prayer that they never appeared in their churches at all.

Saint Adolph founded a *cantorate* at Osnabruck and saw to it that the canonical hours were sung with the dignity and devotion which only the solemnity of the purest Gregorian Chant can bring to the service of our God. Would that a few had a little of his spirit in our own day! Like Saint Peter of Tarentaise and Saint William of Bourges and so many others, he founded numerous charitable institutions in his diocese and had that special love for the poor which characterized the Cistercian bishops of the twelfth and thirteenth centuries. To this he added extraordinary affection and sympathy for the lepers.

His duties frequently took him to a place called Varstonow, and on the way he passed a cottage where there was a leper. He never failed to stop there and visit the poor man, giving him a few words of help and encouragement, as well as an alms and more material assistance. One day, when he came by a strange thing happened. Those who had care of the sick man suddenly took it upon themselves to "spare the Bishop of trouble" of talking to one infested with so unpleasant a disease; and so they decided to leave the poor sufferer in the back room where he was lying in a state of great weakness and tell the bishop that it was useless to try to see him that day. They opened the door for their good visitor and were about to tell him their story when the voice of the leper was heard behind them. He was in his accustomed chair; and no human power had put him there. He was unable to walk or move from his bed. Indeed, it was evident that even now the end of his life was at hand, for he began to thank the good Bishop for all his kindness to him, telling him that it was he who had brought him the strength and courage to end his life in holy and loving patience under the hand of God, to Whom he believed he could now go with full confidence of being accepted into His eternal joy.

Thus it was that the poor leper died a saintly death in the arms of his friend, Saint Adolph, which was taken as an evident indication by all of the latter's own sanctity. The leper's attendants were overcome with sorrow and shame at the attempted piece of selfish trickery, confessed the fault, and made the whole story known everywhere to add to the Bishop's fame.

After his death, in 1224, he was venerated by all as a saint and his cult was officially sanctioned by the Sacred Congregation of Rites. The old menology commemorated him on February 11 and the *Acta Sanctorum* assigns this day to him. He probably died in June.

February 12

Blessed Humbeline, Sister of Saint Bernard

(Sources: Vita Bern 1; Vacandard; Luddy, *Life and Teaching of Saint Bernard*.)

"I don't understand the saints that did not love their families," said Saint Thérèse of the Child Jesus. Leaving aside the question of whether there ever were any saints who did not love their families, with the true love of charity which transcends and often seems to oppose all natural feeling, it is easy to see that Saint Bernard and his brothers, together with their sister, mother and father, do not fall into this category. Indeed, some people might be inclined to reproach Saint Bernard for too much affection for his blood relatives, given, as an example, the overpowering emotion with which he grieved at the death of his brother, Gerard. But we must be careful how we talk about the saints—careful in the first place to see that we really know what we are talking about and really know all there is to be said. The "ruthless" Saint John of the Cross, for example, who is the most uncompromising of men in his sweeping statements of the necessity of detachment from all natural ties ("Forget all alike for the sake of holy recollection"), also admitted that he was fonder of his brother, the blacksmith, than of any other man alive. Nor were the two statements contradictory. There is a sense in which we must be absolutely detached from all natural love, "hating," as the Lord said, our father and mother, but another sense in which, once this universal detachment is accounted for, we must observe a certain hierarchy of loves in which those closest to us have a greater claim on our prayers and attention, even in material things, than others.

Blessed Humbeline was the fourth child of Aleth and Tescelin of Fontaines and was in talent and temperament, as well as in age, the closest to Saint Bernard. A beautiful and talented child, she rapidly acquired skill in music and Latin, besides growing up in the atmosphere of faith and charity fostered by the saintly chatelaine of Fontaines, Blessed Aleth. When that good and holy lady breathed forth her soul into the hands of God, and when Bernard and all his brothers, except little Nivard, entered Cîteaux, Humbeline was left alone with her father and that last brother at Fontaines. The great castle must have seemed empty and sad indeed! It was only a matter of a couple of short years before Nivard was old enough to follow his brothers, and it was obvious that the father would take the same road to the cloister. And Humbeline? In the midst of this family crisis, a young nobleman, Guy de Marcy, appeared to solicit her hand in marriage and was accepted.

In the happiness of her first married years as a noble and popular lady among the noblest of Burgundy, and in a gay and brilliant society in which the women were beginning to play once again an important part, Humbeline yielded to the allurement of the fascinating intellectual and social fashions of her century, the century of "courtly love." It was not hard for human nature to take some measure of complacency in the flattery and attention that began to surround women in society. Humbeline did not mind being put on a pedestal.

But one day the idea came to her that she ought to go and visit her brothers, the monks. Vacandard calls this "a passing whim."[2] William of Saint Thierry says it was "an inspiration of the Holy Ghost."[3] But when Humbeline arrived before the rough gate of Clairvaux, with a cavalcade of noisy attendants whose laughter and empty small talk resounded with the jingling of the bridles under the trees of this valley of peace and silence, Saint Bernard evidently was of one mind with Vacandard, rather than his earlier biographer. The saint shut himself up in his cell and left word that Humbeline was to be told to go home. Bernard was evidently cut to the heart by the emptiness and vanity of this equipage of his sister, not to mention the worldliness of Humbeline herself, and imagined that she had come to patronize her eccentric brothers.

Meanwhile, Andrew at the gate was even more outspoken than Saint Bernard. The holy abbot had referred to Humbeline's attire as "nets for the devil to capture souls"; Andrew referred to it loudly before all present as *stercus*—offal. Humbeline's fall from her pedestal was as abrupt as it was painful. But it is easy to see that there was no real harm to her. She was thoughtless, perhaps, and silly, like most ladies of fashion. But in her, at least, there was no real pride. "If I am a sinner," she said, with crestfallen humility, "well, Christ died for sinners. And if I am a sinner, that is all the more reason why I need advice and help. If my brother despises my body, at least let the servant of God have mercy on my soul! Let him come and command me whatever he wills: whatever he says I will do."

[2] Vacandard, 1:82.
[3] Vita Bern 1.6.

That was all Saint Bernard needed to hear, and apparently William of Saint Thierry was right after all, and not Fr. Vacandard. It was the Holy Ghost that had brought Humbeline to Clairvaux.

A long conversation under the peaceful elm trees in the silence of the afternoon in which the memory of Blessed Aleth lived again among her children had an indescribable effect on Humbeline. When she returned home, it was with the resolution to lead a new life, a life of charity and mortification and Christian piety like that of her mother. She soon fell away from the gay social group of which she had been so prominent a member and devoted herself to the service of God according to her married state, forgetting herself and looking for Christ in the poor and needy and sick. All this was with the permission and approval of her husband. And yet, for Humbeline, it was not enough. Five years passed. Her thoughts began to turn to the cloister. This time, Guy de Marcy put up a sterner opposition but eventually gave in to her desires, and in 1122 she entered the Benedictine convent with the charming name of Jully-les-Nonnains. The word "Nonnain" is best translated by our expression "little nun." The superior of this convent was her sister-in-law, Elizabeth de Forrez. Incidentally, the house was under the spiritual direction of the Benedictine monks of Molesme, particularly Saint Stephen's friend and companion on his pilgrimage, Peter or "Pron," who was a saintly monk.[4] This is worthy of remark because if Molesme had been as bad and as relaxed a monastery as it is sometimes painted, Saint Bernard would never have allowed his sister to enter the orbit of its influence.

Humbeline entered upon her cloistered life with great fervor and far outstripped her sisters in mortifications and penance, seeking the Cross and gracing it with all the fervor of another Saint Andrew. Some of the others were astounded at her fasts, and she wore a hair shirt almost continuously. Indeed, in the milder atmosphere of a Benedictine convent, she was doing all she could to keep up with her Cistercian brothers. One of the sisters reproached her for excess, and Humbeline replied: "For you, my dear sisters,

---

[4] See *Vita Sancti Petri Juliacensis*, PL 185:1264.

whose whole lives have been consecrated to the service of God, this would be good counsel, but for one who has lived so long among worldly vanities, no kind of penance can be excessive." Her use of the word "excessive" here is not to be taken as strict theology. The only virtues in which excess is impossible are faith, hope and charity, but in all other virtues, virtue depends upon moderation, and external penances have to be moderated insofar as they affect our charity. Where penance interferes with charity, in other words, where our sacrifice becomes merely a matter of self-will, then virtue turns into vice. But what Blessed Humbeline evidently meant by her expression was that practically speaking, in her case, she realized her utter inability to make adequate reparation for having given way to the attractions of a vain and sensual world.

In 1130, when Elizabeth left Jully to become superioress of the new convent of Larrey near Dijon, Humbeline stepped into her place, and Jully, under her superiorship, entered upon a period of great prosperity and fervor. There were great numbers of postulants, especially from noble families, and within the next two or three years twelve new foundations were made. One of these, the convent of Tart, was soon to adopt the Cistercian usages, and being the first community of nuns to do so, it was thus the motherhouse of all Cistercian convents. Thus Blessed Humbeline, although herself not a Cistercian, was indirectly concerned in the beginnings of the Cistercian nuns.

The year of her death is not certain, but we know the day: it was in summer, on the twenty-first of August. The tentative date suggested is 1141. Her brothers were called to her bedside, Bernard, Andrew and Nivard from Clairvaux, and perhaps Bartholomew from La Ferte. And as she lay dying, Humbeline gave expression to her realization of the beautiful charity that had existed among all the members of her family and had sanctified them all, but particularly did this charity burn in Bernard, from whom the fire spread to all the rest. "O how happy I am," she said to him, "to have followed your advice and consecrated myself to God! And what a beautiful reward I expect to receive for the love I have had for you in this life! It is to this love that I owe the glory and joy awaiting me in heaven." Here is a strong statement and one that invites deep meditation! We return again to our own age, and to another family of saints, sanctified so largely through their love of one another, and to the words of Thérèse Martin, who was to become the greatest saint of her time: "I don't understand the saints that did not love their families!" And once again we see that fundamental sanity of the old Cistercians whose sanctity consisted not in crushing and exterminating natural affection (for no sanctity could ever consist in this) but in elevating and sublimating it through the renunciation of all *selfishness* in that affection, and the dedication of our whole nature and all its powers and gifts, to God in Himself, and in those around us.

Is it any wonder that Blessed Humbeline died with the words of the beautiful psalm *Laetatus sum* upon her lips? "I rejoice in the things that were said to me: we shall go into the house of the Lord."[5] "We" shall go: plural. And one last reminder of the Little Flower. This "we" inevitably brings to mind her comment on the *Trahe me, post te curremus* of the Canticles. "Draw *me*, and *we* shall run after Thee in the odor of Thine ointments." For when the Lord draws each individual soul, he is never drawing that soul alone, but a multitude of others with it to whom it is bound by bonds of special charity in love in this world and with whom it will be united in a particularly intimate manner in the next.[6]

[5] Ps 121.
[6] *Histoire d une Ame*, ch. 11, p. 202.

March

March 5

Saint Peter of Castelnau, Monk of Fontfroide, France, Martyr

(Sources: Peter of Vaux de Cernay; AASS, Mar. 4:409; Mandonnet.)

Like most of our Cistercian saints, Saint Peter of Castelnau is lost in the obscurity of the past except where he receives occasional mention because of his intimate connection with the beginnings of the Order of Preachers. And here, too, because he is completely overshadowed by the reputation and sanctity of the great Saint Dominic, his own mission and his sanctity are either neglected or misunderstood by modern historians. Saint Peter of Castelnau was called by God, as Saint Dominic was called, to fight the Albigensian heresy, but how different were the two vocations! Saint Dominic's role as preacher and apostle had been cast for him in his mother's womb. Peter of Castelnau, after beginning his career as a canon of Montpellier, left the world and the active life to devote himself to contemplation at the monastery of Fontfroide, in the wild solitude of the hills inland from Narbonne in southern France. From there he had been called back into the world against his will by the express order of Innocent III, together with another Cistercian, Fr. Ralph, and the two were made Papal Legates in Languedoc with full powers against the heretics. Thus he was constituted not a preacher or an apostle but a diplomat and jurist, but in any case, his heart had remained in the cloister.

Consequently, if Saint Dominic was to fight the Albigensians directly with the word of God, Saint Peter (though he too, for a

85

time, joined the band as a missionary), was to fight the heresy indirectly by sacrifice. Saint Dominic and Diego of Osma saw that what was needed to overcome the Albigensians was the preaching of the Gospel and the example of evangelical poverty and holiness of life. Saint Peter declared that what was needed was the blood of a martyr. Both these views were correct. They represented the difference between two vocations. Saint Dominic fulfilled his as everybody knows; Saint Peter of Castelnau also traveled that other road, which he saw God had laid out for him. But his martyrdom ended in obscurity.

Dominic started the Order of Preachers and Peter of Castelnau shed his blood in witness to the faith because of a heresy that is logically enough ascribed to the devil. But that is a rather vague statement, which does not really explain anything to the historian or to the moralist. After all, men are free agents, and it is their free acts, and the motives behind them, that really teach us something about the moral development or degradation of individuals and of society.

It is also easy enough to describe the Albigensian heresy by its doctrines: its belief in two principles, or "gods," one good, the other evil, the former the author of the New Testament, the latter the author and hero of the old. It is not for us to go into the details of their rejection of the Incarnate Christ on the grounds that all flesh was evil and that the Jesus of the Christians was only a man, while the true Christ was a pure Spirit who never walked this earth or ate food (which is evil) among men. What we need to know is, why did these men hold these beliefs which made them reject every Sacrament of the Church, and the Church itself, persecute and mock priests, desecrate churches, and hate the Christian faith? The devil would not have been able to do all this single-handed unless certain conditions had been present and unless God on account of a certain historical situation had permitted it for the punishment of sin. In a word, the situation was frankly that Christian Bishops and Christian priests were too often what they should not have been: they neglected their duties, they were engrossed in the things of this world, they were often the source of great scandal through their ignorance and avarice and sensuality. But even though there was still a great proportion of excellent priests, and many great saints in the Church, the "Gospel was not preached to the poor"—often enough it was not preached to anybody else either. The people were neglected by their pastors.

But it must be remembered that the whole population of Christendom, even though it might be neglected, was full of desire to know God, full of thirst for religious truths and eager for an outlet to their deep and energetic religious instincts.

The result was that they listened eagerly to anyone who had anything to say about eternal truths, and while their pastors neglected to instruct them in these matters, unauthorized laymen did not hesitate to do so. There is nothing so dangerous as a half-truth, and that, as a matter of fact, is the common description of heresy. Now since most of these preachers were half-educated, their ignorance inevitably made them material heretics. Their pride and cupidity and general envy and spite and other motives soon contributed to make the heresy formal. Hence the Albigensians and Waldenses.

These heresies spread most rapidly where people were gathering into towns and where a certain amount of prosperity was coming the way of the common man. They appealed to the fast-forming "bourgeoisie" and the regions where this formation was taking place most rapidly were Languedoc and Lombardy.

In 1203 Peter of Castenau and Ralph left their monastery of Fontfroide as Papal Legates to fight the heresy. They headed straight for its capital: Toulouse. From the outset their mission was a legal and juridical one. They came not to preach but to investigate, apply remedies, impose sanctions. Their first stop then was to find out approximately how many heretics there were in Toulouse, so as to get some concrete idea of the situation. With this end in view, they administered an oath of loyalty to the Catholic faith. At the same time, in order to show that they were in earnest, they threatened with excommunication all who refused to take the oath. This measure was aimed principally at the leaders of the heresy and at Count Raymond of Toulouse and his followers, who were known to be more or less openly allied with the *Cathari.*

Raymond and the others at whom the measure was aimed, all took the oath. Nobody, of course, was deceived by that. But, turning from this temporary stalemate at Toulouse, Peter of Castelnau attacked a far more subtle problem: that of the Bishops of Languedoc who had not only failed to fulfill their ordinary duties but more or less openly favored the heresy and withheld their cooperation in fighting it. Here Saint Peter of Castelnau showed definitely that he intended to be perfectly ruthless and unhesitating in fighting heresy to the death with the most uncompromising measures. He deposed the Bishop of Viviers and excommunicated the Bishop of Beziers. Other priests and clerics were also severely punished.

As a result of these two moves, Saint Peter of Castelnau became universally hated in Languedoc. Loud complaints and recriminations began to go up on every side. This probably was what encouraged Raymond in 1205 to renounce his oath and return to more or less open support of the heretics. By now he had put into practice many of the teachings of the Cathari—especially those concerning matrimony. He had repudiated three wives without even taking the trouble to ask for a divorce and was living with the fourth. He frequented the meetings of the heretics. Once he had appeared in a Catholic church, at Mass, with a buffoon who mimicked the priest and caused a disturbance during the celebration of the Holy Mysteries. He frequently gave expression to the naive beliefs of the Albigensian sect, as, for instance, on one occasion when he lost his temper after waiting a long time for someone who did not show up to keep an appointment: he finally burst out saying: "Anybody can see that this world was made by the devil! Nothing ever turns out the way you want it to!"

Peter returned to Toulouse and managed to argue Raymond, once again, into apparent submission, but by now his health was broken and he had to go to bed. As he lay there, overwhelmed by sickness and exhaustion, and confronted by the hatred and misunderstanding which were the fruits of all his zeal and self-sacrifice, Peter of Castelnau began to realize that his methods were destined to failure. The heresy had taken too strong a hold on the people. The faith was dead. Even the priests had abandoned their churches and bishops their cathedrals. Excommunication, interdict no longer meant much in Languedoc. What was the good of legal measures if the authority behind the law was no longer respected?

Clearly, he had done all that he possibly could, and there was little use wasting his time in further useless efforts. Let the Pope try a new plan of attack, with some other legate as his minister: Peter believed that the best, in fact the only, thing for him to do was to return to the contemplative life, where he belonged. Innocent III did not see things in this light. He replied to an appeal of his Legate, begging permission to retire to Fontfroide, by telling him, in so many words, that at this time action was better than contemplation. As a matter of fact, Innocent III could be very stubborn when his mind was set on an idea, and this time his idea was to use the most vital and energetic religious order in existence—the Cistercians—as a vast reservoir of preachers and apostles to fight the Albigensians.

There was, however, one consolation for the sick and despondent Peter of Castelnau: news came that the simoniac Archbishop of Toulouse, Raymond of Rabastens, had been replaced by the converted Troubadour, the Cistercian monk Foulques of Grandeselve Abbey, a man already renowned for his sanctity and wisdom.

The Spanish bishop and his companion, the future Saint Dominic, were missionaries by vocation, and indeed it soon became clear that the Holy Spirit had raised them up and filled them with the special graces needed to cope with the situation in southern France. For they had been able to diagnose the situation with a sure instinct which Peter and Ralph did not possess. They saw that it was not enough merely to be horrified at the errors of the heretics and to try and pass laws to stamp out their doctrinal and moral abuses. It was not enough to take the Cathari at their worst and view them simply as deluded fanatics whose excesses led to every type of moral turpitude. One had to take them at their best. One had to pick out their strongest arguments and demolish these, leaving the Cathari nothing upon which to fall back, no citadel in which they would be free from attack.

For while it was true that the Manichean system of the Albigensians in declaring that the world and the flesh were evil, and that all flesh appetites were sinful, logically implied that sin was inescapable and therefore could not really be imputed as sin, at the same time prescribed for the *Cathari* or the special caste of the *perfect* a rigorous asceticism and especially the most complete poverty and detachment from all that was connected with the evil material and visible creation. In every argument between Christian apostles and the defenders of Albigensianism, the heretics always pointed to the tremendously strict and zealous life of their "perfect" and brought it into contrast with the luxury and avarice and tepidity that were too often evident in the clerical life of the Catholic Church. It was of little avail to reply by citing the holiness of monks who were hidden away in cloisters from the eyes of men, when bishops and canons and many parish priests displayed their wealth and love of comfort in the eyes of all, who were often cynically open in their practice of simony and other far worse vices. Even though the Albigensians at large were notorious for the worst moral profligacy, the glaring contrast between the voluntary poverty of their "perfect" and the avarice of a great proportion of those Christians whose duty it was to preach the Gospel of Christ was enough to hold in check every attempt to attack the heresy by doctrinal arguments.

Diego and Saint Dominic realized that what was needed was an army of men who were willing to give up everything, renounce the last shred of property, go out among the heretics in all the simplicity and destitution and faith of the first apostles—men as homeless and penniless as Christ Himself. Only such as these could get a hearing.

Peter of Castelnau listened to these views and did a heroic thing. Although he was the Papal Delegate, and consequently *ex officio* the leader of the group, he put himself docilely under the command of Diego of Osma and laid the conduct of the experiment in the Bishop's hands. In June they started out from Montpellier, a Catholic city, worked west, preaching in the villages and towns, disputing with the heretics. At once their apostolate began to create an impression and to make converts. This was what the common people had been waiting for—what they had needed for so long! But the petty Lords of the region, jealous supporters of the heresy, were always a source of danger.

By the time the group of missionaries reached the stronghold of Beziers, with its brown fortress of a Cathedral perched on top of a high, sheer bluff dominating the plains along the Mediterranean, it became evident that Saint Peter's life was menaced as long as he traveled with the others and mingled with the crowds without his former bodyguard. He had long since aroused bitter enmity, and this was the town whose bishop he had excommunicated. When he now appeared in the public streets, arguing against the heresy with his fiery ardor and implacable zeal, the crowds became ugly and hostile. It was decided, for the time being, that he should separate from the little group.

He did so and returned to his diplomatic work, concluding an agreement with certain heretic noblemen at Villeneuve. But early in 1207 he rejoined the other three apostles at Montreal in the diocese of Carcassonne, where a big public debate was held with the heresiarchs, which lasted fifteen days. To make it more formal, the arguments of both sides were taken down and drawn up on parchment and presented to the judges for a final decision. The judges, as it happens, were all Albigensians: what was their conclusion? All the records of the debate were burned without any decision being passed—and this, in itself, was a most eloquent decision!

By this time the apostles were joined by Arnold of Amaury, the Abbot of Cîteaux, and twelve Cistercian abbots and several white monks, who were to be the first contingent of Innocent's projected Cistercian shock-troops against the heresy. Fortunately for the Cistercians, God withheld His grace and allowed their efforts to fail, and they were allowed to return to their cloisters, the project being gradually dropped while Saint Dominic laid the foundations for a new Order specially equipped for this kind of work.

Meanwhile, however, the hour had struck for Saint Peter's final struggle and victory. Count Raymond of Toulouse, with his customary cynical disregard of oaths and agreements, had once again returned to the open support of the heretics. So this time, the Papal Legate fired his strongest bolt: that of excommunication.

Although Raymond of Toulouse attached no special importance to being a living member of the Mystical Body of Christ, he did resent this excommunication as an affront and as a political nuisance. Consequently, he went through the formality of taking another oath, to get it lifted. But this time Saint Peter of Castelnau was accepting no more perjuries. Not only did he ignore this futile gesture, but he confronted the Count of Toulouse in his own court, surrounded by his friends and henchmen, and there publically and solemnly pronounced upon him the sentence of excommunication, branding him with anathema and cursing him out of the Church as something unclean. The fiery Cistercian had signed his own death warrant.

Ironically, the final scene was to be played in the abbey shrine of the gentle hermit Saint Giles, the auxiliary saint to whom all fly for protection from the "terrors of the night," the intercessor whose miraculous aid quiets little children terrified by nightmares and visions of peril and death. But Saint Gilles du Gard, in the hills behind Nimes, was one of the seats of the Count of Toulouse, and hither Peter of Castelnau was summoned in 1208, ostensibly to discuss terms and arrange a reconciliation.

Pleas and subtle menaces left the Cistercian unmoved. Finally Raymond burst into a rage and warned the monk that he might pay for this insulting resistance with his life. There the matter apparently ended.

Then Saint Peter set out from the abbey and started eastward towards Provence. He was accompanied by a solicitous group of friends, together with some armed men provided, against the will of the Count, by the Abbot of Saint Giles. They traveled as far as the banks of the Rhone and then spent the night at Beaucaire. They were at the edge of Raymond's domains, and the atmosphere of the town was that of an armed camp. Saint Peter said Mass in the morning and then descended to the river, preparing to cross. The group that had accompanied him so far now stood by. Then suddenly, several of the armed men surrounded him, and one of them, raising his lance, plunged it into the Legate's side. They were Raymond's men after all. Saint Peter, expiring without surprise or rancor, had time to forgive his murderer before he gave up his soul into the hands of the King of Martyrs.

Innocent III, in a letter to the Bishops of Provence and Aquitaine and all southern France, praised the murdered legate in terms that might almost have sufficed, of themselves, to canonize him. He not only made no question of Peter's claim to the title of martyr but praised the sanctity of his whole life, his faith and zeal, his eloquence as a preacher and his devotion to the Holy See. Indeed, said the Pope, the only thing that prevented his work being supported by miracles was the incredulity of the heretics.

The date of Saint Peter's martyrdom is variously given as January 18 and February 16, 1208. He was buried in the crypt of the Abbey Church of Saint Giles and formally beatified in the Middle Ages. This was reiterated in 1720. His feast is kept by the Cistercians on March 5.

March 11

Saint Stephen of Obazine, First Abbot of Obazine, near Tulle, France

(Sources: AASS, Mar. 1:799 [contemporary life by a monk of Obazine, his disciple]; M. le Cure d'Obazine, *Saint Etienne d'Obazine, sa vie, ses reliques, son tombeau* [pamphlet].)

Saint Benedict says in his Rule that the life of a monk should be a continual Lent, but he immediately added that it is so only for very few. Saint Stephen of Obazine was one of these few: a man whose austerities tend to frighten modern readers. But when we study his history closely we realize what a pure and simple soul his was and how full of kindness and charity. Like De Rance, who is also sometimes accused of being over severe, Saint Stephen was loved far more than he was feared by his spiritual sons. Indeed, their love for him has a character of pure and tender veneration which is seldom accorded to those whose influence over other men is little more than a matter of personal charm and so-called "magnetism." In other words, the love of his monks bears witness to the true spiritual fatherhood of their abbot, this saint who was concerned with the good of their souls above everything else.

Saint Stephen was born at a village near Limoges, in what was then Aquitaine, in 1085—the year of the foundation of Molesme. He was brought up by his pious parents for the secular priesthood.

He led an exemplary life as a young man, but he nevertheless did not completely cut himself off from the amusements and interests of the world, nor was he obliged to do so. However, he soon began to feel that his liking for good clothes, for gay society, and espe- cially for the pleasures of hunting was standing in the way of his vocation. He was born for better things. God wanted more of him that this. Indeed, if he had continued in all these amusements as a priest, he could not be confident of his salvation. Accordingly, as soon as he was ordained, Stephen began to lead a stricter life, withdrawing himself from worldly entertainments and punishing his flesh in various ways. In winter, for instance, he used to break the ice of a frozen river and stand in the water up to his neck. Hand in hand with his growing thirst for penance went a corresponding fervor in prayer, especially in the recitation of the Divine Office. All these things were but indications of the call that was soon to make itself heard, urging him to leave the world altogether and retire to a hermitage. He accordingly went to seek advice about his vocation from a hermit called Etienne de Mercoeur, and the latter told him: "Take care not to delay in following the inspiration of heaven—put your plan into effect as soon as you possibly can. Follow with joy and happiness in the steps of Jesus in order that many souls may be drawn to God by your example."[1]

With his mind made up to become a hermit, Stephen told his project to a good friend, also a newly ordained priest called Peter, and the latter, fired by the contagion of his holy fervor, could not be content to remain behind in the village but asked permission to join him. The permission was readily granted, and on a certain Ash Wednesday, probably about the beginning of the twelfth cen- tury, they gave away all their possessions to the poor, said good bye to their friends, and set out, barefoot, for the mountains. It was not usual, even in the Middle Ages, for one called to a hermit's life simply to leave home and find a cave in the forest somewhere and kneel down and start praying and wait for the ravens to bring him some food like Elias.

[1] Acta SS, *Vita Stephani*, I, 3. AASS, p. 800 d.

Stephen and his friend spent some ten months as members of a small group of disciples of a hermit called Bertrand, who not only gave them spiritual direction and supervised their manual labor but also offered a course of studies. Finding, however, that they were called to a stricter solitude, they left this man and found their way into the mountains behind Tulle. There, halfway between Tulle and Brive, off the valley of the river Correze, they finally came upon a rocky, thickly wooded ravine, practically inaccessible, hidden in the forest, choked with dense underbrush and watered by a little brook of clear water. It was Holy Week when they found this spot, and there they made their preparation for Easter, fasting and praying with nothing to distract them but the songs of the first birds of spring and the garrulous conversations of the stream running among the rocks and watercress. On Easter day, they climbed out of this hiding place and made their way to a village in the valley. There they managed to borrow two pairs of shoes. Having put them on, one of them said Mass, while the other served and received Communion. When they finally emerged from the village Church and returned the shoes, their happiness until that moment, unmixed and perfect, was put to the test of what to most men would have been more than a passing cloud. For in spite of their bare feet, and their hermits' habits, and above all their faces emaciated by much fasting, nobody of the village took pity on them or invited them to share their Easter dinner.

No doubt they were glad to accept this chance of sacrifice, but nevertheless it was somewhat grimly that they began to climb the mountain once again. Halfway up, overcome with weakness and perhaps by dismay as well, they sat down by the road to rest. Then God took pity on them and sent them their Easter dinner, for a woman from the village of Pauliac came by with several big round loaves of bread and a jug of milk. Guessing their plight, she gave them the milk and one of the big, sweet-smelling loaves and went her way, leaving the two hermits feasting in the spring sun.

After that they returned to their diet of roots and leaves in the ravine, which with all its advantages from the point of view of solitude was so well hidden that no one knew of their presence. And of course they had not had time to grow anything; gifts of bread and other simple foods would not have been unwelcome. But Our Heavenly Father again sent them help in due season and inspired a good villager to seek them out with some food. The news that there were hermits on the mountain soon spread, and they might have become in a few months too popular for their own good had not Our Lord foreseen that also and provided for it in His own way. For in a little while another individual appeared on the scene and set up a rival hermitage nearby, and being rather more of a businessman than a hermit, soon began to attract a great following. Finally, when he had gained the confidence of the pious country people and collected a large amount of offerings in view of a Mass he promised to say for his benefactors on a certain day, he absconded with his easy gains and left Stephen and Peter to suffer from the effects of his fraud upon the reputation of all hermits in general. With their credit thus ruined, they were able to sanctify themselves for a long time by the struggle to maintain life in almost total destitution.

Meanwhile, however, they built themselves a cell and a small oratory, and Peter went to Limoges where he obtained from the Bishop, Eustorgius, permission to say Mass in the new chapel. On his return from the city he brought with him one new recruit for their hermitage, a cleric and a former friend of theirs.

This was the beginning of a semi-eremitical community, to which many more postulants soon began to present themselves. Apparently Stephen had anticipated no such thing as this, and the arrival of disciples presented him with a twofold problem. The first, and less important, was that of providing accommodations for them. Their present site, in the narrow ravine, was much too cramped to house more than three or four persons. As the community continued to grow, the site was changed several times until a monastery was finally built on a little plateau that extended like a promontory between the valleys of Vergonzac and Lanteuil, commanding a wooded, undulating landscape of fertile valleys bounded by uplands sparsely covered with scrub oak and box.

The second problem was a spiritual one and more important. It concerned Saint Stephen's own vocation. Seeing that he was pursued into the wilderness by disciples, he began to think of giving up his hermitage and of consummating his holocaust to God among the Saracens, seeking martyrdom in Africa. It is clear enough that this was rather a temptation than a vocation, but it is typical of the interior struggles which souls in the contemplative life have to face at crucial points in their career: God has some special work He desires them to do, and they seem unable to grasp the fact that this work is God's will because it is so entirely strange to their own dreams and ideals and plans for their own future. Peter managed to persuade Saint Stephen that he was called to the direction of souls, the formation of contemplatives, and that was where his duty lay.

Even then Saint Stephen could not quite resign himself to becoming an important person in the small community of souls that God had called to him, and upon their removal to the new monastery he made an unsuccessful attempt to resign his more or less obvious spiritual leadership of the group and get Peter constituted as its head. The argument was finally settled by the Bishop of Chartres, who decided that Peter should be prior and Saint Stephen abbot. He was confirmed as such when he received his abbatial blessing in 1142 at the hands of the Bishop of Limoges, and in the presence of the Cistercian Abbot of Dalon, a white monks' community in the district.

The presence of the Cistercian abbot at the ceremony of Saint Stephen's official installation as superior of the monastery he had founded was no mere coincidence or matter of social niceties. For some time Saint Stephen had been considering affiliating himself with some established Order of monks.

With this in view, he had once made a long and difficult journey in winter across the central mountains of France and into the Alps to the Grande Chartreuse to consult the Prior, Guigo, about uniting his monks to the Carthusians. He made this journey barefoot, taking with him no food and wearing an elaborate penitential machine of wood and iron band which imprisoned his chest and back in its fierce grip until finally, on this journey, it broke three times and he decided that this was an indication of God's will that he should throw the thing away. In any case, he had more important business to attend to than making constant repairs on his private instrument of torture.

Prior Guigo received him with great charity and hospitality, but seeing that Obazine had already grown beyond the limits which the Carthusians had imposed upon themselves (for they insisted on small, and very select, communities), he wisely pointed out that the Cistercians corresponded much better to the end towards which Obazine was evidently tending.

In other words, the life had become essentially cenobitic. Obazine was a large and busy and austere family, rather than a group of solitaries. As for austerity, Saint Stephen indeed had already outstripped both Cîteaux and the Chartreuse in many respects. He ruled his spiritual children with a merciful strictness that was perhaps closer to Saint Columban's than to Saint Benedict's Rule. Saint Stephen believed in corporal punishment—as did Saint Benedict and all the religious orders of the time. Also, according to the custom of Superiors in the Middle Ages, Saint Stephen used to go around the choir personally as *circator* to see that no one had fallen asleep in the almost complete darkness in which the night office was chanted, as well as to regulate the tone and tempo and to see that everything was in good order. If he did chance to come upon anyone overcome with drowsiness, Saint Stephen would not awaken him with any gentle nudge in the ribs. The unfortunate monk would be roused either by a ringing clout on the side of the head or an even more painful blow with a rod of wood. The saint also had no patience with those who allowed themselves to become distracted and dissipated at the Office, and a monk who gave way to laughter in choir was certain to be paid by a good hard blow across the mouth from his first superior.

Obazine soon became famous for the modesty and recollection of the monks in choir.

Penances in the Chapter of Faults were almost universally of a physical nature in the Middle Ages. At Obazine the punishments were simply harder and longer. For example, a frequent penance was for a monk to receive on his bare back a blow of a bundle of switches or of a rod for each verse of the *Miserere* while the rest of the monks chanted that psalm—and in no great haste. If necessary, other psalms were added.

Saint Stephen himself, however, considered all these punishments a privilege and availed himself of them when he could. On

Holy Thursday he used to present himself before his community and humbly accuse himself of all his faults and omissions and then have himself beaten longer and harder than anybody else. This mutual beating was considered by the monks of the Middle Ages as an act of charity, and indeed, in the days when Saint Stephen and Peter had been hermits together, they used to keep one another awake during their long vigils by beating each other with switches.

He had also persisted in many other austerities, including his favorite one of immersing himself in freezing water in the middle of winter, as well as spending entire nights at prayer in the glacial cold of the empty church. In spite of all this, he not only grew to be old in years but he never showed his age. His thick black hair never lost its color or turned grey, and his body never seemed to lose its energy and drive.

Among the numerous postulants who had entered Obazine had been many married men whose wives, inspired by the example of their husbands, also desired to give themselves to this strict penitential discipline. They were joined by sisters of other members of the community, as well as other pious women, and Saint Stephen had a convent built for them at the entrance to the former site of his hermitage, the narrow gorge of Coyroux. On Palm Sunday, 1142, after Stephen's own abbatial blessing, the Bishop of Limoges proceeded to Coyroux to seal the perpetual enclosure of the nuns who lived there under the direction of the saint.

In the meantime he had founded several houses of monks and was to found five in all in the diocese of Cahors, Limoges, Saintes and Angouleme before the memorable year of 1147 when he finally presented himself before Pope Eugenius III at the General Chapter at Cîteaux, and asked to be received with his little congregation into the Cistercian Order. His offer was somewhat overshadowed, no doubt, by the fact that the large and powerful Congregation of Savigny was making exactly the same move at the same chapter. But Obazine was received with joy and charity into the Cistercian family.

From that time on, although some monks of Dalon had previously been at Obazine to instruct them in the Cistercian usages, Obazine had to conform itself to the *Consuetudines* of Cîteaux according to the instruction of officially appointed delegates. To these Saint

Stephen inclined his will and judgment in all obedience and it was not always easy for him to do so.

The monks of Obazine had always fasted all year round, except on Sundays, and he held flesh-meat in such abhorrence that he had never even allowed it to be served in the infirmary.

It was a hard day for Saint Stephen when the first animals were slaughtered at Obazine. But he sacrificed his tastes and principles for the sake of the unity and charity which is the fundamental principle of Cistercian asceticism—the asceticism of obedience and of the cenobitic life, the asceticism of unselfishness and self-effacement, of the family spirit, of toleration for the ideas and opinions and even eccentricities of others, for the sake of Christian unity.

Saint Stephen was seventy-four years old when he fell sick at one of his daughterhouses, Bonnaigue, where he had gone to supervise the election of a new abbot. It soon became evident that this sickness would be his last, and he was in great suffering. Nevertheless, when it happened that the time prescribed in the Cistercian Usages for shaving the heads of the monks and renewing the monastic crown, Saint Stephen, in his zeal for regularity, insisted on having his crown renewed, in spite of the agony it caused him on his deathbed. Surrounded by weeping monks he finally sank down into death with the promise that he would open to them all the gates of Paradise—if they would first gain him admission by their prayers. It was the eighth of March, 1159.

Saint Stephen had been famous for his miracles in his lifetime. He had cured a blind nun at Coyrous by the imposition of his hands. He had miraculously provided food for his community in a time of need. Now, at his death, thousands of men flocked to his bier, and after his was laid to rest favors were multiplied at his tomb and Obazine became an important center of pilgrimages in southwestern France. The sick were healed, the poor were aided in their troubles, prisoners were liberated from captivity through his intercession. Although the abbey of Obazine was destroyed in the French Revolution, the Church remains standing in the center of a small village, and the tomb of Saint Stephen is still a place of pilgrimage. Nor has he ceased to help those who trust in his aid even in this age without faith. A nineteenth-century doctor of the region affirmed that he had always invoked Saint Stephen of Obazine whenever he was faced with any special difficulty and had always received a favorable answer.

March 13

Saint Sancha, Nun of Celles, Portugal

(Sources: AASS, June 4:385; a modern biography of Saints Sancha and Theresa; P. Maria Gloning, *Zwei Heiligen aus koniglichem Hause*, Cist Chronik 9:255.)

The second daughter of Sancho I, King of Portugal, was born at the royal capital, Coimbra, about 1108, and shared in the pious education given to her sisters, Theresa and Mayfalda, who were also to become saints in Cistercian convents. But unlike Theresa and Mayfalda, Sancha managed to escape the sorrow of a political marriage. More fortunate than her two sisters who both were led by their parents into marriages that afterwards had to be dissolved, Sancha preserved the inestimable privilege of her virginity, which she dedicated entirely to Christ, living in pious retirement on the royal property of Alemquer near the town of Jerabica.

Her life in the company of other good women on this modest estate was one of prayer, work and charity. The women spent their time in sewing and recollection, and Sancha especially devoted herself to the care of the poor, seeking out not only the beggars and the obvious paupers but those who were ashamed to make their poverty known. She soon knew all of the poor in Jerabica but very few of the rich.

Each Friday she had twelve poor women to dinner, and herself fasting, she washed their feet and waited on them, afterwards sending them away with gifts of clothing and money. She mortified her flesh by sleeping on a bed of rough cork bark, with a log of wood concealed inside her pillow slip.

Like both her sisters, Sancha is famous for her patronage and help of the mendicant orders, which were then beginning to come into Spain and Portugal. But of the three saintly princesses, it was Sancha who contributed the most to the establishment of the Franciscans and Dominicans in her native land, for it was she who founded the first Franciscan monastery in Portugal. Two of the friars had come over the mountains from Spain, and having approached the Queen at Coimbra, they were sent by her to Princess Sancha at Alemquer. There she received them with great joy and hospitality, and hearing of their designs, she presented them with a little chapel dedicated to Saint Catherine and the land around about it where the two friars settled and established the first community of their Order in Portugal. This was in the year 1216. In the following year, Fr. Suerio Gomez, a Dominican, came over from Spain and founded a Dominican community under her patronage at Monte Junto. From these two centers the Franciscans and Dominicans were to spread overseas to the vast Portuguese possessions that were later to be acquired in Africa and South America, as well as in the Orient.

Yet Sancha's connection with the Franciscans was one of an even more intimate charity than this matter of spiritual and financial patronage. In 1219 five young friars[2] stopped at Saint Catherine's on their way to the Moors and martyrdom. When they presented themselves before the holy princess, she fell at their feet and reverently kissed the hems of their brown robes. Talking together of the Kingdom of God, Sancha and the five friars inspired one another with that intense spiritual fervor promised by Christ to all His children when He said: "whenever two or three are gathered together in My Name, there am I also in the midst of them." How strange it is that in our day when fervent Christians are so eager for the presence of their Lord in their souls, they should concen-

[2] Their names were Peter, Bernard, Accursius, Adjustus and Otto. Their martyrdom took place in January 1220.

trate entirely on a sort of selfish piety, an individual and personal and private quest for consolation, forgetting how much Jesus also insisted that His presence in one soul is inseparably connected with his presence in all other Christian souls and that it is precisely the destiny and vocation of Christians to increase the life of Jesus in one another! With their journey to Morocco financed by Saint Sancha, and their hearts filled with the Holy Spirit Who had come again to them in the miniature Pentecost of their pious conversation—for every meeting of Christians ought to be another Pentecost!—the friars set sail for Africa.

It was the following year, 1220, when Sancha was at prayer one day that her dear friends suddenly appeared to her, robed in blinding white, and wearing the crowns of their victory which they announced to her, thanking her for her indispensable part in it.

As time went on Saint Sancha began to turn her attention to some women who lived in the woods across the river from Alemquer as recluses. These holy women had received the name of *muratas* because of the strange form taken by their solitary life. Each one of them not only lived in a separate cell, but they were actually walled in to their cells, the doorway being filled in with brick or stone and mortar once they were inside so that only a small window was left for air and food and communication with the outside. Hence the name *muratas*. The name of the monastery Sancha founded for them, Celles, or "The Cells," preserves the memory of the old cells in which the recluses lived entombed.

She first gathered these pious women together under the Rule of Saint Augustine, but after her visit to the flourishing Cistercian convent founded by her sister, Theresa, at Lorvao, she received the Cistercian habit from the Bishop of Coimbra, renewed her vow of chastity and made the other religious vows as well, and then proceeded to introduce the Cistercian life at Celles.

One of the most outstanding characteristics of this saintly prioress was her love of hidden virtues and her preference for mortifications that would escape the attention of others. She gave up her practice of frequent disciplines because the sound of the whips could be heard outside her cell, but she retained her hair shirts and girdles of knotted cords. Her object in avoiding attention was that she did not wish, as superior, to seem to prescribe by her example penances that were not only beyond the ordinary Rule but might exceed the strength or generosity of some of her subjects. How well she had understood the spirit of Saint Benedict, who so frequently returns to the prescription that all things must be ordered so that the weak may not be driven to despair and the generous may be able to offer a little more than the bare minimum! Her prayer harmonized with her penances: perfect simplicity marked her posture and all that she did. No loud sighs, no whispered words, no eccentricities, no ecstatic poses.

She shared her sister Theresa's zeal for self-knowledge, a virtue which Saint Bernard, Saint Gregory the Great and Cassian all make the foundation stone of the whole spiritual edifice. The big problem of a religious, or at least of a fervent religious, is the extermination of the more glaring and tenacious of his habits of semi-deliberate venial sin. Since such sins are not fully deliberate, they are impossible to avoid altogether, and our responsibility for them is limited. Yet it must be remembered that there is very often more responsibility on our part than the somewhat easy spirituality of our present day allows us to realize. If, for example, we neglect to examine ourselves, and fail to guard our senses, and are careless about avoiding occasions of sin, then our responsibility for our repeated acts of pride, envy, murmuring, impatience, and petty selfishness will indeed be greater than we imagine. Besides which we will be living always on the boundaries of tepidity and will give much disedification to those who have to live with us. Saint Sancha's insistence on self-examination is interesting to present-day Cistercians because of one detail: she used to examine herself before dinner and before going to bed, times which are now prescribed for the whole Order in the Constitutions. In those days there was no time set aside for systematic examination of conscience.

As superior, Saint Sancha nevertheless rejoiced in performing all the humblest tasks and particularly delighted in helping in the kitchen and in sweeping the house. She accepted sickness and trial with joy, and during her last illness she worked two miracles in the infirmary, saving one nun from certain death by cancer, and to show our merciful God's care for us even in smaller things, she acted as His instrument in curing a young sister's toothache.

She was only forty-two when she died. Saint Theresa came from Lorvao to assist her in her last agony, presenting her at the moment of death with the Crucifix, and saying: "Embrace Him, embrace Him Whom you have loved—gather up your soul, that with your last breath you may breathe it forth into this gaping wound in His dear side!" And so it was indeed. Breathing forth her pure and perfect soul, she flew straight to the Heart of her Spouse on April 11, 1229.

It was evident that Saint Theresa would want to bury her sister at Lorvao, and it was just as evident that the nuns of Celles would want their saintly superior to rest in their own church. Knowing this, Theresa simply stole the body and carried it off to Lorvao. For she obtained permission to stay and wash the body while the nuns went to sing Tierce. At the precise moment when the Sisters of Celles sang *Deo gratias* the nuns of Lorvao were leaving by the front gate with their precious burden.

Her cult was associated with that of her sister, processes being introduced simultaneously. Over ninety well-authenticated miracles were ascribed to them. Sancha was beatified in 1705.

March 18

Blessed Christian O'Conarchy, First Abbot of Mellifont, Ireland

(Sources: V Mal 6 and 15; Luddy, *Life of Saint Malachy* [see also Butler-Thurston, March].)

The story of Christianity in Ireland is a proud one, and it has more than traces of glory: all through that history it is the monk that plays the most active and spectacular part. Nor must it ever be forgotten that there was a time when this far, green island, so remote from the rest of Europe, was its most civilized nation and the source from which Christian faith and Christian culture were to flow back upon the wastes laid desolate by barbarism.

The full richness and vigor of the Christian life was fostered in the great Irish monasteries like Clonard, founded in the sixth century by Saint Finian, Clonfert by Saint Brendan, Bangor by Saint Comgall, Clonmacnoise by Saint Kieran, Arran by Saint Enda; or those founded in the seventh century by Saint Cartach at Lismore or at Glendalough by Saint Kevin. In these immense abbeys—sometimes housing not only hundreds but even thousands of monks at the same time, if we include the brethren in the various dependent houses along with those of the motherhouse as was the ancient custom—Ireland satisfied its burning thirst for sanctity and for truth; for in them was fostered not only a life of intense faith and religious perfection but also a culture so vigorous and enterprising that in the monastic schools were studied poetry, astronomy, music and geography when such things were ignored. in the rest of Europe. Not only was Ireland the "island of saints and scholars" but, as Renan admits, the Irish monks were the "scientific colonizers of Western Europe."

At the close of the eighth century this fair and flourishing culture fell into ruins before the attacks of Danish barbarism, which was only finally repelled by the victory of Brian Boru at Clontarf in 1014. Then came the long, slow work of reconstruction, a work in which one of the most prominent figures was that of Saint Malachy O'More, Bishop of Down and Armagh (see November 3).

This work of reconstruction was to reach its final perfection in the introduction and rise of the Cistercian Order in Ireland, fostered by Saint Malachy and led by Blessed Christian O'Conarchy, the first Irish Cistercian, a title which the holy Bishop of Down might well have envied his disciple, for Saint Malachy himself had been refused permission by Pope Innocent II to take the Cistercian habit at Clairvaux.

Who was this Christian O'Conarchy? He was born in Bangaor, the Vale of Angeles (in County Down)—and the site of the famous Abbey of which Saint Malachy became abbot in the twelfth century. Christian was born about 1100 around the time of the foundation of the Order he was to propagate in Ireland, and it is thought that he was educated at the famous school of Armagh where Saint Malachy's own father, the noble and saintly Mugron O'More, was a lay professor. The young scholar and future Cistercian, tall and of a commanding presence, with a rich and sonorous voice and a heart of gold, had longed since childhood for the contemplative life and enrolled himself among the disciples of Saint Malachy. He soon proved himself so fervent and valuable a recruit under the energetic reformer bishop that the latter made him Archdeacon of Down.

This office of archdeacon upon which Blessed Christian entered in 1132 was equivalent to that of vicar general, and Malachy himself had held it at the beginning of his career. Christian thus became official supervisor of the subordinate clergy, made visitations, conducted courts, punished offenders, examined candidates, fought everywhere for the preservation of the faith, cared for the sick, and watched over the administration of church property.

In 1139 or 1140, when Saint Malachy set out for Rome to render an account of his stewardship to the Vicar of Christ, Christian O'Conarchy and his brother Malchus were members of his entourage. The group crossed the sea to Scotland, traveled south to York where a holy priest named Sycarus, full of the Holy Ghost, uttered many prophecies concerning Saint Malachy and one that deeply affected his companions. This latter was that very few of them would return to Ireland. What then? Would they die in Rome? Die they would, but not before they had first died to all they had ever known, died to themselves in the strictest monastery in Europe, the Clairvaux of Saint Bernard, to enter which, as that holy abbot told his postulants, one had to leave his body at the door.

It was at York also that they met another future Cistercian, Saint Waltheof, then prior of the Augustinians at Kirkham, later monk of Rievaulx and Abbot of Melrose. Waltheof, who had grown up with Saint Ælred at the court of David of Scotland and had that saint's warmhearted generosity and fraternal affection, was greatly moved by the fact that Saint Malachy was traveling on foot. He himself had only a poor sort of a horse, a vicious animal, as black in color as it was in character. But the quality of the gift was enhanced by the charity of the giver, and God, looking down from heaven upon his two saints, blessed the whole proceedings by miraculously changing the horse's disposition—and his color— from black to white. Malachy got good and faithful service from this animal for the rest of his life!

Continuing to France, and passing through Picardy and Burgundy on the road once taken by the great Irish missionaries, Saint Fiacre, Saint Fursey, Saint Fridolin, Saint Gall and above all Saint Columba, they came to the great new abbey of Clairvaux. What were their impressions on first entering that "valley of light" with its seven hundred monks and its severe new building rising out of the oaks and beeches of the forest? All, like their leader, Saint Malachy, fell in love with Clairvaux, and Clairvaux, in turn, took them to her bosom. Above all were they welcome to the heart of the great Saint Bernard, who in the deep and prudent insight of his boundless charity (boundless because there was nothing left of self-love to limit and restrain it), recognized in these souls the great destiny God had in store for them—indeed, the destiny which had already so perfectly worked itself out in the sanctity of Malachy O'More. And when the holy bishop was unable to enter Clairvaux, he left in his place four of his Irish companions, of which one was Christian O'Conarchy.

Nor was this merely a platonic gesture on the part of the Bishop of Down. Unable to remain at Clairvaux himself, he intended that Clairvaux should come to him and to his people in Ireland. These four were to be the nucleus of a new Cistercian colony. "They shall be as seed," said the saint to Saint Bernard, "and in that seed shall our whole nation be blessed."[3]

What a thing it was to live at Clairvaux we may guess from the fact that the colony that was eventually chosen for Ireland, including its leader, Blessed Christian, was by no means eager to leave the cloister of the motherhouse. There were two things that held them back. The first was the presence and influence of Saint Bernard himself; the second was the immense consolation of living

---

[3] V Mal 39.

in a community so phenomenally great in numbers and in fervor. So important were these two facts that the whole face of twelfth-century Europe was covered with Cistercian monks who were carrying as their greatest cross an insatiable homesickness for Clairvaux—the *nostalgia claravallensis*. No doubt the monks who had come from our other great monasteries, Morimond or Cîteaux or La Ferte or Pontigny, were homesick for the house that had seen their first years in religion, but then, at these houses there was no Saint Bernard, under which Blessed Christian now came, which meant one thing in particular: that Clairvaux of all the Cistercian houses was the greatest and most vigorous school of mystical contemplation. It was Clairvaux, above all, that was most acutely conscious of the Cistercian destiny to arrive at intimate union with the Word of God by perfect charity, and it was at Clairvaux, and in the cell of Saint Bernard, that the manner of fulfilling that destiny, dying to self in order to live wholly in and for Christ, was most constantly and most profoundly discussed. It was no little trial to be separated from such a source of fervor and inspiration, and it was precisely this sacrifice that was to be one of the chief elements in the sanctification of Blessed Christian. And such a sacrifice was necessary in order to fulfill in him the very perfection of charity which he would not have reached if he had merely stayed behind at Clairvaux listening to the saint's great doctrine. Not only that, but that sacrifice, on the part of hundreds of others like Christian, was to fill Europe with other schools of mysticism almost as great as Clairvaux; for it is among the filiations of Saint Bernard's abbey that we find the greatest centers of Cistercian mysticism: Rievaulx, for example, and Villers. No doubt Mellifont was another.

However, in a few years, the four Irishmen and nine French monks came to settle in the lovely valley near the Boyne, close to Drogheda, which Saint Malachy had selected as the site for Mellifont—"the fountain of honey." The name itself is full of lyricism that expresses all the freshness and sweetness and strength and goodness of the Cistercian doctrine that was to be preached by word, but more by example, to the hundreds of zealous Irish postulants that were soon to flock to that abbey and its many filiations.

But before that could come about there were difficulties to be overcome. The correspondence of Saint Malachy and Saint Bernard[4] at the time gives us only a vague hint of the cause of the trouble. But one of the things that arose to disturb the peace of the pioneer community was a difference of opinion between the Irish and French monks concerning certain points of the Rule, perhaps according to Luddy,[5] having to do with construction of the new monastery. Was it that the native element wanted the monastery to adopt the old Irish plan, rather than the usual grouping adopted by Cîteaux of the regular places about a central cloister? We do not know. But in any case, it seems that the French monks had the Rule on their side and that Christian sided with them and not with his compatriots. But the upshot of the whole thing was that Christian, the French monks and the architect returned to Clairvaux in discomfiture and almost prepared to give up being pioneers and return to studying the Canticle of Canticles. The wise Saint Bernard evidently saw the good of the humiliation God had permitted for the sanctification of his servants and allowed Christian to remain at Clairvaux and regain his strength and learn yet more of the Cistercian life before sending him back with the architect to Ireland.

Thus chastened by his great sacrifice and the humiliation of a struggle and apparent failure, Christian now went on in the strength of the Spirit of God to accomplish great things for Christ in Ireland. In the first ten years of Mellifont's existence, it became the mother of six filiations: Bective in the diocese of Meath, Boyle in the diocese of Elphin, Newry in the diocese of Dromore, Baltinglass in the diocese of Leighlin, Nenay in Limerick, and Saints Peter and Benedict near Athlone.

Nor could he remain long hidden in the cloister. In 1150 he was chosen to succeed the saintly Maol or Malchus as Bishop of Lismore, soon after which he was constituted Papal Legate. As such, he presided with Cardinal Paparo over the Synod of Kells. In 1157

[4] Bernard, Epp 341, 356, 357, 374.
[5] Luddy, *Life of Saint Malachy*, 85.

came the crowning of all his work as abbot when the great church of Mellifont was consecrated, an event of national importance in Ireland, and presided over by the primate, Gelasius, in the presence of the Ard Ri, Murtough O'Loughlin. Such is the importance of the white monks in Ireland, and it was in this year also that Blessed Christian welcomed his monks into his own diocese with the foundation of Inislaunaught on land given by Donal O'Brian, King of Thomond, the founder of five Cistercian abbeys.

Eventually the Cistercians were to have forty-two houses in Ireland. But meanwhile, Blessed Christian, after a quarter of a century as bishop, retired to the cloister to end his days in that contemplation which he had deserved by such long and faithful service of God in active charity and self-sacrificing labors for his brethren and the church of God. He died on March 18, 1186.

March 19

Blessed Abond, Monk of Villers, Brabant, Belgium

(Sources: Chron Vill, 2.10; Martène, vol. 3; Moreau.)

Like Ida of Louvain, Blessed Abond was the son of an avaricious merchant who was completely unable to understand why anyone would want to renounce all things for God and who lived only for his business. Fortunately, Abond's pious mother saved him from a lifetime in the countinghouse. His father gave him only enough education to make him a useful clerk, but afterwards the boy continued to attend, surreptitiously, a college conducted by priests outside the walls of Huy, where he had been born in 1189.

He spent all his feast days in the church and prayed hiding behind the pillars for fear he would be noticed; when he was discovered he blushed with great confusion, ashamed at having attracted attention to himself. By the time he was seventeen, he determined to enter a monastery of the Cistercian Order and consulted Blessed Yvette, the recluse, who suggested Orval or Trois Fontaines. However, a meeting with Conrad, the Prior of Villers, decided him in favor of that great monastery.

Soon after his religious profession he entered into a calamitous siege of trials and temptations which was to last seven years. Seven years of darkness and horror, in which, no matter where he was turned, he was confronted with all the evils of hell. His vivid imagination seemed to be filled at all times with a nightmare of impurities. But he suffered this heavy cross with faith and patience, going on blindly month after month and year after year until the Lord at last removed the veil of darkness from his soul and revealed how much work had been done in all that time. For refined in the furnace of this trial, he had become one of the "pure in heart, who shall see God."[6] Abond became one of the most remarkable Cistercian mystics of the twelfth century.

He had prayed ceaselessly to be allowed to see heaven, and finally he was admitted to a vision of the saints in heaven and of the most Holy Trinity, Who is their life and their joy. His second vision of the Holy Trinity came one day when he was helping in the kitchen on the Feast of the Nativity of Saint John the Baptist. He happened to pass through the cloister just as the monks in Church were singing the Communion antiphon: *Tu puer*: "Thou, child, shall be called the prophet of the Most High." He instantly felt in the depth of his soul the touch of the Divinity and had barely time to run and conceal himself in the chapter room before the ecstasy swallowed up all the powers of his soul. He remained there for most of the day.

But what was characteristically Cistercian about the mysticism of Blessed Abond was the intimate role played in it by the Blessed Virgin. There is in the present day in the Church a great revival of devotion to Mary, the Mother of God, as our own Mother, and we should be constantly grateful to God for having inspired such a devotion in souls and for having given us such a Mother. But we have yet to rise to the heights of fervor and simple and ardent love

---

[6] Mat 5:8.

which the people of the Middle Ages, and especially the Cistercians, had for the Queen of Heaven as their Lady, as their beloved. This devotion, as we see in Saint Bernard, in the art and liturgy and architecture of the Middle Ages, in the poetry and music of that great age, brought out something in human nature, awakened depths of delicate and perfect love that sublimated all the natural powers of men to the purest heights of artistic expression. Abond's love of Mary had all the delicacy and beauty and sincerity and directness of the thirteenth-century art.

No one who has stood in a Cistercian choir at Lauds, after midnight Mass on Christmas Eve, and sung the glorious hymn of praise for the newborn Son of God, *"O solis ortus cardine,"*[7] will find any difficulty in believing that Blessed Abond saw the Queen of Heaven in a Cistercian cowl, standing near him in choir, singing this hymn with the monks and bowing with them at the doxology.

On another occasion, he asked his beloved Lady for the favor of kissing her hand. Not only did she not refuse him, but to his inexpressible wonder and delight she returned his kiss.

On the Feast of the Purification he was overwhelmed, as it were, with visions. Jesus Himself joined the procession at the first station. Mary appeared with her wonderful Child in her arms in the presbytery as the Mass began. Finally, when the time came for the monks to file back to the presbytery step and return their candles at the Offertory, Abond was so completely lost in ecstasy that his beloved, the Queen of Heaven, came and gave him a friendly nudge and started him on his way, thus saving him from embarrassment and the choir from confusion and disorder.

To love the Queen of Heaven is to be united with the Holy Ghost, Who is her spouse, and with Jesus her Son: This love is all one, and she knows no other love. But to be united with the Spirit of God is to possess charity, and charity necessarily overflows and embraces all our brethren. Abond was as simple as a child among his brethren and showed affection not merely to some but to all, indiscriminately, no matter if they were harsh and unpleasant

---

[7] Sedulius (5th century).

towards him. He was told by the Queen of Heaven how his father was preventing one of his sisters from entering a convent, and he went to great trouble, even getting permission to visit the convent of Ramege and obtain admission for her there, after which he went home and argued his father around to their way of thinking. Many of his confreres were miraculously aided by his prayers, including a novice who feared he would be sent away because of a dangerous illness. He also had the gift of prophecy and the ability to fathom the depths of souls by a supernatural intuition. Both these gifts, again, were intimately connected with his devotion to Mary; in fact, it was through them that the Queen of Heaven made him the special instrument of His Son's mercy for souls. Once, when he was at prayer, Mary appeared to him and urged him to pray hard for someone close to him who was then in great danger. As it turned out later a relative of his had just then fallen into a frenzy and had indeed seemed to have been killed by the violence of the attack. But he recovered long enough to make a confession of his sins before dying.

Two seculars, called Lambert and Godfrey, were trying to gain admission to Villers as novices. They asked the prayers of Blessed Abond. The latter said: "Lambert, you shall not have your desire. And you, Godfrey, will have to ask repeatedly before the abbot finally admits you." As it happened, Lambert died suddenly, not many days later, well prepared, let us hope, by this warning. Godfrey was long unsuccessful in his petitions, although he rallied around him all the friends and relatives he could find who had any influence with the abbot. Finally he was admitted as a lay-brother novice.

After the death of a holy monk called Bernard, in the middle of the night, the community had just returned to bed after taking the body to the church when the soul of the departed monk appeared in glory to Abond and told him of the incomparable joys that were now his in heaven, and from that moment on Abond's longings for the end of his exile and his return to his Father's house became more and more intense.

We do not know the year of his death, but he died on a Friday at three in the afternoon, the hour assigned by the Gospels to the death of Our Savior on the Cross. The date, March 19, assigned to his commemoration by the Cistercian Menology, is purely arbitrary; yet it is not inappropriate that we should celebrate on the Feast of Saint Joseph one who was also so close to the Heart of Mary!

April

April 1

Saint Hugh, Abbot of Bonnevaux, near Vienne, France

(Sources: AASS, April 1:47; an incomplete life from Helinand's Chronicle; Manrique, vols. 1 and 2 *passim*; Le Nain, vol. 6, p. 9f; Chuzel; Dimier, "La Vita Hugonis," Coll 6 [1939]: 214.)

In two generations in the twelfth century the same family raised up two saints called Hugh in the Church of God. The more famous is Saint Hugh of Grenoble, but scarcely less important is our present subject, Saint Hugh of Bonnevaux, the nephew of the great bishop and a Cistercian abbot who is to be numbered among the great patriarchs and peacemakers of the Cistercian golden age. He was one of those monks so remarkable for their simplicity and purity of life and their close union of God who were called to exercise a dominant influence not only over souls committed to their charge in monasteries but also over society at large. The crowning achievement of Hugh's life was that he finally negotiated peace between Frederick Barbarossa and Alexander III, a feat which Saint Peter of Tarentaise had been unable to effect, for he died with this work unaccomplished. The importance of such a work to the Church will easily be seen by anyone who has even a superficial familiarity of the ravages and desolation caused by the schisms fomented by Barbarossa in his time.

Saint Hugh was born in the ancient seat of his noble family, Chateauneuf, dominating the valley of the Isere. Besides his sainted uncle, the family included many other members notable for their piety, not the least of whom was Hugh's grandfather Odilo, who after a career of knighthood, entered the Grande Chartreuse where he evidently did not suffer too much from the strict fasts, since he died at the age of a hundred. There was also an aunt who became the first abbess of Vernaison.

It might have been expected that Hugh would enter nearby Bonnevaux, of which he was eventually to become abbot, but his family had other plans for him. They put him under the care of another uncle, powerful in the Church, the Abbot of Saint-Just at Lyons. He was to supervise Hugh's education for an ecclesiastical career. Unfortunately for these plans, Hugh had heard the call to the silence of the Cistercian cloister, and he secretly left Lyons and fled to the monastery of Miratorium or Miroir.

It is evident from what little we know of the circumstances surrounding his flight that Hugh's family, or at least his uncle in Lyons, was opposed to his entering a Cistercian monastery. But his conversion was a matter of enough importance to elicit a letter from Saint Bernard,[1] in which the abbot of Clairvaux encouraged him to persevere in his vocation. Did Saint Bernard know Hugh personally, or was he a friend of some members of Hugh's family? We cannot tell. The letter does inform us that Hugh was very young at the time of his entrance into the monastery, that is, he was probably a little over sixteen. The most important piece of advice the saint had to give the young novice was that he should pay no attention to the tears and solicitations of his relatives trying to bring him home again. The enemies of a man are those of his own household, the saint said, insofar as they love us not for ourselves but for the pleasure they themselves derive from our presence. Saint Bernard also warns him to avoid visitors, to keep out of the parlor, and to shun those conversations with guests which "fill the ears and empty the mind." For the rest, young Hugh should try to obey his superiors perfectly in all things and put all his trust in God, considering it a kind of blasphemy to fear, even for a moment, that God might fail to answer our earnest and faith-

---

[1] Bernard of Clairvaux, Ep 322.

ful prayers to Him. In a word, it is just the sort of letter one would write to a young acquaintance, scarcely over the threshold of childhood, who had just left a loving and noble family and a life of comfort for the austere routine of penitential duties in a Cistercian monastery. The saint recognizes in him all the necessary courage and goodwill to correspond with his exalted vocation—if only he can be protected against the influence of his parents and former friends.

There is some question about the monastery which Hugh entered. Helinand's Chronicle,[2] followed by several authorities, states that he became a Cistercian at Mazieres in the diocese of Beaune. Manrique holds for Miroir.[3] Strangely enough, the Bollandists quote the ancient hymn, written especially for Saint Hugh's proper office in the Cistercian Breviary where Miroir is clearly intended by a somewhat distorted version of its Latin name,[4] as evidence that he entered Mazieres. The dispute has finally been settled by the discovery of his authentic contemporary biography.[5]

Hugh soon proved himself to be a young man endowed with all the courage and faith and love of God necessary to become a true Cistercian, and he gave himself with exceptional generosity to the observance of the stern Rule of our Fathers. This did not, however, prevent him from suffering powerful interior movements of rebellion and repugnance at his separation from his loved ones.

It is too often wrongly assumed that because sometimes temptations against the vocation are an indication of an ungenerous spirit, they are always so. For although it is quite true that cowardice and self-love and attempts to compromise with God invariably make the burden of fasting and vigils and solitude seem almost unbearable, it is also equally true that sometimes the most generous souls are overwhelmed with the same feelings of repugnance and

[2] PL 212:1078.

[3] Ann Cist, vol. 1.

[4] *Vere plenus munditia Cisterciensi titulum / In domo* Muratoria *subit Hugo vestibulum: / Pastores dant consilia: Liunceli capitulum / Firma fratrum concordia, offert Hugoni baculum.* AASS, Apr. 1:47.

[5] Dimier.

homesickness precisely as a test of their courage and faith. Their acceptance of these feelings with a peaceful heart and a quiet determination to ignore them increases their merit in all the good works they thus perform in spite of every difficulty. It was probably during the course of these trials, at the time of Hugh's novitiate, that someone persuaded Saint Bernard to write him the encouraging letter we have just quoted. But it was prayer and faith that finally brought Hugh's temptations against his vocation to an end. The fact that these temptations came to him as a special trial is made clear by the way they ended: he was granted the grace of a vision of Our Lady, who came to assure him that he would never again have to suffer this particular trial. This is the first indication of Saint Hugh's extraordinary gifts in prayer.

His novitiate did not come to its end without another severe test of his vocation. This time his health was broken by the arduous generosity with which he had not only embraced the burden of our regular penances but added to them, and he became so desperately sick that for a time it seemed that his mind was threatened. Once again, Saint Bernard came to his assistance. It happened that the saint came to visit Miroir at the time, and he helped to nurse the sick novice and prescribed wise mitigations and a long rest, and Hugh recovered his health and strength.

Even then, Hugh was not able to go on peacefully to make his profession at Miroir. Reading between the lines of his story, it becomes evident that his powerful family had not related its efforts to exercise its control over the young man and keep him, as far as possible, within its own orbit. Consequently we find that towards the end of his novitiate, another relative, this time the Cistercian abbot of Leoncel in the diocese of Valence, near Hugh's home, was able to engineer the transfer of the novice to that community, and it was there that Hugh finally made his profession. Apparently, with this compromise, his family let the matter rest, and for the next twenty-three years Saint Hugh was allowed to sink into the peaceful obscurity of the Cistercian life.

The fact that he was allowed the privilege of enjoying so long a period immersed in the obscurity of the common life is itself very extraordinary when we consider Hugh's exceptional gifts, both of nature and grace, which had from the very first moment of his entrance into religion attracted so much attention. God granted him the grace of this long preparation for his career as abbot and peacemaker among the princes of the Church and of the world by giving him a thorough formation as a contemplative.

By the time he became abbot of Leoncel in 1162 he was far advanced in the ways of contemplation and sanctity. But once again, we see that he was a figure of exceptional prominence in the Order by the fact that he received his abbatial blessing from no less a hand than that of Pope Alexander III, who was then at Montpellier. This, of course, was not only because of his virtues but of his noble connections.

It was when he became abbot of Leoncel that Hugh's sanctity, drawn forth from the shadows of the cloister, burst forth upon the world in no uncertain manner. His biographer does not tell us of any miracles at this period, and yet we behold the saint everywhere besieged by crowds who demand his blessing and press upon him trying to cut little pieces of cloth from the hood of his cowl as relics. Evidently, the extraordinary effect produced by this simple and humble Cistercian upon all who came in contact with him is to be traced above all to his deep recollection and union with God. His biographer depicts him to us as being always in the world, as the saying goes, but not of the world. In the midst of the noise and distractions of business and travel he was habitually united with God in simple, contemplative union, which frequently deepened into a real mystical absorption, and he would ride for many miles in the saddle hearing nothing of the conversation about him but firmly entrenched, as his biographer says, in the citadel of divine contemplation. What is more, it is quite evident from this account that Saint Hugh himself was a man of the most perfect and sublime simplicity and that none of this was the product of any special study or effort on his part. It was the fruit of years of fidelity to grace and simple attention to God's presence working in him to produce the wonders of divine union.

As abbot, Saint Hugh set himself first of all to produce a like peace and recollection in the souls of his monks. His first concern was for them to attain to that interior quiet which is indispensable

if grace is to do its work. But the interior and exterior are insepa-
rable, and so, if his monks were to have tranquil hearts, they must
first of all study peacefulness and tranquility of body and learn
that modesty and recollection which keeps us happy and quiet,
just where the Rule would have us be, and not wandering aimlessly around the monastery in a confusion of trivial concerns and
useless errands which only disturb our own souls and make us a
nuisance to everybody we meet.

Saint Hugh also considered it an important duty to provide his
monks with books, and he had his copyists enrich the *armarium*,
or common box, with many works calculated to promote the life
of prayer and contemplation and to assist in the perfect performance of the liturgical services. We have little difficulty in guessing
what these works were—probably something by Saint Augustine
or Saint Gregory the Great and, no doubt, Saint Bernard also.

Saint Hugh was not, however, a great scholar, although his
preaching and instructions were famous not only in the Order but
everywhere he went. The effectiveness of his words sprang not so
much from learning as from what is called "unction." The Holy
Spirit spoke in him, and his simple, direct discourses, eminently
practical, and based entirely on the Gospels and on Scripture as a
whole, with plentiful examples drawn from the lives of the Desert
Fathers, communicated to his hearers something of the ardor of
his own burning love for God. In this respect he was a typical
Cistercian: the sermons of all our greatest saints are characterized
by their simplicity and by the fact that they are completely scrip-
tural and practical from beginning to end.

These same qualities attracted crowds of penitents to him in the
confessional and he achieved real greatness as a director of souls,
not only in the monastery but in the world as well. The great and
the poor, the good and the sinner, came to him with equal confidence and respect. He had a special flair for helping those whose
sins had brought them into grave difficulties and even to the brink
of despair. He was a wise and prudent physician, a good Samaritan
to the weak and wounded, but both in public and in private he
was uncompromisingly strict with the proud and hard of heart.
He had no mercy for those in high places who abused their posi-

tion in order to exploit the poor or defraud or disgrace the Church. He was especially severe with those who were tainted with simony, a vice that was practiced with cynical openness in the Medieval Church.

In 1166, after four short years as first superior of his own monastery, Saint Hugh was elected fourth abbot of the great monastery of Bonnevaux in the mountains near his own home. And it was truly fitting that a saint should become abbot of this nursery of so many saints. It was at this period of his life that the fame of his sanctity became even more widespread and was illustrated with numerous miracles. Indeed, he lost his own health but gained a supernatural power to restore the health of others.

More interesting to us, perhaps, than his many cures of the sick, or his occasional transformations of water into wine which are recorded in his life, are his gifts of supernatural insight into the souls of his spiritual children. Like the Cure of Ars, Saint Hugh possessed an extraordinary insight into souls, as well as the gift of prophecy.

There is, for example, the case of an ex-soldier who entered the novitiate at Bonnevaux under Saint Hugh. The Cistercians were exceptionally broadminded in their reception of novices: unlike the Carthusians, they did not try to exclude from their monasteries all but the most select and special vocations. On the contrary, they readily accepted even the most dubious characters, on the grounds that God's grace could work wonders for them—and it often did. This soldier was by no means a chosen soul or a man of accomplished sanctity. On the contrary, he had left behind him in the world a most unsavory reputation for treachery and violence, and he not only had a long string of misdeeds to his discredit, but he had also made a fair number of enemies. Saint Hugh had not refused him admission, but unconscious of the extraordinary favor this implied, the man did not seize the opportunity offered him and decided to return to the world. Before going, he told the abbot of a dream he had, in which he fell into a well so deep that it took him three days to reach the bottom. Saint Hugh's interpretation of the dream was very simple. "If you leave this monastery," he said, "you will fall into hell."

The man disregarded the warning. He left Bonnevaux. He had not been three days outside the monastery when he was ambushed by one of his enemies and instantly killed.

Yet another novice listened to Saint Hugh's assurance that if he stayed in the monastery the Blessed Virgin herself would appear to him at death and receive him straight into heaven. He remained at Bonnevaux, and the promise was fulfilled to the letter.

One of the monks of Bonnevaux went to his confessor with a sin that was reserved for absolution by the abbot. But Saint Hugh was on a journey. In fact, he stayed away from the monastery too long for the monk to obtain the necessary absolution, for the poor man died before his abbot's return. The night of his return, Saint Hugh had ascended to the dormitory and was in his cell taking off his shoes when, looking out, he saw the figure of the dead monk coming up the steps from the church to the dormitory. The monk went down on his knees and knuckles before Saint Hugh and confessed the sin. The abbot, meanwhile, was so overwhelmed by this extraordinary event that the sleeves of his cowl were drenched in tears, tears of anguished sympathy for this suffering soul. He gave the necessary absolution, however, and then he stretched out his hand to try and touch the figure before him, but it vanished in an instant. The next day Saint Hugh astonished the confessor of the monk by speaking to him of this particular sin that had been on the man's conscience. "Where did you hear that?" the priest asked. "From his own lips," answered the saint.

On another occasion, during the Vigils of the Annunciation, Saint Hugh's devotion was rudely disturbed by an appearance of the devil in the midst of the choir. Greatly saddened by this apparition, and having received an interior revelation as to its meaning, Saint Hugh brought the matter before his monks that morning in chapter. What had happened was this: someone in the monastery had committed a mortal sin and was concealing it from his confessor. The abbot urged the person, whoever he might be, to confess his sin as soon as possible and remove that abominable stain from the community that was even now celebrating one of the greatest feasts of the Immaculate Queen of Heaven. But a few days passed, and the evil one appeared again. This time Saint

Hugh had all his monks retire to their cells after chapter and take the discipline, after which all went to confession at the same time earnestly praying to God to make known who the guilty person was to the abbot. Their prayers were answered; Saint Hugh confronted the man in private and told him point blank what his sin was. The person immediately broke down, confessed and begged for forgiveness, and all was well. So it turned out that the devil had been very useful to Bonnevaux after all, in spite of himself.

The end of Saint Hugh's life, however, was to be crowned with an achievement far greater and far more valuable to the Church than these graces. Ever since Alexander III had ascended the papal throne, the Church had been divided by a schism, which was especially dangerous because Frederick Barbarossa had sponsored the claims of the anti-pope Victor IV in order to further his dreams of a European hegemony with the Pope as his vassal. The entire Cistercian Order, led by Saint Peter of Tarentaise, had thrown its support on the side of the legitimate Pope in 1161, and since that time Saint Peter had done everything in his power to break the schism and effect a reconciliation. The death of the first anti-pope only raised false hopes, however, for Frederick immediately pronounced in favor of a second anti-pope, Paschal III. In 1165, at the diet of Wurzburg, Frederick had even bound himself by oath never to recognize Alexander III or his successors. Saint Peter of Tarentaise finally died in 1175 before success was attained in ending the schism during the reign of the third of Frederick's anti-popes, Callistus III. But Frederick had showed signs of weakening, and his last papal puppet was not a popular figure with anyone except those who were interested in keeping in the Emperor's favor. Attempts to make peace, however, constantly failed when the negotiating parties balked at some detail or other, and matters had reached a deadlock in 1177 when Saint Hugh of Bonnevaux was called from his sick bed to act as go-between, together with another Cistercian, Blessed Ponce de Polignac, Bishop of Clermont.[6]

---

[6] Blessed Ponce de Polignac (d. 1189) entered the Cistercian Order at Grand-selve near Toulouse, where he was remarkable as a director of souls. He passed to Clairvaux as abbot, then bishop of Clermont in central France in 1170.

It was largely because of the immense personal respect of both Emperor Frederick and the Holy Father for Saint Hugh of Bonnevaux that the extraordinarily difficult and thorny diplomatic business of reconciliation was finally carried through without mishap, and peace was restored. This happy event was received with real joy and relief by both the emperor and the Pope. The former solemnly abjured the schism, commended himself earnestly to the prayers of the monks of the Cistercian Order, and wrote to the General Chapter in gratitude for the offices of Saint Hugh as peacemaker, not without mention of Ponce de Polignac.[7] A Papal Bull of Alexander III, which however antedated Hugh's entrance onto the scene, is also included in the compilations of the Statutes of our General Chapters for this period, and in it the Pope praises the work of the Cistercian Order in striving for the restoration of peace.

For a long time Saint Hugh was represented in pictures holding the Holy Crown of Thorns because of the widespread belief that he had been instrumental in introducing the Feast of the Holy Crown into the Cistercian calendar—it is celebrated as a feast of two Masses on the eleventh of August. However, that feast was instituted in the Order some sixty years after Saint Hugh's death at the request of King Saint Louis and then only in the monasteries in France. It was later extended to the Order at large.

Saint Hugh was about seventy years old when he died in the year 1194, and in the old Cistercian Breviary his feast with proper office was celebrated not only at Bonnevaux but also in the whole Order. It had, however, been dropped before the seventeenth century. It is not certain whether or not Saint Hugh was formally canonized, but since if he had been all record of the fact had perished, his title to sanctity was once more confirmed by the Holy See in 1702. His body remained incorrupt until the sixteenth century when Bonnevaux was devastated by heretics and his relics were scattered.

Thomas of Cîteaux's Commentary on the Canticle of Canticles is dedicated to him. He was venerated as a saint. See EM 2.24–26.

[7] Martene, 1:1847.

April 3[8]

Blessed Hermann, Lay-brother of Villers, Belgium

(Sources: Chron Vill, 3.2; Martène, vol. 3; Nimal, 151 ff.)

It is a curious paradox that this poor and humble lay-brother who had embraced the religious state as a Cistercian to die to the world in complete obscurity suffered throughout most of his religious life from an unexpected publicity and fame that resulted from his virtues and sanctity. He was not the only one among our lay-brothers of the Middle Ages—especially in Belgium, where because of the reputation of such men as Blessed Arnulph of Villers (June 30) or Blessed Simon of Aulne (November 6), a Cistercian lay-brother was liable to occupy as important a place in the hearts of a hero-worshiping public as a champion athlete in our own day.

There was nothing of natural beauty or attractiveness to recommend poor Brother Hermann to his admirers, for he had a crippled and misshapen body. But in that body dwelt a soul full of charity and grace that could not fail to manifest itself by a kind of supernatural charm: the charm of humility and simplicity and selflessness. But his whole concern was to escape those who came to ask his prayers and advice as though he were a great saint or prophet and to keep himself hidden and unknown so as to commune with God in prayer. And, indeed, he received great graces of contemplation, together with an insight into the future, and the power to read the souls of other men, for he once advised a religious, whose soul was in danger, to consider the state he was in and rectify his life.

He hated detraction—a vice that has always been heartily despised in all religious Orders but particularly in ours. For it is especially shocking to think that a monk or brother bound to the practice of silence, and to be silent even from good things, "*silui a*

---

[8] This date is purely arbitrary. It is the one given in the old menology.

bonis," as the psalmist says (Ps 38:3), should abuse his permissions to break silence by speaking shamefully or unjustly of his brethren. This sin has always been severely punished in our Order.[9]

Hermann's charity was not merely negative, however: he had a special love for the poor and unfortunate and for all those in trouble or afflicted with suffering and never refused to give all the help or comfort within his power to such persons. As for himself, however, he regarded suffering as a pearl of great price and treasured for the love of God, especially hidden and secret suffering. How many holy brothers there have been like him and who were never even recognized as such by their brethren. Their lives will never be written on earth, but they are written in the book of life, that is, in the very Heart of Jesus Christ, Who is Life itself, and the life of all our hearts and the sanctity of all the saints.

Above all, Brother Hermann had a loyal and tender love for the Mother of God, whom he used to call the Abbess of the Cistercian Order, as indeed she is, for wherever the Rule is kept, and wherever the spirit of our fathers is alive in our monasteries, one may find the same life of prayer and silence and obscurity that Mary led at Nazareth, with Joseph and her Son, the Son of God.

Once, in the course of his sickness, when it appeared that Hermann was close to death, one of his brothers, watching by his bedside, began to weep for he loved the sick brother and did not like the thought of his dying. But Brother Hermann calmly and soberly told him not to weep and said, "I am not going to die yet. But you, you should keep yourself prepared and in readiness, for your death is not far distant." The brother was attentive to the warning, and it was a good thing. For within a few weeks, Hermann was restored to comparative health, and the brother was in his grave.

As time went on, however, it became apparent that Hermann could not live very much longer. Some asked him if he did not fear the flames of Purgatory, but he replied: "No, I have confidence that the mercy of God will give me the reward promised to those who fear Him." He had learned confidence in the Cistercian school:

---

[9] See Statute against detractors, *Nomasticon Cisterciense.*

a true and sound confidence, based on a sure foundation of the filial fear of God, which always seeks to please Him, and trusts in His mercy to make up for all our failures that come from our natural incapacity and weakness.

The many monks and brethren who admired the sanctity of Brother Hermann were disappointed in their hopes of being present at his holy death, for death overtook him when he was at a distant grange. Only two brothers were present, and they testified that the Blessed Virgin had come to receive his soul, not that they themselves saw her, but they sensed her nearness and realized it by the actions and words of the dying brother. And indeed, the presence of the purest and kindest and most perfect of the Children of God, after His own Beloved Son, caused such sweetness and joy in the soul of one of these brothers that it did not leave him for three days.

Some reliable writers, including the Belgian Redemptorist hagiographer, Fr. Nimal, give Hermann the title of "Blessed," but the new menology does not do so.

April 13

Blessed Ida of Louvain, Nun of Roosendael, Belgium

(Sources: AASS, April 2:156; her life by an anonymous medieval writer, based on the notes of her confessor, Hugh; Henríquez, *Quinqua Prudentes Virgines*, edits the same text.)

It would be hard, indeed, to do justice to the long and detailed thirteenth-century biography of Blessed Ida of Louvain[10] by even a lengthy summary. It is one of the most complete accounts of the lives of our Cistercian mystics, and it contains details of many

---

[10] AASS.

mystical graces and semi-miraculous happenings. To reduce all these to a kind of brief catalogue would mean to obscure the meaning and character of the mysticism of this saint under a pile of mysterious charisms. Her life and spirituality are filled with variety and offer much to the spiritual sensation-hunter, but her whole story is dominated by the love of Christ in the Blessed Eucharist and by gratitude for His gifts and mercies to men. Joy and thanksgiving are the mainspring of her mystical experiences and the Blessed Sacrament of His love. We read of her being so carried away with tenderness that she went into the sanctuary of a church in which she thought she was alone and pulled down the suspended pyx, in the form of a dove, in which the Blessed Sacrament was reserved, and covered it with kisses.

On another occasion, she was so overwhelmed with gratitude for the goodness of God that she had a hemorrhage in the throat which robbed her of her beautiful singing voice for the rest of her life.

But to begin at the beginning of her career, Ida's childhood was unhappy. She was born into a bourgeois family, and all the members except herself had nothing but the ordinary materialistic views of their class. They loved comfort, money, pleasure. Ida, on the contrary, with her extraordinary love for God, her desire to praise Him and to do penance and make reparation for sin, soon antagonized all her relatives by leading a life that they thought was insane. She liked to go to church and to stay up all night praying; she liked to sing holy songs and canticles up in her room. She wanted to fast and wear a hair shirt and take the discipline. Indeed, she did go for eleven days with no other food but the flowers of a linden tree. Also, she slept on a mattress of vine branches.

These picturesque penances were nothing to the persecution to which she was subjected by her family—a persecution that was characterized by all the petty spite of the narrow minded. They locked her room when she wanted to go to church, and they shouted and raised an uproar.

Her biographer notes many marvelous incidents in which heaven takes revenge on Ida's behalf, but we need not dwell too long on them, except to remark that once when her father got angry at her for giving away a bottle of wine to a friend, his whole stock of wine went sour in the cellar although it was December, and when one of her sisters had been particularly nasty to Ida, she was awakened in the middle of the night by the Child Jesus who jumped on her bed in great indignation and roughly aroused her to rebuke her saying: "Why did you speak angrily to my spouse and revile her yesterday? Why did you revile her without cause?" Multiple incidents of this kind seem to have had no effect on the family whatever, and hence their number only reduces their credibility. Nor need we dwell on another marvel of her young womanhood, except for the sake of drawing attention to its originality: for Ida, instead of converting water into wine, or filling an empty vessel miraculously with wine, converted beer into wine.

What was more important was the fact that her ardent mystical devotion to the Passion of the Savior bore fruit in stigmatization: she received the impress of the wounds on her hands, feet, side and head. The stigmata caused her almost unbearable pain whenever they were touched by anything, even by her clothes. In order not to attract attention to herself, she prayed for these outward signs to be taken away from her, and her prayer was answered, although she retained the internal pain of the mystical wounds.

Her somewhat Franciscan delight in all living things is expressed in stories of fish coming to play with her and nibble at her fingers when she went to wash some linens in a pond and of chickens coming at her bidding, to stand at the door of a church and listen with attentive reverence to a Mass—at least up to the Gospel, when she dismissed her catechumens and let them go back to their characteristic pursuits. We will not argue that these things are any proof of great sanctity, but they fit in with the vine branches and the flowers and the sweet songs to give her story a charm of its own.

So, too, does the following vision. Ida was in church at the beginning of Mass. Suddenly she was rapt into ecstasy and saw Our Lady carrying the Child Jesus, accompanied by Saint Elizabeth. Saint Elizabeth was carrying a pitcher and basin and a towel, and they all came towards Ida. It turned out that they were going to give the Holy Child a bath. Indeed, Our Lady placed her dear burden in the arms of happy Ida, and she it was who, aided by Saint Elizabeth, bathed the divine Infant. He all the while joyously laughed and splashed and played as little children do, slapping the water with His hands so vigorously that Ida and Saint Elizabeth were soon soaked. After the bath was over and the Holy Little One dried and dressed and in Ida's arms, the Blessed Virgin made as if to take Him again to herself, but Ida would not give Him up. There followed a modest contention between the two, as to who was to keep the Holy Child, which finally ended with Ida coming to herself just in time to adore Him where He appeared before her under the sacramental species at the Consecration. She afterwards related this to her director with the apology that she thought only drunkards and crazy people had such visions.

Her spirituality was predominantly Eucharistic, and she had received the gift of a supernatural sense of the presence of Christ in the Blessed Sacrament when there was no natural indication that He was there. For example, she once visited a recluse who had received permission to have the Blessed Sacrament reserved on the altar in her oratory, but she kept this fact a secret. Ida suddenly felt a deep inner sweetness which told her of the presence of her beloved Lord, and she exclaimed: "My Father is here!" It was evident enough that she was not speaking of the cantankerous old wine merchant whose house she had long since left. After the visit was over, Ida went and bought the recluse a sanctuary lamp.

Suffering under the trials so familiar in the loves of souls dedicated entirely to God, Blessed Ida was once tormented with misgivings on account of her past sins—which certainly were never very grave. At last Jesus appeared to her and ordered her to go to Communion and offer it for the expiation of her sins: they would all be wiped out. She did as she was told and was overwhelmed with the realization of the immensity of Christ's love for her.

A most extraordinary fact about her devotion to the Holy Eucharist was the fact that she received special permission to go to Communion as often as she liked—even daily, which was extremely rare in the Middle Ages. This was indirectly the cause of great suffering to her when, after acquiring a great reputation for sanctity in the world, she fled to the Cistercian convent of Roosendael to escape notice and find more opportunities of pleasing her Lord by the sacrifice of her own will. The greatest sacrifice she was called upon to make was that in the novitiate she was only allowed to have three Communions a year.[11] But Our Lord took no account of this prohibition in her case, allowing her to receive His Body and Blood miraculously with the professed nuns. She could not say whether she was actually in the procession to the altar, physically, or not; but at any rate she made a real sacramental Communion, and it seemed to her that she did so in the ordinary way, but no one in the community noticed it.

Her entrance into Cistercian life was marked by a Eucharistic vision which is not without its meaning. By it she was given to understand something of the importance of community life in the economy of divine grace. Jesus appeared to her and presented her with a pretty coronet made out of intertwined crosses and jeweled flowers. He told her not to fear the austere Cistercian life, assuring her that He would always be with her. And then He explained to her the ineffable mystery of divine charity by which He would give Himself all, entirely to her, and entirely at the same time to each individual member of the community in Communion. It would seem that this entrance into the cenobitic life marked a real advance in the spirituality of one who was already a great mystic, as though her charity had been so far incomplete, since it had not been integrated into any close corporate union with Christ in the other members of His Mystical Body. This fact should remind us Cistercians to be most assiduous in meditating on this aspect of the Holy Eucharist. It is extremely important that we do not confine ourselves merely to striving after the consolation of our own personal union with Christ but always keep in mind that we

[11] The author of her life asserts that this was prescribed in convents of Cistercian nuns. There is no evidence of this in the material we have examined, and the *Consuetudines* of Saint Stephen prescribe at least four Communions a year and advise weekly Communion. When we consider that in those days daily Communion was practically unheard of, and not many priests even said daily Mass, we can see that the Cistercians favored frequent Communion quite strongly.

cannot be truly united with Him as He is in Himself, unless we are truly united by charity with Him in our brethren. No matter how fervent our Communions may appear to be, no matter what lights fill our mind and what ardors inflame our will—as long as we continue to be harsh and impatient and critical of the weaknesses and idiosyncrasies and faults of those around us, we can be sure that our union with God is not yet on a firm foundation. Any system of spirituality which omits this all-important consideration will lead us into dangerous illusion. And never, be it noted, can we make up for any deficiency in charity to those with whom we actually live by our zeal for the salvation of souls at the ends of the earth, although without such zeal, too, we could not call ourselves Christians.

A word about Blessed Ida's prayer. We see her on one feast of Saint Mary Magdalen sitting under a tree and reflecting on all the merciful kindness of God to that great sinner. Filled with these thoughts, she is rapt into ecstasy, and for the rest of the day she lives more in heaven than on the earth. Like all the Cistercian mystics, she drew upon the Liturgy for means to union with God. The liturgical cycle provided her with all she needed to enlighten her mind and inflame her heart and make them ready to receive the visitations of extraordinary grace.

Asked by her director if all these visions and favors did not give her temptations to pride, she replied: "When I reflect on them, I see them as though these favors were not given to me but to some other person." And she added: "As for talking of them, it gives me no pleasure, and I cannot do so without extreme distaste. I can only conceive of telling them to you because you have previously heard all my sins."

It is interesting that at Roosendael her ecstasies gained such command of her that she would go for days in a mystical state which she often deliberately tried to shake off but could not. We find her trying to relax her mind and body by distracting herself, watching little birds and insects. In fact, she had to work as hard to get her mind out of the absorption of prayer as most people do to banish distractions.

Blessed Ida died peacefully and uneventfully after a long sickness. The date assigned to her death is April 13, 1300, but the year is arbitrary. Her cult was confirmed in 1702 by the Holy See, and she is venerated as one of the patrons of Belgium. Her feast is a big day on the calendar at Louvain.

April 18

Blessed Idesbald, Abbot of the Dunes, Belgium

(Source: AASS, April 2:563; a very brief account based on the seventeenth-century Cistercian biographer De Visch.)

O angelica vox, exclaims one of the chroniclers of this ancient Belgian Abbey, speaking of its third abbot, *O egregia summi regis buccina Beate Idesbalde!*[12] "O angelic voice, O most noble clarion of the Most High King, Blessed Idesbald!" One of the few things we do know about this greatly venerated saint is his intense love of sacred chant. He devoted whole days to the ardent study of plainchant, which is a true and perfect preparation for the grace of prayer raising the whole man, body and soul, to God.

Idesbald came from the noble family of the Van der Graacht and was a secular canon at Saint Walburga's in Furnes. It was not until he had reached mature years that he entered the Cistercian Abbey of the Dunes—a name which gives us a clear enough indication of the monastery's bleak situation. It had been a member of the congregation of Savigny, a group of Benedictine houses that all came over to the Cistercians at once in the time of Saint Bernard. Soon after his profession, Idesbald became cantor of the monastery, and in this office he displayed such zeal and love in directing and perfecting the praises of God by his choir that one writer says that

---

[12] John Brandt, AASS, 584.

he received the gift of miracles as a reward for his beautiful singing.

In 1156 he was elected abbot of the Dunes and showed himself to be a prudent and energetic superior, under whom the Abbey made great strides. It was under his administration, in 1165, that Pope Alexander V gave the Dunes many extraordinary privileges and took the house under the special protection of the Holy See.

In 1167, after twelve years as abbot, Blessed Idesbald died in the odor of sanctity and was the first of the three abbots of the Dunes to be buried in the abbatial church. He left his successor one hundred twenty-eight choir religious and forty-eight lay-brothers.

Seventy-two years after his burial the new buildings of the Dunes were completed, and since the old church was to be pulled down, the remains of the saintly abbot were exhumed and translated to the new church. On this occasion, they were found to be in a perfect state of preservation and exhaled a most fragrant and delightful odor. Many miracles had been performed at his tomb, including one where a girl was delivered from the evil spirit. Mass was offered up for her at the tomb of the saint, and soon after the Holy Sacrifice the devil left his prey, leaping out of her mouth in the shape of a toad. The body of the saint was again exhumed in 1624 and was once again found to be in perfect preservation. His title to sanctity was confirmed by the Holy See in 1894.

April 26

Saint Francha, Abbess of Plectoli, Italy

(Sources: AASS, April 3:383, Life by Bertram Reoldi, A.D. 1326; P. Conrad Kolb, "Die Selige Franca, Abtissin, O. Cist," Cist Chronik 8 [1896]: 97.)

In 1173 was born at Piacenza in northern Italy one who was to become a most illustrious and energetic instrument of the Holy Spirit in working for the Cistercian Order in Italy. Not that Saint

Francha was to found many convents, for in fact she founded only one. But her story has some of the familiar characteristics of the exodus from Molesme that was the beginning of Cîteaux.

Born of the noble blood of the Counts of Vidalta, Francha left the world at an early age, entering the Benedictine convent of San Ciro in her native city, where she made profession at the age of fourteen. She applied herself very zealously to the pursuit of perfection in a more or less mediocre community. She was a great lover of prayer and obedience and sternly mortified her flesh, fasting three days a week on bread and water. But the crosses sent us by God are of far more value than the ones chosen by the light of our own myopic judgment, and from her early years until her death, Saint Francha was to suffer much from a disease of the stomach. She was offered medical aid for this at San Ciro, but neither there nor anywhere else would she consent to any other treatment save that afforded to the poor: the use of simple and household remedies.

When she was twenty-three years old, that is, in 1196, the fifty nuns of San Ciro chose Francha for their abbess, and then her trials began in earnest. She was a strict but gentle superior, but all her tact and kindness could not make her swerve from her purpose to see that the Rule was kept as perfectly as the circumstances would allow, and, in fact, San Ciro soon became admirable for its regularity. Most of the nuns loved Francha as a mother. There were, however, some who could not reconcile themselves to this interference with what they considered their "rights" and constantly murmured against the measures she had imposed.

One of the most unpopular of these was a small enough thing in itself: the prohibition of the use of wine to flavor the cooking. However, one day when the irate cook, a member of the dissident party, went to disobey the order and put wine in the simmering pot, the pot was instantly and miraculously emptied before her eyes—or so says the legend.

The greatest of Francha's difficulties came from one of the nuns who was the sister of the local bishop and who used her position to disastrous advantage against Francha, spreading false rumors about her in the town and showing no respect for the authority of one she envied and openly sought to replace as superioress. In this, however, she never succeeded.

Meanwhile, Saint Francha began to see her way out of this unpleasant situation when God sent her a remarkably talented and sympathetic postulant in 1210. This was Carentia, the daughter of Viscount Herbert of Piacenza who, besides being noble and pious, had received an education that was nothing short of astounding in a woman of her time, for she had even studied philosophy and theology. Instead of receiving Carentia's profession at San Ciro, Francha sent her to the Cistercian nuns at Rappallo, on the seacoast, to learn the life with a view to making a Cistercian foundation with her dowry to pay the bills.

Then in 1214, with the permission of the bishop, Francha and Carentia left San Ciro and founded a Cistercian convent at Montelana, just outside the city. Finding life impossible there, they moved to San Gabriele di Vallera, three miles from the city, in the same year, but the General Chapter of 1217 disapproved of this site, and they were forced to move again, to Plectoli, where they finally settled, and where the Church of Santa Maria de Tertio Passu was begun, the bishop laying the cornerstone on March 23. The name commemorated the fact that this was their third attempt to make a foundation.

It was here in a brief space of time that Saint Francha was able to satisfy her desire for penance and prayer—at least to some extent, for Carentia kept a watchful eye on her abbess's health. After the other nuns retired to the dormitory for the night, Saint Francha would secretly receive the keys of the church from the sacristan and return there to spend the night in prayer, in spite of the agony in her stomach and her almost total physical exhaustion. After Carentia forbade the sacristan to give up the keys, Francha entered the church by passing miraculously through the locked doors.

The chaplain of the nuns, a Cistercian monk of the abbey of Columba, did not believe this, and one night he determined to see for himself so he allowed himself to be locked in the church, unknown to the abbess, and placed himself in an obscure corner to await developments. Presently Saint Francha came effortlessly through the locked doors and went to one of the altars where she began to pray. After a time, it became evident that she was struggling with sleep, but she stood up and tied a string to one of her wrists, attaching the other end to a small psalter which she placed on the altar. Then she continued to pray, standing and with her arms stretched out, so that when she grew tired or drowsy and her arms began to sag, the book fell off the edge of the altar and woke her up. But her prayers continued all night long: sometimes her acts of love and oblation and contrition were uttered aloud, since she believed herself to be alone, and the listening monk was able to gain much edification from them although before the night was over he was probably very sorry he himself did not have the gift of passing through locked doors so that he could go and take a little rest.

As if the saint's vigil were not enough of a trial in itself, God allowed her to be frightened by visible appearances of the devil, and once the fiend dealt her such a powerful blow in the face that she fell unconscious on the floor with blood pouring from her mouth.

She had many visions during these long nights, including one of a relative of hers who, having gone abroad on business, fell into heresy through his contacts with all types of people in the commercial world and dying in his sin was condemned to hell. To her intense horror, Saint Francha beheld him being carried away by a devil.

Strict as she was with herself, she continued her unwavering, though gentle, rule of her nuns, insisting above all that they should persevere in love of the Rule and especially in worthily offering up their praises to God in the Divine Office. Meanwhile, as Plectoli gained an enviable reputation for sanctity of life, the nuns of San Ciro regretted their loss and tried to get Saint Francha back, but without success. It was something like the story of Molesme and Saint Robert, but Francha was not called upon to make Saint Robert's sacrifice.

One Sunday in Lent, during which season it had been her custom since her earliest days in religion to eat no cooked food at all, Francha was so sick that Carentia caused some roots to be cooked and served to her. Francha, in doubt as to whether she should break her custom and give in to the desires of her prioress, prayed for God to make known His will clearly to her. Then as soon as she put her knife into the cooked food, drops of blood came forth on the plate. She put down the knife and gently rebuked Carentia, pointing to the portent: "Do not make useless efforts to heal this sickness of mine," she said, "just leave me in the hands of God. Bodily remedies are of no avail against the afflictions sent to us by God for the cure of our souls, and even if they were, it should not be expedient for me to use them. These pains will deliver me from suffering in the next life."

At Easter of that same year, 1218, it became evident that her death was not far off, and confined to her bed, she was gradually devoured by her sickness. When the end came, it was she who comforted her nuns, not they her. The abbot of Columba, their Father Immediate, was summoned, and having heard her last confession, anointed her and assisted at her death. She was in her forty-fourth year and had been three and a half years in the Cistercian Order.

Her body was buried in her favorite place of prayer—before the altar of Saint Michael. In 1266, on the feast of Saint Bernard, the whole church of Plectoli was filled with a delightful odor which seemed to proceed from the tomb of the saint. Carentia summoned the abbot of Columba, and the remains of the saint were exhumed and found to be bathed in a sweet-smelling oil which was collected into phials and occasioned many miracles.

A church was dedicated to Saint Francha and Saint Raymond (not of Calatrava) in Piacenza, and she was beatified formally, according to the ancient code, in 1273. Her feast is kept by the Cistercians of the Strict Observance the day after the Feast of Saint Mark, on which she died.

The somewhat stern spirituality of this holy nun reflects her implacable determination to serve God with all purity and perfection. This was an ideal for which she suffered much, and her story only gives us the bare outline of a life full of trial and sacrifice. But it tells us enough for us to see that her sanctity had the stamp of unmistakable heroism and austerity, which have always been connected with the name of Cistercian, and to teach us that we must all have something of her determination if we are to be faithful to our vocation to the life of penance.

April 29

Saint Robert, Founder of Cîteaux, France

(Sources: William of Malmesbury, *De Gestis Regum Anglorum*, PL 17:9, 1289; Orderic Vital, *Historia Ecclesiastica*, PL 188; EP; EM; Ann Cist, vol. 1; Seraphin Lenssen, "Saint Robert, Fondateur de Cîteaux," Coll 4 [1937]: 2–16, 81–96, 161–177.)

Perhaps the most difficult of the lives of our Cistercian Founders to reconstruct accurately is that of Saint Robert of Molesme, one of the three creators of Cîteaux, and if not the founder of the Order, at least one of the principal initiators of the Cistercian ideal. His long life spent in several different monasteries, and semi-eremitical communities, is checkered with obscure conflicts with the conventional Cluniac monasticism of his time, and the apparent failure of his own personal part in the Cistercian enterprise, when he was recalled to Molesme by the Papal Legate has only made his character more enigmatic to posterity. There are many different opinions and explanations of the vicissitudes of his long career, and some authors have viewed his many changes of domicile with a somewhat critical eye.

Without entering into the details of the polemic that has so long surrounded the history of this great saint, we shall content ourselves with keeping as close as possible to the known facts, as they are presented to us in the documents of the saint's own time, or of the years immediately following his death. Thus we shall be able to avoid the confusions that came in with such profusion in the thirteenth-century interpretations of his career and were amplified by the historians of the seventeenth.

First, an outline of his early career; then we will proceed to the most important period of his life, the foundation of Molesme and

Cîteaux. Robert was born about 1028, not of a Norman family as Manrique would have us believe[13] but of a well-born family of Champagne. His father was called Thierry, his mother Ermengarde, and the latter is supposed to have had a vision of the Blessed Virgin a little before her son's birth, in which Our Lady expressed a desire to be espoused to the child that was soon to be born. This pious legend belongs to the thirteenth century.

When Robert was about fifteen years old, he entered the Benedictine monastery of Saint Pierre-de-Celle, or Moutier-la-Celle, and after ten years he became prior of the community. Years went by, and around 1070, Saint Robert, then about forty-two years old, became abbot of Saint Michel-de-Tennere. It is here that we first begin to get an insight into his personality and his special vocation. A short time after he had become abbot there, Saint Robert was approached by some hermits who were living in the woods at a place called Colan and who desired him for their superior and spiritual director. The delegation from Colan, however, was ill received by the monks at Saint Michel's, who would not allow them to see their abbot at all, and in fact, drove them away with open hostility. Shortly after this we find that Saint Robert left Saint Michel-de-Tennerre for another monastery, Saint Ayoul (Saint Aigulfus).

At once we gather two evident facts from this incident: Saint Robert had some reputation as a director of souls and religious superior, since the holy hermits of Colan were so intent on having him for their abbot that they went to Rome and returned armed with documents from Pope Alexander II which made Saint Robert their Superior. So in 1074 he took up his residence in the woods of Colan. This little community had grown up in those times around a nucleus of two converted knights and a hermit. The two knights, says the story, were one day riding through these woods to a tournament. Though they were blood brothers, or rather precisely because they were blood brothers, the devil began to suggest to each one of them privately the thought of killing the other in

---

[13] Ann Cist, vol. 1.

order to obtain his inheritance. They not only resisted this frightful suggestion, but on returning by the same way, they remembered with horror and compunction what thoughts they had there and went separately to confess them to the hermit who had his cell nearby. Afterwards, they opened their hearts to one another and resolved to leave the world and give themselves to God as solitaries in these woods. By the time Saint Robert came to Colan, one or two others had been added to their number, and it is suggested that one of these was Saint Alberic. The more usual story is that Saint Alberic came to Colan after Saint Bernard.

In any case, one of the first things the new superior did with his community of hermits was to move them to a wooded hillside at Molesme where there was more room for expansion. Here they settled, no longer as hermits, but as cenobites, keeping the Rule of Saint Benedict. As a matter of fact, for the first few years their life was more austere than Saint Benedict's legislation demanded. They dwelt in huts of boughs and had much hard labor, clearing the forest and trying to grow a little food. Their poverty was abject, and often they had nothing to eat at all. However, this state of affairs did not last long.

One day, when the breadbox was empty and there was a good chance that they might starve, Saint Robert told a group of his monks to go into Troyes and buy some food. The only trouble with this project was that they had no money with which to do so. When this was pointed out to him, the holy abbot showed no surprise and not the slightest intention of altering his command. He told them, once again, to go into the city and get some food: God would take care of the financial aspect of the problem. So the monks went, and Saint Robert's faith was more than rewarded. As soon as the barefoot, emaciated monks appeared in the city, word flew from mouth to mouth, and before long they were summoned to the palace of the bishop. This prelate had already seen something of Molesme, and now he hastened to provide the monks with all that they needed. His generosity was the signal for a shower of gifts from all the rich and noble families of the region, so that in an incredibly short time Molesme became not only a solvent but an extremely prosperous community. It acquired not only many rich tracts of land but numerous tithes, parishes, mills, villages and dependent priories.

Saint Stephen Harding's traveling companion, Saint Peter or "Pion" of Jully, was sent to one of these.[14]

It is well known how Saint Stephen was delighted with the life led at Molesme under Saint Robert, but he was not the only saint attracted to the direction of this holy abbot and to his monastery. Whatever else it was, Molesme in its early days was the center of a ferment of religious revival, which was carrying out the same work in Champagne as was beginning to be done in other parts of France by Saint Bernard of Tiron, Saint Vital, the founder of Savigny, Saint Robert of Abrissel, and others. It was from Molesme that there went forth a group of fervent monks to live as hermits in the Alps with Saint Guerin at Aulps. More important still was the fact that the young Canon Bruno from Rheims came to place himself under the direction of Saint Robert for a time. This was the founder of the Grande Chartreuse and the father of the Carthusians. But already when Saint Bruno came to Molesme, attracted by the reputation of Saint Robert, the abbey had grown to proportions and had taken on a character which was alien to his contemplative ideals, and he spent the time (two years or so) at the priory of Seche Fontaine, apart from the hustle of the big, rich monastery.

Manrique and Henriques, reading too much between the lines of the thirteenth-century historians, have presented the sudden decline of Molesme as a real decadence, which it certainly was not. In fact, we must be very careful how we use the word "decline" in this connection. It is undoubtedly true that as soon as Molesme became wealthy, the austere life that was led by the first founders no longer continued there but simply gave place to the ordinary, mitigated Cluniac usages, which were familiar to the many noble postulants who presented themselves there as soon as the place began to have a reputation. But when we speak of the Cluniac usages as mitigated, we must not regard them as relaxed

[14] *Vita Sancti Petri Juliascensis*, PL 185:1261a.

or easy, especially in comparison with the religious life of our own day. It is all very well to sneer at Cluny, but they kept at least the hours of the old Benedictine Fast: that is, they never ate anything before noon, even in summer. During the "fasts of the Order" they did not take their one daily meal until the middle of the afternoon, and in Lent they waited until the evening.

Some Benedictine houses allowed meat, it is true, but Molesme almost certainly did not, although they permitted lard in the cooking—a universal practice. The Cluniac usages prescribed a burden of vocal prayers, beginning in the middle of the night and continuing on through the day, that would appall most modern religious. On an average, these monks had to recite one hundred thirty-eight psalms each day—practically the entire psalter, although the same psalms often recurred. In fact, there is evidence that this backbreaking load of extra prayers and litanies and processions was one of the things against which the Cistercians were reacting, not because they objected to long vocal prayer as such, but because all these extra obligations destroyed the harmony of the Benedictine balance of prayer, work, and meditative reading.

The chief trouble with Molesme, and with the Cluniac system as far as Saint Robert and his sympathizers were concerned, may be summed up in a sentence. The Cluniac monastery had become too important as a cog in the wheels of a complicated feudal society, and its consequent contacts with worldly affairs made a purely religious and contemplative life extremely difficult and uncertain, except in very special situations, as for instance, under an abbot like Saint Hugh of Cluny. In a word, most of the new recruits who came to Molesme were sincere in their desire to fulfil the obligations of their state, but they were inevitably worldly minded and were full of the prejudices and preconceptions that made mediocrity inevitable for them.

Saint Robert had already shown at Saint Michel-de-Tennere that he was weary of a monasticism that compromised with the world and that he longed for a life of purer solitude and union with God. And now, too, there was an energetic and vocal minority in his community at Molesme comprised of men who were even more determined than he was to refuse all half-measures. When Saint

Stephen and Saint Alberic and the others came and put before
Saint Robert their objections to the state of affairs in the community, he heartily agreed with them, and after appointing certain
monks to make a thorough study of the affair, he placed it before
the community at large. The Norman Benedictine, Orderic Vital,
gives a complete account of what then transpired at Molesme.[15]

Having convoked his monks in chapter, Saint Robert laid the
affair before them in few words. They had made vows to keep the
Rule of Saint Benedict, but were they, in fact, keeping that Rule?
There were many things they did which were not prescribed by
it—and by this he meant things that were alien to its spirit—while
many of its prescriptions were passed over and ignored. The chief
of these was manual labor, for apparently, as soon as there had no
longer been any real need for work, to keep body and soul together, the monks had fallen back on scholarly occupations, even
more than these, upon the plain bureaucratic business of admin-
istrating the newly acquired dependencies and estates. We often
tend to idealize the Cluniac monastery as a home of scholarship,
and indeed, so it was; but it was also, and often primarily, a kind
of network of governmental bureaus and offices, in which the
monk substituted for the labor of his hands not study but the business of a feudal civil servant.

And it was at this point that Saint Robert, according to Orderic
Vital, used the strongest language. For since they did not support
themselves by work, and yet lived so well—so much better than
the Rule allowed—how was this possible? Was it not, in fact, that
they were feeding, by their tithes and exploitation of lands and of
the poor, upon the blood of other men? It was his conviction that
they should give up all this and follow the example of the ancient
hermits, living lives of poverty and labor and prayer.

The reply which Orderic Vital attributes to the monks (and his
summary of the dispute is credible) is one which merits to be
studied attentively if only for the fact that its logic is so close to
the familiar arguments of religious in our own day, so hostile to

[15] PL 188:637.

penance and mortification. They began by saying that he was demanding the impossible. He was trying to make them go back to the austerities of the Thebaid, which were beyond the strength of men of their time. Besides, such a rigorous life was no longer needed in the Church. Paganism had been overcome, and the Church was at peace. Such penances were no longer necessary to bring down special graces on the world. Besides—and this being their strongest point—they were living according to usages which had been approved by the Church and which, indeed, had been framed by men who were not only prudent and farsighted directors of souls but were, indeed, canonized saints. After all, they said, was it not reasonable to wear warmer clothing in a cold climate? The Rule itself provided for such variations. Then, too, in northern France there were no olive trees, and therefore lard had to be used in cooking. Besides, if they were going to pray for the world, they were entitled to the world's support; indeed, from Charlemagne on, monarchs and princes had endowed monasteries with ever-increasing generosity, stipulating, however, that certain prayers were to be said for them: it was reasonable to take on these obligations and the emoluments that went with them. And so the argument proceeded.

It soon became clear that there was not much chance of settling the problem by a reform at Molesme itself. Saint Robert and his party were absolutely convinced (and all the early documents, and the later ones too, agree perfectly in this) that the *Cluniac usages seriously disagreed with the letter of Saint Benedict's Rule* and that to live by them was certainly not to lead the contemplative life as the great patriarch had planned it.[16] In fact, to live by these usages might even imply a prevarication against their holy vows. It must not, however, be concluded from this that Saint Robert felt that the Cluniac usages were themselves degenerate or useless. The man who kept them would be, no doubt, a good Christian. But would he be a Benedictine, a contemplative, a man of poverty and solitude and labor and prayer? Would he reach that intimate

[16] Especially see the EP 2, 3, etc. (by Saint Stephen Harding).

union with God to which the first Fathers of our Order so ardently aspired?

Whether or not it was as a result of these discussions that dissension arose in the community forcing Saint Robert to retire temporarily, around 1093, to another hermitage called Aux, or Haur, we cannot say with certainty. All we know is that he did leave his community. To say, as some have said, that his prior, Saint Alberic, in assuming charge of the house, attempted to enforce his notions of reform and was then beaten and imprisoned for his pains, is no more than conjecture. It seems more likely that the beating and imprisonment referred to by the *Exordium magnum*[17] came later. At any rate, the *Exordium* tells us plainly that the reason for it was Alberic's zeal in proselytizing for the new monastery, not reforming the old.

In any case, matters finally came to a head in 1097, and Saint Robert led a delegation of fervent reformers to see the Papal Legate, Hugh, and to obtain his permission to leave Molesme and institute their reform elsewhere. Hugh's letter clearly acknowledges that it would not be possible for them to keep the Rule as strictly as they would like at Molesme and authorizes them to leave.

On the feast of Saint Benedict, March 21, 1098, which was also Palm Sunday, a group of twenty-one monks from Molesme took up their abode in a nearby tract of woods called Cîteaux in the diocese of Langres, not far from Dijon. It was a wild and desolate spot, but there were shelters of boughs and branches like those which had appeared at the beginnings of Molesme a bare twenty-five years before.

Within a little while, Raynald of Beaune and Odo, Duke of Burgundy, came to the assistance of the pioneer community with grants of land and gifts of cattle, but for a long time the monks were destined to live in great poverty. Saint Robert, meanwhile, had been elected abbot and installed by the ordinary of the place. Unfortunately, the monks of Molesme were not going to accept this secession without resistance, and it is quite evident that after

[17] EP 9.

the departure of the reformers for the "New Monastery," Molesme was in a turmoil. They soon sent a delegation to Hugh, demanding the return of Saint Robert, and it appears from the negotiations that took place that the monks of Molesme were aiming not only at the return of their abbot but at the dissolution of the new community, the very existence of which cast such a blot upon their monastic honor. The Legate put the whole matter in the hands of Pope Urban II, who made it known that he desired Saint Robert to return to Molesme, since this was the only way to obtain a return of peace and comparative regularity to that house, but he also indicated that he desired the new community to continue undisturbed. Hugh transformed the Pope's desire into a more or less formal order, and Saint Robert, in humble obedience, complied.

His critics have gone so far as to suggest that his great age had made it impossible for him to bear the hardships of the new foundation and that he willingly accepted this decision; indeed, some have even alleged that the monks of Molesme appeared before the Legate with Robert's connivance. The answer to this accusation is that it is to be traced to a piece of inaccuracy in the account of William of Malmesbury who, in his usual patriotic anxiety to exalt his fellow countryman, Saint Stephen Harding, makes Saint Robert look cheap in comparison, but he does so without any valid evidence. On the contrary, Saint Robert's whole life, at least all that we know of it since his departure from Saint Michel-de-Tonnere, represents a constant striving to get away from mitigations and to embrace a life of greater austerity and sacrifice. Is it likely that, now that he had finally realized his dream, he would have thrown away the fruit of his whole life's work? Indeed it is quite clear that this final renunciation, in obedience to the Papal authority, was the crowning sacrifice of his career.

To complete his story from the pages of his thirteenth-century biographer, not all the monks of Molesme had cause to congratulate themselves on the return of Saint Robert. Once when the holy abbot told the Servant of the Refectory to give some bread to the poor, and the latter disobeyed him, Saint Robert took the bread and threw it into the stream that flowed along the foot of the bluff on which the monastery stood, rather than allow his monks to eat what belonged to Christ in His poor. But under his guidance, Molesme settled once again into a peaceful state, and Cîteaux, through the wise moves of Saint Alberic and the protection of the Holy See, was put out of the reach of any animosity that might have remained in the turbulent element of the community or the local nobility, their relatives.

Saint Robert died on April 17, 1111, at the age of ninety-three, after sixty-six years in religion and forty-four as abbot. At the beginning of the thirteenth century, the monks of Molesme began to promote the cause of his canonization, in which they received the wholehearted support of the General Chapter of Cîteaux, and Saint Robert was raised to the honors of the altar by Honorius III in 1222 by beatification, which in those days was equivalent to informal canonization. His feast is now kept in the Cistercian Order on April 29, when it is usually not liable to fall within Easter week.[18]

Although Saint Robert spent barely sixteen months at Cîteaux, it is safe to say that without him there would have been no Cistercian Order. It was he who as abbot of Molesme attracted to himself the fervent souls who were later to form the nucleus of the great reform. Indeed, Saint Alberic and Saint Stephen were to amplify and concretize the ideal that had always remained somewhat indefinite and half formed in the mind of Saint Robert, but it was from him that the original inspiration sprang. He was truly the father of Cîteaux. And the thing that we, his children, can best learn from him, is his hatred of all compromise. Truly, those who have represented Saint Robert as in conflict with monks who were decadent and totally irregular have missed the whole point of the Cistercian reform. The grandeur of Saint Robert's ideal is that the Cluniac monastic usages, which were not bad but *good*, as far as they went were not good enough for him. The fact that the mitigations of Cluny were all sanctioned by competent authorities, and even had specious arguments of prudence on their side, did not

---

[18] [In the current Cistercian calendar the three Founders, Robert, Alberic, and Stephen, are celebrated on the same day, January 26. —Ed.]

make him content with them. He wanted to give God everything, and that is the purpose of our Order, complete immolation of the body, mind and will to God, without compromise. The Cluniacs tried to alter the letter of the Rule, according to "Prudence," without losing its spirit. Saint Robert and his companions believed, as did a great General of the Reformed Cistercians in our own day,[19] that the best way to keep the spirit of the Rule is to keep the letter as perfectly as possible.

April 30

Blessed Aymon, Monk of Savigny, France

(Source: *Les Petits Bollandistes* 5:105 [based on a contemporary life which is printed in *Analecta Bollandiana* but to which we have not had access].)

When the famous abbey of Savigny, built by the Benedictines among the apple orchards of Normandy, came over to the Cistercian Order with all its daughterhouses in France, England and Flanders, it also brought many living saints, of whom the greatest was Aymon de Landecob. His name tells us that he was born at the village of Landecob in the diocese of Rennes, that is, in Brittany. Like another Cistercian saint of that most Catholic province, Maurice of Carncet, Aymon, although endowed with great intelligence, forsook the opportunities offered him by the life of cleric and scholar and went to Savigny to escape the temptations of a purely natural life by following his own dispositions and tastes in the world of men.

Saint Benedict, as a wise legislator, urges his abbots to try the spirits of their postulants to see whether they be of God, and the trials he suggests are more rigorous than the average person would

---

[19] Dom Jean Baptiste Ollitrault de Keryvallan.

be able to cope with today. Saint Aymon received an ever-more arduous testing of his vocation from the hands of God Himself. He had not been long in the novitiate when he was suspected of having leprosy and was unceremoniously ejected from the monastery. Fortunately, he managed to obtain permission to remain in the shadow of the house he desired to make his home on earth, insofar as we can have a home in this land of exile. There were two monks who really did have leprosy and who were segregated from the community, living in a little hovel in a nearby "desert," that is, in the woods. Aymon received permission to take care of them. It was an arduous enough task in itself, but he added to the arduous and difficult duties he had imposed upon himself as their attendant by spending long hours at night in prayer and meditation.

It was thus that he proved, in the furnace of the trial, the gold of his vocation. Eventually the monks realized that he did not have leprosy after all, and he was admitted to profession and, soon after, to the holy priesthood. He did what all priests should do, that is, he made the Mass the center and whole purpose of his life. And because he did so he was filled with abundant graces from Christ, the source and fountainhead of all life and grace, the principle of all goodness and of the efficacy of all good works. From this overflow of charity, Saint Aymon was blessed with extraordinary gifts in the direction of souls and became in the confessional as famous as the Cure of Ars. Blessed Peter of Avranches, another monk of Savigny, was one of his most celebrated penitents, but Aymon had care of the souls of many laypersons, from the lords of the strong castles of Normandy to the poor and the serfs. Not content to give them the benefit of his inspired judgment and guidance, Saint Aymon prayed for them all as he prayed for himself.

But what of his devotion at Mass? With such great simplicity and purity of heart did this holy monk ascend the altar that he was often granted supernatural revelations of the glory of the work in which he had been chosen by the Son of God to participate. Once, at the *Supplices te rogamus* in the Canon, he saw the altar suddenly surrounded by angels, one of whom took the Host and offered it up to the Father in Heaven, afterwards reverently replacing it upon the altar. They then all retired.

Again at the Consecration he saw the heavens opened, and Jesus appeared and smiled and inclined His head to His poor servant, in whose heart were "felt" rather than heard, but with ineffable certainty, the words "Behold the Son of God Himself, appearing for his consolation!" His whole soul, like melted wax, receiving the impress of this great truth, was so absorbed in the overwhelming presence of Truth itself. When he returned to his senses, he completed the Holy Sacrifice more like an angel than a human being.

Having become Master of the lay-brothers, he suffered great anxiety when a number of his charges gave up their vocation and returned to the world. He could not help accusing himself for their defection, although he was unable to see in what precisely he had been at fault, since he had done everything he could to prevent it. Then, at the Communion of the Mass, he suddenly saw Jesus pierced with nails and bleeding to death upon the Cross, who said to him: "Since I suffered so much for you, it is right for you to set so little store by what you suffer for me." Instantly filled with light and trust and faith, he accepted with a good heart the anguish of these doubts and cares over the sons entrusted to him.

William of Toulouse, a learned doctor from the Norman city of Caen, wanted to enter Savigny. But first he wanted to return to the city and settle his many affairs. He could not be persuaded to keep his hand on the plough without looking back, for very frequently persons with such intentions go back to the world and get so involved in the affairs they are trying to "settle" that they never return to the cloister. Finally, Blessed Aymon himself went to Caen and put everything in order; William remained at peace in the novitiate. This learned man later became abbot of Cîteaux.

Blessed Aymon's holy fear is demonstrated by the diffidence with which he accepted the responsibility for all the relics of the saints in the monastery. His devotion to the saints resulted in the construction of many chapels and churches in their honor in Normandy.

One of his penitents, a holy nun, was on the point of death. He had heard her confession but could not stay at her bedside until the very last as obedience called him back to Savigny. So he, in turn, put her under obedience to remain alive until he could return to her bedside. She lived for several days more until he returned. And then she gave up her soul to God.

The last sickness of the saint himself was a most painful one, and being unable to lie down, he had to spend many months in a chair. This trial he supported with great patience until he finally went to his reward on April 30, 1173. He is still much venerated at Savigny, now a parish church.

May

May 2

Blessed Mafalda, Princess of Portugal, Nun of Arouca, Portugal

(Source: AASS, May 1:10 [based on Henriques].)

Most beautiful of the three pious daughters of King Sancho of Portugal was Mafalda, and her beauty was equaled only by her intelligence and depth of spirit. Indeed, her charm of mind and of countenance and demeanor were so great that her miserly brother Alphonse, who eventually succeeded King Sancho on the throne of Portugal, was not so unkind or unjust to her as he was to her two sisters Theresa and Sancha. Instead of cheating her out of the portion due to her as a dowry, as he did the other two, he even added something to her part.

It is difficult for a princess of royal blood to escape from the world to the cloister, and in the beginning it did not seem there would ever be much hope of Mafalda's doing so. She was resigned to the fate of a King's daughter and entered obediently upon a political marriage that was arranged for her with the young Prince Henry of Castille. However, the marriage had this about it: Henry of Castille was a mere child. As if that were not enough to make it an uncomfortable situation, Mafalda had it on her conscience that he was a close relative. And so, although the nuptials were solemnized at Palencia or Medina del Campo, the marriage was never consummated. Eventually, to her great relief, the activity of politics in the Castillian Court led to the dissolution of the match, and she returned to Portugal.

Now the monastery of Arouca, in a pleasant and fertile valley in the mountains called the Serra de Freitas, had been founded by the Benedictines in 1099. It had been occupied at first by monks, but the community fell into irregularities and tepidity and so degenerated that it was replaced by one of the Benedictine nuns without much better success. In course of time, on the advice of the Abbot of Alcobaça and with permission of the King and Bishop of the place, Arouca became a house of Cistercian nuns, and Mafalda entered as one of their number.

She immediately showed that she was going to be the most fervent type of religious, distinguished for her humility, charity and spirit of penance. Above all, she showed all through her religious life an exceptional zeal for regularity in choir. We say exceptional because by the thirteenth century the influx of royal and noble postulants to the monasteries of Spain and Portugal had introduced, in their favor, certain relaxations of the Rule. Mafalda herself was to receive a special dispensation to retain the use and free disposal of her property and fortune, which were immense. This exception was blessed by obedience and pontifical approval, because of the special nature of her case, and she used her privilege only for the purposes of charity, as will be seen. In her instance and that of her sisters, this dispensation was eminently wise.

She tamed her flesh with disciplines to the point of blood, slept on a mattress stuffed not with straw but with cork, and fasted three times a week. Her great compunction in prayer was accompanied with the gift of abundant tears. She often spent entire nights in contemplation in the convent church and had reason to be sad when the rising sun came peeping through the windows with his prying and curious rays that only served to dispel a far greater and pure light of the spirit. Her greatest devotions were to the Holy Trinity, the Twelve Apostles, Saint Jerome and Our Lady of Silva, venerated in the city of Oporto. To the shrine of the latter the saintly Mafalda presented large sums of money for its embellishment, to the honor of the Queen of Heaven.

This was only one of the many outlets for her charity. Fortunate it was for Portugal that one so insatiable in giving things away had been allowed to retain so great a fortune to dispose of for the glory of Christ. She had a hospice built in the wild mountains behind Arouca, where travelers received shelter, food and services for nothing. She maintained in several places free ferry service over the rivers of Portugal and caused many bridges to be built. Churches, monasteries and hospitals sprang up everywhere, before the magic of her queenly liberality. She greatly encouraged and assisted the Dominicans and Franciscans, who were just then beginning to penetrate into Portugal.

In the year 1252 she made a journey to her favorite shrine of Our Lady of Silva, and while she was returning she fell sick. Forced to remain at a place called Rio Tinto, she sent word ahead to the abbess of Arouca, her executrix as well as spiritual mother. But the latter had been forewarned of the death of her noble subject in a vision and was already on the way to Rio Tinto with several of the senior nuns of the convent.

They found Mafalda on her deathbed, facing with calm serenity her joyful entrance into heaven. "What!" said the abbess to her gently, "you are so joyful now, when all your life you had so great a fear of the dread day of death?"

Then, having given her sisters a most earnest and moving exhortation to cling with their whole heart to the Rule of Saint Benedict as interpreted by Cîteaux, she was placed upon the bed of ashes prepared on the floor and died clasping the crucifix.

According to her own wish, her body was taken to Arouca on the back of a donkey. The legend adds that the donkey entered the convent church with his burden and went straight to her favorite altar, that of Saint Peter, and made a genuflection, getting down on his fore knees before it. Nobody who doubts this story will be excommunicated. Mafalda was laid to rest in a magnificent tomb, and her memory was made illustrious by many miracles and visions in which she appeared, in glory, to her sisters.

She was beatified, by a regular process, in 1792.

May 3

Blessed Alexander of Scotland, Lay-brother of Foigny (near Laon) France

(Source: AASS, May 1:438 [brief account taken from Thomas of Cantimpre, *De Apibus*, 2.10, 13th cent.].)

In the Abbey Church of Foigny, one of the first daughterhouses of Clairvaux, seven kilometers northeast of Vervins in the diocese of Soissons, the faithful have come for centuries to pray at the altar of a Prince of Scotland, Blessed Alexander, whose picture showing him as a humble lay-brother stood above it.

He was not the son but the nephew of a Scottish king, who was childless and without heirs. Of Alexander's three brothers, one had given up everything to live in poverty for the love of Jesus Christ. Another, a Count, had fled the world and the court to become a hermit. The Third, an archbishop, had abandoned all dignities and high ambitions to become a Cistercian monk. There was left, besides the sixteen-year old Alexander, a sister, Matilda. She too was a saint, and it was largely through her that Alexander became one. For she came and spoke to him one day, pointing out that he would soon be the king of Scotland and telling him all that that meant—and could mean. "What will you do, Alexander?" she said, "Your brothers have all chosen heavenly kingdoms, leaving you an earthly one, for which you may lose your soul!"

The young man wept. What, indeed, would he do? He did not want to be king, especially at the risk of losing his soul. The brother and sister fled Scotland together and went to France.

There, living in retirement and obscurity in the peaceful countryside of Brie, their noble birth was hidden and forgotten, and Matilda occupied herself in teaching her young brother to milk cows and churn butter and make cheese. There was a reason why she instructed him in these humble and peaceful arts, for he soon was able to present himself at the Abbey of Foigny and ask for admission as a lay-brother novice without fear that his helplessness in anything to do with labor might betray his origin.

Matilda remained nearby until he was settled in his new life, and then, having made sure that nothing remained to tie him to the world, she bade him farewell and disappeared.

Humble and obedient, Alexander lived the life of a perfect lay-brother, remarkable for nothing but his humility and for his skill in making good cheese. Nobody knew who he was, and the secret did not get out until, on his deathbed, he made known his identity to his prior. However, on one occasion he nearly did give himself away. He was watching over the cows in a distant pasture when a nobleman came riding by in pursuit of a wild boar. He had come far ahead of his fellow huntsmen in the ardor of the chase, and quite near to where Alexander was, he cornered the brute and dismounted in order to finish him with his dagger. Unfortunately, the boar was still too full of fight to be easily overcome, and it soon became apparent that the huntsman's life was in real danger. But suddenly Alexander was there, snatched the dagger from his hand and dispatched the boar with a skill and dexterity and courage that left the stranger astonished.

"My friend!" he cried, "You are no cowherd! Who are you, and what is your name?"

But Alexander, seeing what had happened, withdrew in haste and confusion.

After his death, he appeared to a monk who had come to pray at his tomb for the cure of an ulcerated chest. The saint had two crowns, one upon his head and the other in his hand, and he explained to his client that the one on his head was the heavenly crown he had won by his virtuous and obscure life in the monastery, while the other was the crown of his earthly kingdom, which had not been lost to him by his sacrifice of it but had been returned to him in heaven: so true it is that nothing that we give up for Jesus Christ is ever lost, provided only that there is some value in it; for when we have Him, we have all goodness, all value, all reality, all that is good in anything that we ever had or hoped to have on earth: for in Him is the substance and value of everything that is good. Let us beg Him, then, for grace to imitate Blessed Alexander on earth and to be with him in heaven.

May 5

Saint Martin (*Sacerdos*) [of Finojosa], Abbot of Huerta, Bishop of Siguenza, Spain

(Source: Le Nain, 6:537.)

Saint Sacerdos is the popular name under which is venerated the holy bishop Martin Mañoz y Finojosa, a scion of the nobility of Castilla la Vieja. He was born in the year 1139 and grew up under the care of a most loving and pious Christian mother with his brother, a courtier and knight, and his two sisters Theresa and Eve. Instead of following the usual aspirations to knighthood, Martin was fonder of books and meditation and solitude, and this bent of his was definitely turned into a vocation to the cloister when his father died. The shock of this loss fixed his mind on eternity, and despising all that the world had to offer, he made known his intentions to his mother and brother. He was then twenty years old.

At first he met with nothing but opposition. However, when they saw that he was firm in his purpose, his family did not have the impiety to resist him further, and the mother made a most generous and willing sacrifice of him, taking him to the Abbey of Cantavos and there leaving him with all the ceremonies prescribed by Saint Benedict for presenting the children of the rich to the monastery. Martin, meanwhile, took the Mother of God in exchange for his earthly mother and adopted as his motto for the novitiate: *Si incipis, perfecte incipe*, What you begin, begin perfectly.[1]

In 1164 the community of Cantavos was forced to move because of the poor water supply in that place, and they settled in a new site taking the name of *Hortus Beatae Mariae*, Saint Mary's Garden, called for short Huerta, garden, or orchard. And there, although

---

[1] [Merton credits this motto to Saint Bernard but does not give a literary source. —Ed.]

he was only twenty-six, Sacerdos was elected by the monks to succeed the abbot who had so recently received his profession.

The history of this abbot of Huerta comes to us through official documents which tell us less of his virtues than of the fame of them and the effects of that fame. We read everywhere of the veneration in which he was held by the royalty and nobility of all Spain. We read how, in 1175, the Lords and Grandees of Castille, about to depart on an expedition against the Saracens, came to Huerta for the Abbot's blessing. There was a High Mass in honor of the Holy Trinity, after which Sacerdos gave them their arms and received their requests that they might be buried at Huerta if they fell in battle. In 1170 we read of a magnificent act of donation of King Alfonso of Castille for the building of a vast and noble church, in which the monks are to fulfill the duty which is expected of them by the whole kingdom: to send up their prayers and praises to the throne of God day and night. Yet it is interesting to observe the attitude of Saint Sacerdos towards this donation. He was indeed delighted that a great church should be built to the glory of God. However, the most important thing for him was that he and his monks should praise God in their own souls by their recollection and abstraction from material and distracting cares. Consequently he would not himself take on the charge of supervising the construction of this edifice, nor would he inflict so great a cross on one of his monks. But then, there was no lay-brother capable of undertaking so complicated a task. What then? If it was a question of sacrificing recollection and displeasing God, or sacrificing the new Church and displeasing the King, it was easy to see which this holy abbot would choose. Fortunately the difficulty was overcome when a noble secular, Don Rodrigo Ximenes, later Archbishop of Toledo, took charge of the whole affair.

It will be understood then that it was with the greatest distaste that Saint Sacerdos learned, in 1186, that he had been elected bishop of Siguenza. He only accepted this position under orders from Rome. His first step in the new office was to protect his clergy against the ruthless and unchecked violence of seculars by getting Pope Clement III to force witnesses of criminal assaults on clerics to give evidence under pain of excommunication. Before, they had been terrorized, and culprits could not be convicted.

In 1194, however, Saint Sacerdos persuaded the Pope to accept his resignation and was able to return to the peace and tranquility of Huerta, where he could fill his soul with the infinite sweetness of the presence of God and hide himself in the secret of His face, of whom the psalmist said: *Proteges eos in tabernaculo tuo a contri-dictione linguarum*, "Thou dost protect them in Thy tabernacle against the contradiction of tongues." And that Face, of which we read in the same psalm, *Abscondes eos in abscondite facisi tuae*, is nothing else but the divine Essence, in which we lose ourselves in the luminous darkness of faith, which covers us and makes us invisible to our enemies—and sometimes to ourselves. And so, in these years, Saint Sacerdos was often rapt out of himself in the ecstasy of divine contemplation.

Death finally overtook him in 1210 when he was on a visitation of his monastery of Óvila. He felt the end approaching and set out for Huerta but did not complete his journey, for he died on the way. His venerated body was received with great circumstance by his grieving children and buried in the great church of the abbey.

In 1558 his body was found completely uncorrupted, along with the clothing and crozier with which he had been buried. He was formally beatified with the title of saint and inscribed in the Roman Martyrology in 1584.

May 6

Blessed Ponce de Polignac, Abbot of Grandselve, then of Clairvaux, and later Bishop of Clarmont, France

One of the most fervent monks in the early days of Grandselve, which under the guidance of Blessed Bertrand had become so illustrious a nursery of saints, was Ponce de Polignac, who from the first days of his novitiate gave himself with great love and devotion to the work of crucifying his flesh and purifying his soul to make it a worthy dwelling for the Triune God. And as a young religious, he derived an especial profit from the observance of one of Saint Benedict's instruments of good works, in which we are advised to venerate the older and more experienced monks: *seniores venerari.* The secret of his rapid progress in fervor and spirituality was the attention and respect and love with which he observed and listened to and followed the example of the senior monks.

One of them was the novice master, for whom Ponce had a special veneration. This good old monk had an earnest desire to end his earthly pilgrimage and return to His Father in Heaven, and indeed so intense and gripping was the anguish of this desire that one Holy Thursday when the whole community received Communion, this monk had no sooner taken the Sacred Host into his mouth than he was overcome with longing to see Jesus face to face. Grasping himself by the throat, he spoke inwardly to Christ begging Him for the grace that he might never again swallow any material food after taking this Host into his being.

At once, as if in answer to his prayer, he felt his strength begin to leave him, and right after Mass he had to be taken to the Infirmary, where he died happily on Holy Saturday but not without having revealed his secret to Ponce. He suffered no pain, except in his throat, in the place where he had taken hold of it with his hand.

Before the holy man died, Ponce, with a holy simplicity that was above presumption, asked him to appear to him, if it were God's Will, after his death, and tell him something of his state. And this request was answered within a few days when the holy religious appeared to him shining with a bright and unearthly translucency that made him seem like the purest crystal. He explained that he was thus clad in a spiritual body, which we may take to be nothing but a mystical representation of his charity, just as we read of the saints in heaven being seen with robes, crowns and so on, although their bodies will not actually rise again until the last day. And he said that through every member of this translucent body he saw as clearly as though all of him had been transformed into eyes, so great was the clarity of vision infused into him by the light of glory. And yet there was one blemish, one spot on the heel of one of his feet that was less resplendent than the rest which was, he said, due to the fact that he had not been as generous as he might have been in going to the common labor and had tended to lag behind in the line on the way to the place of work.

In course of time Ponce became abbot of Grandselve, and his strength and faith and prudence and charity were all submitted to a heroic trial during his superiorship, when the Abbey was struck by the plague with so violent an onslaught that forty-five monks died of it in two months. Yet all this took place, comparatively speaking, without turmoil or disorder or any unusual upheaval. So great was the faith of this community that there was not one of those who died that did not yield up his soul to God in perfect peace and tranquility and confidence and resignation, not to mention holy joy and desire.

This was in no small part due to the influence of the good abbot, as we may see from the fact that one of these victims, not many years before, had been terribly tempted to despair of his salvation because of his sins, and Dom Ponce to reassure him had made him a promise which was a good demonstration of his own great faith. For he did not hesitate to offer the salvation of his own soul as a guarantee that the monk would be saved, provided only he remained in the monastery and obeyed the Rule and his superiors.

The saintly abbot had forgotten all about this, until the dying monk relieved him of his obligation, telling him at the same time that he was now not only not afraid of death but eager to enter into the joys of perfect and eternal vision of the infinitely good God, who so loves all His children and made all things out of his pure goodness for our joy and gladness, by which we give Him glory. Indeed, at the point of death, he was rapt into ecstasy, and when he returned to himself, although he was at first unwilling to speak, he obeyed the abbot's command to tell what he had seen and related that Jesus had appeared to him and made him this solemn promise: "All those who persevere in this Order until death, practicing obedience, shall receive from My hands, eternal salvation."

This confirmation of what he had heard from his abbot—or rather from Jesus through his abbot, and now heard from Jesus Himself—has long served as a source of confidence and a spur to the fervent obedience in the monasteries of our Order. Let us never forget that, as De Rance says: "So true is it that obedience is the work of Jesus Christ, and the distinctive character of those who belong to Him, that the devil is capable neither of producing it, nor of counterfeiting it."[2]

So valuable a superior as Ponce was soon chosen for a higher position, being elected in 1168 abbot of his own motherhouse, Clairvaux, the fourth to follow Saint Bernard in that position. Nor did he fail the trust that was put in him. But he was not long at Clairvaux, for another promotion brought him, against his will, to the post of Bishop of Clermont-Ferrand in 1170. There he became distinguished as an arbiter and peacemaker in disputes between abbeys and bishops. Thomas of Cîteaux's Commentary on the Canticle of Canticles was dedicated to Blessed Ponce de Polignac.

He died in May 1181 and was venerated as a saint.

May 10

Saint Peter of Tarentaise, First Abbot of Tamie, Archbishop of Tarentaise (now Moutiers)

(Sources: AASS, May 2:317, Geoffrey of Auxerre, Vita S. Petri, abbot of Hautecombe, former secretary to Saint Bernard and coauthor of Vita Bern, later abbot of Clairvaux and Bishop of Auxerre; *Saint Pierre de Tarentaise*, by a monk of Tamie, an excellent modern biography.)

The curious name of the village where Saint Peter was born—it was called Saint Maurice de l'Exil—springs, perhaps, from the fact that the Roman Empire frequently sent political exiles to that district, and Pontius Pilate is said to have spent a term there in disgrace. The region in question lies in the Rhone Valley, a little south of Lyons, in the neighborhood of Vienne between the river and the Alps. Peter was the son of a pious independent farmer, who,

---

[2] Armand-Jean de Rance, *Explication de la Ste Regle*, Prol.

among his other good works, frequently offered hospitality to the monks of the nearby Cistercian abbey of Bonnevaux when they had to leave their monastery on business of any kind. Bonnevaux had been founded in 1117 when young Peter was fifteen years old, and in the years that ensued, the saintly abbot, John, was a frequent caller at his father's farm. It was from this holy man, says Saint Peter's biographer, Geoffrey of Hautecombe (who was Saint Bernard's secretary and wrote one of the chief biographies of the great abbot of Clairvaux), it was from Dom John that the family learned "to remain at peace with all men, to preach peace to all, and to make peace between those who were at odds: to give assistance to those suffering from injustices, and to rebuke, when possible, those committing it."[3] In other words, the example of a saint, and of his community of fervent Cistercian monks, in the first flower of the Order's energetic spirituality, made a profound impression not only on Peter but on his whole family. Indeed, most of them were destined to become in one way or another Cistercians.

Peter's brother, Lambert, had been destined at first for the priesthood, Peter himself for the farm. But Peter showed an earnest desire to progress in prayer and the knowledge of Scripture. He soon learned the Psalter by heart and recited it daily. Later on he was to penetrate deeper and deeper into the inspired text by reading and rereading Saint Augustine's Commentary, which appears to have been his favorite book outside of the Scriptures themselves.

It was not surprising, then, that this young man should soon express a desire to enter the novitiate at Bonnevaux, which he did in 1122. He was followed there soon after by his brothers Lambert and Andrew, and by his father, while his mother and sister became Cistercian nuns at Saint Paul d'Izeaux. His mother became the first abbess of the Cistercian convent of Betton in 1150.

Peter distinguished himself as a novice by his humility and obedience in a community where there were many saints and where the life was still the hard one of a new foundation. But Bonnevaux was growing, and on February 16, 1132, ten years after Saint Peter had entered the monastery, he set out with twelve other

---

[3] AASS, May 2, vol. 2, 322.

monks and his abbot, Blessed John, for a valley in the high Alps of Savoy and in the diocese of Tarentaise. There, as a result of the efforts of the Cistercian Archbishop of Tarentaise, Blessed Peter (often confused with the saint himself), and Count Amadeus of Savoy, a site for a new abbey had been found and the first buildings had already been made ready for the reception of the colony.

It was a wild enough site, this deep, rocky valley, filled with the sound of the icy torrent fed by the snows of the high peaks that dominated the place from three sides, and yet it was not as perfect a solitude as one might expect. The Archbishop and the Count of Savoy had deliberately sought to establish a colony of Cistercian monks here because the old Roman road from Vienne to Milan, still one of the most important highways between France and Italy, across the Alps, passes this place, and a hospice for travelers was urgently needed. So urgent, in fact, was the need, that the Cistercian archbishop did not hesitate to call upon monks of his own Order to fulfill the task, in spite of the fact that it was something quite foreign to the Cistercian vocation. However, the task was one which practically many a Cistercian monastery undertook, more or less, and it never interfered very much with the contemplative life of the community as a whole.

When Blessed John saw that his monks were properly housed and left them in the charge of Peter as their superior, they found themselves faced with several years of arduous labor if they were to turn the rocky, barren soil into farm land. It was not merely a matter of clearing away the pine forest and rooting out stumps and removing boulders, not to mention tons of loose rock and rubble deposited by glaciation. The chief tasks were to build road and harness the torrent of this and the other valleys belonging to the monks as a precaution against floods and also in order to use them as a source of power. Most of the wheat would have to be grown in a lower valley and then transported to the monastery to be milled. Life in the early days at Tamie was twelfth-century Cistercian life at its most intense: fasting, poverty, long hard winters, prayer, vigils, contemplation, and above all, hard labor to battle the forces of the Alpine weather. In those days, a Cistercian monk had to be not only a saint but an athlete of manual labor and probably no mean engineer besides.

This was the life which Saint Peter led and loved for eleven years. Then God called him from the delights of this holy solitude to a vocation which, though easier in itself, demanded of Saint Peter a far greater sacrifice than anything Tamie had to offer.

At the death of the saintly archbishop Peter (called "the first" to distinguish him from our present subject), the See of Tarentaise had fallen into the hands of an incumbent whose type was all too common in the twelfth century. Like so many of his contemporaries, this individual was a coarse, unscrupulous hireling, without virtue or education, whose only aim was his own enrichment at the expense of the faithful. He had entered the fold, not through the door but rather over the fence of simony, and since his entrance his chief occupation had been to destroy the work of his holy predecessor. In 1141 this Isdrahel, as he was called, was relieved of his crozier by the Holy See, and Peter of Tamie was elected to replace him. Peter demurred, trying to do all that he could to avoid this dignity, but a delegation from the archdiocese presented itself at Cîteaux, to the General Chapter of that year, and Saint Peter's fate was sealed. Under obedience to the chapter, whose orders received the support of Saint Bernard, the Abbot of Cîteaux and Saint Peter's own Father Immediate, Blessed John of Bonnevaux, he accepted the post and entered upon a responsibility which he greatly feared on account of the dangers with which it threatened his own soul.

It was no small responsibility for a man to undertake the care of souls in this mountain diocese. It was relatively dense in population, and the poor soil and hard climate meant that the great majority of the people lived in abject poverty. Besides that, many hundreds of souls were isolated in almost inaccessible mountain villages where, while they had been in many cases deprived of Catholic priests, they were frequently visited by the heretical Waldenses, and heresy was doing a great amount of damage. Even if the Waldenses had not been at work, however, the ignorance of the faith was so great that the true vitality of the Christian life, that is, prayer and the frequentation of the Sacraments, was threatened at its very source.

Saint Peter, living as much as he could like a monk, wearing the poorest of habits, and keeping all the Cistercian fasts, threw open his house to the poor and made up for the lack of manual labor by spending whole days traveling on foot through the mountains, climbing to distant villages where they had not only not received the Holy Ghost but had no idea that there was such a Person. He confirmed thousands of people, adults and aged person as well as children. He raised money to provide books and altar vessels for the neglected parish churches, and Mass began to be said again in many places where it had long ceased to be offered with fitting dignity, or indeed to be offered at all. He continued the work of his Cistercian predecessor Blessed Peter by establishing a community of Regular Canons in his Cathedral and providing for the proper liturgical offices, which had been hitherto neglected by the secular canons, who had regarded their position more or less as a sinecure. He also saw to it that the Cathedral was decorated *ornamentis competentibus*, a fact which is significant and proves that while the Cistercians carried austerity to extreme limits in their own churches, they did not consider this rule to be of obligation outside the Order or attempt to force their own ideals upon the faithful at large.[4]

One of the essential duties of a bishop, and one which was most neglected in the Middle Ages, was the duty of preaching, and Saint Peter made it his business to preach the Word of God wherever he went. Like many of his contemporaries in the Cistercian Order, he had received no advanced theological training, and his sermons depended, for their force, not on learning and scholarship but on faith and long hours of contemplation and meditation of Sacred Scripture, supported by sanctity of life and intimate union with God. In fact, Saint Peter had a kind of repugnance for lofty speculations, and when a sermon had to be preached to an audience of intellectuals, he generally got someone else to do the job. His own ministry was directed above all to the little and the poor, and his sermons were always fundamental. They needed to be, for it must be remembered that there was no such thing as the regular Sunday sermon in the parish churches of the time: most priests never preached a sermon in their whole lives.

[4] AASS, 324a.

An amusing tale illustrates Saint Peter's charity to the poor, which was one of his most characteristic traits—he soon became famous for it in the first years at Tarentaise. At any rate, one day he was invited to dinner at the house of a noble lady, where, thinking that no one was paying any attention to him, he took some bread that was on the table and put it in a bag for the poor. The hostess, knowing what he was about, called for more bread, and presently that, too, disappeared. She sent the servant to get still more. The same performance was repeated over and over. Finally, when the time came to leave the table, Saint Peter could not even lift his sack of bread, and the servant had to help him carry it away.

A section of Moutiers still bears the name of *Pain de Mai* and the name goes back to one of Saint Peter's charitable institutions, his May-bread, or the distribution of food to the poor that was made necessary in that month, when the scant harvest of the previous year had been already entirely consumed and the new crop was just ripening in the valleys.

Every day in May, soup and bread were distributed at the archbishop's palace to several hundred poor. This was not confined to the time of Saint Peter. The practice lasted six centuries and only ended with the French Revolution. When the poor were liberated from the "tyranny" of the Church and the archbishops were all but driven out of their sees, the May-bread *ipso facto* ceased. The poor were then, no doubt, invited to fill their stomach on the speeches of revolutionary orators concerning the way the poor had been starved by the bishops. However, to be just, if there had been more like Peter of Tarentaise, there would never have been a French Revolution. Down through the ages, until that cataclysm, the Isurahels were too often in the majority, and God had His own economical way of getting rid of them.

By the year 1155 Saint Peter of Tarentaise was all but canonized by the people of his mountain archdiocese, and his fame had spread into many neighboring provinces. When, in this year, he was called to the place now called Saint Claude, in the Jura, to settle a lawsuit between two religious communities, of Benedictines and Premonstratensians, concerning the right to fish in a certain lake, Saint Peter, of course, was literally besieged by miracle hunters. He had to take up his position in a room in the tower of the abbey church of Saint Oyen, while the crowd passed up one staircase and filed by him, leaving by another stairway—many of them cured of sicknesses by his touch. Saint Peter, of course, was attributing all this to the merits of Saint Oyen (Eugendius). Meanwhile, the press became so great that a youth was smothered to death in the crowd. Saint Peter made his way through the throng, and carrying the body to the altar of Saint Claude in the church, prayed to that saint, and the boy was brought back to life then and there. The effect of this miracle was tremendous, and indeed, one of its results was an intense devotion to Saint Claude, who had hitherto been quite overshadowed by Saint Oyen, the other patron of the monastery. Indeed, it is as a result of this intensification of the cult that the present town on the site of the monastery bears the name of the once neglected saint.

Much more significant, however, was the result of all this on the life of the saint himself. When he realized what people thought of him, and how they spoke of him, his soul was filled with a terrible fear. No doubt he could not help but feel a certain natural satisfaction in all this—and he wondered if he were not consenting to it, taking pleasure in it for its own sake. Was he not enjoying all this glory as if it belonged to him? He began to be overwhelmed with misgivings. His biographer tells us[5] that he kept asking himself: *Petre, quid actitas?* "Peter, what are you doing? Where will all this lead you?" And he frequently reflected that Christ had told His apostles in so many words that if they were of the world, the world would love its own. These fears could only lead him to one conclusion: he was losing his soul. Under the circumstances, he would be perfectly justified, he thought, in abandoning a post where he was confronted with such insuperable dangers and retiring to a hidden monastery where no one would be able to find him.

Accordingly, one night he simply vanished from Moutiers and struck across the mountain with a guide, penetrated the Jura, and finally found his way north to a narrow valley south of Bale where the little Cistercian monastery of Lutzel was built in such close quarters that the hillside had to be cut away for space to make a

[5] AASS, 326a.

vegetable garden. No doubt the abbot recognized him from having seen him at the General Chapter and connived at his plan. At any rate, Saint Peter sank into the obscurity of community life as a simple monk. He did not even know the language spoken in the monastery (which was German).

Unfortunately, his plan did not work. A sudden inspiration led a friend of the saint to follow his trail to Lutzel. The man took up his position at the gate as the monks went out to work. Sure enough, there was the archbishop. The friend of the saint fell at his feet, imploring him to return to his diocese. All the other monks surrounded them in consternation: as soon as Saint Peter's identity became known, he had to leave. He resigned himself to what was evidently God's will and returned to Moutiers and to his poor— who received him with a most exuberant acclaim!

The famous hospice of the Petit Saint Bernard, which is well known to every schoolboy because of the so-called Saint Bernard dogs, trained to find travelers lost in the snow, was in the diocese which Saint Peter of Tarentaise governed as archbishop, and one of his duties was to provide sufficient funds to maintain this house in existence; for by the time he had entered upon his archepiscopate, it was practically ruined (perhaps because of the tender mercies of Archbishop Isdrahal) and could not carry on its work. The name Saint Bernard, of course, has nothing to do with the great Cistercian: it refers to Saint Bernard of Menthon who reestablished the ancient hospice in the eleventh century.

On one of his frequent visits to the high mountain pass on the slopes of Mont Joux, where this monastery is situated, Saint Peter came upon an old woman huddled in the snow, shivering with cold and weeping with hunger: she had practically nothing to protect her from the icy wind but a few rags. Tears of compassion sprang up in the eyes of the good archbishop. "Poor little mother,"[6] he said to his companions, "Who is going to help her? What shall we do? There is no point in giving her money, she cannot buy

---

[6] *En mater mea . . . me miserum, perit frigore mater mea, quid faciemus ei? Si dederimus nummos, nihil proderunt morienti* (AASS, 324d).

anything here on the mountain, and it will not keep her warm!" But his companions were silent. Saint Peter could not bring himself to follow them as they advanced up the road. Instead, he vanished for a moment among the snow-covered rocks. When he rejoined them, the old woman was wearing his robe, while he, for his part, was left with nothing but a cowl, scapular and hair shirt. It must be remembered that the Cistercians of the twelfth century wore nothing but what was specifically mentioned in the Rule, which says nothing of shirts and underclothing. Perhaps, however, since Saint Peter was on a journey, he availed himself of the permission to wear a pair of breeches. On another occasion, when he gave away his robe in the same part of the mountains, nobody realized what he had done, and he nearly froze to death. He said nothing, but on their arrival at the hospice everyone noticed that the archbishop was ill. He was immediately put to bed and had to remain there several days.

Shortly after Saint Peter's escapade to Lutzel, and his return to Tarentaise, began the long and bitter conflict between Frederick Barbarossa which had been threatening for some time to break out, and which, when it finally did burst into flame in 1159, spread to the whole of western Europe and involved the Church in another of those terrible medieval schisms, each one of which did more and more to weaken the temporal and spiritual authority of the Pope and prepare the way for the cataclysm of the so-called Reformation. In this situation, practically the whole Cistercian Order bent its efforts to the defense of the legitimate Pope (although some of the German Cistercians sided with Frederick)[7] and no one was more active in the struggle than Saint Peter of Tarentaise.

---

[7] A certain Gunther, monk of Pairis Abbey, in the diocese of Bale, near Lutzel, to which Saint Peter fled, wrote a long, bombastic poem in honor of Frederick, the "Ligurinue" (Mig. PL 212). Bishop Blessed Otto of Preisingen, ex-abbot of Morimond, being related to Frederick, was also well disposed towards the emperor and wrote a history of his reign, *Gesta Frederici*. Commemorate him on the actual date of his death, September 22.

To begin with, in 1160, after the spurious "council" of Padua, at which Alexander III was "anathematized" and Victor IV elected Pope, Saint Peter of Tarentaise was practically alone among the prelates of the Empire to raise his voice against this mockery of an election. Not only did he raise his voice, but he began a preaching campaign in the Empire itself, traveling north through Francha— Comte and Alsace—defending the cause of Alexander III, and everywhere he went his mission was confirmed by miracles. Cripples threw away their crutches at the touch of his hand. At Rouffach in Alsace a lame man was healed while he was still trying to force his way through the crowd to get to the saint. Finally, Saint Peter did not hesitate to present himself before Frederick and at- tempt to persuade him to be reconciled to Rome. Great was the astonishment of the imperial court when Frederick not only failed to throw the bishop in chains—where he would have been in the company of all the others who had dared to criticize Barbarossa's anti-pope—but even listened to him with respect and attention. "If I oppose certain men," said Frederick afterwards, speaking of the bishops he had imprisoned, "it is because they deserve it. But would you have me resist God?"[8] All this may be a tribute to the Archbishop of Tarentaise, but it does not explain why, if Frederick recognized God's voice speaking through his servant, the holy Cistercian, he still did nothing to end the schism.

As the struggle dragged on, and anti-pope succeeded anti-pope, the influence of Saint Peter and his Order after him swayed first the churches of England and France,[9] then their sovereigns, to declare in favor of Alexander III and eventually it became clear that Barbarossa's cause was lost. He still stubbornly refused to come to terms. Once again Saint Peter confronted him at Besançon, and the bishop of that place, a partisan of Frederick's who had tried to prevent Saint Peter from coming to the emperor, was sud- denly struck down with a fever and died in the worst possible dispositions. For when a Cistercian abbot came to his deathbed to

[8] AASS, 327e.
[9] AASS, 327e.

hear the bishop's confession and help him make his peace with God, the schismatic prelate raised his hand to his mouth and forming a kind of trumpet, began mimicking a bugle call, and so expired out of his wits. Although this caused a stir, Frederick was still not amenable to terms and in the end Saint Peter died before the settlement of the conflict, which was to be the work of two other Cistercians, Saint Hugh of Bonnevaux (April 1) and Blessed Ponce de Polignac (May 8).

Meanwhile, Saint Peter, now an old man, made frequent retreats to the peaceful solitude of Saint Bruno's retreat, the Grand Chartreuse. He had always had affection for the Carthusians, and now he was received in their monastery where he could pray and meditate and enjoy the fruits of his close union with God. Here he came in contact with the young Carthusian monk who was, like him, to become a saint and a great bishop, Hugh of Lincoln, who was delegated to wait on him and attend to his needs since the saint was chronically ill and needed constant medical attention. As a matter of fact, the details concerning Saint Peter's visits to the Chartreuse and the Carthusians' testimony as to his sanctity are found in the life of Saint Hugh of Lincoln,[10] not in Saint Peter's own. One interesting fact is worthy of special attention: each night, Saint Hugh affirmed, Saint Peter used to say before going to sleep a little prayer which is, in fact, the Post-Communion for the Mass of Ember Friday in September. It is a beautiful prayer: "Grant, O almighty God, that we may be so grateful for the mercies we have received from thy bounty, as to obtain yet greater favors." Strangely enough, this prayer is also the Post-Communion of the Mass *Statuit* of the Common of Confessors Pontiffs, which is assigned in the Cistercian Missal to the feast of Saint Peter himself.

But Saint Peter was allowed only rare intervals of retirement. In 1173 he was delegated by the Pope, together with blessed Ponce de Polignac, Abbot Alexander of Viteaux, the Prior of the Grand Chartreuse and the Grand Master of the Knights Templars, to

---

[10] *Vita Sancti Eugenis Lincolnenis* can be found edited, in Surius, *De probatis sanctorum historiis*, saints of November.

negotiate peace between the warring kings of France and England, Henry II and Louis VII. Henry was the king whose henchmen had recently murdered Saint Thomas à Becket (1170) and now his son Henry Courtmantel had rebelled against him and had taken the field against him with the French forces. Saint Peter made his way to Normandy, where the two sovereigns faced one another on the battlefield. His journey was doubly arduous because of his sickness, and he was obliged to break it for a month at the Cistercian monastery of Preuilly. There the affluence of miracle seekers disquieted the superior of the house who, for all his Cistercian hospitality, did not know where he could get bread to feed such a multitude. The saint told him not to worry, and as a matter of fact the monastery baker did not have to put more than the ordinary amount of dough in the oven for the day's baking: the ordinary ration was miraculously made to cover the needs of the vast concourse of unexpected guests, day after day.

Proceeding to Normandy, Saint Peter left a train of ever-more numerous and more remarkable miracles in his wake. By the time he reached the camp of Henry II, his cowl was practically in shreds, having been cut to pieces by those who had determined not to miss the opportunity of helping themselves from this walking treasury of relics who was the Archbishop of Tarentaise. King Henry finally climaxed the process by falling on his knees before the saint and begging what remained of the cowl for himself. Saint Peter managed to arrange a truce from the Feast of Saint Hilary (January 14) to Easter of 1174, which, in that year, fell on March 24. During that time the two monarchs met for negotiations, and Saint Peter remained on hand.

One day as the peace negotiations were in progress, Saint Peter was among the crowd, and someone brought to him a young boy who had been suffering blindness for the past five years. "What do you want, my child?" asked the saint. "Father, I want to see!" said the little boy. Saint Peter put a penny in his hand, and then moistening his finger with saliva made the sign of the cross on each of the child's eyes and on his head. Meanwhile a deep silence had descended upon the crowd, and the princes had even interrupted their talk. The courtiers stared at the saint and the child as if some strange game were in progress. But their skepticism turned to astonishment when suddenly the boy, looking around, began to cry out in a loud voice, "Mother, I can see, I see all the people! I see everything all around!"[11]

On February 6, Ash Wednesday, the two monarchs received the ashes from Saint Peter's hand at the Cistercian monastery of Montemar, but in spite of all this, the war began again that Easter. Once again, Saint Peter was not to see the successful outcome of his work, which was completed two days after his death. The peace was concluded on September 16, 1174. It was while on another mission from the Pope, at the Cistercian monastery of Bellevaux in Franche-Compté, that Saint Peter was finally called to his reward.

His cause was soon advanced in Rome by the General Chapter of Cîteaux, by King Louis VII of France, and by the abbot of Morimond, Father Immediate of Bellevaux, who had been cured of a disease by touching the cowl of the saint. Alexander III accepted the petition, but the process was delayed by that pontiff's death. Under Lucius III the life of Saint Peter was written by Geoffrey of Hautecombe, but Lucius died. The third Crusade further delayed matters, but finally Celestine III issued the Bull of Canonization in 1191. The feast was transferred to May to avoid conflict with the General Chapter of the Order, which always opened on the Feast of the Exaltation of the Holy Cross (September 14).

May 23

Blessed Aleth, Mother of Saint Bernard, and Tescelin, Father of Saint Bernard, Monk of Clairvaux

(Sources: John the Hermit, *Vita Bernardi Quarta*; Vita Bern 1; Vacandard.)

The portrait left to us by historians of the Lord of Fontaines, Tescelin le Saure, and of his wife, and of the entire household in

---

[11] AASS, 331b.

which Saint Bernard grew up, shows us that medieval Christian knighthood was not an empty ideal. In the last century or two, men have gone to two extremes in their views of this institution. The middle-class sentimentality of the nineteenth century in its attempts to imitate the ancient romances produced a vapid and rather priggish knighthood, theatrical and hollow and dull. The reaction that inevitably followed has tended to view the knight as a barbarian tyrant, exploiting the poor and living like a wolf in his lair. Both views are, of course, false, but with a certain remote resemblance to the truth. For not only were there many medieval noblemen who were little better than bandits, there were also many who were indeed noble and holy men, who made their knighthood something almost sacramental and lived up to it with an intense and charitable fervor which made them real defenders of justice and protectors of the poor, although not the sententious rescuers of maidens in distress that we are sometimes forced to read about, under threat of severe penances, in our high school days.

Geoffrey Chaucer was a very objective man, with a keen eye for faults inherent in a class or a system as such, and while he has little to say in favor of many social types, in his *Canterbury Tales*[12] the knight and the parish priest are the two for whom he has the greatest and most sincere admiration. And in his knight, it is not hard to recognize the dignity, simplicity, kindness, unselfishness and good sense of Tescelin "the Red," Lord of Fontaines, although Saint Bernard's father probably did not have the knowledge of classical literature that his thirteenth-century prototype was able to display on the way to Canterbury.

Tescelin was a vassal of the Duke of Burgundy and lived on an estate built on a small hill, from which it keeps and towers frowned down upon the plain around Dijon, whose walls and spires and pointed roofs with their variegated designs of different colored slates arose not many miles away across the flowery fields and meadows and vineyards.

---

[12] See especially the "Prologue."

The Lord of Fontaines is supposed, by some writers, to have gone on a pilgrimage to the Holy Land, although the story of his pilgrimage is regarded by Vacandard as "apocryphal."[13] At any rate, one reason for the story is to account for the relics of Saint Ambrosian in the chapel of Fontaines castle. Tescelin is supposed to have brought them from Constantinople on his way home from the Holy Land. Whatever may have been the means by which these relics came to Fontaines, the chapel was dedicated to that saint, and his feast was celebrated there on the first of September.

Odo the first and Hugh II, Dukes of Burgundy, recognized the great qualities of loyalty, justice and statesmanship in Tescelin of Fontaines and made him one of their most trusted advisers. And well they might. His honesty and uprightness were so solid that justice seemed part of his very nature. Indeed, it was not merely something that he approved of and followed out of a certain sense of fitness. It was part of his life; it was a deep and insatiable need of his soul, so much so that he could say with impassioned conviction, "I do not understand how it is that certain people find justice a burden."[14] And his soul was so offended at the thought that so many persons forsook justice out of fear or cupidity that it filled him with real grief.

He was, however, a man of war and consequently might be expected to have a certain amount of anger in his makeup. Once, this got the better of him in a lawsuit, and he challenged his opponent to a duel. Not only was he putting himself thus in an occasion of mortal sin, but to make it worse, his opponent was a *bourgeois* and not a soldier, still less a knight. It was a social as well as a religious offense, but to many it would have been a grave dilemma. For once the challenge had been given, by the ordinary fighting code it would be the greatest dishonor to give up the fight, even though there was no honor in overcoming such an antagonist.

[13] Vacandard, 1:16 note: *ce voyage est fort problematique.* The story goes back to the Neapolitan biographer of Saint Bernard, Malabaila (1634).

[14] Vacandard, 1:3.

Tescelin, however, considered not human respect but justice and truth, and when he appeared on the field, he went over to the good *bourgeois* and said, "This has gone far enough. Let us leave it as it is, and I grant you what you demanded of me."[15] Nor did he fear, when the Bishop of Autun hauled the Duke of Burgundy into court for a violation of property rights, to tell the Duke that he was in the wrong.

When such a good and noble man as this presented himself to Lord Bernard of Montbard asking the hand of his fifteen-year-old daughter, Aleth, he was not refused, even though Montbard had destined his daughter for the cloister and all her desires were for the religious life. But she made Tescelin a perfect wife, and indeed her holiness of life was a very important factor in the sanctity of her children, all of whom entered religion, and one of whom became one of the greatest saints on the calendar of the Church.

Not only was she charitable to the poor, but her charity went beyond the ordinary limits. She would visit their cottages, and when there was sickness in the house, she would help with the washing or the housework, and we may be sure that such visits were not marked by that dainty and somewhat clumsy incomprehension implied by our expression, "slumming." Aleth understood what housework was and what sickness and suffering were too. And she was probably more at home with the poor, and the poor more at home with her, than the twentieth-century college girl who has joined the Young Communist League and sets out on an earnest attempt to interest some extremely skeptical "workers" in a few new pamphlets.

Not long before the birth of Saint Bernard, Aleth had a prophetic dream in which she saw the child in her womb under the form of a white dog, barking loudly, and this was interpreted to mean that he would be a great saint and defend the Church like a good watchdog.[16] Medieval dreams were very simple. From his very birth, then, Bernard was her child of predilection. But all her chil-

---

[15] Vita Bern 1.4.
[16] Vita Bern 1.2.

dren received an education of deep Christian piety and charity. They learned to fear and love God and to walk in his sight. Their life was profoundly liturgical, but the word liturgical sounds too academic to describe the harmonious integration of the Church's cycle with the natural succession of the months and seasons of the year. It was not merely a matter of going to the vigils and midnight Mass as they did at Châtillon that Christmas Eve when the young Bernard had his dream of the Nativity. The canonical hours were probably recited in the chapel of Fontaine, if not daily, certainly on any day of importance. And on the feast of Saint Ambrosian, the clergy of the local parish church of Saint Martin's in the Fields were invited to the Castle, and the Office and Mass were sung, after which there was a dinner, which Lady Aleth served with her own hands.

It was in the summer of 1106 or 1107, when Bernard was at Fontaines during the summer recess from his studies with the canons at Saint Vorles at Châtillon, that Aleth surprised everyone by announcing that she was soon going to die. Nobody believed her, but on August 31, the vigil of Saint Ambrosian, she fell ill of a fever and had to go to bed. The feast on the following day was very sad in spite of her own cheerfulness and good spirits. They brought her Communion in her room, gave her Extreme Unction at the same time and retired for the somewhat gloomy banquet. When the meal was over, the guests were conducted by her son, Guy, to the room again, and she told them that her last hour had come. They began to chant the litany, and in the middle of it where they invoked Christ by His Cross and Passion to spare her soul, she began to make a sign of the Cross that was never finished, for her head fell lifeless to her breast.

So great was the respect of all who knew her for her saintly life that no one was surprised when Abbot Jarenton of the Benedictine Abbey of Saint Benigne insisted on burying her in the crypt of his great church which is now the Cathedral of Dijon. And there her relics were venerated by the faithful until the thirteenth century when they were translated to Clairvaux.

Not many years after this bitter blow came the not unexpected request from Bernard that he be allowed to enter the austere monastery of Cîteaux. But Tescelin was saddened and surprised that all of Bernard's brothers followed him there, except little Nivard who was too young to go. And even he insisted that he had a vocation more pronounced and fervent than many of his elders. When Nivard finally departed and Humbeline married Guy de Maroy, the lonely old knight did not need much persuading from Bernard that he too should end his days at Clairvaux.

He crowned his long and venerable life by an act of heroic simplicity in becoming a novice under his son.

He died on April 11, 1121, and joined the small handful of Cistercians who had preceded him to heaven by only a few years. But on earth, his memory, though held in honor and love, never received the veneration accorded to his wife, Aleth, although sometimes he too is called "Blessed."

May 26

Blessed Asceline, Prioress of Boulancourt, near Troyes, France

(Sources: AASS, Aug. 4:661; Life by her confessor; P. Konrad Kolb, "Die Hl. Ascelina," Cist Chronik 4 [1892]: 193.)

Until the time of the French Revolution, each year on the Tuesday within the Octave of Pentecost the feast of "Saint" Asceline was celebrated by a procession from the *Monastère de Dames* at Boulancourt to a chapel in the woods outside the enclosure. There a Mass from the Common of Virgins was said in honor of the saint, at whose tomb in the convent church miracles were still wrought. The French Revolution almost put an end to this cult altogether. There now remains nothing but a few relics venerated in the village church of Vassy (Haute-Marne).

As for the saint herself, her life was written by her own confessor. Not only was he venerated as a saint, but he was buried in the same tomb as his holy penitent, together with Blessed Emmeline, another prioress of Boulancourt. The common sarcophagus of the three was under a consecrated altar dedicated to them on the Gospel side of the high altar of Boulancourt church.[17] All this should serve as some authentication of the life written by Blessed Goswin, the confessor of the saint. In view of the extraordinary statements that are made in it, the reader will find this authentication welcome.

The almost unbelievable amount of time spent each day by the saint in taking the discipline need not retain us long. We can only state Goswin's claim that she began to punish herself in this way when she was a very little child. By the time she was eleven, she took the discipline seven times a day. When she was twenty-eight, she took it fourteen times a day. Elsewhere we read that she spent as much time each day disciplining herself as would be required for the recitation of thirty psalms, that is to say under an hour.

Yet when we compare these claims with those made in favor of some other medieval saints—for instance the Cistercian lay-brother Blessed Arnulph of Villers—we must hesitate to accuse Blessed Goswin offhand of exaggeration. Goswin also tells us that at a certain period of her life when Blessed Asceline was favored with the gift of tears, she used to pray at a place in the church where there was a little hollow in the stone floor. She did not cease her prayers until the hollow was filled with tears. Again, she multiplied her vocal prayers by reciting a psalter each night standing the whole night, saying several hundred *Aves* daily into the bargain, not to mention a thousand on each of Our Lady's feast days, and a thousand on each day within the octave of such feasts. We must remind the reader that this was in the Middle Ages, when people combined extraordinary intensity of purpose, single-mindedness and energy with views that sometimes might appear to us odd.

When these things have been said, we pass on and try to view the saint in a truer perspective than such details would tend to give us. Here again the task is not easy, because some of the chief events of her life are almost entirely without explanation.

---

[17] It has a picture of the three saints in Cistercian cowls.

Asceline was born sometime around 1123 in the village of Laferté-sur-Aube, which was not far from Clairvaux, and as a matter of fact she was Saint Bernard's niece. Her father having died while she was still practically a baby, Asceline was left in the care of a pious mother who went to live at the convent of Boulancourt, taking her little daughter with her. The Augustinian Rule, followed by the nuns of Boulancourt at the time, was flexible enough to allow this.

Asceline grew up in the convent more or less as if she were in her own home, coming and going freely enough to find occasions of venial sin in helping herself to cheese and other foods in the pantry. These sins were not, however, committed, for already in childhood she lived in almost constant contact with the world of the heavenly spirits, and once when she was tempted to stretch out her hand toward the plate she felt an invisible hand pluck her sleeve and heard a voice say, "Don't do that, it is not good for you to do such a thing!"

It happened one day that little Asceline was helping the nuns at work making wax candles for the altar in a building outside the enclosure. The little girl, then eleven or twelve, was busily going about flushed with the natural joy of healthy activity when a young man passing by caught sight of her and was fascinated by her innocent charm. He immediately began to devise some plan for insinuating himself into friendship with her and was so successful as to get himself employed as her music teacher. At the first opportunity, he declared his love for her. Little Asceline had already consecrated her virginity to God, and she had no interest whatever in human lovers, even though their intentions might be good. Was she aware of the character of this particular suitor? Her reply to his proposal has a certain faint irony about it, but it was the unconscious irony of innocence. He had said he loved her and wanted to know if she liked him. She replied that she would like him much better if he wore the religious habit.

Her suitor, with singular stupidity, immediately went and took the habit of religion as a canon, confident that this would immensely enhance his natural charms in the eyes of the young girl. She no doubt was congratulating herself on having won a soul for

God, but an angel appeared to her under the form of a venerable old man and disillusioned her. After that, her suitor left her finding that his cause was lost and came to a bad end. Asceline was deeply affected by this and blamed herself for his fall. She recited a hundred psalters in reparation.

Perhaps this had something to do with the fact that she and her mother left Boulancourt and put themselves under the direction of a hermit, though we are not to imagine that they lived in the woods. During this period, Asceline tried to destroy her beauty which she believed so dangerous by rubbing ashes and lye into her cheeks. But after two years, both mother and daughter were back at Boulancourt.

When Blessed Asceline was about twenty-eight years old, that is to say about 1150, the Augustinian nuns of Boulancourt decided to adopt the Usages of Cîteaux and become affiliated with our Order. This brings us to the most obscure part of her life. It was precisely at this juncture that she left Boulancourt for another convent, Poulangny. This is complicated by the fact that perhaps she was Prioress of Boulancourt. Then again we cannot be certain whether Poulangny was a Benedictine convent or Cistercian. The writer in the *Cistercienser Chronik* believes it was Cistercian. There is no good reason for supposing that the change of rule alone would have been the motive for Asceline's leaving Boulancourt. It appears that perhaps there was some difficulty, some dissension, in the community there which came to a head with the entrance of Boulancourt in the Cistercian Order, causing Asceline to leave for the cause of peace. Later she returned when the hostile elements had left Boulancourt. One may hazard a guess that she had much to do with the introduction of the Cistercian life, and the anger of the opposing faction at her success had caused some difficulties for her.

In any case, we know that she went to Poulangny with the permission and approval of Saint Bernard. The abbess of the house was another niece, Adeline, the daughter of his brother, Guy (Guido). This forms a rather confusing trio of female relatives of the great Cistercian saint—Asceline, Adeline, and Emmeline—all three of them prioresses in neighboring monasteries and two, as we have said, buried in the same tomb! Adeline was apparently not venerated as a saint and does not share the title of blessed which her two cousins enjoyed.

At Poulangny, where Asceline was most zealous with the discipline and where she used to pray until she had filled the hollow in the stone with tears, she also excelled in the more common but more meritorious virtues of obedience and humility. She was sacristan of the convent, a task to which she devoted herself, as might be expected, with the most edifying piety. She wore a hair shirt day and night and was so rigid in her practice of silence and solitude that once, during Advent, when a princess of the royal house called to see her out of curiosity about her sanctity, Asceline refused to go to the parlor, since visits were prohibited in Advent. At least, this appears to have been her reason for the refusal. In any case, it took a certain amount of courage, for the noble men and ladies of the Middle Ages were not in the habit of accepting such slights with equanimity, even from those reputed as saints.

During the four years Blessed Asceline spent at Poulangny, Saint Bernard died, and on the night of his death she saw his soul enter heaven in the form of a dove. She had another vision soon after in which Our Lady and Saint John the Baptist informed her that it was now God's will that she return to Boulancourt. Presumably the difficult situation there had been settled. By this time, she had become very famous as a visionary and many pious and learned churchmen used to seek her advice in spiritual matters. This was a rather frequent practice at the time, for we even find that the General Chapter of the Cistercian Order consulted Saint Hildegard of Bingen concerning the problems of the Order and received her answer in the form of a somewhat lengthy revelation, which, being general in character, provides interesting and useful material for meditation even today.[18] One of Asceline's miracles at this time was to extinguish a dangerous fire, which had got out of control and was consuming some convent buildings, by walking into it with an uplifted crucifix. The flames receded before her as she went, and presently the fire was out.

[18] Canivez, vol. 1.

So widespread was her fame that the Archbishop of Cologne sent a possessed woman from his diocese to be cured by her, and after the success of her prayers, summoned her to visit his archdiocese. She received permission to make this journey, in the course of which she visited several Cistercian houses in Germany and Franche-Comté. At the abbey of Vaux in the diocese of Toul, she had a consultation with a holy monk who, after several years of zealously practicing the Cistercian life, was tempted to leave the Order on the grounds that greater perfection was to be found elsewhere. This insidious temptation had found its way into his mind and gained such a firm hold there that he no longer had any peace. When he began to speak to Blessed Asceline about it, she had another vision and beheld a devil whispering these things into the monk's ear. The expression on her face and the way she told him what she saw carried so much conviction that the monk was instantly cured of his doubts and thankfully returned to his peaceful life as a Cistercian without any further preoccupations about other Orders. After all, God does not bring a man into a thriving and fervent religious community and let him live there in happiness and regularity for years and then suddenly call him elsewhere without any other reason than that the life there might be in itself more perfect.

Whether or not she had been Prioress at Boulancourt before 1150, it is certain that Blessed Asceline had been so for some time by the year 1184.[19] In this position, she long enjoyed the love and admiration of her spiritual daughters. She finally died peacefully on the Friday in the Octave of Pentecost, 1195, having been warned of the hour of her death long before it came. Lest anyone think that the austere Cistercian life is a menace to health, Blessed Asceline, who had fasted and mortified her flesh in every way since early childhood, died at the age of seventy-five.

We do not need to multiply our prayers and penances mathematically as did this saint, but we should certainly strive after something of her spirit. The core of her spirituality was the constant practice of the presence of God. Let us close, then, with the

[19] *Chronicon Claravaliense*, PL 185:1250.

words she once spoke to her confessor. "I know nothing good of myself," she said, "except that I always have God present in my mind."

June

June 1

Saints Bernard, Mary, and Grace, Monk of Poblet (Spain) and his sisters, Martyrs

(Sources: AASS, Aug. 4:452 [based mostly on Manrique].)

The feast of these martyrs commemorates a story that might have been sung in one of the *villancicos*, those simple and poignant ballads that have come down to us from medieval Spain.

Hamed was the son of Almanzor, a Moorish noble, under King Zaen, who ruled the city of Valencia and its surrounding province in southern Spain in the twelfth century. Almanzor himself was ruler of the two towns of Pintarrafes and Carlete, and besides Hamed and another elder son, Almanzor, his heir, had two daughters, Zaida and Zoroaida. Hamed served King Zaen with consummate skill as a courtier and diplomat, and it was in this capacity that he was sent to the Christian city of Barcelona in order to effect an exchange of military prisoners.

Hamed accordingly traveled north to Catalonia. Nearing his destination, having left Lerida, the last Moorish city, he was overtaken with his companions by nightfall just as he was entering the land of the Christians. The party lost their way and ended up in a thick wood where they decided to stop and sleep lest they wander all night in circles. It was a wild place, and their resolution was a good one. They lay down under the trees and presently they slept.

It was about midnight when Hamed was awakened by the sound of singing. From the darkness of the wood there came distant voices, a choir whether of men or spirits he could not tell, singing music such as he had never heard. It was beautiful music, but he was full of fear. His hair stood on end. He did not dare move from where he was. He lay awake listening until dawn, when with the first pale light the music ceased. They then got up and advanced through the trees.

He could not, of course, know that this was one of the feasts of the Virgin Mother of God. But he soon found that the sound he had heard was the choir of the new Cistercian monastery of Poblet,[1] whose monks had been chanting the night office in their plain little wooden oratory, the forerunner of the great abbatial church of the "royal monastery" which still remains to impress visitors to this part of Catalonia.

Fascinated by what he saw, by the quiet monks, by their simple poverty, their silence, their recollection and faith, and awed by what he heard of their life and belief from the abbot to whom he spoke, Hamed began to conceive an ardent desire to know more of their religion and of their monastic virtues. And so having asked if he might stay with the monks, he told his companions that he had fallen sick and would have to remain where he was. They should go back to Lerida and wait for him.

During the several months he spent at Poblet as a catechumen, he soon overcame the struggle with his natural repugnance against leaving his father, his country, his fortune and his career. Nor was he even stopped by the fear of the "disgrace" and, perhaps, material ruin his conversion might bring upon his father at home. On the contrary, he spent his time in diligent study and meditation of the Christian faith and in ardent prayer, impatient for the time when he could be baptized. It was during this time that he read,

---

[1] Poblet was one of the most important Cistercian monasteries in Spain. It is situated in Catalonia in a broad valley seven miles from Tarragona and was founded in 1149 by Raymond Berengar II, Count of Barcelona. The buildings, which still stand, are very impressive. For a short time they housed a community of Cistercians of the Congregation of Sénanque from Fontfroide during a period of persecution of the Church in France at the end of the nineteenth century.

with the greatest interest and most fervent admiration, William of Saint Thierry's beautiful life of Saint Bernard, which, although short and incomplete, is still the one that gives us the truest, most living and most attractive picture of the great saint.

Bernard was the name taken by the Moorish convert then when he was baptized. Not long afterwards, he was admitted to the novitiate. There is much uncertainty about the dates. Let it suffice to know that all this was in the second half of the twelfth century.

Soon after his profession, the former diplomat became cellarer of the monastery, in which position he was remarkable for his almost reckless generosity even more than for his ability. So lavish was he in his gifts to the poor that he was accused before the abbot of having emptied the granaries, borrowing recklessly and without hope of paying, and in fact of having gone bankrupt and ruining the monastery. For his only defense against these grave charges, he told them to look at the granaries and wine cellars. The barns were bursting with grain, the cellars were full of wine and oil, and his coffers with money. Such plenty could only be explained by a miracle. And there were other miracles too. As cellarer, he had charge of the sick, and he had cured several of them with the sign of the Cross.

But his charity was restless and unsatisfied as long as he thought of his family in the south—Moors, living on the edge of hell. And so he received permission to go and try to convert them. His first stop was at Lerida, where he had an aunt. No sooner did she see him than she began to mock and revile him for the coarseness and poverty of his habit. His countenance, once full and handsome, was now thinned with fasting. His bearing had become shy and diffident instead of forward and confident. And yet God gave his words such persuasion of unction and grace that he converted his aunt and traveled on to Valencia.

He received an effusive welcome from his brother. Almanzor thought he had given up the Christian faith and returned in penance to Islam. When he found out this was far from the case, the prince flew into a rage and nearly killed his brother on the spot. However, when he calmed down, he allowed the monk to see his sisters in the hope that their gentleness might influence him where his own rage had failed.

On the contrary, Bernard converted his sisters in a short time to Christianity. They did not immediately make this known to Almanzor. Rather they decided that all three of them must leave and return to Catalonia. And so the two sisters went to Almanzor, persuaded him that it was useless to try and reason with their brother, and convinced him that the best thing to do was to banish him forever from their land. Bernard, consequently, soon left the town under sentence of exile, but he did not travel far. His sisters were to meet him that same night in a nearby forest. This was no small enterprise for two Moorish women who had hardly ever traveled in the streets except in a carriage or a litter, heavily guarded and screened from view. But they managed to find Bernard in the woods with the help of a guide, and there they remained. It would have been impossible for the three of them to start north right away with Almanzor's soldiers combing the country for them.

Their apprehension in this matter was all too well founded. Not many days had passed before Bernard, who was out in search of food, was discovered by a party of armed men led by Almanzor himself. Once again, Almanzor's rage nearly ended Bernard's life there and then, this time with a javelin. But the brother restrained himself in order to drag Bernard back to the town and question him about the hidden place of Zaida and Zoroaida who had now taken the names of Mary and Grace. Refusing to tell anything of their whereabouts, Bernard contented himself with revealing the fact of their conversion to Christianity and his ardent prayer that they might crown their faith with the sacrifice of themselves in martyrdom for the glory of Jesus Christ. It was evident that he had just such an ardent desire for himself, but it was not yet to be satisfied. Only when the two sisters were finally apprehended did the savage older brother try to terrify them by the barbarous death which he caused Bernard to suffer. For before their eyes, the monk was killed by a soldier driving a spike into his forehead. Yet the courageous sisters were only animated by this spectacle to a greater faith, and they soon in their turn followed their brother to heaven, beheaded by the swords of Almanzor's soldiers.

The year 1180 is the accepted date of their martyrdom. Their bodies were left to be devoured by wild beasts but were charitably buried in secret and lay hidden for several centuries. They were finally discovered by a miracle. There is nothing to warrant the assumption that Mary and Grace became Cistercian nuns.

The three were beatified *per modern favoris* in 1701 with the title of saint, and although the date arbitrarily assigned to their martyrdom is August 23, their feast is celebrated in the Cistercian Order on June 1. August 23 is within the Octave of Saint Bernard.

June 7

Saint Robert of Newminster, Abbot of Newminster, England

(Sources: Hugh of Kirkstall, *Narratio de Fundatione Fontanis Monasterii* [in Mem. of Fountains Abbey]; AASS, June 2:46 [a brief *Life*, taken from John Capgrave's *Legenda Angliae* (1516), which follows the old twelfth cent. ms. with some alteration of style]; Dalgairns, "Life of Saint Robert of Newminster" in Newman, 5:429-39 [The latter is based directly on the twelfth cent. ms. of the monk Reginald, but suppressing most of the miracles. Reginald's ms. is a life not of Saint Robert but of his spiritual director, the hermit Saint Godric. The holy abbot of Newminster is introduced in a long digression.].)

One of the English Cistercian saints is the mysterious and attractive monk whose legend, handed down to us in Capgrave's sixteenth-century collection, is full of visions and miracles, but these are only the screen behind which historical facts show us the shadow of a great and holy monk. Fr. Dalgairns fought shy of the miracles in writing his brief life of Saint Robert, and the story loses thereby. Legends may be legends, but their very existence is a fact and a fact of no little importance and significance. Hence their historical value, although it may be oblique and indirect, is nevertheless not to be neglected.

It is a matter of fact, not of legend, that Robert was born in the Craven district of Yorkshire, was educated at Paris and ordained to the priesthood, after which he became a Benedictine at the Abbey of Whitby. Whether or not he was dissatisfied with the life there to such an extent that he left and migrated to Saint Mary's, York, is only a matter of conjecture. At any rate, when Richard, the prior of Saint Mary's, and his twelve companions reacted against the Cluniac regime and asked permission to start a reform on the lines suggested by the newly arrived Cistercians of Rievaulx, Robert heard of it and joined them, not as Dalgairns thought after they had settled at Fountains but while they were still at York in the shelter of Archbishop Thurston's palace.[2]

He was, then, one of the group who traveled to Ripon for the Christmas feast of 1132, and who, on the day after, settled in the wild valley of the Skell with no shelter but the forest trees, no bed but a pile of straw, no covering but his own monastic garments and a couple of blankets between him and the December night. He shared all the poverty, labor and hardship of the precarious new foundation, and those years of struggle were one of the hardest Cistercian novitiates in the history of this strict Order. Here indeed was a life of asceticism when men had to keep the Rule of Saint Benedict to the letter in all its detailed prescriptions, while living in a few huts in a northern forest, huts so lowly that the poorest swineherd might have disdained them. Often starvation stared them in the face, and they had to content themselves with a meal of leaves, herbs and roots boiled into some sort of soup. But after four years the tide turned. Fountains became firmly established and soon was able to make her first foundation. Robert was chosen to lead the colony of monks to Morpeth in Northumberland. Their journey was in the winter, and they arrived at the castle of their protector and sponsor, Ralph de Merlay, about the feast of the Epiphany, 1138. It was probably there that the Bishop of Durham (in whose diocese they were to settle) gave Robert his abbatial blessing. Then in the spring, the new foundation was begun.

[2] *Robertus . . . monachus de Witby qui se egredientibus de cienobio Eboracensi scoiavit* (*Mem. Fount. Ab.*, 60ff; Dalgairns, 9).

It was not as wild a site as the Motherhouse. There were no rocks, no glen, no thick, wild forest, although the land was wooded. It was low rolling country, watered by a meandering river bordered with rich meadows, a pleasant, peaceful and fertile place. The new monastery, "New Minster," had a name that was rather unusual for a Cistercian abbey. Minster simply meant monastery, and hosts of Benedictine abbeys and priories had compound names of which that word was an element. But the Cistercian fashion was always in favor of a more graphic and more romantic name—Valle Crucis, Beaulieu, Jervaulx, etc. Newminster was the only Cistercian abbey in England with such a compound for its name.

Robert was a holy man, strict with himself, kind and merciful to others. He was learned and yet simple. He had written a commentary on the Psalms and a book of meditations, and it is a misfortune that they no longer exist. But like a true Cistercian, he preferred the experiential knowledge of God in prayer to any learning that could be gained from books.

He earnestly strove to dominate and mortify all the desires of his flesh and made a point of never eating to satiety. For though the food of a Cistercian monk is simple enough, there is a big enough quantity of it for him to eat too much of it if he is sufficiently diligent with his wooden spoon. In Lent, Saint Robert fasted all the time on bread and water. His fasts were made more of a penance by illness, and once in Paschal time, he was too ill to eat anything from the common portions. One of his monks asked him if there was not something that he felt he could eat, and he replied after some thought that an oatcake with a little butter on it made some appeal to his appetite. However, when the monk went to get this simple article of food, which even the poorest shepherd would scarcely have regarded as a delicacy, Saint Robert began to reproach himself for self-indulgence and would not eat the cake when it was brought to him.

Once, this holy abbot in his simplicity was in haste to return from a distant grange to the monastery for a big feast and had climbed on the only available mount, an aged packhorse. He then pulled his hood over his eyes and rode along, meditating and conversing with God as was his custom. Presently, a nobleman of the region came along and, seeing the hooded figure in the shabby cowl riding such a poor excuse for a horse, did not recognize the abbot, but stopping him, inquired roughly if the Lord Abbot of Newminster were at the Grange. "He was there when I left," said Saint Robert meekly. Then the nobleman took a closer look at the face in the shadows of the hood and, realizing that he was speaking to the saint, was covered with confusion.

Gentle and simple with others as he was strict with himself, Saint Robert had a deep and burning love for the souls of all those whom God had entrusted to his care, and he prayed for them with more fervor than most monks can muster for their own most urgent needs. Once, it was said, having prayed with tears for a long time in great love and faith for all his sons, it was revealed to him that they would all be saved except two, and some days later two lay-brothers left the monastery.

Like most Cistercian abbots, he could not confine his charity within the walls of his own enclosure. As to so many others of his contemporary Cistercians, the lot of peacemaker often fell to him. Once, for example, in Newminster, he came upon a group of men in the street gathered around an extremely active and malignant little individual who was evidently inciting them to some violence. Saint Robert walked into the middle of the crowd and scattered them to the four corners of the city. He then confronted the *agent provocateur*, who, says the legend, began to grovel in the dust before him like a cringing animal. "Who are you?" said the saint. "You know who I am," said the evil character who was, according to the legend, a devil. Then he proceeded to admit that he had been stirring up the enemies and rivals of a man who had just been married to murder him at the wedding feast. Then the friends of the bridegroom would retaliate and there would probably be many lives lost. Having made this admission, he vanished leaving no trace except that a horse tethered nearby began to rear and kick in the wildest alarm.

Another incident in the life of the saint might have come from the pages of Caesar of Heisterbach. It is related that he looked up one night in the choir and saw a devil peering through the door in the form of a rough yokel, stretching out his neck, grinning fiercely and peering this way and that, being unable to come into the choir itself. Saint Robert began to pray with the greatest earnestness. The devil, finding nothing to interest himself among the monks (it must have been an exceptionally tranquil monastery!), turned to the lay-brothers and displayed, by his horrible laughter, at one who was asleep and gave ironic and clownish applause to another who was allowing his mind to follow distractions wherever they led him. But his greatest pleasure came when, having turned to the consideration of the choir novices, he found one who was turning over in his mind the project of leaving the monastery secretly that very night and giving up his vocation without consulting anybody. Saint Robert saw the fiend reach out with a long pitchfork and neatly spear the soul of the novice and stuff it in a sack. Then he vanished. Saint Robert went to his cell right after the office and sent for the novice, but it was too late. Under cover of the half-light before dawn, he had scaled the wall and was gone. Shortly afterwards, it was learned that he had joined a band of criminals and later on was caught and executed.

Many of the picturesque details of this story undoubtedly sprang from the imagination of the twelfth-century biographer, and, though we have not compared Capgrave's version with the original, it is not difficult to believe that the sixteenth-century compiler added a few touches of his own to the picture. But it would be foolish to suppose that the basis of the legend and its main point are even slightly improbable. The devil may not spear souls with a pitchfork, but that does not make him any less real.

Another vision of Saint Robert's occurred while he was saying Mass. He suddenly beheld a ship badly battered by a storm at sea and on the point of sinking. Right after the Mass, he called several monks and sent them down to the seacoast several miles away to a spot which he indicated to them, and there they found the bodies of the drowned sailors washed up on shore and gave them a Christian burial.

In 1147 or 1148, we know that Saint Robert was in France where he had a long consultation with Saint Bernard and Pope Eugene III. The reason for this journey was a slanderous accusation made against him because of the fact that he had undertaken the spiritual direction of a pious woman. It was much the same as the slander that had been leveled against Saint Jerome, and Saint Bernard, after interviewing the holy abbot, soon realized that God was allowing this trial for the purification of this saintly soul.

During the year 1147, Newminster made two foundations, Salley in Lancashire and Roche in Yorkshire. In 1143, a first daughter-house had been founded as far south as Northamptonshire at Pipewell.

Robert's confessor and director was a hermit, Saint Godric, and the latter foretold the death of his penitent in 1159 and also was favored with a vision at the time of its occurrence, for he saw Saint Robert's soul traveling to heaven like a globe of fire, escorted by angels and rising between two walls of light. Many miracles followed, notably the cure of a boy mute from birth. The boy had been praying to Saint Thomas á Becket, and the great martyr appeared to him and told him to go on a pilgrimage to the tomb of the new saint, Robert of Newminster. He even provided him with enough money to make the journey. Saint Robert was formally beatified according to the ancient code in 1534 and inscribed in the martyrology.

June 12

Blessed Aleyde de Scharbeek, Nun of La Cambre, Belgium

(Source: AASS, June 2:471 [an excellent contemporary life. The name Aleyde, has several variations—Alix, Alice, Alizon, Alizette, Adelaide].)

The life of Aleyde de Scharbeek by a contemporary monk is not only an objective study of a great mystic but also incidentally a brief and concise treatise on Cistercian asceticism. The first chapter, dealing with her monastic virtues, is something that ought to be put in the hands of every monk and lay-brother of our Order. It not only gives instances of her practice of these virtues but sets down with equal brevity and precision a compendium of ascetic theory which is both interesting and practical. In it, for example, is exposed the characteristic Cistercian teaching on the fear of God as a principle of liberation from all our imperfections and deficiencies by giving us that true knowledge of ourselves that makes us turn away from self and desire God with all the ardor of our wills. It is in this sense that filial fear is the beginning of wisdom, and without it love is impossible. In Aleyde, says the ancient writer, fear was the principle from which this love sprang, and then in turn it was through this *love* (not fear) that she mortified her senses and chastised her flesh. This is an interesting and subtle distinction and one which is rather unusual when love is viewed in this juxtaposition with fear. Another interesting ascetical concept is that the light of truth is conceived within her soul by fear (humility), and by love she seeks to give birth to the truth thus conceived. She shows forth in her works and actions the divine life conceived within her and also gains possession of God himself by the merit of her works of love.[3] Space does not permit us to delay longer on this topic, for there are more extraordinary matters in the life of Blessed Aleyde that claim our attention.

She entered La Cambre, near Brussels, when she was only seven years old. Obviously, she could not become a novice at so tender an age. But we know that the Cistercian nuns, unlike the monks, received young children into their care and gave them an education, as for instance Beatrice of Nazareth at Florival.[4] Aleyde was a cheerful and intelligent child and under the guidance of grace soon learned to walk in the presence of God in the way that has just been described. Already by the time she entered the community as a novice, she was well grounded in the virtues. Industrious at all times to please her Lord, she used to say that Jesus had taken three companions with Him to Tabor and she would go the same road with her three companions—manual work, prayer and contemplation. But the quiet and cheerful little sister was to climb not

---

[3] *Veritatis lumine corde sic fulgente oculorumque sciem sursum erigente, jam per amorem perturire quod per cognitionem ante conceperat.* Vita, Cap. 1; AASS, 472e.

[4] See August 29.

Tabor but Calvary. Perhaps it is wrong to make such a contrast, however, for she would probably tell us from her own experience that the two are the same and that the highest consolation is to suffer for the love of God. She was to find in suffering, accepted with love and faith, the quickest way to divine union. She was to be united with Him interiorly by tribulation and exteriorly by labors and suffering of the flesh.[5] She was remarkable for her peaceful diligence and zeal, a diligence which expressed itself not in a restless and fussy concern about doing things that were not prescribed or appointed for her but in carrying out all her common duties as perfectly and unobtrusively as possible.

And then one day, to the horror of the community, this excellent religious was discovered to be infected with leprosy. This was, as her biographer explains,[6] not a punishment for sin but a gift from God to purify her soul and at the same time to isolate her in perfect solitude, that she might live for Him alone and lead a life of pure contemplation, undistracted by any of the material offices of community life.

The first night of her separation from the sisters she nearly died of grief. However, it did not take her long to realize that this was a true sign that God had singled her out as the object of his special love. After a night of great sorrow, she regained her clear realization of God's presence within her and was consoled. From then on, determined as she was to live for Him alone, she soon received the grace to see that she had lost nothing and gained everything by her sickness. From then on, if He had not done so before, Christ began to inundate her soul with mystical joy, particularly at Mass at which she assisted a little apart from the others. Her communions were made with immense fervor, and she prepared for them the whole day before by her deep recollection and ardent desire, neither of which suffered her to be concerned with any earthly consideration. This, of course, was a very special grace of infused

---

[5] *Tribulationibus se Deo siciavit, foris cum laboribus corpus subjugavit.* AASS, 47f.

[6] Vita, Cap. I.

love, and therefore the average religious should not be astounded if he cannot acquire it by his own efforts.

She still went to the altar with the rest of the community, except that she only received the Sacred Host and did not partake of the Precious Blood as did the rest (in those days Communion was given under both species in our Order). This fact caused her some sorrow and even a scruple that her Communion might be imperfect, until Christ reassured her Himself, saying that he was entirely present under the appearances of both bread and wine and could not be divided and that whoever received His body in the Host received His blood as well.

After having spent some time in the infirmary, Aleyde moved to a little house that had been prepared for her next to the convent church. From here, she could hear all the offices being sung in choir, although it seems she was still allowed to go to the church, provided she kept apart from everybody else. When she first moved into this new abode, she was greeted by Christ in a vision, and He assured her that He would be her cellarer and she would lack nothing. As a matter of fact, she was provided with an attendant who took care of her bodily needs and brought her food. Not only did this girl not contract leprosy, but many who were afflicted with the disease came to Aleyde and were cured by her touch.

Once on Easter morning when the responsory, *Surrexit dominus de sepulchre*, was being sung in choir at the night office, Aleyde saw the dark sky open like a sepulcher, and light poured out upon the monastery as from the door of a furnace. The attendant girl was there and seeing all the buildings blazing with this supernatural glow, cried out in terror as if the whole monastery had suddenly caught fire. But Aleyde made her a sign not to be afraid. Then the servant realized that the risen Christ had come to visit the soul of the saint.

As her disease progressed, in spite of all the interior suffering that came with it, Aleyde became more and more firmly founded in spiritual joy and grew daily in desire for heaven and in zeal for the salvation of souls. In these days, the notion of "victim souls" so familiar in Catholic piety at present was unknown. Indeed Blessed Aleyde, like Saint Lutgarde, was one of the first clear instances of such a vocation in the strict sense of one who offers herself to suffer vicariously to appease the divine justice and win grace for souls, and especially to suffer extraordinary sicknesses and trials inflicted directly by the hand of God. But Christ himself made clear to her the meaning and importance of her vocation, so that in 1249 when she lost the sight of her right eye, she offered that loss up for William of Holland, just elected King of the Romans, that he might defend the Church. Later, she was to lose the sight of her other eye, becoming completely blind, and this she would offer for Saint Louis of France, fighting in Palestine.

Before that time, however, her merits were to be increased by the purgatory of infused love, expressing itself in an almost unbearable desire for heaven, a desire which, by the way, must not be confused with the somewhat melancholy overflowing of passion and vague nostalgia which afflicts many pious souls and which may be a more or less sincere yearning for heaven but is not the work of infused love. Rather it has its root in the imagination and the feelings and is sometimes nothing but an unconscious desire for escape from the tedium of everyday life.

However, one night in December, she stood in the door of her little cell and listened to the choir singing the last responsory of vigils for the feast of Saint Ursula and the virgin martyrs of Cologne. Filled with an intense and heartrending desire for the vision of God, Aleyde began to lament that she was not in heaven with these holy martyrs and begged Jesus that she might be with them when she came to heaven. But the voice of Christ replied within her, saying that she would not only be with them in heaven, she would be above them, by which of course He meant to indicate the merit of her long martyrdom and her years of suffering as an outcast of the society. Such statements about heaven, statements in which souls are said to be higher or lower with respect to one another, are hard for us to understand with our earthly notions of dignity. For on earth, social elevation means separation from those who are below. We do not realize that the joy of the souls who are "higher" in heaven—in fact, what constitutes them as higher—is the joy of their greater charity which expresses itself in overflowing into the souls of those who are "below" them. They are said to be higher because they have more to give, more to communicate to all the others. And, of course, this giving of their own joy unites them most intimately and perfectly with all those to whom their joy is given, that is, with all the other souls in heaven. Consequently Blessed Aleyde was promised in effect that she would be closer to the virgin martyrs by being placed higher in heaven than if she had merely been left on the same level with them.

Then on the feast of the Ascension, her attendant noticed that Aleyde, after returning from the conventual Mass, had not broken her fast and asked her why she was allowing the dinner to get cold. "Jesus, who is half my heart, has gone away to heaven," replied Aleyde, "and the other half of my heart has followed him there, so that I am deserted even by myself!" And with this she lapsed into such a depth of mystical joy that she was unable to touch any food for the rest of the day.

By Sexagesima Sunday, 1249, her sufferings had become so intense and the condition of her body so horrible that she was no longer able to leave her cell. Her pains became so excruciating that she believed she was suffering alternately the torments of hell and those of purgatory. But she accepted it all with great joy because of her clear realization not only that it would win grace for sinners, but that without these sufferings of hers certain souls *could not be saved*. The necessary graces for their conversion were made contingent by the will of God upon her willingness to accept these frightful tortures. On the feast of Saint Barnabas that year, she received Extreme Unction, but it was revealed to her that she had still one more year to live and suffer. It was then that she finally went blind, and in the last months when her body had been reduced to a mass of corruption she sang continuously, praising God and magnifying His Name until the promised day, June 11, 1250, when she finally passed to her victory and her reward.

Her long-standing veneration was confirmed by two beatifications, one *per modeum favoris* in 1702 and the other by a formal process in 1907. Her feast is celebrated by the Cistercians of the Strict Observance on June 12 with the rite of three lessons.

June 12

Blessed Placid of Rodi, Abbot of the Monastery of the Holy Ghost, Ocra, Italy

(Source: AASS, June 14:104 [contemporary life].)

Like many other Cistercian saints, for instance Pope Blessed Eugenius III, Blessed John of Caramola and Blessed Arnulph Cornibout, the lay-brother of Villers, Placid of Rodi came of very poor parents. His father was a peasant, his mother a pious Christian woman, fearing God and zealous in doing His will in all things. Her third son, the little Placid, was soon sent out to watch the flocks of sheep in the hills, and the Holy Spirit of charity was so strongly burning in his heart even in childhood that he often gave away his dinner of bread to one of the other little shepherds and came home in the evening joyful at having fasted and offered a sacrifice to God and given his bread to Jesus in his little brothers.

He was not fond of boisterous games, but he loved to sing, and he would go about the flowering fields singing the *Pater Noster* and glorifying God by his simple joy. So eager was he to learn new ways of praising God that he would stop the school children and ask them about their lessons and learn from them how to pick out the words in the Psalter so that at length he became able to read the Psalms. They became his constant prayer. Patient and humble with everybody, he never argued with those who rebuked or injured him. He obeyed the counsel of the Lord that tells us not to resist evil but to overcome evil with good. He was pleasant and openhanded with everybody, sharing all that he had with those who, by some marvel, were even poorer than himself.

As he grew older, he began to look about restlessly for some way to serve God more completely, and the first thing that came to his mind was a pilgrimage to Saint James of Compostela in Spain. He spent a year with the brothers at that shrine, but on his return home he fell ill with a painful sickness that kept him in bed for five long years. During much of that time, he was so weak that he could not even lift his head without help. Having emerged from the crucible of this trial, he once again set out on a pilgrimage, this time to Rome. Then from the shrines of the two great Apostles, Peter and Paul, he went east into the wildest part of Italy, the mountains of Abruzzi, and climbed the steep, fir-clad slopes of Monte Corno, where he spent a year in fasting and prayer under the direction of a hermit. Even then he did not settle down. Returning north to Rome, he fell into spiritual dangers when a woman fell in love with him, and fleeing from her into Tuscany, he ran headlong into the nets of other temptresses, who found him out in a retreat on Monte Casentino.

By now he was twenty-four years old. It was the year 1218. In a resolute attempt to find perfect solitude, he returned again to the Abruzzi and discovered a cave, almost completely inaccessible, halfway up a cliff. Only a daring and experienced climber could hope to get to it. For twelve years he lived here in peaceful and unmolested contemplation until inevitably the fame of his sanctity began to be spread abroad. People came climbing up the cliff to ask his prayers and advice. Finally, a certain priest called Simeon lost his footing while trying to scale the dangerous crag and fell to his death. Overcome with the thought that he should have been, indirectly, the cause of this death, Placid came down out of the rock and dwelt in a hut in the woods, living on grass and roots, wondering if he were to be damned as a murderer. It was here that Jesus appeared to him one day and spread out a scroll before his eyes saying, "Read this, Placid, thou servant of God!"

"Lord," said the holy man, "I cannot make out this language."

But the Lord enlightened his understanding, and he read there a record of all his prayers and merits. "Do not be afraid, Placid, my servant," said Jesus, "for as thou hast prayed to Me, so have I prayed to the Father that thy faith may not fail."

From then on he continued his life of prayer with an increased courage and ardor, the Psalter ever in his hands, and he would often stop at a verse and reread it over and over again, burning with intense inward joy and consolation, filled with the light of the Holy Spirit. Indeed so great was his simplicity, that the Holy Ghost often was seen coming down upon him in the form of a dove. And this, as his old biographer explains, was most fitting since birds of a feather flock together, and Placid was as simple as a dove.

During the last thirty-seven years of his life, Blessed Placid never slept in a bed nor did he even stretch out full-length on the ground but slept crouching or sitting down. He never ate meat and not only avoided wine like poison but he never even drank his fill of water. During his lifetime, he made one hundred fourteen forty-day fasts during which he partook of no cooked food at all and many others in which he ate nothing but subsisted on liquids only.

He was often tempted and persecuted by fiends. Indeed, sometimes he would look up and see whole hordes of devils charging down the mountain upon his poor cabin, but he would turn away in scorn and murmur a verse of a Psalm, knowing that faith was an impenetrable armor against all the devils in hell and believing in and using all the grace that comes to us in the inspired words of Scripture.

Meanwhile, the relatives he had left for God's sake were gained to him in charity by the strength of his prayers and example. Many of them began to come to him for help and advice. Some he sent on pilgrimages, others settled with him in the woods of the Abruzzi, and these were the nucleus of a new monastic community which he instituted in 1222[7] at Pretola, the monastery of the Holy Spirit of Ocra, more accurately Val d'Ocra.

As soon as the community took shape, he made a journey to the Cistercian abbey of Casa Nova and had his monastery affiliated to the Cistercian Order and thus insured the permanence of his work. But the devil did not miss this opportunity to try and destroy his peace of mind, reproaching him for throwing away "his" monastery, "his" work, and giving to others the fruits of superiorship that might have been "his" alone. "*Male fecisti*," said the fiend, but

---

[7] Janauscheck, 248, says he cannot be strictly called the founder since the house was presented to him by Berard, Count of Alba. But surely Blessed Placid deserves the credit for instituting a new community by his own work and not as an offshoot of an already existing monastery. The erection of building is only secondary in the foundation of a monastery. What is more important is the group of monks who occupy the building.

Placid made the sign of the Cross and Beelzebub went away. He lived on in peace and joy, the patriarch of his happy, religious family, joining them in their common labors until his holy death in 1248.

After he had breathed forth his soul and the body was washed, the monks took his body to carry it out to a chapel in the woods. As they came forth from the monastery, a sudden wind swept down the mountainside and through the forest, so that the whole mountain seemed to sigh, and as they passed between the trees, the tall oaks and firs miraculously bowed not as with the wind all in one direction but towards the bier in which the saint was carried, some this way and some that. But all bowed as he passed by. His relics are still venerated in the church of Pretola, where the walls are decorated with fourteen paintings commemorating his life and miracles.

June 16

Saint Lutgarde, Nun of Aywieres, Belgium

(Source: AASS, June 4:187. Thomas of Cantimpre, the author of this beautiful biography, met Saint Lutgarde through Jacques de Vitry. He became an Augustinian at Cantimpre, then on the advice of the saint was ordained priest. In 1232 he entered the Order of Preachers of Louvain. He studied four years under Saint Albert the Great, the master of Saint Thomas Aquinas, and then became Saint Lutgarde's director. But all his life, she remained his spiritual mother, and he did not cease to take spiritual direction from her. H. Nimal, *Vies de quelques-unes de nos grandes Saintes au pays de Liège* [Dessain, 1898], gives a complete French translation of Thomas's *Vita* with a few useful notes.)

Without any question, the most extraordinary and most important figure in Cistercian mysticism of the early thirteenth century was Saint Lutgarde. She was as famous in her day as the stigmatist of our own century, Theresa Neuman, and for much the same reasons.

Even before she entered the Cistercian convent of Aywieres, and while she was still a Benedictine nun at Saint Catherine's, Touyres, Lutgarde's sanctity and mystical graces had given her a wide reputation, and we read of important secular and ecclesiastical figures traveling long distances to visit and consult her. And so in Saint Lutgarde we have an example of a very extraordinary and special vocation, the vocation of a soul called in a particular manner by Christ to a life of intimate union with Him in His sufferings in reparation for sin. The great affluence of graces, so called *gratis datae*, and the intimate personal control of her life by Jesus in His Sacred Humanity appearing visibly and almost daily to her, places her in a certain manner beyond the orbit of the ordinary Cistercian vocation.

Her story is, nevertheless, in many respects both more instructive and more inspiring to a certain type of Christian soul than the more obscure and less dramatic lives of some of our great saints. In the first place, it brings home more cogently and more vividly to the imagination the closeness of Jesus to humanity and His intense desire to pour out His special graces upon souls. In the second place, it reminds us most forcefully that we are all called to suffer in union with the suffering Christ in His Body, the Church, to make reparation for sin and to win graces for sinners. The extraordinary heroism of someone like Saint Lutgarde is intended, in the plans of God, to inspire us all each in his own manner to follow her example of self-sacrifice as best we can, even if it is only a matter of accepting the common routine of religious life in the spirit with which she accepted her astounding preternatural sufferings.

Another thing is that Saint Lutgarde and her contemporary mystics represent a new development in Christian piety. Nowhere before their time do we find so clear and uncompromising a statement of the ideals of abandonment and victimhood with Jesus in the sense in which these have become familiar to modern Catholics, although of course from the time of the first Apostles and especially of Saint Paul, all the greatest saints have practiced both these essential features of Christianity.

With Saint Lutgarde and the mystics of the thirteenth century, the principal novelty is their double insistence on the eminently passive character of those sufferings and on the intensity of personal union with the Humanity of Christ, of espousal with Him in suffering. In a word, it is with these mystics that we first begin to see to any large extent in the Church that thirst for suffering which, with a constant, impatient and insatiable desire to die for Christ, does not seek martyrdom in the arena but rather offers itself to Jesus, begging and even provoking Him to let loose upon it a sea of sufferings of His own choosing, interior or exterior, culminating in a death for and by love.

We find none of these things explicitly in this particular form even in Saint Bernard in spite of his evident influence on these Cistercians brought up in his school of mysticism. Saint Bernard seeks active immolation by the Rule and the mortifications it prescribes and above all by obedience. He accepts and even courts sickness and suffering but in a somewhat different spirit—the spirit of a soldier of Christ entering the battlefield rather than of a passive victim lying down on the altar and awaiting the fall of the knife. Saint Bernard's love of the Divine Humanity is rightly regarded as laying down the foundations for devotions to the Sacred Heart, but we must remember that with him the love of Jesus is still only a stepping stone to union with the Divine Word. Saint Lutgarde is not only content to let Christ in His Humanity be the beginning and end of all her striving, but in her devotion to the Sacred Heart, it makes its appearance in an explicit and definite form with the famous "exchange of hearts." Finally, Saint Bernard constantly insists on a mysticism that transcends all visible or imaginable apparitions. He devotes like space in his existing graces *gratis datae* and advises his disciples to avoid all desire for them,[8] while devoting themselves to the earnest quest of the mystical marriage[9] which is for him nothing but the ordered development of the life of Sanctifying Grace and the seven Gifts in an exalted sphere which it is beyond any human power to reach by its own efforts.

[8] SC 46.8.
[9] See especially SC 32.

But Saint Lutgarde's mysticism is an almost unbroken series of visions, revelations, ecstasies and preternatural visitations of suffering, together with gifts of discernment of spirits and of prophecy. Clearly, Our Lord destined Saint Lutgarde not only to sanctify herself but also to accomplish by her extraordinary union with Him special effects in the Church.

Space hardly allows a detailed study of her mystical life, and what follows may seem a rather crowded and fragmentary series of miracles and revelations. If so, it is because we have followed somewhat closely the pattern of the great contemporary biography of the saint by the Dominican, Thomas of Cantimpre. This work, besides being one of the literary masterpieces of the thirteenth century, is the production of a noteworthy scholar and director of souls and one who knew Saint Lutgarde personally and intimately. Therefore, everything he says about her is to be taken as exceptionally trustworthy, and it is confirmed in any case by the unanimous testimony of such contemporaries as Jacques de Vitry, Blessed Foulques of Toulouse and scores of religious and secular persons cited as having benefitted by their contact with Lutgarde and by her intercession for them.

Lutgarde was the daughter of a well-to-do bourgeois in the town of Tongres. The fact that the other mystics who resemble her so closely, like Blessed Ida of Louvain, Blessed Ida of Nivelles, Blessed Beatrice of Nazareth and evidently Saint Gertrude also, belonged to the same social order offers food for thought to the historian who likes to trace a parallel development in the social and religious spheres. A direct and continuous devotional tradition is evident from Saint Lutgarde to Saint Margaret Mary down to and including Saint Thérèse of Lisieux, who, though she represents a distinct development into something quite new, nevertheless preserves its essential element in her notions of abandonment and victimhood.

Lutgarde's father was a businessman, and his ideals were those of the world. He wanted his daughter to be comfortably settled in life, to receive a little education and culture and to make a good marriage and live prosperously. As a matter of fact, his daughter was endowed by God with equal beauty of soul and of face. For her own part, she was not averse to her father's ideas, and she had a natural feminine weakness for pretty clothes. But the influence of her pious mother eventually prevailed upon her to enter the religious life as a Benedictine nun. Although she was only twelve years old, she was just reaching what was in those times an age when marriage was nothing unusual. Evidently, too, she was received at Saint Catherine's convent not as an aspirant to the vows but rather as a boarding student confided to the care of the nuns with a view to remote preparation for the religious life. Consequently, she was allowed frequently to receive the visits of a wealthy and noble young man who wanted to marry her, and for her own part she was by no means disinclined to listen to his conversation and proposals.

Then one day, an extraordinary thing happened which completely changed her mind and her life. Since the days of Saint Margaret Mary, representations of Christ pointing to His Heart pierced for the love of man have been familiar to every Catholic. In Saint Lutgarde's time, such things were unknown, and she was certainly one of the first great mystics to be vouchsafed the grace of this vision of the Sacred Heart. It was while she was in the parlor talking to her young friend that Jesus appeared. He showed her the lance wound that pierced His Heart and spoke to her saying, "Daughter, give up the vain love of creatures. Contemplate here in this wound what you must love, why you must love. I promise you that you will find therein the purest delights."[10]

From that day on she repelled all the advances of her suitor, which had now become odious to her, until he, infuriated by her resistance, attempted to kidnap her one day when she was out of the convent on the way to the house of her sister. The rejected suitor appeared on the road accompanied by a group of armed men who surrounded her. But she leapt from her horse and escaped into the woods while the cries of her own terrified companions eventually put the suitor himself to rout together with his followers.

This incident alone, together with Lutgarde's conversion and the intense piety of the life she now began to lead at Saint Catherine's, was dramatic enough to make her famous everywhere in the district.

---

[10] *Blanditias inepti amoris ulterius non requiras: hic jugiter contemplare quod diligas: hic totius puritatis delicias tibi spondeo consequendas.* Vita 1.1.2.

People already were speaking of a prophecy that had been made of her that she would be a second Saint Agnes. For her own part, she completely renounced all human friendships and began most earnestly to apply herself in all things to please Christ, her divine lover, asking Him among other things to send her humiliations, to make her repulsive to men and to allow her to share in His humiliations in His Passion. This in itself is significant enough, when we reflect that the first steps in conversion of the average twelfth-century saint always implied something active like fasting and disciplines or long prayers.

Meanwhile, the skeptical and somewhat worldly nuns of her convent smiled at her newfound fervor and assured her that she was going through a "stage" that would soon be over and that she would once again act like everybody else. Saint Lutgarde, tempted to discouragement and fear by what she heard, was reassured by a vision of Our Blessed Lady, who assured her of protection against any further relapse into a tepid and unspiritual way of life. The promise was fulfilled. From now on until her death, Saint Lutgarde persevered and continued to advance daily deeper and deeper into the immense kingdom of the love of Christ, with all the extraordinary graces He had in store for her. Constant union with Jesus in prayer was for her a matter of great ease by reason of her mystical state. She was often seen praying surrounded by an ethereal light. One feast of Pentecost, when the *Veni Creator Spiritus* was intoned, the nuns who had told her her piety was only a "phase" were suddenly startled to see her body slowly rise several feet above the floor and remain there suspended in midair while her ecstatic soul was completely lost and absorbed in God. "*Felix Lutgardis*," cried Thomas of Cantimpre, "*cujus corpus et anima exultaverunt in Deum vivum!*" It is a fine ejaculatory prayer. "Happy Lutgarde, whose body and soul exulted in the living God."[11]

One night in the grip of a violent fever and soaked in perspiration, she feared with the general weakness of the flesh—indeed with natural prudence—to get up and go to the night office in

[11] Vita 1.1.10.

choir. But the voice of Jesus rebuked her, "Arise, why do you lie there? Arise and pray for sinners wallowing in the mire of their sins." She made her way in spite of great weakness to the church, and there at the door she was greeted by a vision of Christ on the Cross covered with blood. He drew her to Himself, pressed her lips to His pierced side, and she was inundated with strong floods of His grace.

While she was still at Saint Catherine's, the famous exchange of hearts took place. It had as its prelude several other graces. First she had received the gift of healing. But so many people came to her to be healed that it interfered with her life of prayer. So with a familiarity that is rather astounding, she simply asked Jesus to exchange this grace for one that was better suited to her own tastes. What would she like? Well, she thought she would try the grace of understanding the psalms without having learned Latin. Immediately, she began to receive the most profound and penetrating lights concerning the sacred text in choir and elsewhere. But Saint Lutgarde was not an intellectual. These brilliant intuitions were something so foreign to her mode of prayer and union with God that they simply embarrassed her. So she began to desire another exchange.

"What then do you desire, my daughter?" Christ asked her.

"Lord," she replied, "only one thing—Thy Heart."

"But then," said Jesus, "I must have thy heart in return."

"Take it all, O Lord, but do Thou so closely unite Thy Heart's love to my poor heart that I may possess my own heart still in Thee, ever safe in Thy protection."[12]

There is more in this sentence than a delicate and pious piece of ingenuity, a pretty turn of phrase. It expresses the paradox of Christian mysticism which is at the very climax of the doctrine of Saint Bernard, namely that perfect love of God, being a perfect union of wills with Him, must result actually in the annihilation of our will in His Will because the two are one. And yet this annihilation

[12] *Ita sit. Domine, Sed tamen ut cordis tui amorem cordi meo contemperes et in ter cor meum possideum: omni tempore tui munimine Jam securum.*

can never mean a confusion of our person with God. Indeed, we not only remain distinctly ourselves in this annihilation of ourselves, but we become more perfectly ourselves than we ever were before it. This must inevitably be so if all the divine perfections belong to us and if we have become gods by grace as He is God by nature.

Nowhere in this record are we told so important a detail as when Saint Lutgarde made her profession at Saint Catherine's. It must have been right after her change of convent. But at any rate, so great was the impression she made upon the nuns there that when she was barely twenty years old she was elected first superioress, that is prioress of the community, and she held this position for about four years.

About the year 1210, Lutgarde was advised by a learned priest, Jean de Lierre, to leave the Benedictine life. He felt that she was out of place in the convent of Saint Catherine, in spite of the good she was doing there. She belonged not in this ordinary and more or less worldly atmosphere but in a convent of Cistercian nuns where every detail of the life was designed to strip the soul of attachments and to favor recollection and interior peace by offering almost unlimited opportunities for sacrifice of one's own will. His advice was that she enter the community at Aywieres.

Unfortunately, Aywieres was a French-speaking convent, and Lutgarde spoke only Flemish. It therefore appeared to her much more sensible to enter some house like Herkenrode,[13] where she would be able to understand others, and make herself understood

---

[13] Herkenrode, founded in 1182, was one of the first houses of Cistercian nuns in the Low Countries. It was most famous for the *Miraculous Host*, which is still venerated in our own day, at the parish church of Hasselt. Having been profanated, this sacred Host bled miraculously. It was taken solemnly to Herkenrode, and many miracles accompanied its passage. Placed on the altar of the convent church, it was venerated by thousands of faithful Christians, and once a great concourse all saw Christ Himself appear to their bodily eyes on the altar crowned with thorns. The Host has remained intact for seven centuries and has occasioned many miracles. During the French Revolution, it was hidden in a tin box, sealed in the wall of the stigmatic of our Order, Blessed Elizabeth of Spalbeck. (Canivez, 129).

otherwise than by the conventional system of signs when necessary. But the choice was not up to her. Jesus, who was ruling her every movement by His immediate direction, had already decided otherwise. His voice was heard within her saying, "Lutgarde, go to Aywieres, or I will forsake you."[14]

Actually, the wisdom of this choice soon became evident. Lutgarde was not only withdrawn from that part of the country where she was well known and had many friends, but she was even set apart, in a sense, from those who lived with her in the same house. Later on, too, as the fame of her sanctity also burst forth upon this region, she would have been an obvious choice as abbess either of her own house or some filiation. But since she did not know French that was impossible. Jesus wanted her to be busy with Himself alone, a favor He had refused Saint Bernard, Saint Peter of Tarentaise and so many other Cistercian mystics who groaned under the burden of their active works for souls.

Her mystical formation had begun when she was still a Benedictine, but it had not gone beyond the bounds of favors that are, after all, granted to a comparatively large number of holy souls, if we except levitation, which is not an everyday occurrence in most convents. Now as a Cistercian she was to begin a career of truly extraordinary mystical graces.

To begin with, it seems that it was only after she became a Cistercian that her vocation as a victim for the sins of the world reached its full development and assumed its direct and explicit reference to the Albigensian heresy, which was then at its worst and which became for a time the prime object of her reparatory sufferings. Furthermore, her victimhood had its positive side, which was to win grace for those engaged in every kind of active work for the Church but especially for the newly founded Dominican Order, the Order of Preachers. Blessed Jordan of Saxony, the second general of the Preachers, was an intimate friend of Saint Lutgarde and depended on her prayers, commending his whole

---

[14] *Volo ut ad locum Aquiriae finaliter pergas, et nisi facias, ego to deseram.* Vita 1.2.22.

order insistently to her, and she offered special prayers daily for them. Jordan called her the "Mother and nurse of the Friars Preachers."[15] We have seen her intimate connection with the Dominican Thomas of Cantimpre, and one of her directors was also a Dominican, Fra Bernard.[16]

It was at Aywieres, then, that Saint Lutgarde undertook three seven-year fasts, in reparation for the sins of the world and to win grace for the people of her time. The first began as a result of a vision of Our Sorrowful Mother, who appeared to the saint and so stirred her with a vision of such unhappiness that Lutgarde cried out: "Most Blessed Lady, why is thy face so pale, O Full of Grace?"

Our Lady replied, "Alas, my Son is once again crucified and spat upon by heretics and bad Christians. Offer yourself as victim and fast for seven years to appease the anger of my Son, Whose hand is ready to fall upon the world."[17]

Saint Lutgarde, in willing obedience to this demand from heaven, began her long fast on bread and the common drink of the convent which, as it happens, was a weak beer. This in itself was not what was most extraordinary about her fast, for it received the stamp of an authentic supernatural character by the fact that she was totally unable to swallow any other food or drink for that period. Besides this, the only effect upon her physical constitution of this meager diet was that she grew stronger and healthier on it than she had been for a long time before. Later, she undertook two more seven-year fasts on bread and a few vegetables.

In the intense onslaught of infused mystical love, Saint Lutgarde suffered an almost unbearable desire for the death that would liberate her from the limitations of this life and unite her perfectly with her Beloved, and she frequently prayed for death with an entirely pardonable and understandable selfishness, which is more of a virtue than an imperfection, until one day Jesus appeared to

---

[15] *Ipse,* [Jordanus] *ei super omnes femines confidebat, adeo ut eam totius Ordinis Predicatorum matrem constitueret se nutricem. . . .*

[16] Vita 1.1.6.

[17] Vita 2.1.2.

her showing her His wounds and saying, "Behold, my beloved, how my wounds cry out to you that the shedding of My Blood be not in vain or My death unprofitable."[18]

As was frequently the case in her visions, Saint Lutgarde did not understand at once what our Lord meant and asked for an explanation. He said, "You must work and shed tears to appease the anger of My Father and keep Him from condemning sinners and obtain mercy that they may be converted and live."

From then on, Saint Lutgarde, like Saint Mary Magdalen de'Pazzi, preferred to live and suffer for the love of Christ, rather than to die and enter into heaven, because on earth she could share in His passion and win more merit for sinners, at the same time increasing her power to help them in heaven.

The gift of tears is a great grace to which many souls aspire and which Saint Lutgarde possessed in a high degree. Day after day she would become so afflicted with sorrow for the sins of the world and with compassion for the suffering caused by sinners in the Sacred Heart of Jesus that she would weep for hours. But once again Christ Himself intervened to lift her above this grace which, holy as it is, still partakes too much of human weakness. He told her, "I want you to cease weeping for sinners. Continue your prayers for them fully and quietly, and thus you will appease My Father's anger." The flood of tears ceased. Lutgarde's compassion was sublimated to something infinitely more interior and more spiritual.

Her compassion led her to pray with special fervor and insistence in behalf of the agonizing and of the souls in Purgatory. In the case of a dying nun at Aywieres, Lutgarde was privileged with a special revelation concerning the power of the communal prayers for the agonizing as recited in religious Orders. The poor sister was having a hard death until the community arrived, praying, in procession, in the infirmary. Then Lutgarde saw the devil visibly take to flight. He said to her on his way out, "Consider how I tormented

[18] Vita 2.1.6.

this soul until the arrival of this mob, which has broken all my power."[19]

Many were the souls liberated from Purgatory who testified, by appearing to Saint Lutgarde or to others, that they owed their deliverance to her prayers. Not the least of these was Pope Innocent III. Before the news of that mighty pontiff had reached Belgium, he appeared to Saint Lutgarde and told her that he was in Purgatory and was condemned to remain there until the day of judgement unless someone interceded for him. Of course, Saint Lutgarde did not hesitate to come to his aid, and with the desired effect.[20] It was Innocent III who had marshaled the forces of the Church against the Albigensians and the Waldenses and who had so strongly favored the foundation of the Dominican Order. In his fight against heresy, he had had much to do with the Order of Cîteaux and had failed in his attempts to get the Cistercians out of their cloister and into the active ministry to combat heresy by the apostolate.

Another suppliant who came to Lutgarde for her help was a Cistercian abbot, Simon perhaps of Foigny,[21] who had been condemned to a long term of punishment because of the violence and harsh severity towards his monks. "Lord," cried Saint Lutgarde, "take away all the consolations Thou hast destined for me, and give them to this poor soul. I shall not cease to weep until he is delivered." Simon went to heaven.

Saint Lutgarde also enjoyed the grace known as the discernment of spirits. There was a nun at Aywieres who, as one might have reason to fear in an atmosphere of popular mysticism, had been misled by her imagination and by the devil into a kind of spurious spirituality which eventually bore fruit in a series of extremely peculiar visions and ecstasies, remarkable most of all for their eccentricity. St Lutgarde was praying for her when Our Lord appeared to her and said: *Illuminare his qui in tenebris et in umbra*

---

[19] Vita 2.1.15.
[20] Vita 2.1.7.
[21] Vita 2.1.4.

mortis sedent.[22] Lutgarde had to go and find one of the nuns who knew Latin in order to discover what this meant, and even then she was not quite sure what she ought to do about it. She continued to pray. The spirit of illusion who was causing all this trouble appeared to her and admitted that he was feeding the poor nun with lying visions. Saint Lutgarde, refusing to trust his word, told him to prove it by appearing to Holy Brother Simon of Sulne. Presently Blessed Simon came to Aywieres and asked to see Saint Lutgarde. He knew all about the sister with the visions. In the presence of a group of worthy persons, that nun was brought before Saint Lutgarde and Blessed Simon. As soon as she appeared among them, the false mystic suddenly became as rigid as a board from head to foot, and was, as it were, frozen stiff in a diabolical trance. Not only was she unable to answer their questions, but it was even impossible to pry her mouth open with a knife. Everybody in the room was seized with consternation, and all, in a body, fell upon their knees and began praying. It was as the fruit of these prayers that the unfortunate nun was liberated from the devil and returned to her normal state, took nourishment, and began to lead a regular life again.[23]

Thomas of Cantimpre was able to follow her subsequent career in religion, and he affirmed that she eventually became a very edifying religious.

Among other graces received by Saint Lutgarde was that of stigmatization. When she was twenty-eight years old, she was consumed with desire of martyrdom and was praying for it in her dormitory cell with great intensity of desire when a wound suddenly opened in her side, and blood poured forth in such quantities that all her clothes were drenched with it. It was revealed to her that, because of her desire, she would receive the reward of a martyr in heaven, even though she never suffered actual martyrdom.[24]

---

[22] Luke 1:7.
[23] Vita 2.1.10.
[24] Vita 2.1.21.

One might continue a long list of such charismata, but lack of space would necessarily turn the account into a kind of catalogue which would only make all these marvels seem somewhat trite. One thing, however, from which the average reader will profit is a consideration of the immense importance of the Divine Office in the mysticism of Saint Lutgarde. So great was her fervor in choir that one day a nun of the opposite side of the church looked over and saw a great flame shooting out of Saint Lutgarde's mouth. So overcome was the poor sister by this astonishing manifestation of grace that she collapsed in a dead faint. No doubt most of us will have to be content with the warmth of devotion less perceptible both to others and to ourselves, but we can at least imitate Saint Lutgarde's faith in the holiness and power of the sacred text which is the basis of our office. She loved the psalms, even though she did not, as a rule, understand them. All day long she practiced constant union with God by ruminating on fragments of the inspired text. She had probably never read Cassian, whose recommendation on this point is famous, but she frequently had the verse, *Deus in adjutorium meum intende*, in her mind and found it a most effective weapon against the devil. She received many revelations concerning the Office and the words of the psalms and canticles and hymns.[25] The Blessed Mother of God appeared to her and encouraged her to say with special devotion the words of the Te Deum, *Tu ad liberandum suscepturus hominem non horruisti Virginis uterum*: For Thou in order to deliver man didst not abhor the Virgin's womb, as these words were most pleasing and gave great honor and joy to Our Blessed Lady.

But we must not think that Saint Lutgarde was spared the ordinary trials of monks and religious in choir. Like all the rest of us, she had to fight distractions, which only served as another proof of the truth expressed by Saint Teresa, that in themselves, distractions are by no means incompatible with close union with God, as long as they are completely involuntary.[26] After all, it is physi-

---

[25] See Cassian, Conf 10.10.
[26] Teresa of Jesus (of Ávila), *Way of Perfection*, chap. 31.

cally impossible for a normal human being to avoid distractions altogether for any length of time, and the ability to do so is only had by virtue of a supernatural grace: any other instances of prolonged and complete avoidance of distractions by so-called "natural" means would probably be attributable to some pathological abnormality or to the devil. But in any case, Saint Lutgarde suffered intensely because of the fruitlessness of her struggle to dominate her wandering imagination at prayer, and she even got the whole community to pray for her. Eventually, Our Lord Himself appeared to her to assure her that her prayer was pleasing to Him in spite of her involuntary distractions.[27]

All her mysticism revolved around the liturgy and was closely interwoven with the liturgical cycle. Five years before her death, on the third Sunday after Pentecost, when the Gospel of the wedding feast is sung, Saint Lutgarde told Sybille de Gages: "On the Sunday when this Gospel is sung, I shall be admitted to the banquet of the Lamb." Exactly five years later, Sybille remembered these words, when the Gospel was sung, and Saint Lutgarde lay stretched out in her bier in the middle of the choir.

Before this time, she was to complete the third of her seven-year fasts. Also as she continually advanced in mystical contemplation, she gave, from time to time, indications of the state of her soul which made these lofty graces in some sort comprehensible to others. For instance, she once told one of the sisters how it was that Jesus appeared to her in her visions.

"In the twinkling of an eye, an overpowering flash of splendid light appears, in which I see, like lightning, the ineffable beauty of my glorified Savior. If this vision lasted more than a second, it would cost me my life. After the apparition, my spirit remains full of light, but when I seek, in this light, and try to find again what my eyes saw in that instantaneous flash, I no longer find it."[28]

---

[27] Saint Lutgarde unreasonably strove to keep all thoughts, good or bad, out of her mind. God does not demand the impossible. Vita 2.2.17.

[28] Thomas of Cantimpre compares this to Song 3:6: *Anima mea liquebacta est ut dilectus locutus est*. Vita 3.1.9.

Again she said: "The eyes of Christ blaze with such tremendous fire, that their splendor would dim the light of the sun, as the sunlight puts out the pale light of the stars."[29]

Small wonder that the soul that saw these glories was little troubled by the loss of her bodily vision. Eleven years before her death, Saint Lutgarde had been struck blind in both eyes, but she accepted this trial with patient joy, for the love of God, who promised her, in return, that she would never see Purgatory even for a moment.

A year before her death, Jesus appeared to Saint Lutgarde and gave her instructions how to pass her last days. She was to spend them in thanking Him for His graces: a thing she could not adequately do without the assistance of the prayers of the saints. She should also pour herself out in prayers for sinners, and finally, spend the year in ardent longing for the joys of heaven. Those who want a good method of preparation for death would do well to make a note of these three simple points: meditation and practice of them will be of far greater utility than any number of prolonged vocal prayers or even of exaggerated self-examination and self-reproach for past sins.

On June 16, 1246, Saint Lutgarde passed quietly to her eternal reward, and not without signs and miracles. She told Sybille de Gages[30] several days before her death that she saw the whole monastery full of the radiant souls of saints, including many of the sisters who had gone to heaven from Aywieres. She was a long time in ecstasy before dying, and at that moment when her soul left her body, many nuns in different parts of the convent felt, as it were, most clearly and sensibly the presence of Christ among them, coming to claim the spouse He had redeemed.

The first miracle was not long in coming. During the washing of her body, which preserved an amazing lifelike beauty, a nun with a crippled hand happened accidentally to touch the saint's

---

[29] Vita 3.1.9.

[30] See the old Menology, October 9. She was venerated with an immemorial cult and was therefore entitled to be called Blessed. Before entering Aywieres she had been a noble lady in the world, then a canoness at Nivelles.

body with that hand, and was instantly cured. Saint Lutgarde appeared to Elizabeth de Wans,[31] a nun of Aywieres, revealing that she had not only escaped Purgatory but had delivered many souls from it on her way to heaven. She also appeared to another nun, and said: "Follow me." The sister died a most holy and edifying death nine days later.

Another nun went by night to pray at Saint Lutgarde's tomb, and prostrating full length in the dark she accidentally struck her eye against a sharp iron point protruding from a candlestick: in intense pain, she begged the saint to save her from blindness. Not only was this prayer answered, but within an hour all pain was gone. Many miracles were worked by the touch of Saint Lutgarde's veil. Pilgrims came in great affluence, bringing lilies (her favorite flower) to her tomb at Aywieres until the time of the French revolution. Her feast is celebrated in the Cistercian Order and in the diocese of Malines, Liege and Namur. Her title to sanctity was officially recognized by Rome, without judicial process, in 1584, and her name was inscribed in the Roman Martyrology by Molanus and Baronius.

Saint Lutgarde is one of the special glories of Cîteaux and one of our favorite saints, and well might she be so, for her life remains as a constant inspiration to all who embrace our life of prayer and penance.

Let us not only seek to follow her in the magnitude of her generosity and the fervor of her love for the Sacred Heart but also trust in the power of her intercession to make this possible for us, who are so far from her perfection.

---

[31] Menology, July 5—She had been a Benedictine.

June 17

Saint Teresa, Infanta of Portugal, Nun of Lorvão

(Sources: AASS, June 4:365 [biography written in modern times]; M. Gloning, "Zwei Heiligen aus Koeniglichem Hause," Cist. Chronik 19 [1908]: 225.)

Of the three saints[32] who were daughters of King Sancho of Portugal, Teresa is the one who attracts the most attention. Probably this is partly because of the fact that, being the eldest child, she exercised a natural dominance over her sisters Sancha and Majalda, but her influence was especially strong in matters of religion. The princesses were brought up more or less in seclusion in the palace at Coimbra, where Teresa was born around 1178. Even in the natural Order, their training was of a kind to direct them in the ways of simplicity and virtue, and it is perhaps surprising to read of royal princesses being taught how to sew and cook and spin when the daughters of grocers and mechanics in our own day too often scorn these household arts as being beneath their dignity. The religious education of the future queen was not neglected, and they were quick in corresponding to grace. They loved prayer, spiritual reading, and holy Mass, and their conversations were most often about saints and heaven and God. Above all, they took advantage of their position to give alms in profusion. That all these things were more than mere pious hobbies is proved by the sincerity and zeal with which they applied themselves to purifying their hearts and doing all things out of love of God alone.

It is remarkable that both Teresa and Sancha were models in "Self-custody," or the virtue which Cassian calls *discretio* or the "mother, guardian and guide of all the other virtues."[33] Since pu-

---

[32] Saint Sancha (March 13) and Blessed Majalda (May 2).

[33] Cassian, Conf 2.2, *De discretion*: [*Discretio*] *cogitationes hominis universas actusque discernens, cuncta quae gerenda sunt praevidet et perlustrat. . . . Omnium namque virtutum genetrix, sustos moderatrixque discretio est.* PL 49:52–28.

rity of intention depends upon the ability, first of all, to see through all the artifices of self-love and the devil, we can never attain it without this *discretio spirituum* or ability to know at once when we are deceiving ourselves in practicing works that appear to be righteous. And to be frank, Saint Teresa of Lorvão needed to be equipped with the virtue of self-knowledge and the habit of wise self-examination, because her position brought her into many dangerous situations.

The first of these, and the most perilous to her soul, came when she was barely thirteen. At that age, she had to enter into a political marriage with the seventeen-year-old King Alphonso IX of Leon, her second cousin. Teresa, of course, was completely ignorant of the irregularity of the match which was the will of her parents, not her own, and which was, moreover, sanctioned by two bishops, though more or less unofficially. In other words, no dispensation was obtained. The marriage meant, of course, the sacrifice of many of Teresa's favorite mortifications: her hair shirt, her long vigils, fasts, sleeping on the floor, and so on. The renunciation of her own will undoubtedly more than made up for the cessation of these external practices: indeed, it does not take much imagination to conceive how much of a sacrifice was involved in this marriage.

Teresa had become the mother of three children before the political enemies[34] against whom the marriage had been directed, as the basis of an alliance between Portugal and Leon, finally reached the Pope who had the match dissolved.

Meanwhile, as a reminder to Sancho I and the others in responsible positions who had allowed the marriage to be solemnized, divine Providence visited Portugal with almost every imaginable evil, from earthquakes, which leveled whole towns and cities, to tidal waves, plagues, drought, floods, plagues of locusts, disastrous fires, and invasion by the Moors.

In 1196, then, Saint Teresa, leaving her husband, returned with her three children to Coimbra, where she also acted as mother to the younger members of the family of eleven who had been born to King Sancho and Queen Dulce. She was able to return to her

---

[34] Particularly the House of Castille.

semi-secluded life of prayer and almsgiving and works of penance, but what was more important, she began to turn her eyes toward the religious life. It was evidently going to be a little difficult for one in her position to make a clean break with the world in which she had so many real responsibilities, and the first step was more or less indefinite. It took the form of a charitable foundation.

There was in a mountain valley behind Coimbra an ancient monastery which was supposed to have been founded in the time of Saint Benedict himself. It had long been a fervent community of Black Monks, who had even gained the respect of the Moors, in past years. Now, however, the recent wars had driven the monks to another site, and the abandoned monastery attracted the attention of the Infanta Teresa.

Having first interested several noble ladies of the court in the idea of becoming Cistercian nuns, and having sent them to make their novitiate in two Spanish convents of the Order, Carrizo and Grandefes, Teresa then obtained a colony of nuns from those two houses and went with them to establish a new foundation at Lorvão.

Saint Teresa herself, since she had not made any novitiate, could not join them as a nun or make profession. It seems her intention was not yet to do so, for at first she joined the community only as a *familiar*, or family sister, that is, as a layperson more or less informally connected with the community, leading a penitential life and sharing the labors of the nuns.

The little colony was impressed and a little frightened by their first sight of Lorvão. It was a lovely place, that wild ravine. The buildings clung to the rock. Under the bright Portuguese sky the cliffs were dazzling in the sun, and here and there clumps of flowering shrub bloomed on the rocks. The level places were green with wild olive, and the silence of the glen was broken by the music of waterfalls, pouring in cascades from the spring in the monastery itself and escaping down the cliff, dividing into lesser falls and streams, and disappearing in the green woods of the lower valley.

When the noble ladies who had newly made their profession as Cistercian nuns (Teresa's sister, the princess Blanca, was among them) came to the edge of the cliff and looked over at the breathtaking drop into the ravine, when they surveyed the narrow winding path, with a sheer rock wall on one side and the abyss on the other, they drew back in fear. They were almost ready to return to Coimbra, rather than attempt that perilous descent on mule-back, but with the encouragement of Teresa's words and example, they started down into the valley of Lorvão.

The fact that Saint Teresa had not yet taken the habit becomes easily intelligible when we consider what happened after the death of her father Sancho in 1211. Evidently, Teresa had been expecting trouble from her brother, who now ascended the throne as Alphonso II. The new king was a weak and irascible character, and he seems to have disliked his two sisters, Teresa and Sancha. At any rate, he now set himself to cheat them out of what was due to them and to Teresa's children in Sancho's will. He meant, in short to possess himself of their estates by force. Thus not only Lorvão was menaced but also Alemquer where Sancha was living in retirement. Teresa had kept herself free not only in order to defend the rights of her children but also to secure the possibility of retirement in the various foundations which she and her sisters had in mind. She was aided against her brother by the soldiers of her former husband, the King of León.[35] It is not necessary to go into the details of the conflict; but once again we must remember that this was another trial, placed by Providence in the path of the saintly Infanta, to test her virtue and her loyalty to God.

It was not until 1229, after the death of Sancha, that Teresa was finally able to take the Cistercian habit, which was given her by the Benedictine Bishop John of Sabina, in the presence, it is believed, of her former husband King Alphonso of León.

From then on Saint Teresa gave herself entirely to the life of contemplation and penance. She might well have become prioress of the community over which she had always exerted a strong moral influence even before she formally became a nun, but she always refused this high office, preferring to remain a simple religious. She did however accept the positions of cellaress and portress.

[35] Alemquer was defended by Knights Templars.

It was her special joy to keep strictly and perfectly all the details of the community, and she was especially eager to benefit by the humiliation of public penances. And when we speak of public penances, we must remember that, in those days, it was more than a matter of kneeling at the door of the church after dinner or accusing oneself, publically, of some infraction of the Rule. Saint Teresa sometimes received the discipline on her bare shoulders, in chapter, at the hands of nuns who had been her former ladies-in-waiting. As a true Benedictine, Saint Teresa had forgotten all distinctions of social class and rank.

Now that she was at last able to sever all her connections with the world, Saint Teresa discouraged the visits of her noble friends and relatives from Coimbra, and so intense was her desire to be rid of everything that savored of the world and its ways that she refused even to let money touch her hands.

Her greatest care was to keep her mind in peace and recollection, united with God outside of choir, so that when she went to Church she might acquit herself of the principal duty of a Cistercian, which is to praise God in the divine office with all one's heart and soul.

She especially loved all hard and menial work and made the ordinary penances sent by providence, like the blazing heat of the Portuguese summer and the cold of the mountain winter, her chief mortifications of the flesh. However, she also fasted all day on Fridays, meditating on the Passion of Our Lord.

She did not despise the simple, fundamental practice appropriate to the so-called purgative way, the constant remembrance of our approaching death. Can a Benedictine ever afford to neglect this easy and simple method of keeping his passions and his self-love from creeping up on him without his being entirely aware of the danger? We do not, of course, need to do all the things Saint Teresa did: she used to put ashes in her food, to remind herself what her body would eventually become, no matter how well it was fed. Her tomb had already been prepared for her, before the altar of Our Lady of the Rosary,[36] and she used frequently to lie in

---

[36] Probably the first such feast to be so dedicated in our Order.

it praying and meditating on the day that was to come when she would be placed in that position and remain there for good. One practice of hers that we can imitate is frequent meditation on the prayers for the agonizing and the rites of Extreme Unction and burial: for the great wealth hidden in these liturgical treasures is not for the dying and the dead alone but also for the living who must one day die.

Hagiographers have made the phrase "she took the discipline to blood" tiresome and trite by repetition, but when Saint Teresa of Lorvão went about her convent with her hair shirt clinging to the drying blood on her shoulders and eating into the raw flesh of her back, it was no trivial penance.

Her sanctity was corroborated by several miracles in her lifetime, the most remarkable of which was the instantaneous cure of a paralytic. This man was a beggar who came to her asking for alms when she was portress of the convent. His paralyzed arm was healed as soon as she placed the gift in his hand. The news of this soon spread and brought crowds of sufferers to the convent to be healed. She also obtained by her prayers the return to life of a nun who had died suddenly without the benefit of the last sacraments. The sister revived long enough to make her confession and receive Extreme Unction and Viaticum. Later on, a nun with an injured leg was cured when she put on a robe that had belonged to the saint.

God granted Saint Teresa twenty-one years of the pure contemplative life as a simple nun before calling her to heaven, in 1250. By that time, the ex-queen of Leon was seventy-two years old, but her energy and fervor were most extraordinary. Like Saint Benedict, she aspired to die on her feet before the High Altar, or at least—as it happened—on her knees there. She had requested to be taken to the Church when she felt that her end was near, and while she stood before the altar, with the sisters reciting the prayers for the dying around her, her agony began. She fell to her knees, supporting herself on a large Crucifix, and while all the sisters, at her request, were singing the *Magnificat*, she joined in with them and finally expired after breathing the words: *Suscepit Israel puerum suum.* (He hath received His child Israel.)

Such was the end of this truly valiant nun, in whose veins ran the blood of a race of warrior kings, but whose heart was filled with an even more generous love for the crucified Christ. And indeed we cannot deny to Saint Teresa of Lorvão the quality of true greatness, true heroism. A blind youth, to mention one of her posthumous miracles, made a pilgrimage to her tomb: he drank from a glass that had been used by the saint and regained his vision. Ninety-seven miracles were brought forward in favor of the two Holy Queens Sancha and Teresa when their joint cause finally came up, in Rome, in the seventeenth century. Clement IX accorded them the title of saints in 1705.

June 30

Saint Arnulph, Lay-brother of Villers, Belgium

(Sources: AASS, June 7:566 [Life by his contemporary, Goswin the Hunch-back, Cantor of Villers; Nimal gives a French translation of the biography of Goswin]; Chron Vill, 3.1.)

It must be said at once that, although Blessed Arnulph is certainly the most spectacular lay-brother our Order ever produced, he stands well outside the Cistercian tradition of simplicity. His life written by the cantor of Villers, Goswin the Hunchback, who was a great admirer of this incorrigible self-torturer, is an extraordinary document. It is not altogether an incredible record, although at times Goswin lays himself open to suspicion of exaggerating out of sensationalism or, even more, in order to raise a laugh. Nevertheless, when all is said and done, it is hard to determine just what we are to think of Blessed Arnulph.

First of all, who was this astounding lay-brother? He had been born in the slums of Brussels and had grown up among evil companions. He had fallen deep into a life of sin, but grace had rescued him while he was still in his teens, and he had come to Villers and entered the lay-brothers novitiate filled with an extraordinary order for penance. He soon signalized this fact by binding himself up from head to foot so tight with knotted cords that he collapsed. The cords had bitten into his flesh and he was covered with blood. All this, of course, had been done without permission. After this, although his penances were unabated, his biographer assures us that he always had permission for them. If we are to take Goswin's word for this, then Arnulph's superiors must have been thoroughly convinced that this lay-brother had a most extraordinary vocation, and this fact alone should be enough to remind us that what follows is not proposed to lay-brother novices, or to anybody else, as a model for imitation.

But what of his superiors and this question of his extraordinary vocation? We need only say that Arnulph lived at Villers under three of its greatest abbots and at the very peak of the monastery's fervor and prosperity. One of these, Walter of Utrecht, died in the odor of sanctity and is commemorated in the menology of the Order.[37] It cannot be said that these men were altogether imprudent or irresponsible. Did they think Arnulph had a very special vocation? Evidently they did. For he was soon sent to a distant grange, not in order to do any special work but in order that he might be practically alone and have an opportunity to give himself freely to his penances and prayers. It was a very small grange, where he had only three companions. Furthermore, Goswin assures us that for certain periods he was dispensed from manual labor entirely in order to devote the time to his special austerities. Is this credible? In the thirteenth century there were many members of the Order who lived as recluses, under obedience to an abbot, and led precisely this kind of life. Besides, Goswin was writing shortly after Arnulph's death, and these "permissions" must have been at least credible, or he would not have attempted to foist them upon an audience that was well able to be judge of the facts.

After these preliminaries, what was it that Arnulph did in his strange zeal? He slept on a bed of pointed stones. He dined on

---

[37] Born in 1221. Old Menology, November 13.

bread that was so stale that it was thrown to the dogs, and his portions of vegetables were put to one side to rot for a few days so that they would be sufficiently disgusting for his penitential appetite. When eating, he used to force his stomach to accept this filth with exclamations of "Here it comes, stomach! Take it whether you like it or not!"[38] Although he was neither educated nor especially intelligent, he had an extraordinary inventiveness when it came to devising hair shirts. To begin with, he had not only hair shirts but hair drawers, hair stockings and even hair socks. One of his hair shirts was made of intertwined, knotted horsehair cords, which must have been even worse than it sounds, since the grangemaster took it away from him, much to his distress. Arnulph got the shepherds to kill all the hedgehogs they could find and bring him the skins: out of these he concocted another hair shirt. But the worst of all was apparently one made out of a rusty coat of mail, decorated with hedgehog quills. His ingenuity in inventing disciplines kept pace with the examples we have just seen. He started with holly branches, but after all, that was relatively commonplace.[39] Then he beat himself with thorns, finally with an iron scourge decorated with hedgehog quills.

The worst of all was the length of time he devoted to these scourgings. In Lent, for example, having arisen from his bed of stones at the proper time, he put on his hair shirt and prayed until tierce, that is, about seven in the morning. After that, retiring to a special cell, or stone hut apart from the grange, he stripped off his clothes and took his discipline and beat himself, with intervals for repose, in which his blood-covered body had an opportunity to feel the biting cold. This went on for hours—in fact, it continued all the time Arnulph should have been doing some useful work in the fields and did not cease until the middle of the afternoon, that is, time for Vespers. This was followed by the one regular meal of the day, which Arnulph took in his usual style. Allowing for exaggeration in Goswin's account, we repeat that the circum-

---

[38] Vita 1.3.25.

[39] Ida of Louvain (April 13) had also punished herself in this way.

stances under which it was written make it at least to some extent credible.

Once a monk from Villers presented himself at the grange looking for Brother Arnulph. He asked the brother in charge of the horses where he was.

"He is in purgatory" said the brother.

"In purgatory!"

"Yes, over there, in purgatory." The brother pointed to Arnulph's hut. The monk approached and heard the sound of the scourge. He knocked on the door, and the scourging ceased. Arnulph put on his robe and opened the door.[40]

"Brother! What are you trying to do?" cried the monk, "do you want to kill yourself?"

"No," said Arnulph brightly, "I am killing sinners."

As a matter of fact, Arnulph used to encourage himself, during his beatings, by shouting the names of those for whose intentions he was thus macerating his flesh. Goswin assures us that after it was all over, his flesh would miraculously heal in a few hours, but this is one miracle that is too convenient to be altogether plausible without some further substantiation.

One thing, however, is quite evident. Arnulph was burning with an intense zeal for souls, which also found its outlet in an equally reckless generosity to the poor. Here again, the question of official permission raises a few difficult problems.

Once, for instance, Arnulph gave away forty-two loaves of bread in one fell swoop to the poor. Villers was a big, rich abbey and was famous for its organized charity, but nevertheless, forty-two loaves of bread when distributed in a manner not provided for by the routine of the house, by a more or less irresponsible lay-brother, were a loss that would scarcely go unnoticed.

Goswin says that Arnulph had permission to make this gift if he could do so in secret. But afterwards he was proclaimed in chapter, and the abbot, who presumably gave him the permission, penanced him for it. If his action had been under obedience, why was he

[40] Vita 1.3.25.

penanced? Setting aside the possibility that someone else had given him the permission, there is a chance that the same superior both granted him the permission and gave him the penance—the latter in order to avoid trouble with the more prudent members of the community. The solution is that the penance was, for Arnulph, not really a penance at all, since it consisted in being put in solitary confinement in a hut near the gatehouse. After all, if the superiors had been following a systematic policy of isolating Arnulph from the rest of his brethren for the sake of his penances and contemplation, this gesture might at the same time satisfy others that a penance had been given, without any injustice to the brother.

As a matter of fact, Arnulph went off to his new cell with the remark that he was now, like Saint Peter, a gatekeeper, and presently he had one of his spectacular visions while he was alone there.

It must be observed that the characteristic of Arnulph's mysticism was a tumultuous and exuberant joy, which used to take such possession of him that it simply burst out in spite of all he could do. Far from agreeing with Moreau[41] that these outbursts were signs of mental derangement, we are inclined to think that they set the seal of credibility on Arnulph's whole story. After all, it is a well-known fact in mystical theology that such manifestations can be truly the product of special charismata, and Cassian tells us that they were not infrequent among the ancient hermits. One might reply that this does not prove them genuine in Arnulph's case: but the authority of Fr. Moreau is not sufficient to prove the brother a madman. After all, Moreau disqualifies himself as an authority on mysticism by the statement that Saint Bernard himself was not a mystic.[42]

On this particular occasion, one evening Arnulph was praying in his solitary cell when suddenly Our Lady appeared before him, bearing in her arms the Holy Child. Arnulph was overwhelmed. He began to shout and clap his hands, intoxicated with delight. When the Blessed Virgin offered to place the Child Jesus in the

[41] Moreau, 104.
[42] Moreau, 97.

poor Brother's arms, he was beside himself. "Oh no!" he cried, "Oh no! It is too much! Grace is enough! Grace is enough!" And indeed, he all but exploded with joy. He could not contain the immensity of the exultation that filled him. Is it, after all, hard to believe that a man should go wild with happiness when suddenly confronted with the pattern and exemplar of all joy, made flesh for love of him? Arnulph ran around his cell and flung open all the windows and began to cry out at the top of his voice, calling all men who loved God to hasten and come to his cell, for they would find there what they were looking for, and their search would be at an end.

The brothers at the gate, who were just about to retire for the night, looked out, then gazed at one another and shook their heads in pity: it had affected his mind.

This ebullient joy was more embarrassing to Arnulph and to the community when it seized him in choir. At such times he could not stand still, and he would be smiling and jumping about in his stall and even laughing and softly clapping his hands. It got so bad that he was unable to stay in the chapter room for sermons on big feasts, because as soon as someone would mention the joys of heaven, or the goodness of God, or even the names of Jesus or His Blessed Mother, Arnulph would be overcome with delight, and these paraoxysms of enthusiasm would begin to make themselves noticed.

This bonanza of joy lasted about seven years in Arnulph's life. If it is fortunate that most of us do not receive the same grace, and in the same measure—for it would make community life unnecessarily complicated—we can at least nourish the spirit of interior joy, as Arnulph did, by devotion to the joys of the Blessed Virgin. In fact, after he had spent long years in loving meditation on the traditional seven joys, he had a vision of the Blessed Mother, in which she informed him that she would be greatly pleased, and her Son glorified, if he would also meditate on the seven joys in the glory of heaven. The first of these is her own glory, which is above all the glory of the angels and saints. The second is the fact that by her own joy and glory the beatitude of every other soul in heaven is increased. Then she rejoices in the love and service given to her by everyone in heaven because she is the mother of their King. The fourth joy is in the perfect unity of her will with the Holy Trinity, Who is Charity, so that all that is willed by the infinite love of God is willed by her, and conversely, everything that is willed by her is willed by the Blessed Three. The fifth joy follows from this one and is greater still because it consists in sharing joy with others: it is the joy she takes in the fact that everything she asks for her children and servants on earth is granted by the Holy Trinity. The sixth joy is her closeness to the Holy Trinity, the very fact of which makes her closer and more intimately united with all the other saints in heaven, both intimately and as a community. But the crown and perfection of all her joys is the seventh, the absolute certainty that these joys will never be diminished or taken away.

This is a beautiful devotion offered to our meditation. It cannot help but teach us charity if we penetrate below the surface of these seven mysteries of love; and in so doing, it will prepare us for heaven, which is nothing but charity—participation in the Charity Who is God, with and through Mary and her Divine Son. And when we finally, by God's mercy, enter into that joy and glory, our very arrival there will bring an accidental increase not only to the joy of all the saints but to that of our most Blessed and Sweet Lady, and even to the Holy Trinity itself, humanly speaking.

Before closing the annals of Arnulph's life, one well-known story of the holy lay-brother of Villers should be mentioned. It concerns his charity to the poor.

One day he was sent on a rather long series of errands with a wagon, with a load of fruit from a grange to Villers and thence with a load of bread to another grange. On the first lap of his journey, he acquired some pigs, more or less unofficially, which he planned to give to some poor people whose cottage lay on the second lap; in other words, after his call at Villers. But it was imperative that the pigs should not be discovered. Arnulph had tied them up in sacks, but if one wishes to conceal a pig, it is not sufficient merely to make it invisible. The animals set up a chorus of squeals that seemed to grow louder and louder as they approached the monastery.

Arnulph finally turned on them and said: "Listen to me, pigs! If it is God's will for me to give you to the poor people, you are to stop that noise, and be quiet. On the other hand, if it is not His will, just continue as you are doing." The noise immediately ceased, and all the while Arnulph was loading bread on top of them at the monastery, the pigs lay with the silence of death.

For all that, when Goswin came to write about the virtue of obedience in his hero, he was not able to collect any concrete details but merely set down a few edifying generalities. If we grant that all Arnulph's exploits were blessed by obedience, we are still forced to characterize his thoroughly extraordinary spirituality in Goswin's own terms as a kind of "holy obstinacy."[43] In other words, if his superiors would not give him permission to beat himself half to death, he simply pestered them until they did.

Perhaps this does something to explain the failure of the probable attempt to canonize Blessed Arnulph—not that the actual details of his life ever seem to have come under discussion, even at the General Chapter. A tradition at Villers, noted by Molanus[44] in the seventeenth century, held that Arnulph's cause was brought up before the General Chapter, and it was turned down because "too many canonizations might make sanctity seem of little account." This was taken up by Henriquez[45] and magnified into a *statute* of the General Chapter. Such a statute, of course, never existed. Fr. Seraphim Lenssen[46] believes that the canonization of Arnulph was probably suggested and vetoed, above all, since an office was composed in his honor, probably by his admiring cantor-biographer.

In any case, this holy lay-brother must stand apart as a kind of curiosity in the history of the Order. It is a pity that the lay-brothers who achieved renown and veneration in our Order were all more or less outside the limits of true Cistercian spirituality. The true

[43] Vita 2.3.19.

[44] Joannes Molanus, *Natales Sanctorum Belgii, et eorundem chronic recapitulatio* (Tornacii, 1616).

[45] *Fascicules Sanctorum Cist.* 1, Introduction.

[46] See Lenssen, Coll 6, 11.

Cistercian lay-brother-saints have all remained anonymous. The reason is not far to seek: it is part of the very obscurity and simplicity which are essential to our vocation, particularly to that of the *conversi*. The accounts in the *Exordium magnum* of many of the virtues of individual brothers, who have remained nameless, remain to give us a true picture of Cistercian sanctity in the twelfth and thirteenth centuries, but unfortunately there is no place for them in this volume. They are, however, familiar to all members of our Order from the Cistercian Necrology, read daily in our refectories.

July

July 8

Saint Theobald, Abbot of Vaux-de-Cernay, near Paris, France

(Source: *Les Petis Bollandistes* [Account based on a contemporary life to which we do not have access].)

It is said of Saint Theobald that, after Saint Bernard, no other saint had such great devotion to the Virgin Mother of God. And we know that his conversion to the monastic life was the result of a miracle in which her intercession obtained for him the grace to see the futility of his way of life. For Theobald de Marly was a great knight, related to the famous Montmorency family, and like most noblemen in his time he had been brought up in the arts of fighting, riding, jousting, hunting, and all the skills appropriate to the life of a feudal lord. And yet he had also always had great devotion to Our Blessed Lady.

So one day while he was riding to a tourney, he passed a church where the bells were just being rung for Mass. He stopped, dismounted, and entered. He heard the whole Mass with the greatest devotion and love, for it was a Mass in honor of the Queen of Heaven. But when he proceeded on his way to the tourney he was astonished to meet a group of his friends coming from it. They, in turn, came forward with smiles and congratulations to felicitate him on his victory in the lists. Amazed at what he heard, and yet finally convinced that they meant what they said, the only solution that presented itself to his mind was that his place had been taken by his guardian angel, wearing his armor and colors, and jousting probably much better than he could have done! In any case, he

247

was so moved by this marvel that he promised the Mother of the Savior that he would enter religion and soon presented himself at the Cistercian Abbey of Vaux-de-Cernay, situated in the pleasant wooded country west of Paris, in which is now the diocese of Versailles.

All we know of his fervent novitiate was that he was like wax in the hands of his superiors, so perfect was his obedience and submission to their least desire, in accordance with the Rule. Nor was it long after his profession that he was elected abbot. In his new office, he took every possible opportunity to practice humility, continuing to perform in his turn the simple and ordinary duties of servant of the church, dormitorian, servant of the refectory and so on, duties which involved waiting on tables, lighting candles for Mass and covering the altar afterwards, and other simple functions. During the construction of a new dormitory he assisted the more skilled monks who were working as bricklayers by acting as hod-carrier for them. He was proclaimed at the General Chapter of the Order for the "excessive" poverty of his habit.

As abbot, also, he showed great zeal in promoting the honor and glory of the Mother of God, and he desired that the monks who worked at copying and illuminating manuscripts in the scriptorium of Vaux-de-Cernay should decorate the name of Mary with an especial loving care and elegance. He has left us another trace of his devotion to the Queen of Angels in a beautiful ejaculatory prayer to her, which runs: *Nomen suave Sanctae Virginis, nomen venerabile, nomen benedictum, nomen ineffabile, nomen amabile in saecula saeculorum!* "O sweet name of the holy Virgin, venerable and blessed name, ineffable and worthy of love for ever and ever!"

Whenever he passed the High Altar and the Blessed Sacrament, he would say: "Blessed be Jesus Christ, the Son of God, who by His temporal birth filled with ineffable glory His most noble and illustrious Mother."

When someone reproached him with loving the Mother of God excessively, he replied simply: "It is only Jesus in her that I love." But it is impossible to love God to excess. In fact, if it were possible, we should exert all our efforts to do just that. And so, in loving Jesus in Mary, and loving her in Him and for His sake, it is impossible to love too much. Charity is an end in itself, teaches Saint Thomas, and like the other theological virtues, we can never have too much of it.[1]

Saint Theobald had many visions and received many high graces of prayer, one of which was a vision of the Blessed Trinity, in which it was revealed to him that the beautiful canticle of the Three Children, from Daniel, which we sing as a tract on Ember Saturday in Advent, and on other Ember Saturdays, was most pleasing to the Three Divine Persons and that God received much honor and glory from the singing of this tract by choirs of fervent monks on earth. But the glory of God, as far as we are concerned, is our sanctification, and if He tells us that some activity of ours gives Him glory, He also means by that that we are brought closer to Him by it, for this is what He wills, in His infinite love for all His poor creatures. And consequently, this vision of Saint Theobald's means that the fervent and intelligent singing of this wonderful canticle can bring us close to God and fill us with incalculable graces.

Saint Theobald's whole heart was in the monastery, where he could pray in peace and dwell in the presence of God all day long. When he had to be out in the world, he would say to himself: "O my soul! Thy well-Beloved, whom thou seekest, is not here. Let us go back to Vaux-de-Cernay, for there thou shalt find Him, and speak with Him, and see Him by faith, in thy prayers."

Yet even in the world he was always united with God. Once, at the court of the holy King of France, Saint Louis, Theobald was rapt out of himself and into ecstasy by some sweet music played by a court musician, so that the good king said afterwards that his friend, the Abbot of Vaux-de-Cernay, truly possessed the gift of turning temporal into eternal delights.

Theobald, in his great charity, used to besiege God most effectively in his prayers, and Queen Margaret of France attributed to his intercession the birth of her children after a long barrenness. By praying all night, he completely overcame the temptation of one of his novices to leave the monastery. But who can count or

[1] Saint Thomas, *In Rom*, 12.1.

estimate the graces won, for his monks and for all the people of his country and the whole church, by the prayers of so good and simple a man?

He maintained the spirit of Saint Stephen, Saint Alberic and Saint Bernard in his monastery of Vaux-de-Cernay. We have seen him coming into conflict with some of the less fervent members of the General Chapter: and among these and their subjects Vaux-de-Cernay was frivolously called the "prison of the Order." And yet so happy and peaceful a spirit reigned there that many monks changed their stability and passed over to that house from less rigid communities.

He died in 1247, and at the translation of his relics his cowl was found uncorrupted. And among the many pilgrims to his tomb, princes of the royal house of France were to be seen earnestly begging his intercession for them in heaven. Let us not fear to do the same.

His long-standing veneration as a saint was officially confirmed by the Holy See in 1702.

July 8

Blessed Eugenius III, Abbot of Tre Fontane, Italy, Pope[2]

(Source: Saint Bernard, Epp [*passim*]; Eugenius, Letters, etc., PL 180; Philip Jaffe, *Regesta pontificum romanorum* [Leipzig: Veit, 1885; reprint Graz: Akademische Druck- u. Verlagsanstalt, 1956.] [http://works.bepress .com/david_freidenreich/18]; Vacandard, especially vol. 2.)

It is not possible to give a detailed account of the career of this greatest of Cistercian Popes, although it would be both interesting

---

[2] [This article on Blessed Eugenius III appeared in *Cistercian Studies Quarterly* 44.2 (2009): 174–80, and is used here with kind permission of CSQ. —Ed.]

and valuable to have a complete study of Eugenius III quite apart from the life of Saint Bernard. As it is, the fact that he is usually treated as a kind of satellite of the Abbot of Clairvaux throws the pontificate of Eugene III into a more or less false perspective. It is true that when the cardinals, in a moment of grave crisis, secretly and in haste elected the obscure Abbot of Tre Fontane to the papacy, within two days of the death of Lucius II, in 1145, as a consequence of wounds received in a battle with the Roman "republicans," they must have intended to put the Order of Cîteaux in the Vatican, rather than the ex-canon of Pisa, who happened to be abbot of the nearest community of White Monks in Rome. Nevertheless, Eugenius was a holy and courageous man who, although not endowed with the genius of a Gregory the Great or an Innocent III, nevertheless joined to his native ability and honesty the determination of a saint to fight for the interests of God and His Church in a time of great danger. Without the influence of Saint Bernard, his task would have been harder, no doubt, but he would have been nonetheless a good, perhaps a great, Pope.

Bernardo Pignatelli had been born of poor parents and did not receive much education, but by his holiness and hard work he managed to arrive at a canonry and provostship at the cathedral of Pisa. It was here that he came under the influence of Saint Bernard, and at the synod of Pisa in 1134 he received a Cistercian vocation and followed Bernard to Clairvaux.

There is a tradition that he had the humble office of tending the furnace of the calefactory, or warming room, at Clairvaux, but in 1140 Saint Bernard appointed him to lead a colony of monks to Rome, where Innocent II was interested in founding a Cistercian monastery, somewhere in the vicinity of the city. The first site chosen was at San Salvatore, eight miles from the great Benedictine abbey of Farfa, and it was a good enough place for a monastery. Dom Bernardo set to work, and his monks had already finished the foundations for a new cloister when they were unexpectedly ordered by the Pope to move to another far less desirable place. This was the ancient monastery of Saint Vincent and Anastasius, in a little valley a few miles outside of Rome towards Ostia. It was built on the site of Saint Paul's martyrdom and took its name "Tre

Fontane" from the three fountains that the legend says sprang up where Saint Paul's head bounded three times after it had been severed from his body.

This had been a Benedictine abbey, then had been tenanted by a Greek community, and more recently had been occupied by Cluniac monks. All of these had found the place practically un- inhabitable, and the Cluny community had been decimated by malaria. The White Monks settled here, out of obedience to the Pope, and at once began to suffer from the unhealthy situation.

Sickness became so prevalent that the harassed abbot finally wrote to Saint Bernard for permission to call in doctors and pur- chase remedies from secular pharmacists. Saint Bernard replied in characteristic style with a refusal,[3] which he explained on the grounds of poverty, adding that God always provided some natural remedy in unhealthy places and they should use the com- mon herbs they found around them. The monks of Tre Fontane did without doctors and survived. Nevertheless, in our own day, the situation has been greatly improved by the planting of euca- lyptus trees.[4]

Another trial of the new abbot was a rebellion on the part of one of his monks, who not only disobeyed him but publically insulted him. Dom Bernardo took this with patience and humility but nevertheless administered a moderate penance. The offender was demoted and not allowed to intone anything in choir. At this, the recalcitrant monk, who had never previously been able to be moved by pleas or threats to give his voice, now began to roar out antiphons and psalms out of turn, disrupting the whole choir. Having been punished for this by being ordered to take his meals apart from the community and at a different time, the trouble- maker insulted the abbot again, in chapter, and finally left the monastery, asserting that the only reason he had come to the new foundation was to see Rome.

[3] Bernard of Clairvaux, Ep 345; SBOp 8:286; Letter 399 in *The Letters of Saint Bernard of Clairvaux*, trans. Bernard Scott James (Kalamazoo: Cistercian Pub- lications, 1988), 458.

[4] By Dom Edmond Obrecht, who afterwards became Abbot of Gethsemani, Kentucky. He died in 1935.

The future Eugenius III was able to accept all these trials with equanimity, but nobody foresaw for what great responsibilities he was being prepared. No doubt he had been aware of the revolutionary ferment in the nearby city. He was soon to be thrown into the midst of the political whirlpool.

His first problem was to deal with the Roman "republic" and Arnold of Brescia, and this was a peculiarly modern difficulty. Arnold of Brescia was a brilliant and severely ascetical man, a pupil of Peter Abelard, and not without a certain tendency to mysticism. Seeing the abuses in the ecclesiastical life of his time and burning with an earnest and sincere desire to do something about the social problems that were everywhere clamoring for settlement, he conceived an oversimplified social panacea, which ascribed all the ills of the age to the avarice of ecclesiastics and planned to cure them all by giving secular powers full right to dispossess the church of all its property. The church should return to a condition of complete evangelical poverty and let the secular power take care of material things. It was not he who had first fomented the republican movement at Rome. Indeed, the revolution that was going on at the time of Eugenius's election had nothing to do with Arnold, who was then in exile.

Eugenius, forced to leave Rome where the mob was rioting and sacking the palaces of cardinals, made it his business to attack the problem on both fronts by excommunicating the patrician Jordanus in Rome and Arnold of Brecia, then in refuge in Switzerland. This brought Arnold to his feet, seeking reconciliation, at Viterbo, in the same year, while the people of Rome, momentarily disgusted with the republic, renounced their aims and made peace with the Pope. Unfortunately, Arnold, while doing this penance in Rome, joined forces with the Roman republicans, and the trouble began afresh. It was to last all through the reign of Eugenius III.

Arnold was once more excommunicated in 1148. Several times peace was made and broken. The Pope entered Rome for short periods, then left, again in exile. Arnold's policy was to undergo a certain evolution, which we need not study here. At one point, in his desire to completely despoil the Pope of all temporal power, he sought to put his party entirely at the service of the Emperor, and the advent of Barbarossa might have favored this alliance but for the shrewd diplomacy of Eugenius, whose treaty with Frederick I in 1153 made such an event impossible. Then, turning back to the Roman proletariat, if the term may be used somewhat anachronistically, Arnold hoped to form, with their aid, a sort of republican-Europe that might bear certain analogies to a fascist state. Eugenius did not live to see the final overthrow of this earnest reformer. In all this struggle, Eugenius was fighting his own battle with little more than a few words of encouragement from the Abbot of Clairvaux; nevertheless, it must be remarked that Saint Bernard himself was a truer reformer than Arnold of Brescia, whom he resembles in some respects. The significant difference is that Saint Bernard saw all the abuses that Arnold was fighting and fought them in his turn, but he did not make any of Arnold's mistakes. Also, his influence effected only good, and Arnold's was almost entirely harmful.

The second great enemy Eugenius had to face was heresy, and during the year 1145, at the Pope's command, Saint Bernard made his apostolic journey through the south of France where, although the effect of his own personal sanctity was great, the roots of the heresy itself remained intact, and after Saint Bernard's departure, the evil sprang up again in all its virulence.

The fall of Edessa in 1144 had made a new crusade necessary if the Christian control of the Holy Land was to be maintained. Louis VII of France was probably the chief promoter of the holy war and exercised his influence to get the Pope to command Saint Bernard to preach it. This too was a mighty undertaking. Eugenius was to see its failure and share that burden with Saint Bernard.

In 1147, Eugene, in exile, attended the General Chapter of the Cistercians, not as Pope but taking his rank as an ordinary abbot. All through his pontificate, he had continued to live as a Cistercian, as far as he could. Underneath his pontifical garments were the Cistercian cowl, scapular and robe, and in the Pope's bed chamber, the costly bedclothes concealed a plain straw mattress.

In 1147 and 1148 the Councils of Treves and Rheims brought several important problems before the Pope. In both cases, Saint Bernard was there to dominate the situation, and it was Bernard who settled the difficulty of Gilbert de la Porres's teaching on the Holy Trinity. In all this, the Pope was by no means an idle spectator. Especially in the case of Gilbert, the council was divided between Saint Bernard and the French bishops and theologians on one side and the cardinals on the other, and Eugenius had to act as arbiter in a particularly tense situation. In the end, he not only facilitated the issue by pinning Gilbert down to the crucial point of his doctrine—the question whether he did or did not teach that God's essence was really distinct from His existence—but when Gilbert capitulated under the withering fire of Bernard's zeal, Eugenius handled matters so that the bishop, thanks to his docility, was able to make a graceful retreat.

More amusing was the heresy of Eon de l'Etoile, a Breton nobleman, who, having heard in Church the priest speaking of *eum qui venturus est judicare saeculum per ignem*, interpreted the pronoun *eum* as *Eon* and decided that he must be the Messiah. His case also was settled at Rheims.

Eugenius long cherished the ideal of so many modern popes: to see a reunion with the Greek schismatics, and during his pontificate, a delegation of bishops from Armenia came to consult him at Orvieto, but nothing came of it. The Pope also had many Greek Patristic texts translated into Latin.

To avoid bringing in further small details, which would reduce this article more or less to a catalogue of obscure historical events, we may sum up the pontificate of Eugenius III as one of considerable energy and firmness in the face of multiple grave problems. Eugenius was one of the great medieval Popes, and in an age of extremes, he was among the saints of the Vatican, not their opposites. He was a saint because of his uncompromising honesty and zeal for God and His Church. If, on the other hand, he had the humility to continue to seek advice from his former abbot, and to take it and apply it, he nevertheless showed independence and initiative whenever it was needed and was, in his own right, a diplomatist and statesman of great ability.

But underneath all this was a soul filled with the simplicity and austerity and faith of the first Cistercians. The election of Eugenius may have caused universal surprise in Rome, at Clairvaux, and above all at Tre Fontane, but when he came to die on July 8, 1153, at Tivoli, it was easy to recognize that the Holy Spirit had been at work in his choice and had continued to work through his pontificate.

His memory was held in veneration, even in rebellious Rome, for his simplicity and generosity, and the church of Pisa celebrated his feast centuries before he was finally beatified formally by Pius IX in 1872.

Eugenius has been called one of the greatest and most afflicted of popes, and that by one who was himself a saint: Saint Antonine. Vacandard sums up his pontificate in these positive terms:

> His reforms display a talent bordering on genius. As an administrator he succeeded in putting an end to the abuses that filled the Roman curia with a commercial atmosphere: and under his reign, avarice gradually disappeared from the sacred college. . . . His efforts in the political sphere were no less happily crowned. He put down the Roman revolution almost without the shedding of blood. . . . In the sciences, Eugenius III, far from being behind his times, was ahead of them. . . . At his death, Eugenius bequeathed to his successors the most profound lessons in administrative wisdom; he bequeathed them, besides, something which the abbot of Clairvaux believed to be more important than anything else— the example of his private life, which was, as they used to say in the middle ages: "A mirror of holiness."[5]

July 9

Saint Albert, Lay-brother and Hermit of Saint Andrew of Sestri, near Genoa, Italy

(Source: Cist. Chronik 28, 161 [account based on a ms. life, now at Genoa, by one of his contemporaries].)

Long before the Cistercians came into existence, Saint Benedict himself founded the ancient abbey of Saint Andrew, on what was then an island close to the mountainous shores of Liguria, known

[5] Vacandard 2:505.

as the Italian Riviera. As time went on the island became joined to the mainland, and with the coming of the Cistercians to Italy, Saint Andrew's became the third monastery of the White Monks in that country. Its greatest glory was to be a humble and uninstructed lay-brother, who came to the monastery as a shepherd boy so shy and unused to the ways of civilized men that the brethren almost refused to admit him into the community on the grounds that he was "more like a wild beast than a man."

Indeed, his life in the mountains and forests of Liguria had been most primitive and yet at the same time most holy and pure. Born of poor mountain shepherd-folk, sometime between 1160 and 1170, he had early acquired a deep and fervent devotion to the Mother of God and developed the habit of sanctifying his whole day by saluting her and lifting his heart to her each hour with an *Ave Maria*. And when he was sent out to watch the sheep, he drove them deep into the woods so that he could devote himself, undisturbed and unobserved by men, to prayer which was his only delight. From childhood, too, he began to tame his flesh with fasting and abstinence: and although the diet of a Ligurian peasant is simple enough to seem like an extreme mortification, in itself, to most men, he further curtailed it, living on roots and berries and a few vegetables.

One day when he had come down from the mountains into some primitive village, perhaps to some fair or market, he heard a wandering minstrel singing to the people in the public square the story of a Provençal nobleman, called Theobald, who had left the world and the career of arms and gallantry to become a hermit. This fired his simple heart with the desire to leave all things, his parents and his flocks, and retire into absolute solitude with God alone. And at that very time Providence aided and directed him in his design by sending to the house of his parents a stranger, from whom he learned of a certain hermit living in the mountains. To this holy man he directed his steps and put himself under his care in spiritual matters. But he had not been with him on the wild and isolated mountain for very long before he had a dream that settled his vocation once and for all as a Cistercian. He dreamt he was up in a tree and that an eagle flew down to him, bringing him a certain religious habit he had not seen before, and this dream the hermit, his director, interpreted as a sign that God desired him to enter a monastery. So he left the mountains and went down to the seacoast to the monastery of the White Monks at Sestri, a village that took its name from the fact that it was at the sixth milestone out of Genoa, of which city it is today a flourishing suburb.

The holy Abbot of Saint Andrew's soon saw what great promise of sanctity there was in this pure and primitive soul, and he ignored the objections of some of his monks who considered the poor shepherd's simplicity somewhat excessive. And, indeed, all his life Saint Albert was to be one of those religious upon whom many members of their community tend to look askance because, no matter how hard they try, they are always set apart from the rest by something extraordinary (which estranges them from others). Whose is the fault? There is no fault, really, unless it be on the part of those who consider themselves "normal" refusing to try and understand and make allowances for someone so completely different, by nature and upbringing, as well as by grace, from themselves. This is simply one of those little things that arise in every community, and for which the only remedy is Saint Benedict's *patientissime tolerent!*—let them bear one another's peculiarities with the greatest patience.[6]

But the rash judgments and criticisms of his brethren were always to be an important factor in the sanctification of Saint Albert. For after a fervent novitiate, he was made assistant to the cellarer and thus assumed a charge of considerable importance, materially speaking, in the community. Now there is nothing so sanctifying, for a contemplative soul, as to be thrown unexpectedly into a position requiring a certain amount of active labor and business ability, for which he is completely unsuited in every way. This was the case with Saint Albert. The combination of his mysticism and spirit of evangelical charity, with the charge of that office in the community which most closely affected the stomachs of his confreres— namely, the provisions and the cooking—could not help but produce a situation of rare difficulty, both for him and for the

---

[6] *Infirmitates suas, sive corporum sive morun, patientissime tolerent.* RB 72.5.

community. In the first place, he gave free rein to a reckless generosity to the poor that soon emptied the storerooms of the monastery. At least such was the impression gained by some of the monks, who menaced in that most delicate and sensitive part of the body, the stomach, and fearing to have to fast far more than the Rule prescribed, hastened to the abbot with loud complaints about the new cook. Albert was summoned to the superior's cell. What was the meaning of these reports? Were they true? Were the storerooms indeed empty?

"Well," the brother replied cautiously, "there is a certain foundation of truth in what they say." When the abbot asked him what he meant by "a certain foundation of truth," Albert did not commit himself by a direct reply but merely invited them all to come and inspect the storeroom. The cellars so recently certified to be empty by so many sincere and righteous, if hungry, religious were found to be well stocked and full of provisions.

On another occasion, a great disturbance was aroused in the community when the mystical cook prolonged his thanksgiving after Holy Communion until twelve o'clock. The good brother was roused from the delights of divine union and summoned to the abbot's cell.

"Brother Albert," said the Reverend Father, with more than academic interest, or impersonal curiosity, "what are the monks going to have for dinner today?"

"Come and see," said the holy brother with placid confidence. They arrived in the kitchen in time to see an angel standing over the uncooked food make a sign of the Cross, by which everything was instantly and completely cooked and made ready to be served up to the brethren.

Often, too, Albert was sent out fishing, or went by boat to Genoa, and on one occasion the perfection of his obedience—for he was always perfectly obedient to his abbot and to all the brethren too—received a mark of supernatural approval. The abbot commanded him to leave the boat and go hastily to shore on some special errand, and he spread his cloak on the water, glided rapidly over the waves and reached land in a moment of time. Once, too, he left his sack of bread in the house of a poor sailor, whose hunger got the better of his virtue, so that he emptied the sack of all its loaves and substituted stones for them. Albert came and got the sack, and was almost immediately approached by a beggar, asking for an alms. He reached into the sack and pulled out a fine loaf of bread, which he presented to the poor man.

In 1211, with the permission and approval of Abbot Lambert, Saint Albert was allowed to retire to a cave in the mountains to live as a hermit, but that did not sever him from the monastic life altogether. On the contrary, he remained under obedience to the abbot and came to the monastery on Sundays and feast days for the Offices and Mass. In other words, he was in much the same position as any lay-brother stationed at a grange outside the enclosure of the community itself. In this solitude he spent twenty-eight years and reached the highest sanctity. Nor was his life easy by any means: he was often cut off from the monastery by snow or storms and several times was in grave danger of death from starvation, but his faith and confidence in the Mother of God delivered him from all his difficulties. Indeed, once she appeared to him in a dream when he was dying of hunger, and taking from a golden chalice a morsel of food, she placed it in his mouth, and thereafter he felt no more need or desire of food until relief came from the valley below. His great sanctity and purity of life drew all the peasants of the mountain region to him for help in their trials, and he was once asked to intervene against the plague of foxes that were devastating all the barnyards for miles around. Saint Albert went to the edge of the forest and in a loud, clear voice delivered an imprecation against the foxes, which from that time on ceased to raid the chicken coops of those peasants altogether.

But there were more than foxes in the mountain forest. Once a wolf came down into one of the villages and, snatching up a child in his jaws, was running off to the woods with his prey when he was stopped by the holy hermit, who commanded him in the Name of Jesus Christ to let the child go. The wolf obeyed and went back to the woods.

Above all, we can see what was God's purpose in drawing this holy man, like so many others of his time, into complete solitude in the fact that hundreds of sinners came to him for advice and consolation, and his influence, example, words and prayers did a tremendous amount of good. Nor must we ever forget what a great spiritual power our holy lay-brothers exercised upon souls in the Middle Ages, not merely indirectly but directly and by immediate contact. We have only to consider some of the saintly lay-brothers of our Belgian monasteries, like Blessed Simon of Aulne, who was called to Rome and consulted by the Pope himself [Innocent III]. But, curiously enough, one of the many sinners that came to see Saint Albert was the very same minstrel who, years before, had sung the romantic tale of Theobald, the nobleman who became a hermit—the story that had induced the saint to leave the world. And now Saint Albert himself brought about the conversion of this wandering singer.

Saint Albert finally died in 1239 and was buried in the cave where he had lived. It immediately became a shrine and a place of pilgrimage, and even today, the feast of Saint Albert is the biggest day of the year in Sestri. It is celebrated as a Double of the First Class with octave in the diocese of Genoa, and on that day, enthusiastic crowds of peasants in their picturesque traditional costumes flock to Sestri for a day of festivities in which natural and supernatural rejoicing are harmoniously blended in a manner that is gradually being forgotten in a materialistic and pagan world. Saint Albert was formally beatified with the title of "saint" by Pope Innocent IV in 1244 and is, curiously enough, the only Cistercian lay-brother to enjoy this title.

His feast is celebrated by one of the smaller Cistercian congregations but is absent from the Breviary of the Strict Observance. It is greatly to be desired that such a gap in our liturgy should be filled: for after all, the Cistercian Order is the one in which the lay-brothers and choir religious live together on the greatest plane of equality and familiarity and it is odd that at least one lay-brother of our great family should not join his brethren of the choir in the liturgy. Meanwhile, let us not hesitate to add our prayers to those of generations of pious and fervent souls who have made him the patron of those sunny and flowering shores of northern Italy.

July 16

Saint Stephen Harding, Third Abbot of Cîteaux, Founder of the Cistercian Order

(Sources: EP; *Consuetudines I*; *Charta Charitatis*, etc., by Saint Stephen himself, see *Nomasticon Cisterciense*, or Philippe Guignard, *Monuments Primitifs de la règle Cistercienne* [Dijon: Darantiere, 1878]. Also PL 166; EM; William of Malmesbury, *De Gestis Regum Anglorum*, bk. 4 [PL 179:1278]; AASS, April 2:493; Dalgairns; Coll [*passim*]; Manrique, vol. 1.)

Manrique, the annalist of the Cistercians, drew an ingenious analogy between the first three fathers of the Order and the Three Persons of the Holy Trinity.[7] Saint Robert was the Source and Father of the Cistercian ideal; Saint Alberic suffered that it might live; Saint Stephen possessed the energy and charity and, indeed, the consummate genius necessary to put this ideal into practice in the foundation of one of the great contemplative Orders in the Church. This work of diffusion more than corresponded, in a vague analogy, to the work of the Holy Spirit. It was the actual work of the Spirit of God in and through Stephen. It is certainly no fiction to say that the Spirit of Love lived and worked in the soul of this great saint with a special directness and intensity. We have several extremely important documents from his hand which express his genius, every line of which breathes a spirit of apostolic and contemplative charity which reminds one of the early Church by its stress on the basic concept of mystical oneness in Christ. Not that Stephen's writings are those of a speculative mystic, like Saint Bernard, far from it. They were all practical, but then, love is practical, and mysticism is nothing but love. The spirituality of Saint Stephen, then, is the mysticism of love in action, love sacrificing itself for others (instead of talking and rhapsodizing about sacrifice), love working to bring others into unity, and above all, love

---

[7] Manrique, vol. 1, p. 6.

that breaks silence only to talk of deeds, not to talk about itself, about love in the abstract, with a capital "L."

That is why Saint Stephen, when he does take his pen in hand, writes about the Rule and how to keep it in its letter and in its spirit. To him, loving Christ meant doing Christ's will, and Christ's will, for Benedictine contemplatives, is the Rule of Saint Benedict. God's will for Saint Stephen and his companions in the twelfth century was the reestablishment of an integrally monastic life in the Church by means of the strict observance of the Rule of Saint Benedict. The Cistercians were not alone. The Spirit of God was working in that age, with an especial intensity in the eleventh and twelfth centuries, to enkindle strong flames of contemplative love and prayer and penance. The Camaldolese, the Vallombrosans, the Carthusians, the Orders of Grandmont, and the Congregations of Tiron and Savigny[8] were all to spring up in those days, along with the Cistercians. All of them had ideals of great loftiness and purity; none of them was to achieve such a widespread diffusion and to influence so many souls, and indeed have such a mighty effect on the course of Christian and even political history, as the Cistercians. All that was, of course, largely due to the magnetic influence of Saint Bernard of Clairvaux; but insofar as Saint Bernard was a propagator of the Order and a founder of Cistercian monasteries, he was only building on the firm foundation laid down by the saint who had formed and trained him for the Cistercian life: Stephen Harding, the third Abbot of Cîteaux.

Saint Stephen was, it is said, the child of noble parents in southern England. Whether or not that is true, we know that he went as a child to be educated at the priory of Sherborne, in Dorset.[9] He is supposed to have been born about ten years before the Norman Conquest (that is, about 1056), and it is said that he left England after an insurrection against the Conquerors. He passed to Scotland,

---

[8] The Savigny congregation came over *en bloc* to the Cistercian Order in 1147.

[9] Sherborne did not become an abbey until 1122. At the present day it is a boys' school.

or perhaps to Ireland, to continue his studies.[10] Fr. Dalgairns, in his English life of the saint,[11] infers that Saint Stephen was already disgusted with Benedictine life as he had seen it at Sherborne and had given up the thought of his vocation. In any event, we next find him attending the schools of Paris and there, according to William of Malmesbury, he did definitely receive a vocation to devote himself in some way more closely more perfectly to God,[12] *Divini amoris stimulos accepit*.[13] The vocation was not clear or well defined: it was just an urge, a persistent inward ache, a striving after something which he could not quite define. All in all, it can be summed up as a strong awareness that he was not in the place God had destined for him. Leaving Paris, he started visiting the shrines of various saints in the lands of Champagne and Burgundy, and there he made friends with another devout traveler like himself. The two decided to go together on a pilgrimage to Rome. Saint Stephen and his friend Peter, afterwards also venerated as a saint under the nickname of Saint Pron (a corruption of Peter), undertook this arduous journey, maintaining silence all the way except for the daily recitation of the psalter, from which no difficulty involved by their travels could dissuade them. The detail about their absolute silence may perhaps be an exaggeration, but the daily psalter, which has little of the extraordinary about it in any case, is vouched for in early documents, particularly in the contemporary life of Saint Pron by a Cistercian monk.[14]

Returning from Rome to Burgundy, Stephen and Pron stopped at the recently founded monastery of Molesme, of which we have reason to believe that they had probably heard before, since the monastery rapidly became famous in Burgundy. However, their

[10] Luddy, 19, says that "Scotia" meant Ireland as well as Scotland. See the *Kalendarium* (Martyrology) of the primitive Cistercians; see Guinard, 325; XVI Kal. Aprilis: *In Sancti Patricii episcopi* announces the feast of Saint Patrick by recalling his death "in Scotia."

[11] Dalgairns, 7.

[12] William of Malmesbury, *De Gestis Regum Anglorum*; PL 179:1287.

[13] PL 185:1257–70.

[14] PL 185:1257–70.

discovery of Saint Robert and his fervent community is sometimes represented as having been a complete surprise and almost an accident. Whatever may have been the actual fact, they both joined the community and found in it the peace that they had so long sought—at least they found that peace for a time. Manrique incidentally relates, without any foundation, that Saint Stephen's friend (he did not know Saint Pron's name or history) had tried to dissuade him from entering the monastery and had become estranged from him when he disregarded this advice.[15] Manrique was plainly unacquainted with the facts related in the life of Saint Pron discovered since his time.

It is difficult to say at precisely what stage in the development of Molesme Saint Stephen joined the community. The life of Saint Pron tells us that Pron spent part of his novitiate in a priory, depending on Molesme. In that case, Molesme had already traveled far on the road to prosperity by the time he entered. On the other hand, the usual opinion is that Saint Stephen became a member of the community during the purity of its first fervor, that is, shortly after the removal from Colan, which took place in 1075.

Eventually, of course, the monastery became filled with converted knights, men of sincere but conventional piety, who knew nothing but the usages of Cluny and were not prepared to accept anything that conflicted with this familiar standard Molesme, from a fervent community of penitential and contemplative monks, fell to the level of an ordinary Cluniac monastery.

William of Malmesbury, who is the best contemporary authority for information about Saint Stephen Harding, represents him as the first mover of the reform at Molesme. He it was who initiated and dominated the conversations in which the fervent minority in that community complained to one another that the Rule which was read every day in chapter was not being kept in their daily life. It was Saint Stephen who, together with Alberic, placed the matter before Saint Robert.

---

[15] PL 185:1261.

Saint Stephen, according to William of Malmesbury,[16] modestly but firmly advanced a series of arguments that attacked the very essence of the Cluniac usages by denying that they were a valid interpretation of the mind of Saint Benedict, and indeed all the early documents concur in affirming that the reformers at Molesme considered that the Cluniac usages had so distorted the letter and spirit of the Rule that it *was impossible to follow them and be a true Benedictine.* In other words, to keep the Cluniac usages was to violate at least the spirit of the Rule of Saint Benedict. Saint Stephen was, of course, a prominent member of the delegation that accompanied Saint Robert to Hugh, the Legate of the Holy See in 1097, and obtained official approval to leave Molesme and start a new foundation, on the grounds that it was impossible to initiate a successful reform at Molesme.

The arrival of the monks at Cîteaux and the nature of the new site, in the marshy woods belonging to the Viscount of Beaune, have been sufficiently described in the lives of Saints Robert and Alberic (April 29 and January 26). Stephen Harding was made subprior of the new community, Alberic was prior, and the first abbot was, of course, Saint Robert, the director whose reputation and influence had attracted them to the religious life in the first place.

After the departure of Saint Robert, forced by obedience to the Holy See to Molesme, which had fallen into a state of turmoil in his absence, Saint Stephen became prior under Saint Alberic, and we have every reason to believe that it was during his priorate that Saint Stephen was also concerned with problems of liturgy and monastic customs which he finally settled once and for all in his masterly *Consuetudines.*[17] The fact that 1109, the date of his election as abbot, in succession to Saint Alberic, is also the date of his edition of the Bible means that Saint Stephen had spent much of his time as prior on this work of revision and correction of the Scripture text, for details of which we refer the reader to the *Compendium*

---

[16] PL 179:1287.
[17] PL 166.

of the History of the Cistercian Order (p. 59). We need only remark that this work of revision and correction, which has been praised as one of the most masterly pieces of biblical scholarship of the Middle Ages, is an interesting revelation of Saint Stephen's spirituality. It indicates his concern to have his monks study and meditate on Holy Scripture in its authentic and purest possible text and proves that Saint Stephen was the enemy of vagueness and carelessness in spiritual things. Although scholarship as such was foreign to the Cistercian ideal, Saint Stephen did not hesitate to throw himself into this exceedingly intellectual task when there was question of the spiritual formation of his monks.

The zeal that prompted Saint Stephen's revision of the Vulgate text is not unrelated to another reform for which he is far more famous: his extreme simplification of the Liturgy and of Ecclesiastical architecture.[18] But here again, the same burning desire for solidity and truth in spiritual things was expressing itself. And, in the first place, we must realize that all the monastic reforms of the time were tending in the same direction. Saint Stephen was by no means alone in his liturgical revolution: but of all the reformers he was the most uncompromising and the most drastically complete.

A few words will suffice to give an idea of the extent of his revolution. We have but to glance at the basilica of Cluny with its bas-relief, its statues, stained glass, mosaics, marqueterie: huge chandeliers of gold and crystal hang from the ceiling. The altar is covered with splendid cloths, and the vessels of the altar are pure gold, studded with precious jewels. The vestments of the ministers are heavy with cloth of gold or shimmering with silk and velvet. Jewels flash on mitre and crozier-crook. Organs and other musical instruments accompany the choir, and the monks are vested in splendor on all great feasts. All this luxury represents immense expenditure. Of course, the monks believed it was all for the glory of God. Did not all these things raise the heart up to God? Even if

---

[18] Anselm Dimier, "Saint Etienne Harding et ses idees sur l'art," Coll 4 (1927): 178–92.

the answer to such a question were necessarily true, there was one consideration of far greater importance. How many men dedicated to God were feasting their eyes on this worldly gorgeousness, under the pretext that it helped them pray, and yet were blind to the ragged and starving beggars at the door of the Basilica and to the blackened and bowed serfs in the fields, broken by penury and oppression. Oh, it is true, Cluny did much for the poor, but for Saint Bernard, as long as there was one man starving, there could be no excuse for throwing away money on jewels and gold for the altar of God, for such gifts would never please the Lord Who came on earth and died that we might learn charity.[19]

What a contrast to all this, then, was the Cistercian church. The walls were bare of all sculpture and painting and mosaic. For two centuries the General Chapter was to fulminate dire penances against abbots who had allowed themselves to be persuaded to accept gifts of stained glass windows in churches of the Order. So far from being decorated with carpets or tapestries or even with flowers, the sanctuary was completely bare. Indeed, the altar itself, outside of the time of Mass, presented the aspect which it now has only on Good Friday. It was stripped bare. There was nothing on it but a Crucifix. On each side of the altar stood two large candlesticks of iron or wood, high enough so that the candles reached about to the level of the feet of the figure of Christ on the Crucifix, but the candlesticks themselves, it must be noted, stood not on the altar but on the floor of the sanctuary, to either side of it. In the sanctuary there was also a *piscina* or basin needed for emptying vessels used in the liturgical functions, like the lavabo basin, for instance. Beside the credence, there was also an *armarium* or cupboard where the chalice and various books and other things necessary for the Mass were kept. There was no tabernacle on the altar, but at least by the thirteenth century the custom prevailed in Cistercian churches of reserving the Sacred Host in a ciborium suspended within a golden dove that hung from the ceiling of the church directly over the altar.[20]

[19] Bernard, Apo 12.
[20] See Fulgence Schneider, *L'Ancienne Messe cistercienne* (Koningshoeven, 1929), vii, 264.

What was the reason for such strictness? Why did the Cistercians have to go to the extreme of having plain linen vestments, all the same color, and without decoration? Why this exaggerated simplicity? Saint Stephen would have answered in the first place that contemplative monks should not need pictures and statues to lift up their hearts to God, much less stained glass windows and circusy decorated vestments and gorgeous altar vessels. These things might be helpful for people living among the distractions of the world, but to monks, living in habitual recollection, they were more likely to cause distraction and keep the mind wandering away from God in a mass of trivial and curious details. On the other hand, it is a matter of experience that the simplicity of the early Cistercian churches which still survive is of a kind to raise the heart to God with singular effectiveness by virtue of the very absence of details and curiosities.

The reason is that the harmony and interrelation of simple masses of masonry disposed in the most perfect architectural balance presents to the eye a far more spiritual beauty than the accumulation of colors and the display of jewelry which must often have spent itself in something verging on vulgarity. The early Cistercians, however, did not enter into speculations on these things. Their chief motives were poverty and simplicity. They were trying to keep the Rule and the Gospel to the letter, and that was all.

As soon as he was elected abbot, Saint Stephen began to show himself to be an even stricter and more uncompromising reformer than Saint Alberic, although that holy abbot had never been a lover of compromises by any means. However, Saint Alberic seems to have raised no objection when Duke Odo of Burgundy, one of the first and greatest benefactors of the New Monastery, desired to come and hold his court there. On the other hand, when Hugh, who succeeded Odo as Duke after his father died on his way to the Holy Land on a Crusade, announced his intention of coming to the Monastery and holding his court there, Saint Stephen politely informed him that he would not be welcome. It is generally thought that this was taken by the Duke as an insult and that it resulted in the withdrawing of his support from the monastery. We do know, as a matter of fact, that under Saint Stephen Cîteaux went through the most crucial trial since its foundation. God evidently wanted to prove this great saint and his companions in the crucible of real hardship and to set the seal of His approval upon the Order; for there is no surer sign that a good enterprise is willed by God than the fact that it meets with opposition and difficulties, in spite of all the goodwill and prayers of those who undertake them.

Saint Stephen's faith was quite equal to the test of poverty. An old story tells how one day, when there was no food in the monastery, and no money either, the abbot gave a monk three pennies and told him to take them and go to Vézelay and spend them in purchasing three wagonloads of food.[21] When the monk asked how he was expected to drive so hard a bargain as this, Saint Stephen told him to trust in God. The monk went to the market with his three pennies, but he did not even have to spend them, for he met a man who, learning of the plight of the monks, introduced him to a dying man of some means who, on his very deathbed, was glad to assure his salvation by an act of charity and changed his will to make the monks of Cîteaux his beneficiaries.

Poverty and the direst need of his monks could never be for Saint Stephen a reason for compromise with his moral principles. Once when a brother who had been sent out to beg for food in a moment of extreme necessity returned with two mule-loads of provisions, Saint Stephen sent them back where they came from, with all their load intact, as soon as he learned they were the gift of a priest who had gained his position by simony.

The early Cistercians, however, were filled with the gift of fortitude, and their hardships were to them a source of sweeter consolation than they had ever known before. One Pentecost Sunday at Cîteaux the monks sang in choir with transports of joy that were all the more intense because of the fact that they knew there was nothing in the house to eat and that there would be no dinner and that, what is more, nobody cared. The Bread of angels was all they desired. For the rest, the Holy Ghost would take care of them. And He did. When they came out of their simple wooden church, they found that a benefactor had brought ample supplies to the monastery gate.

[21] EM 1.22.

Cassian says that if we want to have our minds clear and free from distractions when we are at prayer, we must get the habit of controlling our thoughts and imagination outside the time of prayer and emptying our minds before we ever start to pray.[22] Otherwise, the very struggle with distractions will itself be an insupportable distraction. Saint Stephen is famous for a little gesture he had acquired to remind himself of this on entering the church. At night, when going from the cloister, after the communal reading into choir for Compline, he used to touch the doorpost with his hand, and when someone asked him why, he said it was in order to leave all his worries and cares at the door of the church.

As years passed, Cîteaux had lost several of its monks. Lenain calculates that some seventeen or eighteen had died since the first foundation, and if that is the case, by the year 1112 there would only have been three or four left.[23] But in any case, the almost universal criticism and calumny directed against the reformers of Cîteaux had made the New Monastery so unattractive to postulants that they stayed far from the door. Eventually even the strong convictions of Saint Stephen Harding were a little shaken by this state of affairs. After all, he was faced with the fact that his critics were not merely the malcontents of Molesme. Many holy and prudent and altogether estimable men were of the opinion that the Cistercian reform could not be the will of God since it was so far beyond the strength of ordinary men. Was it, indeed, an exaggeration? Had the devil taken advantage of his inborn fervor and idealism to lead him into a trap? The fact that no vocations came to the monastery gave Saint Stephen a very cogent reason for believing that God did not favor the reform. He might well have allowed criticism and poverty to continue, but if the New Monastery was His will, surely He would provide for its survival by choosing souls to come and lead this austere life of prayer and penance.

Eventually, another of the monks fell sick and came to die. Saint Stephen approached this brother, as he lay on his deathbed, and in simple faith asked him, in the name of Christ and in virtue of

---

[22] *Quales orantes volumus inveniri, tales nos ante orationis tempus preparare debemus*, Cassian, Conf 9.3.

[23] Lenain, *Essai de l'Histoire de L'Ordre de Cîteaux 1* (Paris, 1696).

holy obedience to make known to him, after his death, if their manner of life was pleasing to God. The brother, with equal simplicity, promised to do this if Saint Stephen would help him with his prayers. A few days after the monk's death, Saint Stephen was at work with his monks and gave the signal for the customary rest period. Then withdrawing a little from the others, and recollecting his thoughts, he renewed his conscious communion with God. Suddenly the monk who had just died appeared before him in a blaze of glory and revealed to his father abbot that the Cistercian life was indeed pleasing to God and was His will. For his own soul was now in the bliss of heaven as a reward for his sacrifices and labors and prayers at Cîteaux, and presently God would give a more tangible confirmation of His approval by sending them many vocations. Thus it was that in the fifteenth year after the foundation of Cîteaux, the future Saint Bernard presented himself at the abbey's wooden gate with his thirty companions. The lean years were ended. From now on God's favor shone upon the new foundation in all things, material as well as spiritual.

Perhaps the conversion of the son of one of his closest friends, Tescelin of Fontaines, did something to pacify the insulted Duke Hugh of Burgundy. But at any rate, within a short time, Cîteaux was not only firmly established in its own right but was able to make its first foundation: La Ferté. The Church of La Ferté was consecrated in 1113. In 1114 Pontigny was founded in a wide fertile valley in the vicinity of Auxerre. In 1115 Saint Bernard was sent to found Clairvaux while Morimond, the fourth of the original abbeys that were to serve as the basis of the Order, came into being in the same year.

Having consulted the superiors of these four houses, Saint Stephen drew up the famous document known as the *Charter of Charity*.[24] Here in a few pages of powerful and concise thought, the great abbot laid down the basic lines along which the Cistercian Order was to develop, and the very first thing he had to say was that the monasteries issuing from Cîteaux and depending

[24] PL 166:1177.

upon it in all spiritual things must be bound together not merely by social ties of material expediency but by supernatural charity. The object of their union is not merely the material well being of all the individual communities—still less must the Order be allowed to degenerate into a system by which the archabbey carried on the economic exploitation of a large territory through its subsidiary houses. On the contrary, if they are to be welded together in an Order it is always with a view to their own ultimate end in life, union with God, contemplation in this world, the life of glory in the next. But what is the principal means God has given them for attaining this twofold end? The Rule of Saint Benedict.

What is the connection of the *Charter of Charity* with the Rule of Saint Benedict? Is it something added to the Rule? No, it is simply a practical application of the Rule to a particular group of religious communities formed into an Order. It is a manifesto, declaring that all the houses of this Order shall interpret the Rule in the same sense as Cîteaux, that all shall make use of the Usages and Customs of Cîteaux and the same liturgical books. Nowhere in this document do we find a trace of belligerent assertion that the Cistercians have the best or most literal interpretation of the Rule. Saint Stephen is not concerned with comparisons with Molesme or Cluny: he is not trying to outshine monastic competitors. His purpose, in issuing such a manifesto, is to guarantee the preservation of that peace and harmony and concord without which the contemplative life is absolutely impossible. He foresees that problems and questions concerning the Rule must necessarily arise, and he is intent on providing a means for settling them without unnecessary dispute and of protecting the literal observance of the Rule against mitigations on one hand and eccentric severities on the other. In other words, the *Charter of Charity* set out to protect and foster the pure contemplative life in our Order first by insuring true peace between all its members, second by guaranteeing that the Rule, the means for arriving at contemplation given by God to this particular group of monks, should be maintained in all its purity.

Apart from this spiritual interdependence, the houses of the Order were to maintain their autonomy, especially in the economic and material sphere. There would never be a question of the motherhouse living on the work of the monks of a filiated community, except, of course, in case of some emergency. Legislation provided that all the houses should contribute to the aid of any one community that fell into grave economic difficulties. But Saint Stephen set up a simple and powerful machinery to protect the observance of the Rule and Usages in these houses—a system which worked admirably well for several centuries: indeed, the surest proof of the efficacy of this system is the fact that its neglect was one of the chief reasons for the decline of the Order. The supreme authority in the Order was not the Abbot of Cîteaux but the General Chapter, whose members were the superiors of all the monasteries in the Order and which met annually at Cîteaux on the Feast of the Exultation of the Holy Cross. The chief business of the General Chapter was to pass legislation clarifying questions of regular observance, but above all to correct all deviations from the Rule and Usages in the various houses of the Order and punish the offenders. The General Chapter was even empowered to excommunicate the Abbot of Cîteaux and his whole community if the need should arise. The General Chapter, however, would never have been able to function properly without the assistance of the regular annual visitations prescribed for each house, to be carried out either by the Abbot of Cîteaux or by the Father Immediate of the various communities, that is, by the abbots of their motherhouses. It was on the findings of the Visitors that the General Chapter based its decisions and legislation.

With the phenomenal spread of the Cistercian Order in the first half of the twelfth century (fifty-one new houses were acquired by the Order in 1147, and at the death of Saint Bernard in 1153, there were three hundred forty-three abbeys in the Order, spread all over Europe from Norway to Spain and from France to Hungary and even Palestine), it would have seemed to be difficult to carry on this system of visitations with the regularity desired. On the contrary, however, a glance at the statutes of the General Chapter for the twelfth and thirteenth centuries will show, by the details of the penances and corrections imposed upon abbots even of the most remote houses—and especially of such houses—that the visitations were being carried out in perfect order and with all their desired effects. The records of Cistercian houses in England and Wales, for example, show ample evidence of visitatorial activity in the deposition of abbots by visitors. Wales, being a remote and rather savage land, possessed a group of Cistercian monasteries largely recruited among the Welsh mountaineers, and these houses, by reason of their isolation and of the peculiarity of their inmates, were a thorn in the side of the General Chapter. But we would not even know this if these monasteries had not been constantly and regularly visited and if the troubles in them had not been brought before the Chapter and summarily corrected by severe measures.[25] In the year 1188 we even read of a descent of special visitors upon England sent by the General Chapter. And when John, abbot of Fountains, failed to make a visitation of his foundation of Kysakloster in Norway, he was severely penanced by the General Chapter, although he had every excuse for omitting the visit because of the political difficulties which had led to the suppression of his own monastery by King John Lackland.[26]

The same arguments have been raised to suggest that attendance at the General Chapter was neglected by many abbots, or was, indeed, impossible. Not in the Golden Age of the Order. Abbots who failed to attend the General Chapter received severe penances, and most of them were so eager to be present at Cîteaux on the Feast of the Exaltation of the Holy Cross that we occasionally read of superiors undertaking long hard journeys in spite of bad health, and even dying on the way to or from the Chapter.

It was also under the direct supervision of Saint Stephen that the book of Usages or *Consuetudines* was compiled between the years 1120 and 1125. The chief concern of the Usages is to ensure the perfection of the choral services and of the liturgical functions in the sanctuary, and it is these that occupy most space in the volume. In many situations where the Rule has nothing definite to prescribe, such as details of posture in choir during Office and Conventual Mass, the Cistercian Usages follow the Usages of Cluny, which, in these matters, are very similar to the other sets

---

[25] David Knowles, *The Monastic Order in England 638–1658* (Cambridge: University Press, 1940).

[26] See Knowles.

of monastic usages known in the early Middle Ages. However, in all the important features of the monastic life, especially in the celebration of Holy Mass and in the distribution of activities throughout the day, the Cistercian Usages represent a drastic simplification of all that Cluny practiced and admired. Liturgically, the Cistercians continued to base themselves on the Gallican Rite, especially that of the Church of Lyons, but their rites were immensely simplified and purged of superfluities as compared with the practices of Cluny. But the biggest difference between the Usages of Cîteaux and those of Cluny are those which concern manual labor, silence, fasting, abstinence, and monastic poverty.

In 1133 Saint Stephen, being about eighty years old and having completed his work, resigned his abbatial office at Cîteaux in order to spend his last days in preparation for eternity completely occupied with God alone. His brother abbots very unwillingly acceded to his request and elected a successor, a learned and seemingly able man, Abbot Guy of Trois Fontaines. For some reason, God allowed their choice to fall on an evil subject, and Guy had to be deposed almost at once. The cause has been so jealously kept hidden by the fathers of the Order that no one has ever managed to discover what it was, but Guy's name is obliterated from the list of abbots of Cîteaux.

Raynard, one of the great legislators of early Cîteaux, followed him in office, but Saint Stephen did not live to see the fruits of this able and holy abbot's labors. The patriarch of Cîteaux died on March 28 in great peace and quietness. Practically his last word was a gentle reproof of some monks who thought he was unconscious and declared by his bedside that he was a saint.

The Order was long in recognizing this sanctity officially. Apart from the wave of enthusiasm that swept all the Cistercian houses and led to the canonization of Saint Bernard, we find that our fathers in the first two centuries of the Order's history showed themselves singularly unwilling to undertake causes of canonization even for the honor of our holy founders. Saint Robert was raised to the honors of the altar largely through the efforts of Molesme, and other canonized Cistercian saints achieved this distinction in the Middle Ages only because of the work of seculars in promoting their causes. However, Saint Stephen was finally officially numbered among the saints in 1584, and in 1625 the General Chapter gave him a feast of twelve lessons. At present [c. 1954] he enjoys a feast of the highest rank in the Order, that of Sermon Major with Octave, celebrated on July 16, given by Baronius as the date of his canonization.[27]

July 16

Blessed Alan of Lille, The Universal Doctor, Lay-brother of Cîteaux [#2]

(Sources: *Opera*, PL 210, preceded by biographical studies, etc., by Oudin and De Visch; Jean-Marie Canivez, "Alain de Lille," *Dictionnaire de Spiritualite*, vol. 1.)

It is no inconsiderable paradox that one of the famous men of his time should have left us not one single reliable detail about his life. His retirement from the university world, where he had made a great name for himself as a popularizer and a kind of medieval encyclopedist, to the Abbey of Cîteaux, where he died as a lay-brother, has been called into question. And this should not be surprising, because in the account of his life given as a preface to his works, which fill an entire volume of Migne's Patrology, Alan of Lille is confused with the monk of Clairvaux, Alan of Flanders, and the dates and facts of the latter's life are dragged in to complicate the whole problem beyond measure. Alan of Flanders was also borne at Lille and also became a Cistercian, and he lived somewhere about the same time, but there the resemblance ends. Alan of Flanders ended his life as a bishop, and there is no difficulty in proving that he was a Cistercian.[28]

---

[27] [Today Saints Robert, Alberic, and Stephen are celebrated together as Founders of Cîteaux on January 26. —Ed.]

[28] PL 210.

What might appear to be at first sight the strongest proof of Alan of Lille's status as a member of the Order is the fact that his tomb occupied a very prominent place in the abbatial church of Cîteaux until it was destroyed in the French Revolution.[29] It bore a figure of the great doctor who was depicted in the habit of a Cistercian lay-brother, bearded and holding a rosary in his hand, and an inscription declared that he knew everything there was to know—*totum scribile scivit*—and died in 1294. Unfortunately, this tomb was erected over Alan's bones several hundred years after his death by the Abbot Jean de Cirey, and it is impossible to confirm the date which it bears, since by all accounts Alan flourished at the end of the twelfth century rather than by the thirteenth. A glance at his works, in any case, will confirm this. There is scarcely a trace of scholastic method in his writings. They are more or less collections of allegorical glosses on Scripture and Theology after the manner of the pre-scholastic ages. In any case, the accepted date of his birth now seems to be 1115, so that if he died in 1294 he would have been one hundred seventy-nine years old. Our lay-brothers frequently live to a grand old age, but none of them have as yet gone much beyond a hundred.

Even then, Henriques, undaunted by the difficulty of dates, managed to effect a compromise between various alternatives offered him and ended up by asserting that Alan of Lille died in 1294 at the age of one hundred sixteen.

Without entering into the intricacies of the problem, since we do not have the necessary documents at hand to settle it ourselves, we can only quote the two best living authorities on the subject, both of whom agree that Alan of Lille died as a Cistercian lay-brother, although they do not concur as to the exact date. The New Menology says he died on July 16, 1202, and Fr. Jean-Marie Canivez, OCR, writing in the *Dictionnaire de Spiritualite*, gives the date as 1202 or 1203.[30]

[29] Edmond Martène, *Voyage Litteraire de deux Benedictine de la Congregation de Saint Maur*, 2 vols. (Paris: Delaulne, 1717), 1:214.

[30] Jean-Marie Canivez, OCR, Alain of Lille, *Dictionnaire de Spiritualite*, vol. i. 270.

This entitles us to consider the question closed and to accept Alan of Lille definitely as a convert from the university world to the humble life of a lay-brother. But that does not mean that we must swallow the legend of how his conversion took place, nor the even stranger one of his fabulous journey to Rome.

The story of Alan's conversion would not be unlikely if it had not been related to many other saints before him—especially of Saint Augustine. Alan was supposed to have been walking on the banks of the Seine one day, meditating on a great lecture in which he would make the mystery of the Trinity quite plain to the minds of a vast audience. The project, at least, sounds like Alan. He was definitely a popularizer, and the subject was just the sort of thing to attract him. However, as he walked up and down meditating on his topic, he observed a little boy playing by the bank with a toy spade. He had dug a little hole and was scooping the water of the river into the hole. And as fast as he scooped, the water sank into the sand, and the hole would never fill. Alan asked him what he was trying to do: did he want to get the whole river into that little hole he had dug?

The child looked up and answered him: "That would be just about as sensible as what you are going to attempt tomorrow morning with your idea of making everybody understand the Blessed Trinity."

Alan was so shaken by this incident that he could not deliver his lecture at all, and a few days later he disappeared, never to return again to the world of learning. The "Universal Doctor," the famous theologian, preacher, naturalist and poet, had gone to seek peace in the obscure and humble life of a Cistercian lay-brother.

Tradition has it that he was a shepherd, and legend adds that he accompanied the Abbot General of the Order to Rome, but this part of his story has all the earmarks of a good daydream. Alan is supposed to have entered Cîteaux incognito, and so far no one had discovered who he was. Having accompanied the Abbot General to Rome, he had dismounted at the door of the hall where a great disputation was to be held against "some heretics" in the presence of the Pope no less! Suddenly overcome by curiosity—or prompted by the Holy Spirit, perhaps—Alan "borrowed" the gown of a Doctor and put it on over his lay-brother's habit against the feeble protests of the Abbot General, whom he accompanied into the hall. Then the debate began and proceeded according to form, until it began to be apparent that the "heretics," whomever they were, were winning the argument. Then suddenly Alan stood up and cried, "*Jube Domine Benedicere!*" He was asking permission to speak. The horrified Abbot of Cîteaux tried ineffectually to get him to be quiet and sit down, but it was too late: the Holy Father had already given his permission to speak. Needless to say, Alan's defense of the truths of the faith was brilliant, astounding, magnificent! Finally, one of the heretics, reduced to a state of helpless confusion, cried out: "Either you are the devil or you are Alan!"

"I am not the devil," replied the "Universal Doctor," "but I *am* Alan."

It all sounds like the evening meditation of a tepid religious on a particularly dull day.

The conclusion of that part of the legend is typical. Alan returned to Cîteaux, where instead of looking after the sheep he now had two clerics working for him as secretaries, taking down his dictation as he composed his monumental works.

Having presented this fable for what it is worth, we may proceed to a brief consideration of the works of Alan of Lille. It need be no more than brief, because it is almost certain that none of them were composed at Cîteaux, and few of them have much to offer that really belongs to the tradition of Cistercian spirituality. When the General Chapter had just issued statutes to restrict the writing of books and of poems, even by choir monks, it is not at all likely that a lay-brother should be encouraged to compose a long didactic poem of several thousand lines like the *Anticlaudianus* of Alan of Lille. Lay-brothers in those days were not even allowed to read books, and in fact they were not even allowed to learn to read at all.

The most valuable work of his from the point of view of the spiritual life is his commentary on the Canticle of Canticles. The whole *Elucidatio* is in praise of Our Lady and reflects not only a fervent devotion to her but a deep interior spirit and a clear-sighted penetration into the glories of Mary, who is here considered among other things as the model of contemplatives. The most important thing about this commentary is that Alan did not hesitate to proclaim the doctrine of the Immaculate Conception, and indeed his name was called into court, when the dogma was defined in the nineteenth century, as one of its defenders in the Middle Ages.

His treatise on the "Six Wings of the Cherubim" was naturally confused with Saint Bonaventure's tract *De sex alis seraphim*, but the authorship is clearly conceded to Alan of Lille. The two tracts bear only a superficial resemblance to one another: Alan's is concerned with the interior life and Saint Bonaventure's with the virtues of prelates and religious superiors.

Besides his sermons, only a few of which are printed in Migne, Alan composed a kind of dictionary of Theological Allegories and a compendium of Moral and Dogmatic Theology, along with a manual for preachers and a long treatise in apologetics, *Contra haereticos*. One of his most famous works is the *De planctu naturae*, a dialogue between himself and "nature," in which "nature" justly complains of all that she has had to suffer from the vicious and perverse inclinations of fallen man.

The *Anticlaudianus* is typical of the twelfth-century renaissance, and its method has something in common with that of the great Cistercian Fathers, who often more or less consciously had in mind some classical model which they were turning inside out in order to purify and sublimate it. Thus William of Saint Thierry's *De natura et dignitate amoris* contains, among other things, an implicit criticism and condemnation of Ovid's *Ars amatoria*. Here Alan is reversing and reapplying the fundamental device of Claudian's *In rufinum* to the ends of a Christian moral theme. The poem became very famous and is even thought to have had some influence on Dante.

July 24

Blessed Baldwin of San Pastore, later Cardinal of Rieti, Italy

(Sources: Saint Bernard, Ep 201; AASS, July 4:451; Janauscheck, 222.)

On July 24 the Cistercian Order celebrates the feast of a holy disciple of Saint Bernard, Blessed Baldwin, about whom unfortunately nothing more is known than what is given in the lessons about him in the night office, and even they are inaccurate. This dearth of biographical materials is common among our Italian saints.

What do we know about him? He was an Italian nobleman; his brother became Abbot of the great Benedictine Abbey of Monte Cassino and was later elevated to the dignity of Cardinal. But there have been many noblemen, whose brothers were Cardinals, who yet failed to achieve high sanctity, or for that matter, any degree of sanctity whatever. We know that Blessed Baldwin certainly aspired after sanctity since he traveled from Italy to Clairvaux to renounce all the ambitions and pleasures of the world and fight under the standard of obedience and monastic poverty with Saint Bernard as his captain. And we know that Saint Bernard had a great respect and affection for this monk, from a letter written to him by the saintly Abbot of Clairvaux, praising his virtues and declaring how high a value he placed upon his services. Quotations from this letter go to make up the third lesson of Blessed Baldwin's night office.

We also know that he is buried in the cathedral of Rieti in central Italy in a costly marble tomb, before which a light is kept constantly burning. His head is kept in a silver reliquary, and his relics are exposed at intervals to the veneration of his many devout clients, for whom he does not neglect to perform miracles. In other words, as in the case of other of our Italian saints, we find a flourishing cultus but no biography.

The breviary and the old Menology and the Bollandists, in fact most of the historians of the Order, all declare that Baldwin was sent from Clairvaux by Saint Bernard to be abbot of the monastery of San Matteo, attached to the church of San Pastore at Rieti. He is supposed to have introduced the Cistercian usages to this old monastery and to have become its abbot. He is consequently known as Baldwin of San Pastore. And yet there is no record of San Pastore having become a Cistercian house before 1218,[31] which, although we do not know the correct date of Blessed Baldwin's death, was long after that of Saint Bernard, his contemporary. But the old Menology says Blessed Baldwin died in 1140.[32] It is easy to see why there is no record or mention of Abbot Baldwin in the archives of San Pastore.

Reliable historical documents do tell us, however, that Baldwin was sent by Saint Bernard to be prior of Chiaravalle near Milan. Chiaravalle is the Italian equivalent of Clairvaux. And it seems possible that from there he did go to Rieti when, for a brief interval, San Pastore did make a move towards adopting the Cistercian usages. But Baldwin died and the attempt was given up.[33] However, his virtues and sanctity had won the hearts of the people of Rieti as they had won Saint Bernard's, and the pious citizens showed their love for him by the veneration paid to his memory. And so, if we have no glowing accounts of his virtues, visions and miracles, if we have no written records of his humility, his charity, his love for the poor, is this to stop us from praying to him? Is it not enough for us that we have the example of the faithful and of our Order to guide us? Let us, then, not neglect to pay our homage to this little-known Cistercian and to do so just as readily as we would show our veneration and respect for one like Saint Peter of Tarentaise, whose life is more widely known and whose deeds are more universally remembered and acclaimed.

[31] Janauscheck, 222.
[32] The New Menology Catalogue, 36, hazards no date except "xiith century."
[33] Janauscheck allows that this is possible.

August

August 1

Blessed Ponce de Leras, Lay-brother of Silvanes, Southern France

(Source: *Cartulaire de l'Abbaye de Silvanes*, Supplement, *Chronicle* by the monk, Hugh [12th century], concerning the foundation of the Abbey of Ponce.)

One of the most dramatic conversions of any Cistercian from the world to the cloister was that of the nobleman Ponce de Leras, whose power and title had served him only as an excuse for brigandage and highway robbery for all the early years of the twelfth century.

As we ascend the River Aveyron, from the Garonne basin, we come into a wild and rocky country of lofty uplands, or "causes," intersected by the deep gorges of streams and covered with scrub oak and bitter-smelling box trees. Far back in these hills, towards Lodeve, stood the castle of Leras on a rock above a narrow pass, twenty-one-hundred feet above sea-level, near the village of Pegairelles. This was the repair of Ponce de Leras. It was impregnable. From the top of this towering rock, safe behind the thick walls of his keep, the brigand could have defied the armies of England and France together, if he had enough of a food supply to wait them out. From this retreat, he issued forth by night or by day to plunder the farmers or the other lords of the region, to hold up wayfarers and merchants and churchmen and every likely prospect. Those he did not openly rob he would swindle or cheat or bully out of their property, for he was without scruple. And besides this criminal career, he had a long list of other sins to blacken his name, until suddenly one day the fear of God pierced his flesh, and the word of God entered in even to the marrow of his bones, until he withered and dried up like grass, and he cried out with the psalmist against the thorn that dug deeper and deeper into his flesh the more he turned to get away from it: *Conversus sum in aerumna mes dum configitur spina!*[1]

So powerful was the grace of repentance that in order to escape the torture in his conscience, there was no way but to make restitution of all he had stolen and leave the world. Having obtained his wife's consent to this plan, and having confided his children to the care of a religious community, he began his sweeping campaign of restitution and penance. First he announced an auction of all his possessions—those that were rightfully his—and when this was over with, he divided the proceeds among the poor and the sick and churches and various monasteries of the region around Rodes and Lodeve. Attracted by the news of what was going on, his relatives flocked to Leras, where they found that what they could hardly believe was indeed true; and so complete, sincere and fervent was the conversion of the ex-brigand that six of his relatives were also touched by grace and threw in their lot with him. Wherever he went, they would go and live a life of solitude, penance and prayer.

The next thing was the public restitution of all that he had stolen. He caused to be announced in all that part of Languedoc and southern Auvergne that on Palm Sunday, at Pegairolles, he would make good all claims against him for robbery, theft, brigandage and other injuries. And indeed, on the morning of Palm Sunday, an immense crowd was gathered before the church at Pegairolles, headed by the Bishop of Rodes. It was with no small astonishment that they beheld Ponce de Leras enter the square with his feet bare and one of his six converted relatives beating him over the bare back with rods. Presenting himself before the bishop in this humble

---

[1] Ps 31:4. "I am turned in my anguish, whilst the thorn is fastened," Douay.

guise, the Lord of Leras made a public and general confession of all his crimes and sins in the accents of the deepest contrition—a confession that was punctuated by the heavy blows of the rods falling rhythmically upon his blood-covered back. After that he made restitution as he had promised, at the same time falling at the feet of those he had injured and begging their forgiveness. There must have been many flocks of sheep and goats and many yokes of oxen changing hands in the market place of Pegairolles that day! Ponce had been a great thief.

Finally, when the work was almost done, there was one man standing before the penitent, who waited to hear him speak, and, hearing nothing, said: "Do not fear, make your claim!"

"I have no complaint against you," was the answer, "you were always very good to me."

"You are wrong," said Ponce quickly, "Do you not remember that on such and such a night, a certain number of sheep disappeared from your fold?" And he went on to mention several other thefts.

A light began to dawn in the eyes of his interlocutor, who then exclaimed with more admiration than resentment: "So that was where they went! I never suspected you!" And instead of taking back his sheep as his just due, he received them in gratitude as a gift from heaven and went about everywhere, after that, proclaiming the goodness and holiness of Ponce de Leras and praising him as his benefactor.

Then came the penance. On Holy Thursday Ponce and his companions washed the feet of thirteen poor men and gave them a dinner, in honor of Our Lord's washing the feet of his Apostles and instituting the Sacrament of His Love, for Ponce was to rely more on charity than on beatings to make reparation for his sins, since he had read that to the one who had loved much, much was forgiven, and the charity was the plenitude of the Law which he had so often broken. He resolved to reply on nothing less.

But now, on the night of Holy Thursday, keeping in mind the great anguish of Our Savior in the Garden of Olives and the high priest's palace, Ponce and his companions without lying down to rest started out barefoot and penniless on the road to the plains, thus beginning their pilgrimage to Compostela. It was a terrible night indeed, for they got lost in the wild country, a storm overtook them among the rocks, and they nearly met death in the ravines but suffered all joyfully until dawn brought them exhausted and bleeding to the shrine of Saint William in time to adore the relic of the True Cross with the faithful there. After Easter, which they celebrated with the greatest devotion, they pursued their course to Compostela, across the Pyrenees, begging as they went. They never asked for more than their needs, and when they received more, they tried to give it back, fearing the least shadow or suggestion of avarice or of reliance on anything but the pure mercy of Jesus Christ, Who had told them, and was telling them every moment in the depths of their souls, to consider the lilies of the field and the birds of the air and to seek first the Kingdom of heaven and all their material needs would be added unto them, for their heavenly Father knew that they needed all these things. Let us meditate long upon this example of poverty, which teaches us that the root and soul of poverty is trust in a loving and merciful God and which will warn us against mistaking a penny-pinching avarice for this holy virtue, so necessary to all religious: for without faith and loving confidence in God, poverty can never be anything but a subtle form of avarice.

The Archbishop of Compostela was able to give them some more precise directions as to their vocation, urging them to settle down in the solitary state to pray. But he suggested that they return to France where they knew the language of the people and where their example and precepts could be of more benefit to those around them.

Accordingly, after a long journey to the famous Mont-St-Michel on its rock in the sea off Normandy and to the shrine of Saint Martin, the founder of monasticism in Gaul, as well as that of Saint Martial at Limoges, Ponce and his companions came once again into the rocky hills behind Lodeve. There they received many hospitable offers but accepted that of Lord Arnold of Pont-de-Camares, who gave them land in a narrow wooded valley called Silvanium, or Silvanes, from the woods (*silvae*) that were in it. Ponce promptly changed the name to Salvanium, suggesting salvation (*salus*), and settled there to build a monastery at the confluence of a little brook with the main stream that watered this solitude.

The life was as hard as that of any monastery begun with little money in desolate and rocky woodland, and to add to their difficulties, the country was soon struck with a famine. Hundreds of poor people gravitated to Silvanes from Lodeve and Rodes and even so distant a place as Beziers, down near the sea. With all these guests camping in the valley and their own meager food supply beginning to dwindle, the monks began to fear lest the crowds, unable to satisfy their hunger, might turn on them and kill them out of rage. And some were abandoning the monastery by night and escaping the whole problem by flight into the hills until the crowds departed. But at this Ponce was greatly indignant. Upbraiding them for their lack of faith and charity, he announced that he would sell the monastery and everything in it and divide the proceeds with the poor and after that, die with them if there was no further help from heaven. But he did not have to go to such lengths. As soon as Lord Arnold heard the news that Ponce had set out from Silvanes on his donkey to effect this sale, he sent orders to stop him at all costs and then practically emptied his own granaries to feed all who were in the valley. But the wealth of Arnold would never have sufficed to outlast so long a famine if the monks had not repeatedly seen the grain multiply in the bins and between the millstones, miraculously, before their very eyes.

As time went on, Ponce decided that Silvanes should be affiliated to a regular order, and in 1136 he traveled to the Grande Chartreuse in the Alps to consult the holy prior, Guigo. This prudent saint sent Ponce back to Mazan, a Cistercian foundation made by Blessed John of Valence, when he had been Abbot of Bonnevaux, and there the abbot received Silvanes into the Cistercian Order as his daughterhouse.

Ponce's work was not yet done. Refusing the habit of choir religious, much less the charge of superiorship which one might logically expect to fall to his lot, he took the humble habit of lay-brother in order to be the servant of all, like his dear Lord who had come not to be ministered unto but to minister. And thus he ended his days in holiness and peace and great sanctity, sometime after 1146.

The ancient diocese of Lodeve used to keep his feast on September 18, though August 1 is the traditional date of his death.

August 2

Blessed William, First Abbot of Rievaulx, Yorkshire, England

There is a very well-known story of one of Saint Bernard's miracles, which concerns his famous letter to Robert of Châtillon, the young monk of Clairvaux who had been spirited off to Cluny, in the abbot's absence, by the prior of that great Abbey. The saint happened to be outside the enclosure of Clairvaux and in the hills behind the monastery when the Holy Spirit, working in his heart full of grief at this defection, inspired him with the words that are so well known to Cistercians. This letter was dictated to the abbot's secretary, William, who happened to be at hand. But the remarkable thing about it was that, along with Saint Bernard's inspiration, had also come a torrential downpour of rain. Yet the saint did not give up his dictating, nor the secretary his rapid writing, and the whole letter was taken down *in imbre et sine imbre*, without a single drop touching or blotting the parchment.

Who was this secretary? He was one of the many monks attracted to Clairvaux from England. It is thought by some that he had been a pupil of the great scholar, Henry Murdac of York—the same who was soon to become a Cistercian himself and would eventually be one of the greatest abbots of one of our greatest abbeys, Fountains. William was a monk of talent, ability and piety. He had a special proficiency in "plain chant," which led to his appointment as associate reviser of the Cistercian Choral Books, a post of the greatest importance since it affected the whole Order at a time when the peculiarly simple and pure and austere form of chant which has characterized our Order from the beginning was still in process of formation—or rather re-formation from the manuscripts of the earliest times.

In 1133 a noble Yorkshireman, the Knight, Sir Walter Espec, bereaved of his only son by a riding accident, determined to spend what would have been the son's inheritance in founding monasteries. He owned some forest land watered by the little river Rye which was just the kind of solitude that attracted the monks of the new Cistercian Order, whose fame was beginning to reach the northern counties of England, so long deserted by the monks.

William was chosen by Saint Bernard to lead the colony that was to found the first of the great Cistercian Abbeys of Yorkshire. And it is strange that it is these northern abbeys that are the most famous, although the Cistercians had already established themselves at Waverley, in Surrey, and Tintern, in Herefordshire. Yet the southern abbeys never achieved the recognition won by the Great Schools of sanctity at Rievaulx and Fountains. We know of no saints or blessed at Waverley or Tintern: the ones that must have flourished there were truly hidden.

Among the woods and steep hills of Rye Valley, William and his monks soon built a strong community, the very existence of which was a challenge to priests and scholars and monks and laymen, soldiers and nobles and even princes in all the north, at York, Durham, and at the court of Scotland. Within twelve years, Rievaulx numbered three hundred monks, including the famous Maurice, subprior of Durham, and so great a scholar that he was called the "second Bede," but above all, the noble Saint Ælred, who had come from King David's court to become one of the greatest mystics and theologians and directors of souls in our Order—and one of the greatest of the English saints.

William became a man of great influence in northern England and Scotland, and the Church owes much to his work in those lands which had threatened for centuries to fall back into complete and pagan savagery. He was an important factor in the revival of the Christian England of Bede here in the north. In 1136 he took over the famous Scotch abbey of Melrose, and made it Cistercian at the request of the King. He also founded Wardon, far south in Bedfordshire, and Dundrennan. But above all, it was his influence and example that led to the foundation of Fountains by the heroic prior of Saint Mary's, York, Dom Richard.

When he died in 1143, this holy abbot left to his successor a great and fervent community of three hundred monks and many lay-brothers: a community filled with the spirit of Cîteaux and Saint Benedict, and admirable, above all, for its charity and for the equality and true brotherhood existing between men of every social rank and class in the cloister, whether they had been nobles or serfs in the world. Indeed, this was one of the things that most astounded the Middle Ages about the early Cistercians, just as this spirit of Christian brotherhood had amazed the pagans of imperial Rome.

Jocelyn of Furness in his *Vita Waleni*, or Life of Saint Waltheof, relates two visions of that holy abbot in which was revealed to him the sanctity and glory of Blessed William in heaven. One of these visions is related to our account of Saint Waltheof (the following day), and the other may serve as a conclusion to these few words on the first Abbot of Rievaulx.

Saint Waltheof was on a visit to his motherhouse, Rievaulx, in the summertime. It was midday. The monks had finished their repast and had gone up to the dormitory for the meridian, or rest prescribed by Saint Benedict during the summer months. Saint Waltheof, having remained behind to pray in church, did not want to waken the monks by going up to the dormitory late, and so he sat down in the cloister and tried to sleep there. Unable to do so, he turned his mind to prayer in the peaceful sun-dappled shade of the cloister with nothing to disturb him but the songs of the birds in the thick Yorkshire woods in which the abbey lay deeply hidden. Suddenly he saw someone coming towards him, and it was no natural apparition, for the figure of this monk shone with a glorious light, and his garments were resplendent with jewels, and on his head there was a brilliant crown. He was followed by a throng as gloriously arrayed as he was. Waltheof rose and approached him with a respectful *benedicite* and asked him who he was.

"Do you not know your good friend, William, the first abbot of this monastery?" was the reply. "And these," he added, pointing to those who came after him, "are the holy monks and brothers who were my spiritual children." He went on to explain that each jewel in their garments represented a soul saved by their words or example. Let us not forget this last when it seems to us that our life is fruitless because we cannot see its fruit. Prayer, vicarious suffering and example are the greatest works of the Cistercian, band his example is his most effective, indeed, most often his only sermon.

The holy abbot William concluded his conversation with his friend by explaining that they all came to visit their monastery three times each year, for it was there that they had merited heaven.

August 3

Blessed Waltheof, Abbot of Melrose, Scotland

(Source: AASS, Aug. l:242, Joycelyn of Furness, *Vita Waleni*, 12th century.)

Readers of the series of lives of English saints, brought out in the last century under the direction of Cardinal Newman, may be surprised that we do not give Waltheof the traditional title of saint which was used by Fr. Delagairns and which dates back to two English martyrologies and to the statement of Chalemot that he was canonized.[2] The martyrology of Richard Whitford (1526) tells us that Saint Waltheof's feast was kept at York on August 3. However, since Chalemot is apparently wrong, and since the title of saint was only a matter of popular usage and was never officially confirmed by Rome, we follow the new Cistercian Menology in calling him "Blessed." The name Waltheof is probably now correctly pronounced Wal-teff, and it is found in varying forms as Waldef, Walthen, and Walter, but the latter is probably a mistake. The Latin form of the name is Walenus, and our present article is based entirely on the beautiful *Vita Waleni* by the twelfth-century monk, Jocelyn of Furness Abbey in Lancashire.

Waltheof was one of Saint Ælred's closest friends at the court of King David of Scotland. His birth and position made him even more liable than Ælred to advancement in political and court life,

[2] Chalemot, August 1.

for after the death of Waltheof's father on a Crusade, his mother had married the king and became Queen of Scotland. However, Waltheof, unlike Ælred, was not even tempted by the pleasures of court life and cultured society. He seems to have been one of those shy, retiring people who are so often thought unsociable. When the court went hunting, Waltheof, we are told, used to get lost on purpose and go off in the woods to think and pray by himself. He seems to have hesitated some time in leaving the world altogether, but the issue was precipitated by the fact that a young lady fell in love with him and presented him with a ring. Waltheof, with the usual awkwardness of his type, made the mistake of accepting the gift for the simple reason that he did not know how to refuse. His fear of offending the young lady only put him in a worse position than ever, and finally he had to insult her in order to get out of it. Since his acceptance of the ring, everybody had taken it for granted that he intended to marry the girl: so finally, one day he publically threw the ring in a fire. After that, even if he had not worked up enough decision to leave the court, he would certainly never have had the courage to stay.

He crossed the borders of Scotland and entered the monastery of the Augustinian Canons at Nostel. Soon after his ordination to the priesthood, Waltheof was chosen prior of the Augustinians of Kirkham. He was a fervent and prudent religious, a wise superior, and an enlightened director of souls. In short, it soon became evident that he was a man of eminent gifts. But the greatest favors given him by God were the mystical graces which began at this time. It was at Kirkham, for instance, that he had a vision of the Child Jesus, smiling and holding out his hands upon the altar, right after the consecration of the Sacred Host at midnight Mass on Christmas Eve. It would seem that the Divine Infancy even more than the Passion dominated the mysticism of the Cistercians, especially in the twelfth century—this is certainly true when we consider the frequency of visions in which not only the Holy Child but also His most Pure Mother appeared to our saints. A proof that Waltheof had overcome his shyness and hesitancy by this time is to be found in his action in a singularly tricky emergency. One of the priests of the community while saying Mass had just consecrated the Precious Blood when, to his utter dismay, a good-sized spider dropped into the chalice before it could be covered. The prior was summoned, and with hesitation he told the priest to go on with his Mass and consume the spider along with the Sacred Species. The priest did so without mishap, and the event was regarded as somewhat supernatural, although it is prescribed that the priest should do this *if he can* without nausea.

In 1143, on account of Waltheof's reputation for sanctity and ability, as well as on account of his former connections, he was elected, much to his own sorrow, Archbishop of York, but he did not need to fear the dignity. The election was successfully contested by the King of England for political reasons (since Waltheof was stepson of the King of Scotland), and in the confusion, Waltheof made off from Kirkham and entered the Cistercian Order not in one of the nearby houses in Yorkshire but at Wardon, not far north of London, in Bedfordshire.

The entrance of Blessed Waltheof into the Cistercian Order brought many trials and hardships, interior and external. If ever a vocation was tested, it was his. In the first place, all the peace and consolation that had accompanied his life according to the mild Rule of Saint Augustine gave way to repugnance and difficulty. His physical weakness and his rather sensitive temperament found the rigors of the Cistercian labor and vigils and fasting a heavy burden. Then there was the silence and austerity of the Cistercian community life. Worst of all, the mystical favors that had been showered upon him at Kirkham now left him altogether and gave place to intense dryness and discouragement and disgust. On every side he seemed to be hedged in by doubts and fears. His soul was tormented by a constant vicious circle of arguments. Was the Cistercian life too austere? Had the White Monks not made prayer impossible by excessive severity to the body? After all, if the body is broken by inordinate penance, the mind cannot concentrate upon anything solid, let alone direct itself constantly to God. "Oh shameful thing," Saint Ælred would have answered him, "to seek for spiritual graces by the rule of Hippocrates!"[3]

---

[3] *O rem prudendam! Secundum regulas Hippocratis gratia quaeriter spiritualis.* Spec car 2.5.

The graces of prayer are pure gifts of God, and in giving them He takes no account of bodily sickness or health. Only the attachments of our weak will impede Him in distributing these favors, and one of the greatest hindrances to advancement in prayer is futile solicitude about our health. Instead of considering the flowers of the field and the birds of the air, who do not have to toil and spin and sow and reap to be cared for by our heavenly Father, Waltheof was wasting time in useless anxiety. However, this was probably no sin on his part, since it was almost certainly not deliberate or consented to, and doubtless it constituted, unknown to him, a great grace, and a form of passive purification. Other forms that this anxiety took were scruples about having left Kirkham on the grounds that he had deserted his spiritual children who needed him, or that he had shown ingratitude to God for the graces He had bestowed on him there. Finally, he was haunted by the fear that everybody else could read the struggles going on in his mind and that they were scandalized by his weakness. In short, Blessed Waltheof, as a novice at Wardon, was going through one variation of the struggle which must, usually, sooner or later, be faced by every Cistercian, whether in the novitiate or after it, and whether the trials be concerned with the vocation as such, or with stability, or with obedience, or chastity.

As if all this were not enough, Waltheof's brother, who happened to be the Lord of the land where the monastery was situated, took it into his head that it was folly for the young priest to become a Cistercian. In his brotherly solicitude for poor Waltheof, then, he came storming down to Wardon and roundly upbraided everybody concerned, asserting that Waltheof had been nearly killed by the Rule of Saint Augustine and would certainly die if he remained among the Cistercians. But his most forceful argument was that, unless Waltheof was sent away from Wardon, he would personally come with his men and burn the monastery to the ground.

The Abbot of Wardon knew enough about medieval knighthood to realize that in such cases these people generally kept their word, and Blessed Waltheof passed from Wardon to Rievaulx, Yorkshire, being now safer than the south.

In 1147, Saint Ælred, Waltheof's childhood friend, and now Abbot of Rievaulx, was having trouble with the superior of his filiation at Melrose. Abbot Richard of the famous old monastery on the Tweed, newly refounded as a Cistercian house, had proved himself too much of a martinet. He was one of those harsh, bad-tempered disciplinarians who make the Rule an end in itself and like nothing better than to assert their own power over others at the expense of peace and charity and the spirit of prayer and true regularity and everything else that befits a house of contemplatives. Every line of Saint Benedict's portrait of the true abbot warns us against this type of counterfeit. In this particular case, the offender was deposed and replaced by the gentle Waltheof, who proceeded to give an example of what a Cistercian abbot should be: a man mild but firm, loving the Rule and the brethren, hating all irregularity and vice with an implacable hatred, but full of tolerance and understanding for human weakness and failures.

A typical precept of Blessed Waltheof was his categorical prohibition of the least word or sign about any fault of anyone in the community, once that fault had been duly proclaimed and expiated in chapter. His aim was to promote a spirit of perfect peace and mutual charity and to extirpate the habit of continual criticism of others. He used to say that anyone who reproached or mocked a brother for his faults once they had been publically acknowledged was on a par with the devils in hell, for that is precisely the function of the evil spirits, for all eternity.

His constant meditation on the humility of Christ, and his life of intimate union with Him, which was now far more perfect than before, since he had emerged from the crucible of his purifying temptations, had filled Blessed Waltheof with the modesty and gentleness and humility of the Divine Savior, and he radiated the spirit of Christ wherever he went. He had a special love for the simplest and humblest members of the community, and for that reason, his greatest joy was to be among the lay-brothers, of which there were many at Melrose. He delighted in giving them frequent conferences in their chapter room and in receiving them for direction—and considering the numbers at most of our great Cistercian abbeys, it must have been rather a rare thing for a lay-brother to get to see his abbot, even for a few minutes of private conversation in the twelfth century. Blessed Waltheof saw to it that this was not so at Melrose. Indeed, he was so much more at home with his lay-brothers that he was able to open his heart to them more readily than to anyone else, and many of the details of his own inner life of prayer come to us from shy and artfully disguised anecdotes in his talks to the rough Scotch *conversi* of Melrose, but they had enough native wit to guess who it was that their abbot was referring to when he began a story with some such words as: "Somebody I know once had a vision. . . ."

Blessed Waltheof's life is especially interesting to us because of the details Jocelyn gives us on the intensely liturgical character of the saint's mysticism. His visions not only followed the feasts and mysteries celebrated by the Church in the course of the year, but his greatest graces generally had, as their mainspring, some verse or sentence from the offices of the great feasts. These words not only touched off, as it were, the blaze of light and love kindled in him by the Holy Spirit on these occasions but also served to re-ignite the same fire in his memory for years to come. Thus, he was always tremendously stirred by a beautiful oration of the ancient office and Mass of the Vigil of the Epiphany: *Corda nostra splendor futurae festivitatis illustret,*[4] because one year these words had sent him into ecstasy, and he had beheld in a vision the three Kings coming to see the Christ Child and offering Him their presents and adoration. It was the same with the Collect from the Mass of Holy Saturday, which takes up and resumes the wonderful theme of the *Exultet* in the words *Deus qui hanc sanctissimam noctem gloria Dominici resurrectionis illustraasti,* etc.[5] These also occasioned a similar vision of the Easter mystery. It is interesting to notice that in both these occasions the saint received an illumination that was more or less explicitly promised by the prayers in question. And these extraordinary favors are nothing but a clear indication of more ordinary lights and graces that are the proper fruits of a sincere and complete liturgical life for all the Christians who wish to lead one with pure hearts, in a spirit of faith and love, and on a basis of compunction and humility.

---

[4] This Collect is not in the present Cistercian Breviary, which has the same as the Roman Breviary and Missal on this day.

[5] Both the Roman and Cistercian rites keep this same oration in our time.

But a spirit of penance and sorrow for sin is essential if the liturgical life is to be something more than pious diletantism, and Blessed Waltheof had that spirit to an extraordinary degree. He always approached the Sacrament of Penance with the deepest and most humble contrition, even for the slightest faults, and never omitted to do severe penance.

As abbot, he had a privilege which is not the lot of the ordinary Cistercian monk: he could directly give alms to the poor. Indeed, that has always been one of the duties of a Cistercian community. But the year 1154 brought more than an ordinary occasion for charity to the poor. Scotland was struck by a famine, and four thousand starving men and women came and camped in the meadows and pastures along the Tweed, outside the enclosure wall of Melrose. Blessed Waltheof immediately had the livestock slaughtered and distributed all the cheese and butter they had at hand. Large quantities of bread were baked, and the wheat reserve was soon attacked. Days passed, however, and the supply of grain never diminished. More and more bread was baked: the granneries were as full as ever. This went on for three months until the time of the harvest.

Several miracles of this kind are attributed to the holiness of Blessed Waltheof, including more than one multiplication of loaves in the abbey guesthouse. There was another famine, in which the monks agreed to give up half their daily portion of bread to feed the poor. But that day, after the bread had been distributed, when the monks entered the refectory at dinner time, each one found a freshly baked loaf of bread at his place—a fact for which there was no natural explanation.

One of the most famous visions of Blessed Waltheof occurred at Rievaulx. He had gone to the motherhouse in Yorkshire and according to his usual custom remained in church after the community had retired for the night. When all was silent, he went into the chapter room to pray at the tomb of the saintly founder of Rievaulx, Blessed William.[6] While he was absorbed in prayer,

---

[6] Blessed William, English by birth, had been Saint Bernard's secretary at Clairvaux and, as such, had taken down the famous letter *in imbre et sine imbre*, in a rainstorm, without getting wet (Ep. I to Robert of Châtillon). He was also

Waltheof suddenly heard the sound of singing voices, and the song they sang was of such loveliness that it nearly separated his soul from his body. Going out into the cloister, he beheld a procession of monks, shining with the light of the glory of heaven, filled with the ineffable bliss of the vision of God, coming towards him in grand, stately elation, chanting the words of the Apocalypse: "Give praise to our God, all you his servants, and you that fear Him, little and great, alleluiah! For the Lord our God, the Almighty, hath reigned!" At the head of the procession was his friend, the abbot William, and with him were many other monks of Rievaulx that Waltheof had once known there. There was one in the crowd he did not recognize, however, one who shone with a greater and more perfect glory than any of the rest. While he was wondering who this one might be, he was told that it was a monk who, in his lifetime, had always been considered a more or less insignificant and useless member of the community, and who, therefore, had never been entrusted with any special employment. Hence he had the great grace of always remaining obscure and profiting by the full measure of merit attached to the common rule and the common work and the common routine from day to day.

After about ten years as Abbot of Melrose, Blessed Waltheof was again elected to a bishopric, this time that of Saint Andrew's in Scotland. Saint Ælred used his authority as Father Immediate to press him to accept, and this time there were no political obstacles, but Blessed Waltheof had a better reason to offer. He said he had a revelation that he was soon going to die. Early in 1159 he developed a painful sickness which slowly grew worse as the year advanced. In July it became apparent that his revelation had been correct: he could not live much longer. He was anointed on the Feast of Saint Peter in Chains. Lying on his death bed, smiling and lifting up his hands to heaven, he thanked God for all the trials and sufferings of his life as for the most precious of graces, and if

---

an authority on plainchant and assisted in the revision of the antiphonary undertaken by the early Cistercians. He was sent to found Rievaulx in 1132, formed Saint Ælred to the Cistercian life, and died in the odor of sanctity in 1145. See August 2.

no other proof of his holiness were to be had, this alone would be enough. The heartfelt realization of the value of our temptations and sorrows is a greater gift than that of miracles. Having earnestly exhorted his monks to strive in all things to maintain unity and charity in the house and in the Order, Blessed Waltheof lingered on for two more days, consumed in the furnace of a terrible fever, and then passed into the glory of perfect charity, which is heaven, to praise God forever.

Blessed Waltheof was buried in the chapter room, and so great was the concourse of the faithful to his tomb that his successor finally had to prohibit seculars from coming into the chapter room—which, in any case, was rather irregular, if it was allowed indiscriminately. Thirteen years after the saint's death, his body and clothing were found uncorrupted in the tomb, and forty years later, in 1207, the same miracle was verified once more. The monks of Melrose celebrated two feasts in his honor: the day of his death and the feast of the translation of his relics.

Among the posthumous miracles related by Jocelyn, a large number were cures granted to Blessed Waltheof's beloved lay-brothers. One of these with an incurable sickness that might possibly have been cancer prayed at Saint Waltheof's tomb by night and eventually fell asleep on the tomb itself. When he awoke, his disease was cured, and all trace of swelling had gone.

Then there was the case of a man who tried to cross a flooded river on horseback. He was swept away by the current and nearly drowned but invoking "Saint" Waltheof he was suddenly deposited safe and sound on the river bank. The great martyr of Canterbury, Saint Thomas à Becket, repeated for Blessed Waltheof the favor he had gratuitously done for Saint Robert of Newminster. A client of the martyred archbishop was on a pilgrimage to Canterbury when Saint Thomas appeared to him and told him to go to Melrose and make his petition of Blessed Waltheof instead.

August 10

Blessed Lawrence, Lay-brother of Clairvaux, France

(Source: EM 3.15; 4.33.)

It is rather by virtue of liturgical etiquette than for any historical motive that Blessed Lawrence is commemorated in the Cistercian Menology on August 10, the feast of the great Martyr Saint Lawrence. We do not know the date of this holy and simple brother's death, but he was long venerated by the monks of Clairvaux and by the faithful as a saint, and his popular *cultus* earns him the title of Blessed.

He was one of those gentle and humble Cistercians who were formed to the religious life by Saint Bernard and whose beautiful lives fill the pages of the *Exordium Magnum* with the fragrance of a most perfect simplicity. He is truly one of those "little ones" that make the sanctity of the twelfth and thirteenth centuries so attractive—and a close spiritual relative of those meek and joyful brethren of Saint Francis of whom we read in the *Fioretti*.

He was a man of deep interior life, devoted to prayer, and perhaps because of this he was chosen, at one point in his religious life, as custodian of the tombs of Saints Bernard and Malachy in the abbey church of Clairvaux, for the relics of the holy abbot and his friend, the Irish bishop, had become the object of constant pilgrimages. In the long and lonely hours of the night, however, there was hardly anyone to prevent Brother Lawrence from becoming absorbed in prayer, and we are told that he received such great grace of compunction that the stone floor was often wet with his tears.

Blessed Lawrence was one of those who recognized his sins and God's great love and mercy in pardoning them, and such a realization was enough to make his heart almost break with love and gratitude.

However, his prayer was not all consolations. He had his trials. And like Saint Teresa of Ávila, one of them was to be confronted with the devil in visible form. The *Exordium Magnum* does not hesitate to admit that he was very frightened. He made the sign of the cross, and asked the apparition who he was, as if he didn't know! The evil spirit was not reticent or shy. He enumerated all the terrible evils and misfortunes that had fallen upon Job and said: "I am the one who did all that," with the all-too-evident implication that he was on the point of repeating his performance, with a few embellishments, here and now, with the poor little brother as his victim. This was too much for Brother Lawrence. He took to his heels: "But of course," as the *Exordium Magnum* hastens to explain, "he was only a novice in the spiritual life."

This was not the first time the fiend had tried to trouble the monks and brethren of Clairvaux and disturb their prayers and contemplation by filling them with turmoil and fear. He had appeared, for instance, in the form of a goat, prancing in the choir and making faces in front of Blessed Gerard of Farfa.[7] But then, Blessed Gerard was no novice; he was old and experienced in the life of prayer, and he had learned, as also Saint Teresa had learned, to despise the devil, for all the devils in hell cannot do us as much harm as the smallest venial sin. We mention Gerard of Farfa because after his death this holy man appeared in glory to Brother Lawrence and foretold that he too would eventually find a high place in heaven. But before vanishing, Blessed Gerard remarked that, at his own death, the infirmarians had been in too much of a hurry to get him out of the room where he had died and had taken his body out to wash it before he had actually breathed his last.

One of Blessed Lawrence's most important and arduous functions had been to serve as messenger and letter carrier for Saint

[7] *Blessed Gerard of Farfa,* (Menology, December 7) was an Italian, who began his religious life as a Benedictine at Farfa, near Rome, a powerful and famous monastery and a great center of learning. Gerard, seeking a stricter and more contemplative life, came to Clairvaux where he edified all for many years by the great simplicity and purity of his soul. He lived to a venerable old age. The incident here related of him took place when he was ninety. He was buried, among several others venerated as saints, in the new cloister of the abbey as soon as it was finished.

Bernard. The great Abbot of Clairvaux was so important a figure in the political and religious life of his time that he corresponded with kings and princes and prelates in every part of Europe, and many of these letters were extremely important and were entrusted to a special messenger. Lawrence thus traveled many hundreds of miles along the glorified footpaths that went by the name of roads in the Middle Ages when traveling was an arduous and dangerous business.

After the death of Saint Bernard, he was sent by his prior on an important mission to the King of Sicily. And it was on this mission that he underwent one of the great trials of his life. Arriving at Rome, he learned that the King, who had been a good friend of Saint Bernard's and to whom perhaps Lawrence himself was known, was dead. And suddenly the devil, not now in visible form but working much more subtly and effectively, filled the soul of the poor brother with great fear and uneasiness. He realized, all at once and with extreme clarity, just how small and helpless and alone he was, all by himself in a strange city, heading for a destination where perhaps he would be ill received, unknown, rejected, left perhaps to perish. God allowed all this, in His wisdom, to purify Lawrence's soul of what was evidently a strong natural reliance on himself and his own experience and his usefulness to Saint Bernard.

And now the brother fell on his knees and began to call upon his holy abbot in fervent prayer, saying:

> My Father, my Father, you were the chariot of Israel and the horseman thereof; why have you abandoned us? What shall I do, holy father, poor and miserable as I am, and lacking in all counsel! When you were living, I used to go without fear into any country of the earth when you commanded me, and because of you they gave me a fine welcome everywhere I went. When I was bearing your greetings and your letters, kings and bishops and everybody received them as blessings from heaven itself! Now you are no more, and all my credit has vanished away! No one will help me: I am nothing but a poor stranger. And this King who was such a good friend of

of yours: he's dead. Who has taken his place? Some child who, perhaps, does not even know who you were.[8]

But here comes the core of the whole problem, although we must not be too ready to ascribe the exact sentiments to Brother Lawrence, since the words are those of the writer of the *Exordium* (thought by some to be Blessed Helinand, February 3). "If I go to him, and am sent away empty-handed, after all this long journey and all my troubles, what will I do? To think that I used to return to Clairvaux from such missions so successful! And on the other hand, if I go home to Clairvaux without having seen him, they will accuse me of being lazy and stupid. So please hasten to my assistance, and give me your advice, and do not despise the tears of your poor little servant."

That night, when the unhappy brother was asleep, Saint Bernard appeared to him in great glory in a dream and gently reproved him for his lack of confidence: "Why do you not trust in God's mercy, and in my help?" he asked. "Do you think my power is less, now that I have entered into the powers of the Lord, than when I was on the earth? Go on to Sicily, you will have complete success: and by that you will know that it is indeed I who send you."

The good brother awoke in great joy and consolation, his heart full of faith, and set out for the south; and on the road, as he left the city and struck out across the Campagna, among the ancient shrines above the catacombs and the pagan tombs and the places hallowed with the blood of so many martyrs, he fell in with some merchants going to Sicily, and they, hearing he was from Clairvaux, treated him royally all the way. The new King not only received him well, as Saint Bernard had predicted, and satisfactorily completed the business for which Lawrence had been sent but even opened his treasury and gave him a large sum of money as a contribution to help in the building of the new Abbey Church.

As if this were not enough, on his return through Rome, Blessed Lawrence was far from being left lonely and ignored. He was received by Cardinals and princes of the Church, and loaded with

[8] EM 4.33.

presents for his famous abbey, not the least strange of which was a gift of ten Indian buffaloes.

His journey back to Clairvaux, driving these strange beasts, was not the least wonderful achievement of his life. The Indian buffalo is a very powerful relative of the ox, with long curving horns, and in the wild state is strong enough to kill a tiger. Even when tame, it has some erratic habits. It is very fond of reposing in the water of streams or marshes or immersing itself in deep mud. It is at its happiest when it is completely covered by nice, muddy water with nothing but its muzzle protruding above the surface for air. Although it has a very thick hide, it is bothered by flies, and this is one reason for its love of mud: for it likes to coat itself all over with mud which dries and forms an effective protection against these insects. With all this, it often does not hesitate to leave whatever task has been allotted to it and settle in the nearest river or swamp, so that its Indian drivers, when using it as beast of burden, are careful to see that whatever it carries is waterproof.

We do not know if Br. Lawrence had much trouble of this kind, although it is almost a miracle that he ever got such creatures beyond the Po Valley. However, he had two little boys to help him keep the buffalos in order all the way to Clairvaux.

His biggest danger was from bandits, and when he was entering upon a certain country infested with them, he prayed fervently to get through in safety. Soon afterwards, two men appeared on the road before him, holding lighted tapers, and after awhile they vanished, which vision he took for a sign that his prayer was answered.

Nevertheless, he was soon surrounded, as he had feared, by bandits, who descended upon him and his precious buffaloes from every side. Fortunately, however, the honest men of the district, hearing that he came from Clairvaux, banded together and came to his rescue in time.

The poor brother had feared to return to Clairvaux in disgrace, but actually, when he arrived with his charges, he was met with openmouthed stupefaction (*cum omnium ingenti stupore*), for this was the first time buffaloes had ever been seen north of the Alps. The account in the *Exordium* goes on to say that the buffaloes settled down and became acclimatized so that soon Clairvaux was able to send some buffaloes to other parts of France.

As for Blessed Lawrence, he was already an old and venerable man, and this feat may be regarded as the climax of his life of service to his abbey: the rest of his days were spent in peace and complete obscurity, until his holy death, of which we know neither the day nor the year. But he was venerated with an immemorial cult.

August 21

Blessed Gobert, Monk of Villers, Belgium

(Source: AASS, Aug. 4:370. *Chronicon Villarensis Monasterii*, longer contemporary life, and copious notes; Martène, 2:2, a shorter contemporary life by an anonymous monk of Villers.)

This holy man was one of the many convert knights who by their simplicity and generosity in the service of Christ fill the annals of Cistercian history with the "good odor" of Our Savior's charity. Gobert D'Aspremont was the son of the Count of Aspremont in Lorraine, and his father picked him out for a military career in preference to his elder brother, later Bishop of Verdun, who was destined for the Church. Gobert, then, became a soldier and arrived at knighthood. But like so many of his kind, instead of being brutalized by a fighting life, he sublimated his activities and refined them by a sincere spirituality, and the motive power of that spirituality was a loyal devotion to the Virgin Mother of God.

His love for her, and for Christ in her, made him even in the world a man of prayer and good works. He was most liberal in his charity to the poor, which was a sincere and Christian charity and not mere philanthropy. He loved the poor.

Like so many of his contemporaries, he took the Cross and set out for the Holy Land. His choice of an expedition with which to make that journey was an unfortunate one, for he joined up with Emperor Frederick II, who had been using the promise to go on a crusade as a political tool in obtaining certain things he wanted from the Church. But he separated himself from Frederick in Palestine when the latter threatened to fight the Knight Templars instead of the Saracens. Later, Gobert visited the Holy Place at Jerusalem. On this crusade he learned by heart the Little Office of the Blessed Virgin, which he continued afterwards to recite daily. On his return, he went on to the shrine of Saint James Compostela, across the Pyrenees, before returning home. By this time, he was not only daily attending Mass, at Prime, wherever he happened to be but also receiving Communion every day: a rare thing indeed for an age when even some religious houses did not allow Communion more than once a month, or even less frequently.

Such were the effects of this manner of life that by the time he was once again in Lorraine, he had decided to leave the world: all that remained was to find a suitable cloister. It was from a holy Beguine in the town of Nivelles that he heard of the Cistercian monastery of Villers in Brabant, and thither he turned his steps. Henceforth he would be able to assist at Matins without having to travel through dark streets in the middle of the night.

He immediately edified all by his humility and love of obedience, which he based upon four principles. The first was an uncompromising loyalty to the Rule, every deliberate violation of which was, to him, a sin of pride. Second, he would never look down upon, despise, or even patronize those who were, in one way or another, situated below him. Third, he would never place himself above his equals. And fourth, he would never try to put himself on a level with those who were above him.

He put this last item into practice, especially where the priests of the monastery were concerned. He himself never received the honor of Holy Orders, and to the end of his life he would wait at the door of the refectory, at times when the monks were not entering "in community," and would not wash his hands at the little fountain placed there according to our usages until all the priests had gone before him, irrespective of their rank of seniority in the community.

His humility with his equals was shown by an occasion when he was traveling with an irascible monk called Peter. The latter had charge of their common funds, and one night at an inn he ordered a dinner that seemed to Gobert to be a little extravagant for two monks. He said nothing at the time, but the next morning he mentioned the matter with great meekness and diffidence to his companion. The latter became very angry and refused to answer anything. In fact, he brooded over this "insult" for the next three hours. Finally, the time came for them to dismount and kneel at the roadside to say their office. But Gobert, who was filled with compunction at the memory of Our Lord's admonition that if any man comes to the altar and remembers his brother has something against him, he should leave his gift and go first to be reconciled with his brother, begged Frater Peter's pardon on his knees and in tears for having offended him. His companion was touched by this and came out of his black mood, and all was once again in peace. Let us learn from Blessed Gobert a lesson in abandoning our own judgment for the sake of charity.

He was as impulsive as he was simple in his desire to do everything in the way most pleasing to God, and when he found that he sometimes became drowsy in choir, he took to putting pepper on his tongue to keep himself alert. He had to be forbidden to give the clothes off his back to the ragged poor he met in the wintertime, and so, with a typically medieval impulse, he used to take off his cowl and carry it in order to share some of the cold with those he could not relieve. Once he gave a pair of shoes to a poor Beguine who came begging at the gate of Villers. She complained that the shoes were too hard. Gobert instantly ran to get a pot of oil to soften them up for her. On his way back, he met a friend of the monastery and hid the pot hastily to avoid comment on his charity; but in bowing he spilled the oil all over his cowl and was much ridiculed both for his mishap and for what the bystanders considered an "eccentric" excess of charity to a poor old woman of no account.

So great was his zeal for the salvation of a brother's soul that when one of the monks apostatized, and would not listen to any of Gobert's arguments, the ex-knight pursued him down the road with entreaties to come back and then finally picked him up bodily, put him on his shoulders and carried him back to the monastery on the simple theory that Jesus had done this with the lost sheep, and it had proved effective then: why not also in this case? It succeeded. The monk stayed.

No one has thought of calling Gobert a martyr, but indeed he was in a broad sense a martyr to his charity. Alice of Burgundy was infringing on the rights of the monastery of Gembloux in her attempt to do good to another religious house, and because her intention was, in itself, pious she could not be persuaded that the means were not justified by the end she had in view. Gobert went out to defend the rights of the monks, as he was qualified to obtain a hearing by reason of his noble origin.

But on the way his horse, which was a wild and cantankerous beast, suddenly broke away and threw his rider. Grievously injured and covered with blood, Gobert would not be persuaded to discontinue his journey, and indeed he went straight into the presence of the Countess with blood streaming down his face and smeared all over his cowl.

"Who has done this to you?" cried the Countess, aghast at such a spectacle. "You have, my Lady!" he replied bluntly. And then he proceeded to explain why he had come. She yielded to his argument and to his charity. But it cost him his life.

Returning to Villers, he went to the infirmary, where he lingered for some time in great pain, which he suffered with the most edifying patience. Finally he died on the feast of Saint Bernard, 1263, and left his brethren on earth with a face full of smiling joy to join the great Cistercian saint in heaven.

August 22

Saint Bernard de Candelada, Monk of Valdeiglesias, Spain

(Source: AASS, Aug. 4:369.)

On August 20 the universal Church celebrates the feast of the great Saint Bernard of Clairvaux. On August 20 the village of Candelada in Estremadura, Spain, also celebrates the feast of Saint Bernard, its patron. This saint is also a Cistercian monk and also a great miracle worker, but unlike the Abbot of Clairvaux, nothing is known of him at all, except a few vague indications of what his life must have been. However, in his case, there seems to be just enough material in these indications to allow some reasonable deductions about him.

Although we do not know the date of his death, much less of his birth, nor even the exact century in which either one occurred, we know he was a monk of Valdeiglesias, who was admitted to the Cistercian Order in 1177.

Probably in the thirteenth century, then, he was sent by his abbot with a colony of monks to make a new foundation, called Grandis-silva, in Estremadura. Whether he went as superior of that group or not, we cannot tell. But one thing is known: the monks who founded Grandissilva were surely united with their Lord Jesus Christ upon His Cross, for the community was destroyed by plague. Whether all the monks were killed, or whether it was at this time that Saint Bernard died, there is no telling. But in any case, he was sanctified by struggle, bitterness, failure, and perhaps by the sacrifice of his life.

There are several pictures of him in the church of Candelada, and the chief of these, behind the high altar, depicts him not in his cowl, as one might expect, but in scapular and ready for work.

His chief feat, however, and the only one which legend particularly ascribes to him, is that he walked on the water of the river Alberche in Estremadura. The menology adds to the story the detail that he not merely walked on water but spread his cloak on the water of the river and used it as a boat.

This, then, is all we know. And yet there is something attractive in the very mysteriousness of this saint and in the hints offered to us by these poor, dry crumbs which the Bollandists have managed to get for us. A monastery wiped out by plague. A saint walking on the waters of the river Alberche. . . . But let us not fall into the traps spread out to capture an imagination by such harmonious names as "Estremadura" and "Valdeiglegias," which, incidently, means "Valley of Churches."

One more fact about Saint Bernard of Candelada: he is invoked against rabies.

August 26

Blessed John of Caramola, Lay-brother of Sagittario, near Naples, Italy

(Source: AASS, Aug. 5:369.)

The Abbey of Our Lady of Sagittario owed its name to its miraculous origin. For one day (says the legend) a hunter was going through the forest in the mountains of this wild section of the old Kingdom of Naples and, shooting an arrow at some quarry, was astonished when the arrow turned in midair, flew back and struck him without harming him. Then, stooping down to pick up the arrow, he perceived a little image of Our Lady lying at the foot of a chestnut tree. So impressed were the people of the region with the news of this portent that a monastery was built on the spot called Our Lady of the Archer, Sagittario. This abbey, in its quiet and sunny forest, high in the mountains of southern Italy, was to become famous as the shrine of a holy lay-brother, John Caramola, who had previously lived as a hermit higher up on the same mountain at a spot where, for centuries, the faithful visited the site of his retreat and prayed under an olive tree planted by his hand.

The touch of this tree cured quartan fever. For hundreds of years, also, they chanted a beautiful proper office for the saint down in the Abbey church, recalling the day when first the joy of those ancient Cistercians burst out with the words: *In coelorum rosario, rosa novella ponitur: in sanctorum collegio, novus santus colligitur.*[9] "A new rose is placed in the rose garden of heaven, and there is gathered a new saint into the company of the saints!"

He was a Frenchman of the South of France, born at Toulouse. Somehow he left his family, his home, his native land, like Abraham. Guided by no one knows what inspiration, he found his way to southern Italy and into the mountains behind Naples. He settled for a while in the little town of Chiaramonte, living as a secular, earning his bread as a day laborer, which had evidently been his occupation before leaving home. The only thing remarkable about him was his exceptional honesty and purity of life. He was one of those simple and perfect and humble people, of whom there are so many among the poor: people who have surmounted their economic poverty by poverty of spirit. And yet they are men who are completely unconscious of their virtue, perhaps even unconscious of the very existence of the abstract term "virtue." John Caramola was such a one. And how much God delights in such souls we know by the fact of His having chosen one of them, Saint Joseph, to be the foster father of His son. We are told of John that, when working in the vineyards on the hillsides around Chiaramonte, he would not even help himself to one bunch of grapes.

After some time he decided to become a hermit. And so he climbed into the mountains and settled high up above the valley and the little town, high above the monastery of Sagittario. There he lived in silence and prayer. Sometimes people brought him bread; sometimes he had to come down to beg for a little. He never asked for more than crumbs. Indeed, all he ate was a little bread, perhaps a few handfuls of crumbs, and all he drank was a little cupful of water from the spring. This was his daily meal. Between meals he did not even drink any water.

[9] Antiphon of the third nocturn.

It was sometimes hard for him to provide for even so simple a meal as this. We read of his coming down to Sagittario in the middle of a blinding snowstorm to ask for the crumbs that might be lying around in the breadboxes, only to be told that there was no bread in the monastery itself, and the crumbs had all been served to the sick in the infirmary. The monks were not absolutely without food: they had some vegetables to boil for themselves. We are not told whether the poor hermit partook of these or not.

He had other troubles. Some robbers decided, in their lack of faith, that this hermit was undoubtedly putting up a false front and probably had some money and food hidden in his cell somewhere. So they attacked him and ransacked his poor little dwelling, where they found, of course, nothing at all. Furious at themselves as well as at the hermit, as if he were to blame for not having a hidden treasure, they gave him a savage beating and left him senseless on the ground. And yet, when the victim of this attack was questioned about the identity of his brutal attackers, he simply kept quiet and refused to give them away.

He was famous for his gift of prophecy, and it seems that God had given him this gift, as He had to several others of the early Cistercians, for the purpose of righting wrongs done to the Church. The Countess of Chiaramonte, long childless, came to ask the hermit to pray that she might have children. He predicted that her affliction would end when she had restored certain rights to the Church in her lands. And his prediction was fulfilled.

After many years in his hermitage, with his legs partly crippled, and with constant suffering from sickness, he was admitted to the monastery of Sagittario as a lay-brother, and there the monks were able to observe his virtues at close range. His silence was something phenomenal. He seemed like a man without a tongue. He would go for days in such recollection and absorption that everyone was in amazement at his quiet, peaceful immobility in God. Yet he was conscious of nothing, least of all that he was remarkable in any way. He had forgotten himself entirely.

He continued his fasts. He brought with him his bed, which was square, four feet each way, and did not permit him to stretch out in any direction. Besides that, it was concave in the middle. But he never seemed to sleep on it anyway. In fact, there was no one at the monastery who ever saw him asleep.

Finally, in the year 1339, he died. The night of his death was a wild one and the wind roared into his cell, blowing out all the lights at the moment of his departure from this world. But it was long before miracles were obtained through his intercession. Frater Thaddeus, a philosophy student at the monastery, fell ill with dysentery and became so weak that his life was despaired of. Indeed, he was having hemorrhages and had to be supported by two other monks when he did so. But suddenly, in this condition he thought of Brother John of Caramola, and to the astonishment of all, he rose up and got out of bed and walked unaided down to the church, where he cast himself down before the saint's altar. The sign of the Cross having been made upon his stomach with the relics, he was cured. Then there was a man with an ulcerated arm who, to escape the threat of a barber-surgeon who wanted to cut his arm off entirely, prayed to John of Caramola and had the ulcer cured by the touch of the hermit's staff.

Meanwhile, the last relatives of the holy man, near Toulouse, had a vision in which they saw a venerable old man in the habit of a Cistercian lay-brother carrying a staff and surrounded by a heavenly light. He told them that he was their relative who had so long ago left Toulouse and that he had died in a Cistercian monastery. Not knowing what to do, but filled with an earnest desire to visit the tomb of one who had so obviously become a saint, the poor folk set out for the nearest Cistercian monastery, which was Grandselve, a few miles up the river towards Agen.

There they were allowed to consult a holy lay-brother, also called John, who had the gift of prophecy, and he, after some prayer, discovered to them that their relative had died at Sagittario. Thither they accordingly went. Let us leave them in prayer before the shrine of their saint, whose saint whose image stood with those of Saint Bernard and Our Lady in a special chapel, and let us not fail to trust in him also. The years mean nothing in heaven, and neither does space, and John of Caramola in his simplicity is as close to us as he ever was to those who wondered at the fact that he never slept and never spoke: in fact he is much closer.

August 29

Blessed Beatrice, Prioress of Nazareth, Lierre, Belgium

(Source: *Vie de la Blessed Beatrix*, by a Monk of Lérins [based on her auto-biography]; Plogaerts.)

One of the "five prudent virgins" whose lives were collected together in a book by Chrysostom Henriquez[10] was Beatrice of Nazareth, who ranks as one of the great Flemish mystics of the thirteenth century.

Beatrice was born in Tirelemont, Brabant, on the Feast of the Immaculate Conception, 1229, and indeed long before her birth she had already been consecrated to the Mother of God. So pious were her parents, indeed, that her father was to found three Cistercian convents and to die in the habit of a Cistercian lay-brother while her two sisters joined her in the cloister; one of her brothers became a Premonstratensian canon and the others are thought to have become Cistercian lay-brothers like their father, commemorated as Blessed Bartholomew in the abbey menology.[11]

Beatrice, a shy and pious child, loved Christ in the poor, for she had a lively and loving faith, nourished by her habit of pondering the phrases of Holy Scripture which she heard and read. She would introduce poor beggars into the house and give them a place by the fire and offer them her own food. At the death of her mother she was sent by her father to the school of the Beguines at Leeuwen and there learned not only to read and write but also acquired a thorough knowledge of Latin, without which it was impossible to

---

[10] *Quinque Prudentes Virgines* (Antwerp, 1630). The five are: Blessed Ida of Louvain, Blessed Ida of Nivelles, Blessed Ida of Leeuwen, Blessed Beatrice, and Blessed Aleyde.

[11] *Menology*, August 24; see also Plogaerts, 15. The convents he founded were Glorival, Maagdendael, and Nazareth. He ended his days as a lay-brother in the service of the nuns of Nazareth.

be accepted as a postulant at many convents at that time, notwith-standing the false opinions concerning the lack of all feminine education in the Middle Ages.

But when her father founded his first Cistercian convent, endow-ing the ruined Benedictine monastery of Florival for the reception of a colony of Cistercian nuns, Beatrice became a boarder with the sisters and under their direction lived a more or less strict life, keeping many points of the Cistercian Rule, although still only a child. Although the Rosary as we know it had not yet come into use, little Beatrice used to daily recite the hundred fifty Aves that made up "Our Lady's Psalter" and did so prostrate on the cold stone floor of the abbey church until she was forbidden to do so for the sake of her health.

She soon developed a great desire to do penance and punish her flesh, and so she fearlessly set about some very austere mortifica-tions, beating herself fiercely with holly branches until her body was covered with blood, wearing a tight girdle of knotted cords, and filling her bed and clothing with holly leaves. She would also go out into the garden and kneel in some hidden corner for long hours in the snow or with the rain pouring down from her head and shoulders and soaking her to the skin. This did not fail to have a bad effect on her health, but although she was consumed with a burning fever, she could not be persuaded to forego a single one of the regular exercises.

She had long desired to enter the Cistercian Order and become one of the community at Florival, but her natural timidity as well as a humility born of grace made her hesitate and reflect upon this step, devoting a whole year to preparing her soul before she pre-sented her request to be admitted. At first it was refused on account of her poor health, but she argued with such simple faith and such intense earnestness of desire, that God would give her the neces-sary health, that her pleas could not be refused.

Soon after her religious profession, an important change oc-curred in her life. She was sent to the famous convent of Ramege to learn the art of illuminating manuscripts. It was in the scriptorium of Ramege that Blessed Ida of Leeuwen had added, to the distinc-tion of her sanctity and beautiful spirituality, the humbler glory of a most proficient copyist and illuminator. Beatrice was probably sent with several other nuns from Florival to learn this art and form a scriptorium at their own convent, which they successfully did. Father Canivez tells us[12] that even the schedules of profession, written out by the nuns of Florival, to be sung at their profession day and placed on the altar, were works of art. Many of them are still preserved.

But the most important thing about Beatrice's stay at Ramege was that it brought her into contact with the great mystic Ida of Nivelles. Blessed Ida soon recognized the depth of spirituality in this young sister and loved her because of the great graces that she foreknew would be bestowed upon her by God. Indeed, she even told the young nun just when these graces would first come to her, warning her to purify and prepare her soul, because the Lord would give her a new and incomparably profound and intimate knowledge of Himself during the octave of His Nativity.

Beatrice did, indeed, earnestly prepare herself, but on Christmas day not only were there no exceptional graces or consolations to be had, but she could not even pray. Her soul was invaded by a paralyzing dryness and seemed surrounded by the dark waters of hell. Nor did the situation grow any better for the next two or three days but rather worse. Then finally, one evening at Compline, she was turning over in her mind, according to the habit she had formed from childhood, a responsory of the liturgy (at present it is the fourth of the night office of Christmas Day: *Propter nimiam charitate*: "Because of His exceeding great love with which He hath loved us, God the Father sent His Son in the likeness of sinful flesh to save all"). And then, for no strictly liturgical reason, she associated this by chance with something from the liturgy of Paschal time that came into her head at the moment: *Et David cum cantoribus cytharam percutiebat in domo Domini*:[13] "David with the singers played upon the harp in the house of the Lord." At that moment it seems that a burst of flame shot forth from the tabernacle and

---

[12] Canivez, *L'Ordre*, article on "Florival."
[13] See *Breviarium Cisterciense*, Pars Vernalis.

set her heart on fire with a joy so immense and powerful that she was rapt completely out of her senses in an instance and, the office ending, fell on her knees in her stall and remained there even while everyone else filed out and went to bed. Hours later, her absence from the dormitory was discovered and the sisters found her still kneeling, apparently lifeless, in the same position. She came to herself in the infirmary and told them what she had seen: for she had been present and assisted at the joy and exultation of the angels of heaven surrounding their Queen and the Child Jesus and praising the love of God in sending His only Son to redeem mankind. For days afterwards, and indeed all her life, she had only to remember this first foretaste of glory and her heart would become light with pure joy.

Nevertheless, ecstasies are not perfection of virtue and sanctity, nor do they guarantee us against temptation or great imperfection or even sin. Saint Gertrude had to struggle all her life against stubborn and seemingly incurable imperfections, temptations against patience and even against fraternal charity, temptations to fear and despair; and all the while she was being visited by frequent visions and raptures. Blessed Beatrice, on her return to Florival, was deluded by the devil into a false humility which told her that she would be attracting too much attention if she spent long intervals in prayer before the Blessed Sacrament, and consequently she began to curtail her visits to Jesus in the Tabernacle and even omit them altogether.

And Blessed Beatrice, desiring "not to attract attention," deprived herself so drastically of the food of the soul that soon she became indifferent and tepid in all her religious life. Her Communions were ill prepared and her thanksgivings short and cold. Finally, one day she was kneeling in choir and saying to herself: "I shall not go to Communion tomorrow. I went twice this week, and both times I did not take time to prepare: it is too late to make a good preparation now: and besides, I am tepid after receiving Communion." But one of the other nuns received a supernatural intuition of what was going on in the soul of her sister and gave her an urgent warning that she must by all means go to Communion the next day. Beatrice was startled and frightened and made a fervent

Communion, after which she received grace to see what a mistake she had made and resumed her long visits and began to receive Communion almost every day.

The way she distributed her time at this period of her life could serve as a model for any religious in our Order—or any other. Although she spent much time in adoration before the Tabernacle, she did not, on that account, neglect her spiritual reading: for the two go hand in hand. They should be well balanced, however. Her reading was meditative rather than studious. She did not apply herself to her books with the intense concentration of the scholar but read prayerfully, pausing to ask for light and to reflect on what she read but making notes at the same time, copying down whatever impressed her most.

Most of her reading was Holy Scripture. She made every Sunday a day of recollection and retreat, on which she examined herself on her faults and progress of the past week and took a few effective resolutions. She habitually meditated on the Passion of Our Lord: for five years, she took no other topic. And besides that, she associated the various hours and times of the day, especially the canonical hours, with the phases of His Passion. At Compline she was with Him in Gethsemani, during night Office before the high priests, at Prime she saw Him judged and scourged for our pride and self-indulgence, and so on throughout the day. Her prayer was mostly affective, and she talked with Our Lord, pouring out her heart to Him in simple and direct and loving words.

Her meditations sometimes produced some rather elaborate devices to help her in the way of perfection, like her "interior monastery," of which Reason was the Abbess, Wisdom the Prioress, Prudence the Sub-Prioress and so on. Chapter of Faults was held every evening after Compline.

Here life was not all consolations and fervor. She was tried by several long periods of dryness and passive purification, during one of which, lasting three years, she became almost persuaded that heaven was closed to her utterly.

Then one year on Ascension Day, her heart was pierced like that of Saint Teresa of Avila by a fiery dart, which in her case came not from the hands of a seraph but from the tabernacle. After that immense joy, she entered into a period of intense physical and moral suffering.

She founded Nazareth, the third convent endowed by her father, in 1220 and was superior there until her death in 1268.

On Christmas Day of 1267 she had collapsed after receiving Communion and was taken to the infirmary where she lay all but dead, with no sign of life except the beating of her heart, for days and weeks and months. Finally in July she returned to herself and received the Last Sacraments before passing joyfully into the glory of her Spouse on the twenty-ninth of that month.

She was venerated with an immemorial cult and has left posterity an autobiographical account of her visions and revelations.

September

September 8

Blessed William of Saint Thierry, Monk of Signy, near Rheims, France

(Sources: PL 180:205 and PL 184:365; Vita Bern; Étienne Gilson, *The Mystical Theology of Saint Bernard*, trans. A. H. C. Downes [New York: Sheed & Ward, 1940], Appendix 5; Justin McCann, Introduction, *The Golden Epistle of Abbot William of St. Thierry*, trans. Walter Shewring [London: Sheed and Ward, 1980].)

All our early Cistercians have been much neglected even in their own Order, but perhaps the most neglected of all, when we consider how great a claim to our attention is made by his writings and doctrine, has been William of Saint Thierry. Here is a mystic and theologian with all the power and genius of the great theologians of Saint Victor, whom he closely resembles, and one who, at times, is in no respect inferior even to Saint Bernard or Saint Anselm. It has remained for one of the soundest and most able Catholic Philosophers of our own century, Étienne Gilson, to evaluate William of Saint Thierry at his true worth. Let us hear what he has to say of William in his valuable Appendix which he devotes to him at the end of his book, *The Mystical Theology of Saint Bernard*:

> He is a very great theologian [and Gilson is by no means careless with his superlatives], in whom firmness of thought goes hand in hand with a remarkable power of just expression.
>
> Intimately connected with Saint Bernard, in full accord with him on the principles of the mystical life and the solution of its problems, he knew how, in the midst of his unreserved

327

admiration for the Abbot of Clairvaux, to preserve an absolute
independence of thought. For William of Saint Thierry has
everything: power of thought, the orator's eloquence, the
poet's lyricism and all the attractiveness of the most ardent
and tender piety.[1]

William of Saint Thierry has everything! Indeed it is true: there
is not a line of his writing that is not filled with the light and unction of the Holy Spirit, and yet this great mystical theologian is
practically unknown, even to the average Cistercian monk, when
his beautiful *Meditative Orationes*,[2] for example, ought to be engraved in the hearts of every Cistercian, even from his novitiate
on, or at least from the moment he has acquired enough Latin to
understand them. Who was this saintly theologian? What kind of
a person was he? To begin with, he was Saint Bernard's first and
best biographer. No one has yet equaled his brief, unfinished Life
of the great abbot, whom he preceded through the portals of heav-
en.[3] This Life is a real masterpiece, one of the finest things in medieval literature.

Its character and atmosphere, as a matter of fact, have influenced
the Office of Saint Bernard in our breviary and have colored our
whole view of the great abbot ever since. What a joy it is to look at
the twelfth century and Clairvaux and Saint Bernard through the
eyes of one so simple, so joyful, so clearheaded and pure of heart
as William of Saint Thierry, for whom the whole world was radiant
with the glory and goodness of the divine mercy. His pictures of
Clairvaux are unforgettable: indeed, the only living pictures of
many a Cistercian, especially Saint Bernard's brothers, are to be
found in a stray phrase or sentence of William's *Vita Bernardi*.

Apart from a few dates and uncertain facts as bare and dry as
dust, all we know of Blessed Humbeline, Blessed Nivard, Andrew,
Tescelin, Aleth, and all the rest, to say nothing of the wonderful
history of Saint Bernard's conversions of his other friends, is built

---

[1] Étienne Gilson, *The Mystical Theology of Saint Bernard*, trans. A. H. C.
Downes, CS 120 (Sheed and Ward, 1940; Kalamazoo, MI: Cistercian, 1990), 198.
[2] PL 180:205.
[3] PL 185:221.

on a few vivid lines of William of Saint Thierry. And yet from a few words of his, we feel we have a complete picture of Humbeline; for example, we seem to know her well.

Born of noble parents at Liege, about 1085, William went to France, perhaps to study at the hill town of Laon, where many famous scholars and teachers were gathered in the shadow of the cathedral. And William admits that when he was there, he nearly took the same path as Abelard, so seductive was the charm of learning for its own sweet sake in this new spring of philosophy and humanism that was filling the eleventh and twelfth centuries with its fair flowers. But, unlike Abelard, William recognized the temptation of *curiositas* in time and turned to another school to learn the one science that included and vivified all others: the love of God, who is himself perfect and infinite truth, and whom we can only truly possess by love. So he entered the Benedictine abbey of Saint Nicaise at Rheims. There he became a most edifying and regular monk, distinguished for his love of the Rule (which was there kept according to the Cluniac usages) and of the brethren, as well as for his learning and skill in various sciences, including dialectics, theology, and even medicine. It was not long before his piety and ability were recognized, and he became Abbot of Saint Thierry near Rheims in Champagne.

There Abbot William showed himself a zealous teacher of Christian perfection, equaling in his fervor and wisdom the great Benedictines, his contemporaries, Hugh and Richard, and the other great theologians of the School of Saint Victor in Paris. Saint Thierry became known as a most regular monastery. It was inevitable that William of Saint Thierry should soon become a friend of another learned and holy Benedictine, William of Champeaux, himself a philosopher from Saint Victor, who was ordinary of the diocese in which Clairvaux was situated. It was through William of Champeaux that he met Saint Bernard.

We know from the *Vita Bernardi*[4] what were his first impressions on coming over the brow of the hill and seeing below him in the wooded hollow the plain monastery buildings and barns, the

---

[4] Vita Bern 1.7.

workshops, stables, fields, gardens, orchards, pastures, all full of busy monks and resounding with the cheerful, wholesome music of labor and yet no sound of a human voice; and we know what were his reflections on this picture of charity, so ordering things by the loving observance of a common Rule as to produce the paradox of hundreds of monks living as true solitaries, yet in a community in which all were constantly together and no one was alone! But what was his admiration, his awe, rather, when he entered the poor "leper's hut," where Saint Bernard was confined to rest and recover from his infirmities by order of the General Chapter: William approached that place as if it were "the altar of God." This was the beginning of a famous and most fruitful friendship, one which produced many great books in defense of the truth and at least one miracle.

The miracle was this: Saint Bernard once heard that William was dangerously ill and in bed at Saint Thierry. He nevertheless earnestly desired to see him and talk with him at Clairvaux of the things of God, and accordingly, he sent his brother and cellarer, Blessed Gerard, off to the Benedictine abbey with the somewhat cavalier promise that if William would come to Clairvaux, he would be cured—or at least have the satisfaction of being buried among his best friends. The humorous reservation was simply a cloak for a promise that might otherwise have seemed presumptuous, but William had no doubts in his mind. Rising from bed, he made the journey to Clairvaux with the greatest difficulty and pain, but on his arrival he was cured.

It was during this time, when Saint Bernard's sickness had enforced so much inactivity upon him, that he was meditating and planning his sermons on the Canticle of Canticles. This had long been a favorite subject of study with William also, who in fact compiled two commentaries on that book: one of selections from the works of Saint Ambrose, explaining various passages of it, and the other of selections from the works of Saint Gregory the Great. Besides this, he also composed a commentary of his own. All three are to be found in Migne's *Latin Patrology*.[5] But the two saints spent

---

[5] PL 180:473; 15:180–441.

many hours in the cottage at Clairvaux, talking of the glory for which all are born, the perfect participation in the divine nature of love.

Some of William's best known works belong to this period: they are the ones included in Mabillon in his edition of Saint Bernard and are found together with the works of the Abbot of Clairvaux in Migne.[6] For it was at this time that William wrote the *De contemplando Deo* and the *De natura et dignitate amoris*. The latter work has the characteristic Cistercian and twelfth-century stamp upon it, imposed by the social context in which it was written, of beginning with a conscious appeal to nature and then from this starting point ascending to the supernatural and transfiguring nature by subjecting it to grace. William's treatise on the *Art of Love* is a conscious challenge to the fleshly love and prudence of Ovid, just as Saint Ælred's *Spiritual Friendship* is a challenge to Cicero. For William's point is that man was made by nature to achieve perfect happiness by love, but that since the fall, what appeals to the senses and passions produces only a caricature and degradation of the true love which, instead of giving us joy, gives us only infinite misery by enslaving us to what is beneath us. In our present fallen state, our nature still tends by its own natural movement to love; but original sin has so vitiated and blinded us that all our love, instead of tending to God, tends to self. It is self-love that is the seed of ultimate damnation and if we want to be happy we have to root out and entirely exterminate self-love and relearn the true love that self-love has obliterated from our memories. We have to recover charity. How is this to be done? Of course, the whole aim of the law of God and of the grace of Christ, which enables us to fulfill that law in and with him, is to do this work of reforming the shattered image of God in us. But William is especially concerned with the means of doing this work. Now if we want to learn a science, we go to school. And if we want to learn charity, there must be schools of charity.

Monasteries are such schools, but in them we learn not so much by books and conferences as by actions, by obedience. For since

---

[6] PL 184.

the main problem in gaining charity is the overcoming of self-will, obviously we can best expedite matters if, from the very outset, we commit all our will into the hands of a superior and obey him according to our Rule.

Ars est artium ars amoris ("The art of all arts is the art of love").[7] And since this art was implanted in our very nature, even though we seem to have lost it, if we would find it we must seek it again within ourselves, for it is there but covered over by the disfigurement of self-love. Hence, the next step for William of Saint Thierry, as it was for Saint Bernard, is for us to know ourselves. *Nosce teipsum* is the basis of all our meditation and of our prayer, not in the sense that we are the ultimate end of all our investigations (God preserve us from such a doom), but we come to know God through knowing his image which is implanted in the depth and center and in the very substance of our souls.

It is in the question of the divine image within us that William takes a slightly different course from Saint Bernard. He is in the first place more speculative than the abbot of Clairvaux. And then, like Saint Ælred, he keeps closer to the traditional lines laid down by Saint Augustine by considering the trinity of powers in the soul, intellect, memory and will, in their analogy to the Holy Trinity who is also with us by grace.

The distinctive feature of William's doctrine is the importance he gives to the Augustinian notion of *memoria*. This memory is by no means merely the faculty of recollection of past things that we usually speak of by that name. Rather it is that very consciousness of self, of existence, of one's own being, and of the metaphysical fact of being itself which lies at the very heart and core of all the activities of the human mind and is in a sense the principle of all thought. More than that, it is the faculty of recognizing in ourselves the latent presence of God.[8] Now, buried deep in this *memoria* is the "light that enlightens everyone coming into the world" (Jn 1:9). Right in the very center of our souls, truth itself, God, is to be found

[7] PL 184.
[8] Gilson, 204.

in his image, the root of our very being. The whole purpose of our lives is to penetrate through the confusion and darkness of our passions into the depth and peace and tranquility of this center and find that image once again. In other words, our whole intellectual and spiritual life begins when we re-establish contact with God present within us.

In this sense, then, the *memoria*, which contains this principle of all thought, God himself, resembles the Father. The intellect, which realizes this presence, corresponds to the Son. The will, which then turns to God present in us, in our *memoria*, and directs to him all the power and ardor and desire of which our whole being is capable, is like the Holy Spirit. And then we begin to live, for then all our powers are once more directed to their center, their true end. All is harmony. We have peace, "the tranquility of order," because we love. And in thus loving we are acting like God, whose infinite and perfect activity is his love of himself in his three persons.

In other words, William of Saint Thierry has worked out the one fundamental practice underlying all Benedictine spirituality into a mystical doctrine of the greatest beauty and subtlety. What he has done has been to explain to us what is really meant by the "realization of the presence of God." Of course, the most important factor in the working of this regeneration to supernatural activity within us is grace. And this leads us to William's Christology.

How do we get grace? By faith. But where do we get faith? William does not go into the intricacies of explaining how it is that, although we must make a free and meritorious act, grace must always come first to inspire that act. In his psychological approach to faith he goes straight to the root of the matter: the Cross. Christ demands faith of us and himself gives us the means to acquire it. "For it is not difficult for someone to entrust himself to One whom he sees going before him in merciful love [*pietate*]."[9] We believe in him, hope in him, love him, because we see how much he has loved us. But let William speak for himself:

[9] Gilson, 204.

Everything that Jesus did, everything he said on this earth, including all the insults He suffered, being spat upon, and struck, dying on the Cross and being buried, was nothing else but the love of the Father speaking to us through the Son, by which love our own love is awakened and lifted up even unto Him.[10]

It is not merely the love of a man for us that we see on Calvary, for that would not be enough. We see in Jesus the love of the infinitely powerful and merciful God for us. And thus our response to this love is more than gratitude and sympathy: it is complete confidence in the power of him who sent Jesus to save us and confidence in his mercy, because we see that he has not hesitated to sacrifice his only-begotten Son to redeem us. Only God, says William, deserves the name of Lord, because only he can save those who serve him.

But now let us see with what subtlety and penetration he goes into the depths of the mercy of God for us. "Thou alone art Lord, for with thee alone does *domination over* us mean *salvation* for us: for us to serve thee, is nothing else but to be saved by thee."[11] This is the substance of William's doctrine on justification and recalls Saint Bernard's dictum: *Consentire enim salvari est.*[12] To consent to God's mercy, to his graces, to the love He offers us, is to be saved. We are justified and glorified by *allowing* God to pour out his infinite love upon us.[13] And that means by corresponding with all his graces, by believing what he wants to tell us concerning his great love for us, and acting on that belief. *Haec est justitia filiorum hominum: ama me quia amo te.*[14] Justice, says William, for the sons of men means to love God, because God loves us. And why is love the beginning and end of all? Why is it that God wants only our love, asks us only for our hearts? Not because he needs our love, but because we need to love him if we are truly to live.

[10] William, Contem 10; Sch 61 bis.
[11] Contem 9; Sch 61 bis.
[12] Bernard, Gra 1.2; SBOp 3:167.
[13] See Bernard, Gra 1.2; SBOp 3:166–7.
[14] Contem 10; Sch 61 bis.

"Thou hast first loved us in order that we might love thee: not because thou needest to be loved by us, but because the only way we can become that for which we were created is by loving thee." [15] This love is true wisdom, and if it begins with the realization of the meaning of Bethlehem and Calvary, it continues and grows in us in proportion as we share in the graces of Bethlehem and Calvary. But both are perpetuated upon our altars. "To eat the Body of Christ," says William, "is to become the body of Christ and the temple of the Holy Spirit." [16] Therefore God dwells in us, and the more he dwells in us by this intimate union, in which we actually "become the flesh of Christ," the more we will find strength and light to progress in virtue, that is to say, the more we will love what is good and spiritual and despise both the prosperity and adversity of this world. It is remarkable what great importance William puts on the Holy Eucharist in the spiritual life. For him it is the quickest way to perfection, to wisdom, to true union with God. If this mysticism is based on the realization of the presence of God within us, it is obvious that, since he sees clearly that the Eucharist is what makes us most perfectly and most truly temples of God by making us "the Body of Christ," the Eucharist will be the supreme means to nourish the divine life and presence within us.

Nevertheless, William is also, of all the Cistercian writers, the one who has the most to say about the Holy Spirit. Here, too, his doctrine is extremely illuminating and important because of the clear distinction he makes between human and divine love. Human love is an affection, implying movement towards an end, contingency and change, imperfection. God's love is his own eternal and unchanging and perfect substance. Now one of the great weaknesses of the spiritual life of most people who have advanced a certain distance towards perfection but seem to be able to get no further is the natural tendency to reduce God to a human level and consider his love for us only in terms of a human affection. God's love is not an affection; it is himself. And he loves us, not

[15] Contem 10; Sch 61 bis.
[16] Nat am 13.38.

as we love by moving towards some object of desire but by drawing us into himself, that is, by making us participate in his infinite
love for himself and for all things in him. And it is the Holy Spirit
that performs this wonderful work. William writes:

> Thou dost love thyself, O most dear Lord, in thyself, when
> from the Father and the Son proceeds the Holy Spirit, the love
> of the Father for the Son and of the Son for the Father: and so
> great is this love that it results in oneness: and so great is this
> oneness that it results in an *homoousios* that is, one same
> substance for both the Father and the Son. And thou dost also
> love thyself in us, sending the Spirit of thy Son into our hearts,
> crying out in us, from the sweetness of love and from the
> vehemence of the good-will thou hast breathed into us: "Abba
> Father!" And thou dost make us thy lovers in such a way that
> . . . we have full confidence in the fact that all that belongs
> to the Father, belongs to us, and call upon thee with the same
> name, by grace of adoption, as that which is used by the only
> Son by reason of his very nature.[17]

And yet this hardly begins to give us an idea of the richness and
beauty of the doctrine of this saintly mystic, whose every line is a
cry of love for God so full of light and joy and ardor that it lifts
our hearts up to heaven on the wings of divine grace and desire,
and we long for that perfect vision, the very thought of which was
the daily bread on which this saint was nourished all his life.

But to continue the story of that life: it was inevitable that he
should desire to enter Clairvaux, and he soon asked the abbot
to accept him as a novice, which Saint Bernard refused to do,
believing that William would do much more good by his fervor
and regularity as abbot among the Benedictines than as a simple
monk at Clairvaux.[18] But when, in 1135, William retired to an ob-

---

[17] Contem 11; Sch 61 bis.

[18] William had participated in a reform movement of several Cluniac houses
in the province of Rheims, inspired by the Cistercian reform, but remaining
within the Cluniac congregation and observances. A small General Chapter
was held on the model of that instituted at Cîteaux. The fact that Saint Bernard

scure new foundation, the Cistercian abbey of Signy in the forest of the Ardennes, Saint Bernard showed neither surprise nor disapproval.

William was by that time nearly fifty, and the change was hard on his health and constitution. He was not able to bear the full burden of manual labor, and as a fortunate consequence for us, he was forced to do a great deal of writing. Indeed, his most fruitful and prolific period of writing was in the Cistercian monastery of Signy, where he produced eleven treatises, including one *On the Holy Eucharist*, two *On Faith*, one *On the Nature of the Soul and the Body*, a *Commentary on Romans*, and a polemic against Abelard's heresies, as well as the beautiful *Golden Epistle* to the brethren of Mont Dieu Charterhouse, a treatise on prayer and the contemplative life which was long erroneously attributed to Prior Guigo of the Grande Chartreuse.

Williams's holy death took place on September 8, 1148, and was followed by miracles. He was venerated with an immemorial cult.

September 29

Blessed John of Montmirail, Monk of Longpont, France

(Source: AASS, Sept. 8:86; Life of a monk of Longpont, 13th century.)

The story of Blessed John of Montmirail, written by an unknown monk of Longpont, near Soissons, shows us a nobleman and soldier who was a mixture of ingenuousness, passion, impulsive sincerity and well-meaning stubbornness, all of which, transformed in the crucible of his conversion from the world, made him a saint.

---

wanted William to carry on with this same work indicates that the early Cistercians did not hold that the mitigated Cluniac usages were in themselves useless or decadent.

This prince of the royal blood and descent of Charlemagne had once saved the life of King Philip Augustus of France, when they were surrounded by the soldiers of Richard Coeur de Lion at Gisors, Normandy. Great soldier and powerful lord that he was, and filled with the ideals of his time and class, he had once spent the immense sum of a thousand pounds upon a single tourney. But the rebukes of a holy priest he knew finally succeeded in converting him from his vain love of power and repute in the world. His conversion, however, was marked by a piece of typical impulsiveness that showed at once his sincerity and his complete lack of discernment in spiritual things. For, in an intense desire for the grace of compunction for his sins, he begged the Virgin Mother of God to appear to him in a vision and tell him that he was damned (without this being actually so, of course), so as to frighten him into repentance. Instead of answering this idiotic prayer, God sent him a physical affliction, an intense, inexplicable and apparently incurable pain in his side, which afflicted him for four years until he was relieved of it by the prayers of a holy recluse.

By that time he had entered upon a career of reform and penance. He had abandoned fighting and jousting and all his other expensive entertainments and turned the Castle of Montmirail in the rolling, wheat-growing plains of the province of Brie into a hostel for pilgrims, a refuge for the poor and a hospital for the sick.[19] He drove out all usurers from his domains, and while treating his own body with the utmost austerity, sleeping on the floor, wearing a hair shirt, and spending long, cold nights in prayer, he also helped to tend the sick who were sheltered under his roof. This was not without its difficulties: for in spite of his goodwill, he was once so overcome by the smell that filled the room where the poor patients lay that he escaped to the fresh air in disgust. The woman whom he had put in charge of the place followed him and cried out in derision: "What are you afraid of, you great soldier? Is it your sins, perhaps, that overwhelm you with their

---

[19] Saint Vincent de Paul also resided here for some time when he was chaplain and tutor to the Condi family. They acquired the estate in the seventeenth century.

evil smell?" He returned inside without a word, thereafter often kissing the foulest of sores and wounds upon the bodies of the sufferers.

Another vivid picture of his character: riding from Oisy to his village of Alcimont, to sit in judgment upon the cases and disputes of his people, he is met on the road by twenty-five lepers. Dismounting, he distributes to them all his money, kissing their hands, while his companions stand apart at a safe distance. But a few hundred yards along the road they meet one more leper, too weak to keep up with the rest, who cries out piteously for alms. The lord of Montmirail says: "I have no more money to give. But I will ask something of you: give me your coat, in exchange for mine." So the exchange was made, and the lord took his place in the seat of judgment at Alcimont, wearing a leper's coat. But it was not a very successful court from the point of view of the various plaintiffs; they pleaded all day, and every case was dismissed without issue because John de Montmirail was lost in God.

It was about this time that he began to think of leaving the world, and he sent one of his men to consult a holy hermit about the advisability of the lord of Montmirail's embracing the estate of a solitary in the woods. The hermit's answer was as vehement as it was definite. No! Never! He himself, said the holy man, was thoroughly disgusted with a state in which his soul, constantly and furiously attacked by evil spirits, was at every moment of the night and day in the gravest peril of sin. It was not good for man to be alone. Let the Lord of Montmirail become a Cistercian monk, *militans sub regula vel abbate*,[20] as Saint Benedict has it: "fighting under a rule and an abbot."

On Ascension day, probably in the year 1210, John de Montmirail was received as a novice at the priory of Longpont, a daughter-house of Clairvaux, in what is now the department of Oise, a considerable distance from his castle and lands.

He began at once to add enthusiastically to the penances prescribed by the Rule. In the refectory (such enthusiasm almost

[20] RB 1.2.

always starts in the refectory) he ate little or nothing, and the portion he did eat, he made almost tasteless by filling it with cold water. The prior took him to task for this and finally told him to eat, at least, all of his bread.

The Rule provides for a pound of bread a day for each monk, but in the Middle Ages the pound was not standardized, and could be anything up to thirty ounces. John found himself with much more bread than he could comfortably eat. However, out of obedience, he ate every bit of it, in spite of the difficulty. Later, when the prior sent him a fish, he also obediently ate that: in fact, he also ate the head, the tail and the bones.

It happened that one of his relatives entered the monastery, and this monk, Frater Amandus by name, as a token of love and respect for his famous relation, took to oiling his shoes for him surreptitiously during the night. John was very upset and went to the prior complaining that he had come to serve and to get away from being served. He wanted the whole thing stopped. The prior gave him a prudent and successful solution, telling him to go, that night, and perform the same service for his relation. And after that John was able to take care of his own shoes once again without interference.

As a monk, John held some office that sent him frequently outside the monastery with the prior and cellarer, and on these excursions he had many opportunities to show his humility in that impulsive and dramatic way that the medieval saints could carry off so well because they were so childlike in their sincerity. One day John and the Cellarer of Vauxcelles were entering Cambrai. There was a group of idlers and vagabonds loitering on the drawbridge over the dry moat, and seeing the two poor monks they started calling out after them "Hauy! Hauy! Hauy!" which, as the learned commentator in the Bollandists explains, in the most unnecessary note in the history of hagiography, was a cry of mockery—*vox illusorum*. The same commentator also produced a story, not in the anonymous "Life," of how the soldiers of the Count of Flanders fled from the miraculous rainstorm produced, at the siege of John's castle at Oisy, by the prayers of the White Monks at Vauxcelles: the fugitives took to their heels in the pelting rain with cries of "Helpt! Helpt!" which says the note, *sunt voces Belgicae quae latine adjuva reddes!*[21]

But in any case, to return from this digression in linguistics, the cellarer of Vauxcelles felt very embarrassed to have people shouting "Hauy! Hauy!" at him as he was going by and urged his companion to make haste and get into the city. But John turned back, snatching with great zest at this opportunity for humiliations and crying: "Go on! Go on! Shout at the top of your voice, for I am the greatest of sinners, John de Montmirail!"[22]

In the ordinary course of a monk's life he may expect most of his opportunities to practice humility and obedience and self-denial at manual labor. John not only made much of these but found others. We know that when he was still in the world he wore not only a hair shirt but hair breeches and hair stockings, so fearsome that when he had them on he could not ride a horse. Perhaps he continued to wear them at Longpont. But in any case, one day the community was going out to work in single file, as usual, and they came upon a dead animal of some sort, which produced a sickening stench that turned the stomachs of most of the monks. While the rest of them had their hands or their sleeves or their coarse handkerchiefs at their noses, John the later Lord of Montmirail dragged the stinking carcass off to a safe distance and buried it. Another time they were at work in the fields, and John, apart from the rest, had the good fortune to see a very loathsome leper coming through the fields. Instead of leaving him a wide berth, he went up and gave him a friendly kiss—for the old days of giving money and exchanging cloaks were gone—and then escaped with his hood down over his face, for fear that the act of virtue be recognized as his and he might lose the merit.

He had many real trials, not the least of which was the enmity and ingratitude of his own son, who disputed with the monks of Longpont the possession of a farm which John had given them. The new Lord of Montmirail refused to let the monks come near

---

[21] AASS, Sept. 8:202.
[22] AASS, Sept. 8:227.

the place and threatened violence if they did. John, at the head of a group of secular workmen, went to the farm and began to make the necessary repairs on the roof and was spared. But his son did not have any more than this purely negative respect for his father. Once when John was traveling and stopped for shelter at his own castle, the door was slammed in his face. On another occasion he stopped at the castle of his wife, a very hot day. The Lady-in-waiting returned to the door and told him that My Lady of Montmirail would be unable to receive My Lord John today, as she was all in a sweat—for even ladies sweated in the Middle Ages. (They did not begin to *perspire* until the seventeenth century.) John traveled on to the castle of his mother-in-law, who was more kindly disposed. And when she asked to what she owed the honor of this visit, when he might have stopped at his wife's place, he replied: "O, you are not all in a sweat!"

But on this occasion he had a chance to do more than exercise his irony. The noble lady had condemned a robber to have his arms and legs cut off, and he was even now imprisoned in the castle. Hearing of it, John began to beg for mercy for him. She consented to have the man brought forth from his cell, and the poor wretch immediately flung himself on the floor at her feet begging for pity. John lost no time in joining him in his position on the floor, making, if possible, even louder and more heartrending supplications, and she consented to free the man on condition, as John suggested, that he take the cross and go to Palestine, which he gladly did.

Once when his prior asked him what he would like to be if he could not be a Cistercian, he replied that he had often thought of becoming a "ribald," that is, a member of the lowest and poorest class of foot soldiers, to whom fell all the most dangerous and dirtiest and worst tasks, with the consequence that they lived practically like slaves or animals and were extremely reckless and desperate characters. The prior expressed great surprise and asked him if he would wish to spend his time trying to stupify himself with drinking and gambling and cursing and violent living. John replied, "There are ribalds and ribalds," and went on to explain that he envied the extreme difficulty and humility (of the lot) of those who lived soberly and virtuously in that state, hidden and almost crushed under their great burden of degradation. "Such men give very great glory to God," he said.

After seven years in the monastery, and in the twenty-fifth of his conversion, John de Montmirail died on the Feast of Saint Michael and All Angels, 1217, with so high a reputation for sanctity that his body was soon translated from the cemetery to the chapter room and from there to the Gospel corner in the sanctuary. His cause was introduced at Rome but was abandoned, probably for lack of funds. In 1891, his long-standing cult again came to the attention of the Holy See, and he was beatified *per modum processus*. In 1567 the Calvinists attacked Longpont and burned all the relics, including those of Blessed John, on the steps of the high altar.

October

October 3

Blessed Godfrey the Sacristan, Monk of Villers, Belgium

(Sources: Chron Vill 2:4; Martène; AASS, Oct. 1:484; Nimal, 80.)

This great Cistercian mystic who is, like all true mystics, admirable most of all for his charity began his religious life in the Benedictine Abbey of Saint Pantaleon at Cologne. But after some time he began to feel that he was called to a life of stricter penance and of more intimate union with God, for he did not here find the full peace that his soul desired. Thirsting for that peace, he prayed the Holy Spirit to enlighten him, and his prayer was answered by a vision of the Abbey of Villers and all the people in it and of the life that was led there, so detailed that he might have lived there all his life and not been better acquainted with that great school of sanctity.

It was with great joy and enthusiasm that he entered this new home and set himself to observe, admire and imitate the virtues of the holy monks who had come there before him. Humility is not an adequate description of this, the most characteristic and necessary virtue of a cenobite: let us say that Godfrey had that reverential love of his brethren that honored Christ in all of them and found all its joy in being edified by their slightest virtues. How full of this spirit were the early Cistercians! And it is this that makes the cloister an earthly paradise. For what is paradise but the vision of God? And how can we better see God on earth than in our own souls and in those of our brethren? For the desire of heaven in our own hearts is Christ living in us, and the desire of

heaven in the hearts of others is Christ living in them. And since
there is no man on earth, however wicked he thinks he is, that can
prevent himself from desiring heaven, at least implicitly, we see
Jesus in all the desires of all men for happiness. We see Him, in
some sense, glorious in the desires of those who desire happiness
where it is to be found, and we see Him crucified in the desires of
those who seek peace where there is no peace and happiness where
there is only an endless circle of frustration, that is, in sin. Godfrey
had this vision of God in other men, and therefore he loved them
all.

There is one Sacrament that nourishes this virtue of charity and
one Sacrifice that was given us above all that the unity of charity
might bind us forever to one another in Christ: the Sacrament of
His Body and Blood, and the Sacrifice of the Mass. Now there is
one significant ceremony in this Sacrifice that the early Christians
considered very important and that we have almost altogether
forgotten. Fortunately it is preserved in our Cistercian ritual, whenever anyone receives Communion; and that ceremony is the *Pax*,
or kiss of peace. There was trouble at Villers, a conflict among
brethren, and Blessed Godfrey said a Votive Mass of the Holy Spirit
for the one who was most intimately concerned in this misunderstanding. That monk was not present at the Mass. But when the
saint came to the time when the kiss of peace was given, he seemed
to see this brother before him and seemed actually to give the *Pax*
to him. Let us learn, from the sequel, the significance of this little
ceremony. This kiss of peace, which is a symbol and integral part
of Holy Communion, liturgically speaking, served mystically, in
this case, as the proximate means by which the peace of God was
restored to the heart of that monk, who was afterwards found in
perfect tranquility and joy, the misunderstanding having died out
in mutual forgiveness.

We might expect that Blessed Godfrey took an exceptional pleasure in the holy *mandatum*, in which those appointed as servants
of the refectory for the week that has finished and the one that is
to come, both wash the feet of all the monks, in memory of the
charity of Jesus in washing the feet of His disciples. What incen-
tives to fruitful meditation are to be found in the beautiful antiphons which are sung during this ceremony, which is so rich in

graces for those who give it their loving and faithful attention! As a reward for his devotion to this Sacramental, Godfrey was granted an exceptional favor by Our Lord, Who appeared to him when he was alone in the sacristy after the *mandatum*. Kneeling down before the good monk, girt up with a towel as He is described in the Gospel, Jesus offered to wash his feet.

Godfrey's immediate reaction was that of Saint Peter: *Domine! Tu mihi lavas pedes,*[1] and the Lord answered him as He had answered Saint Peter: "If I do not wash thy feet, thou shalt have no part with me." How well we see the heart of that great saint and Prince of the Apostles in his childlike and impulsive charity with which he answered that statement! If washing was to be a condition of union with God, then let him be washed all over! *Non solum pedes, sed et manus et caput!* And Godfrey too was thus received into the Kingdom of God, which is nothing else but the participation in His charity for all men. For Jesus told him, as He had told the disciples, "As I have laid down My life for you, so you must lay down yours for your brethren."

Great was the charity of this monk after such favors! But there were many more of the same nature. There was the time he came down to church to light the lights for Matins and found the vigil light before Our Lady's altar extinguished and the whole church in darkness.[2] But a lighted candle suddenly appeared in midair before him, which he took in his hand and thus found his way to the Lady Chapel, to set things right.

So great was his joy in approaching and entering the church for that greatest of all works of charity, the Divine Office, that Jesus was frequently seen accompanying him. Indeed, once our Lord's footprints were left indelibly impressed on the stone floor of the church, where they were afterwards surrounded by a railing. A little verse telling of the miracle was engraved in the stone, together with the Psalm verse: *Adorabimus in loco ubi steterunt pedes ejus!*[3]

---

[1] Jn 20:12.

[2] Evidently the Blessed Sacrament was not reserved in the Church of Villers at that time.

[3] Ps 131:7.

Once, at Mass after Consecration, Blessed Godfrey had the privilege of holding the Holy Child as Simeon had held him, visibly and evidently in his own hands. And then, immersed and absorbed as he was by ecstasy in the Divinity of Him whom he held, in His Humanity, in his hands, he understood the feelings of holy Simeon, *Tenebat a quo tenebatur.*[4] He held Him by whom he was maintained in being.

What was Blessed Godfrey's manner of prayer? He once gave an explanation of it to Dom Thierry von Lurke, an ex-canon of Bonn, who had entered our Order.

Like all the Cistercian mystics Godfrey's mysticism was strictly liturgical. And yet he combined this liturgical character with a prayer utterly simplified, discarding all more or less natural acts of the imagination, reason, will, and so on. When Dom Thierry asked him how to pray, Godfrey told him: "Speak no words at all, but simply *call to mind* the Lord in one of His mysteries, the Nativity, the Epiphany . . ." and so on.[5] We are not to take this as meaning that we are to exercise our imagination in constructing a vivid sensible picture of the mystery, although that may be useful in its place. Godfrey is describing a prayer of a more mystical character, in which the soul, unified and gathered up into one simple act of faith, hope and love that defies analysis, loses itself in the general and peaceful contemplation of Jesus, whom this simplified act of loving, trusting faith makes really and actually, but darkly, and without images or anything sensible, present to her in one or another of His mysteries. The soul can remain in delight and peace in this general, obscure awareness of Jesus' presence for hours at a time, even though the body may be engaged in other occupations than prayer; and this simplified prayer, which is infinitely more fruitful in graces for ourselves and others than laborious meditations or elaborate acts of this or that virtue, is perhaps what Saint Benedict had in mind when he insisted that our prayer should be "short and pure" and that, for the rest, we should keep in the presence of God.

[4] Chron Vill, 2: 4. Martene, 3: 1341. See *Senex puerum portabat, puer senem rogebat*, 2nd Responsory, Vigils, F. Purification. Cist. Brev. Pars. Hiem.
[5] Nimal, 82.

As the end of his life approached, Blessed Godfrey received from the Blessed Virgin the grace of a revelation that he would soon die. It was at the night office of the Feast of the Annunciation, and he was taking great delight in the singing of his neighbors and the other monks, when he saw the lovely Mother of Christ and the Queen of all Cistercians walking in the choir and distributing consolations to his brethren. He himself, hypnotized by the beauty of our Blessed Lady, got up and followed her out of choir, but she turned, and said gently: "Go back, now—for this is not yet the time for you to follow me to your reward." He was left with the assurance that that time would soon come.

Nor was he mistaken. For on Good Friday he nearly collapsed but was able to continue fasting until the next day, when obedience sent him to the infirmary. On Easter Monday he received Extreme Unction, and his infirmarian was afraid to go down to the refectory at supper time, for fear that he would never see Godfrey on earth again. But the monk assured him that this would not be so. And, indeed, during supper the infirmarian looked up and saw two venerable men entering the refectory, one of them a monk called Cesarius, who had died recently, and Godfrey was the other. "I have kept my promise," he said, "you have seen me again, and now I am going away to heaven."

At the washing of the body, his was flesh found to be covered with livid traces of his flagellations, and as a result of a revelation, he was later buried among the saints venerated in the church of Villers. His death occurred about 1200.

It is a strange thing that although Blessed Godfrey is known and venerated throughout the Order as "the Sacristan," nothing has come down to us concerning his functions in this important office, except that his most famous vision of Jesus washing his feet took place in the Sacristy. And yet the office of sacristan is one to which the Cistercian usages devote many pages of detailed instruction, thereby showing the respect and importance it holds in the Cistercian life.

The Sacristan is almost always a priest, and the very nature of his duties, which bring him and keep him close all day to Jesus in the Blessed Sacrament, and make him in a special manner the servant of our Eucharistic Lord and of those who bring Him to our altars, should fill him with that sweetness and charity which characterized the soul of the Blessed Godfrey.

October 8

Saint Martín Cid, Abbot of Valparaiso, Spain

(Source: AASS, Oct. 3:947. A few notes on the scant material provided by Manrique and various martyrologies.)

One of the many Cistercian saints who suffered from the liturgical accidents that befell our Order in the nineteenth century revisions of the Breviary was Saint Martín Cid, who used to have a feast of twelve lessons but is now reduced to a simple commemoration. He long enjoyed considerable veneration in Spain, but like several other of our saints, much less is known about his life and virtues than is known about some who enjoyed far less important *cultus*.

Who was he? His nationality is not certain, but the name Cid may be presumed to be a Spanish title, indicating his nobility. Before we go on to the many doubtful statements about him, let us say what is accepted with more or less certainty regarding his career.

He began his religious life in Spain in an abandoned robber's cave between Salamanca and Zamora, which he and several companions turned into an oratory and hermitage. As time went on, they made additions to their retreat, building a hospice for travelers and the poor, and here these holy men cared for the wayfarers whom Providence brought to their door, with all Christian charity and tenderness. All this was financed by Martín's own money, which was probably not too great a sum. But in any case the little community soon attracted the attention of King Alphonso VIII of Castilla y León. This monarch provided the monastery with a handsome endowment and then, in conjunction with the Bishop of Zamora, arranged for its affiliation with the Cistercian Order in 1137. Either some monks were sent from Clairvaux or Martín and his disciples joined some Cistercians who had already settled at Valparaiso (Valley of Paradise), and the community began to flourish under the new usages with Martín, its founder, as abbot. They continued to maintain their hospice and to devote a large amount of their time to the care of the poor. This was not really an exception to the Cistercian or Benedictine practice, as a matter of fact, for in most Cistercian monasteries the guesthouse was also a hospital, and the brothers and monks serving there were usually skilled physicians and pharmacists. Saint Bernard had counseled his abbots not to bring in doctors to treat their monks, as this was not appropriate to an Order vowed to poverty, and far from suffering from this, the Cistercians had brought many benefits to themselves and others by becoming as good of doctors, if not better, than most of them could have called in from the medieval towns or other monasteries.[6]

This monastery of Valparaiso, then, grew and flourished under its holy abbot, after whose death, in 1152, there were many miracles and a strong liturgical veneration.

As for the apocrypha, it is impossible to accept both the following stories at once, although many have tried to do so. The first says that Martín went from Spain to France and entered Clairvaux, under Saint Bernard.[7] Martín is then supposed to have been sent to Spain to make a foundation for Clairvaux. Even if we accept this, it cannot be reconciled with the following story, which is so glibly attached to it, namely that, having reached Spain he was discovered all alone in a cave by King Alphonso, half-starved with fasting and beating himself with a scourge.[8] After all, when Saint Bernard made his foundations, he did not send out one monk all by himself. In short, Saint Martín Cid is one of those whose virtues we must take on trust. His cult was confirmed by equivalent beatification in 1702.

---

[6] Ep 345 [James 388], 2.
[7] Hugo Menard, *Mencl. Benedictimum* (quoted AASS, Oct. 3:948).
[8] Henríquez, *Menologist*, October 7.

October 13

Saint Maurice, Abbot of Langonnet and of Carnoet, Brittany, France

(Source: AASS, Oct. 5:378 [based on the *Secunda Vita* by Abbot William of Carnoet, d. 1382; the *Prima Vita* was unearthed in the library of Troyes in 1880 by Dom Plaine and has furnished materials for a more complete account edited by Abbe LeCam in 1924 and published by Bayon-Roger of Lorient (Morbihan, France)].)

In the year 1116 was born, of poor and pious parents in the little Breton village of Loudeac, a child who was destined to be the patron saint of Breton mariners sailing the coastal trade back and forth from Bordeux and Spain. Maurice Duault received a good education in Brittany and at Paris, was raised to the priesthood and the doctorate, but left the world at the age of twenty-seven to enter the Cistercian monastery of Langonnet, then recently founded (1136). About his life here we know nothing except the significant fact that, only three years after his profession, he was made abbot of the monastery and retained that position for thirty years. During this long period of time he was not only the spiritual guide of a fervent community but to some extent the friend and counselor of churchmen and princes. Documents dated 1161 and 1166 show that Saint Maurice was chosen as arbiter in disputes concerning property or jurisdiction by the canons of Nantes, the Benedictines of Quimperle and the Bishop of Quimper. Conan IV, duke of Brittany, frequently visited the man of God and followed his counsel.

The career and achievements for which he is venerated as a saint were all crowded into the last fifteen years of his long life. His publically heroic sanctity, so to speak, did not begin until he was fifty-six. But we can be sure that it rested upon the foundation of thirty-three years of obscure and humble and laborious virtue, lightened by prayer and the delights of the spirit in contemplation, and all of this, like a true contemplative, he kept to himself, like the prophet who says, *In corde meo abscondi eloquia tua, ut non peccem tibi*: I have hidden Thy words in my heart, lest I sin against Thee.[9]

Just at the time when Maurice was beginning to think of giving up his office and retiring, Conan, Duke of Brittany, came to him with the offer of a large tract of forest land at Carnoet, and a sizeable endowment if he would consent to found a Cistercian monastery in that place. Maurice was not unwilling to do so, and taking a colony of monks, he moved to the wild new site and began to clear the ground for a new community.

Unfortunately, the new venture was barely begun when Conan died, and the help promised by him did not materialize. In spite of the desire of some of the monks to return to Langonnet, Maurice decided to cast all his care on the Lord and continue the work he had begun for His glory. And indeed, God did not desert them. But before Carnoet was firmly established, they had many trials to undergo.

First, there were wolves in the forest, and these animals ferociously attacked not only their flocks but even some of the monks. A lesser danger, perhaps, was that of the numerous rats that infested the river bank on which the monastery was built. These not only made dangerous inroads into the small supply of grain but even ate the monks' shoes while they were asleep.

Finally, the monks came to their father abbot and announced their despair in the face of these two problems. What was to be done? There was only one thing, they thought. The abbot would have to curse the wolves and the rats and destroy them by the power of God.

Saint Maurice was not of this opinion. Far from it. He remonstrated with his sons, telling them how God had created all these animals, and in doing so He had seen that they were good. *Erant valde bona!* The monks pointed to the wounds inflicted by the wolves. The abbot considered. Finally he consented to curse the wolves because they were attacking men. And he had no sooner

[9] Ps 118.

done so than two great wolves were found dead without a mark on them outside the monastery.

With the rats it was different. The abbot bluntly told his sons that they had better look after their shoes if they did not want the rats to eat them. But that did not help. Monks cannot stay awake all night on account of shoes and rats. So he cursed the rats also. And then two crows, huge, black and terrible, appeared over the monastery. So frightful was their aspect that they merely had to look with their piercing eyes at the places where the rats were hiding, and the rats walked right out and died. Then the crows carried them away. Thus far the old legend. But whatever the details were, Saint Maurice did liberate his community from these two dangers.

A more important and difficult liberation was that of a Breton islander from a spell cast upon him by a so-called prophet who lived in an isolated part of that strange Celtic coast and practiced magic. The islander, exorcised and delivered, entered the monastery as a lay-brother and defended himself from then on against all attacks of the evil one by the strong and certain weapon of obedience. He never again left the enclosure of the monastery. Nor did the death of Saint Maurice deprive him of his confidence and trust in obedience to the saint's successor.

Saint Maurice died in 1191, about seventy-five years old. Through his intercession, miracles were worked in all parts of Brittany. One of the most dramatic was the return to life of a drowned youth brought by his mother to the holy abbot's tomb. So great was his fame, and so important a place of pilgrimage did his monastery become, that its name was changed to Saint Maurice de Carnoet. And we may see that already the Order was tending to relax Saint Stephen Harding's prohibition against any statues in our churches by the fact that the statue of Saint Maurice was placed over the high altar for the greater devotion of his many clients throughout the centuries that were to come.

It is not certain whether he was canonized, but an equivalent beatification in 1702 confirmed his title of "Saint."

Of the eight monasteries of the Cistercian Order founded in Brittany in the first half of the twelfth century—all directly or indirectly through the influence of Saint Bernard's spiritual daughter, Ermengarde, Countess of Anjou—Langonnet is the only one that survived the Revolution intact. The buildings, now the property of the Holy Ghost Fathers, have the same aspect today as when, in 1790, the religious who dwelt there "were forced to quit their retreat, bearing with them the esteem and the regrets of all upright men."

Today, at least eighteen towns and villages in Brittany have shrines of Saint Maurice, to which the faithful flock in large numbers on the occasion of the annual procession, or as it is locally called, "*Pardon*, of Saint Maurice."

October 16

Saint Hedwig, Duchess of Silesia, Foundress of Trebnitz in Poland

(Source: AASS, Oct. 6:198. Life by a contemporary Cistercian monk of the monastery of Leubus.)

If the Cistercians had ever had a Third Order, its most illustrious member would probably be Saint Hedwig. One would also include Saint Malachy and Saint Edmund of Canterbury, whom the Order adopted from the beginning. But Saint Hedwig was more than a friend of the Order and an admirer of its spirit. She lived the Cistercian life just as completely and fully as many saints of the Order, certainly as fully as Saint Teresa of Lorvac or her sisters Saint Sancha or Blessed Mafalda. In fact, but for an accident, Saint Hedwig would have been able to make her profession under the same terms as did these Portuguese princesses: namely, retaining the ownership and use of their properties in order to be able to dispose of them for charity. Somehow, while Sancha, Teresa and Mafalda received dispensations that enabled them to do this, Saint Hedwig was never able to do so. However, she did the best she could to live the same life as the nuns. A house was built for her nextdoor to the convent, and in the Cistercian habit and under the Rule she followed all the exercises, all the fasts, and did all the penances of the Order. Indeed, her exclusion from a company of nuns she revered as great saints, and of whose number she considered herself unworthy to be one, only added to the merit of her heroic and admirable humility.

Hedwig (born about 1174) was the daughter of Berthold, the Marquis of Moravia and Count of Tyrol. Her sister was Queen of Hungary, and that made Hedwig the aunt of the great Saint Elizabeth of that country.[10] Hedwig herself had been married at the age of twelve to Henry, Duke of Silesia. After they had six children, they took a vow of chastity before the Bishop of Breslau, and Henry, under the influence of his saintly wife, also gave himself over to a life of penance and good works. One of their numerous religious foundations was Trebnitz, and they endowed it heavily enough to enable the Cistercian nuns to feed one thousand poor people to live according to the Rule and Usages of the Order.

Like all the saints of our Order, in fact like all true saints of any time or place, Saint Hedwig was a person of astounding simplicity: simple in the intense directness and sincerity of her humility and love. And yet we must not judge the old saints by the apparently extraordinary character of their external actions. In the present age there is a considerable reaction against all that is astonishing or surprising in an external way; and it is a good thing, too, because nowadays we are not simple or sincere enough anymore to do such things in the spirit of a Saint Francis humiliating himself by walking into a town naked, or Saint Bernard, in an outburst of holy love for the Queen of Heaven, entering the Cathedral of Speyer just as the Salve Regina was ending and adding to it on the spur of the moment the inspired cry: *O clemens! O pia! O dulcis Virgin Maria!*

Now Saint Hedwig was completely lost in admiration of the nuns of Trebnitz. How holy they were! And poor Hedwig! How

---

[10] She was also the aunt of the unfortunate Agnes of Merania, whose illegal marriage to King Philip Augustus led to the interdict laid upon France by Innocent III in 1199.

backward in the service of the good God! How cold! How stupid! And so she thought that the only hope for her was in the prayers of the nuns. The very ground they walked on was holy to her. After one of the good sisters got up from her knees in church and went away, Hedwig would surreptitiously go over and kiss the place where she had been kneeling. A nun came back to church, secretly, when all the others had gone to the refectory, and found Saint Hedwig kissing the place where each nun stood in choir. She would also reverently kiss the dirty towels thrown aside by the sisters to be washed. She washed her face in the water the nuns had used to wash their feet.

In a word, everything that the nuns had touched or used became, in Hedwig's eyes, an object consecrated, blessed, a sacramental, a means of grace. It was the same with the poor. Her house was frequently filled with beggars, paupers, cripples, and the sick, and the saint either waited on them at table or sat down with them, using, after them, the same drinking cups, the same eating utensils, preferring to drink out of cups that had been used by those with the most loathsome diseases. After these dinners, she would gather up the crumbs left by the poor and eat them as if they were holy. For she well knew that Our Lord said: "Whatsoever you do to the least of these My brethren you do it also to me."[11] If we really love any person, we show our respect to their body as well as to their spirit. Love is too realistic to separate a human being into two things which, existing separately, do not and cannot make up a person: the body and the soul. Love loves persons. Now if we love the Divine Person of Jesus Christ Our Lord, and despise His Body, and attack and injure Him in it, can our love be true? All Christians are members of His Body, and all persons are also potentially His members. And if we want to love Christ in His members, we must pay to His members the honor we owe to Him. Saint Paul insists on this, and Saint Benedict echoes him: *Honore invicem praevenientes*: vie in honoring one another.[12]

---

[11] Matt 25:50.
[12] Rom 12:10; RB 72.4.

It is simply a question of using faith in our relations with others. Only faith can give us the necessary principles for charity. For there is no person, however perfect, in whom we cannot find many faults and imperfections if we look only at his natural endowments—if we consider him according as he affects us and our limited and fluctuating tastes and feelings. But there is no man in the world, however great a sinner, in whom we cannot find, if we see him as someone created and cherished by the infinite love of God, many virtues, many qualities, many things that will take away our breath in admiration and make us want to fall down and worship the Creator whom he reflects.

Saint Hedwig was indeed no fool, to have such reverence for other men and women. Far from it: in that reverence she possessed the secret of true joy. For not even the love of God in Himself can give us peace if we destroy and deny it by despising our neighbors. But if, in spite of our other negligences, say in the virtue of religion, which is only a moral virtue, we truly love and worship God and serve Him in our brethren, we shall find that the theological virtue of charity covers a multitude of sins against the moral virtues.

To continue with Saint Hedwig's charity: she visited even her enemies in prison (rather her husband's enemies, for surely she had none!) And by night she stealthily visited the rooms of her sleeping servants to find out little needs they might have in the way of clothing or other necessities. Once, by miracle she brought back to life two criminals that had been hanged by her husband's orders and Duke Henry, in admiration at the miracle as much as at the excess of pity that overstepped all civil laws, ordered that in the future, every time Hedwig passed a prison, the doors were to be thrown open and all the inmates released, for love of her.[13]

When she was injured or hurt by anyone, she never showed any impatience or resentment but only a sort of mild surprise,

---

[13] AASS, Oct. 8:242a. The first of these miracles was attested to before the Roman Curia by an eyewitness. As for Duke Henry's gesture, it had in it as much comical despair as admiration. We are not to imagine that Hedwig started a series of circular tours of all the jails for the pleasure of seeing the doors open at her passage.

and she would say: "May God forgive you! Why do you do such a thing?"

As for her penances, she often went about barefoot, even in winter when the ice and snow cut her feet and made them bleed. Nor are the winters of Silesia by any means mild. She wore a coarse shirt of horsehair and beat herself with the discipline until her back looked as if she had been attacked by a lynx. But there was one amusing incident connected with her abstinence from all wine or strong drink. Duke Henry was rather like those monks Saint Benedict complained of, whose prejudice would not permit them to believe that water was not most injurious to health. Now when Henry heard that his wife was drinking nothing but water, he became very excited and determined to find out if this monstrous information were really true. In order to do so, he crept up behind her when she was at table and suddenly snatched her drinking cup and brought it to his lips. It was wine—or rather, when he tasted it, it was wine, although when it was on the table it had been water. For the Lord showed, by this little miracle, how pleased he was with his servant Hedwig and her abstinence. This was, of course, before she took the Cistercian habit.

She had a most faithful and loving devotion to the Holy Sacrifice of the Mass, which must undoubtedly have been the source of all her great charity towards her neighbors. For the Holy Eucharist is the Sacrament of charity, the Sacrament of unity and peace, given to us, as the Fathers of the Church so well realized to unite us *to one another in Christ.*

To all her other virtues was added the crown of a perfect trust in God's goodness and a perfect abandonment to the dispositions of His merciful Providence. She was most patient and resigned when Duke Henry was captured and imprisoned by his enemy, Conrad of Masoria, and eventually he was delivered by her prayers.[14] Having predicted that her son, Henry, would die by violence, she astounded her nuns by the calm with which she

---

[14] Henry had been at war with Conrad of Marsovia for the possession of Cracow. A party of Conrad's men surprised Henry at prayer in a church and led him a prisoner to Plock in 1229.

received the news of his death in battle at the hands of the Tartars.[15] "Why are you disturbed?" she asked them, "God can do whatever He pleases with His creatures. Would you want me to go against His will?"

After a long sickness, in which she was visited and consoled by the Mother of God and many of the saints, she died on October 15, 1243. But both the Roman and Cistercian calendars postpone her feast to the following day.

Saint Hedwig was canonized by Clement IV on March 26, 1267. She is venerated as the patroness of Silesia and one of the patronesses of Poland. In the nineteenth century a congregation of Sisters of Saint Hedwig was founded in her native country, dedicated to the charity which was her chief characteristic but in a more purely active form. They follow the Rule of Saint Augustine and devote themselves to the care of orphans.

October 23

Blessed Bertrand, Abbot of Grandselve, near Toulouse, France

(Source: AASS, Oct. 10:339. A contemporary life, made up entirely of statements of the saint himself on his deathbed and incidents following his death; written by one of his monks.)

The ancient abbey of Grandselve began as a Benedictine foundation, but within a few years it adopted Cistercian usages and eventually became a member of the Cistercian Order about 1143, first under obedience to the Abbot of Cardonia, and then when that did not prove satisfactory, as a daughter of Clairvaux. This is the bare outline of a story between the lines of which we read the record of a life of struggle, difficulty and sacrifice for the perfection of the contemplative ideal in that monastery: the life of the holy

[15] Ps 113.

abbot Bertrand, who worked thirty years to bring about this affiliation with Clairvaux.

In the first place, Grandselve was founded in the midst of the
region that was infested with Albigensianism. It was about halfway between Toulouse and Montauban, in the flat, yellow plain
of the Garonne, a land of vineyards and squat brick farmhouses,
a land of violent passions, too. In those days it was a center of
heresy. Later, Montauban was to become a stronghold of Calvin-
ism. Toulouse, in our own century, has merited in another sense
the nickname given to it because it was built of bricks: *la ville rouge*,
the red city. It is a center of radicalism.

That Abbot Bertrand found his responsibilities to weigh heavily
upon him, and judged his task full of insuperable difficulties, may
be gathered from the fact that he once even abandoned Grandselve
and went as far away from Languedoc as he could get, even as far
as Sicily, where he made an unsuccessful attempt to start another
monastery. About a century later, another Toulousain, Blessed Jean
of Caramola, was to make nearly the same journey, but he was to
remain and arrive at high sanctity at Sagittario, a Cistercian monastery near Naples. But Blessed Bertrand eventually returned to
Grandselve and to the difficulties with the neighbors in that fierce
country and even with his own monks, many of whom resisted
all his attempts at a complete Cistercianizing of their monastery
until a few years before his death.

Who was this holy man? What kind of person was he? Simple,
humble, courageous, obscure, lost in God, living for God alone
and in continual intimacy with Him, forgetful of himself, throwing
away his life, so to speak, for the sake of leading men to God by
prayer and penance. He was typical of those early Cistercians, the
patriarchs of the early twelfth century: he was another Alberic,
a Hugh of Bonnevaux, a John of Valence, an Amadeus, a Stephen
Harding all over again. We might have said another Bernard, but
Saint Bernard was more than a typical Cistercian—he was in a
class by himself.

Asked on his deathbed whether God had ever shown him any
extraordinary favors in his life, Blessed Bertrand at first merely
turned his face to the wall without answer. But finally to satisfy

his monks and get rid of them, he admitted that as far back as the beginning of his profession, he had received the grace to meditate daily upon the Gospel with such joy and attention that no distraction, no thought of his relatives or of the world, could move him from his contemplation; however, he did not say that the distractions never came to him. Saint Gregory the Great remarks: "We must take great care in cutting away all useless thoughts: but, nevertheless, *they can never be eliminated altogether.* For the flesh continually generates superfluous cares and distractions, which the spirit, with the razor of solicitude, must shave away."[16] In other words, we can no more prevent the appearance of distractions in our mind, to tempt us, than we can stop our hair from growing; but we can keep ourselves clean-shaven by simply turning away our wills from them and never accepting them so that we eventually arrive at the recollection we desire and with which this holy abbot was blessed, in which these distractions are forgotten as soon as they arise and never make any impression on our will, vanishing without trace like the shadows of clouds traveling across the country on a windy day.

This did not satisfy his monks: they continued to inquire. He admitted, then, that he had also received the grace, and had it for many years, of never hearing the Holy Name of Our Savior without getting tears in his eyes, from the realization of all the goodness contained in that name. A true disciple of Saint Bernard, the author of the beautiful *Jesu dulcis memoria*, chosen by our wise and prudent Mother, the Church, as the hymn for the Feast of the Holy Name. Indeed, there never was, nor ever can be, a true Cistercian or a true Christian, for that matter, the very foundation of whose spirituality is not a deep and personal affection for the human Jesus, Who so often emphasized the fact that he was the "Son of *Man*": for without His Humanity, we could never hope to arrive at the Word, the Divinity, the Spouse and everlasting joy of our intellects and immortal wills.

More than this, however, the holy man often saw Jesus and His Blessed Mother. Once, for example, in choir, on a Monday evening

[16] Mo 5.33.

at Vespers, the deeply moving Psalm *In exitu*[17] had just been intoned. Blessed Bertrand looked up and there was Jesus, walking down the church between the two choirs. How happy was the monk that evening, and with what joy did he not sing! It was with no little surprise that he afterwards found out, on inquiry, that the other monks had failed to see the Savior.

Jesus also frequently appeared to him while he was saying Mass, and often, too, when the holy man would be traveling the white and dusty roads of Languedoc, among the endless vineyards and rolling low hills, he would look up into the bright sky and see the heavens open and look straight into the courts of our Heavenly King and see Jesus there, smiling down upon him.

His visions were not always comprehensible to others, or even to himself. Two months before his death he had a rather strange one. "I saw Jesus," he said, "standing in a certain place. He was just like Himself, good and kind and merciful. All around him there were a lot of empty mansions. Then He said to me: 'Speak!' And I said to Him: 'But what shall I say?'—'Just speak,' He said, 'and I will give you the words.' So I opened my mouth, and the words that came out were: 'The name thereof is bitterness.' And having said that, I perceived that all the mansions were suddenly filled with rejoicing souls!" What was the meaning of the words? Perhaps a reference to Clairvaux founded in the *vallis absinthialis*, the valley of wormwood, but certainly, in a general sense, a reference to the Cross without which we cannot be saved. By his intercession, many souls would take up the Cross as Cistercians and get to heaven.

On July 3, 1149, an old friend, an abbot, turned up at Grandselve unexpectedly. "Ah!" said Bertrand, when he saw who was there, "you have come to bury me." It was true. And after the holy man died, this visiting abbot also had a vision of many sheep feeding peacefully in the pleasant pasture: souls saved by Blessed Bertrand's prayers, his sacrifices and his example.

His work did not end with his mortal life. There were still many thinking of breaking away from the Cistercian Order; there were

---

[17] Ps 113.

still others who were even tempted to abandon the religious life altogether.

One day, after None, as the tablet was struck for work, one of the novices remained, as it were, in a stupor, sitting in the novitiate. The others shook him, poked him, pushed him around, received no sign of response and decided he must be dying. They rushed to the superior with this information. But the novice was not ill. Soon he began to talk: "*Domine . . . Domine sancte Bertranne!*"

"Do you see Father Abbot?" they asked him.

"I hear him," he replied. He did not answer some other questions but soon, suddenly, burst into a flood of tears, saying, "*Domine Jesu, non sum dignus, non sum dignus!*"

As he began to recover from his ecstasy, the novice told them he had seen Jesus and Mary and Blessed Bertrand, and that the latter had told him to "tell the brethren to remain in the Cistercian Order." Then they asked him the reason for his sudden tears, but by now he had come to himself fully and refused to say anything, except that he had entertained the notion of leaving the monastery but had now utterly given up any such notion.

The holy abbot also appeared to another novice in the infirmary, after the latter underwent an intense spiritual crisis in which the whole infirmary was attacked by devils, which had to be driven out by the community and their superior with holy water. The novice was then consoled by a vision of the saint in heaven, offering up Holy Mass, served by angels. In fact, both novices had seen him vested for solemn Mass: for it was his special glory in heaven to be a "priest forever according to the order of Melchisedech." This is, of course, to be taken in a mystical sense: he did not offer Mass in heaven as he did on earth.

Blessed Bertrand was venerated with an immemorial cult and his feast was marked by proper antiphons and collects (memorably at Lauds and Vespers) at Grandselve.

Let us not forget the example of so holy and perfect a life as that of this good abbot. Let us never forget his simplicity and faith, which was nourished entirely by his love for the Son of Mary, and let us beg him to intercede for us, that we may follow him to those joyful mansions of heaven, by the narrow way of the Rule and the crosses of our obscure and humdrum life, never fearing these and never despising them either, remembering that if, in this life, "the name thereof is wormwood," we shall be anointed, in heaven, with the oil of eternal gladness in the vision of Jesus, Who is infinite charity, and the vision, in Him, of all the souls saved by our love, and whose love has saved us and brought us to this glory. Not the least of these last may be Blessed Bertrand of Grandselve!

October 25

Saint Bernard de Calvo, Bishop of Vich, Spain

(Source: AASS, Oct. 12:21. A long study, including the Latin translation of a contemporary Catalan life of the saint, and the account of his miracles compiled in 1244 by Raymond of Capraria.)

The Monastery of Santes Creus (Holy Cross) stands in the middle of a wide and fertile valley in the foothills of the Pyrenees, near Tarragona. Its great abbatial church enshrined a relic of the true Cross and a thorn from the Savior's crown. There, too, are the tombs of the Kings of Aragon, who made Santes Creus their "Royal Monastery" in the thirteenth century. One of these kings, James I, was to have as his close friend and adviser in diplomatic as well as religious matters its abbot, Saint Bernard de Calvo.

Born of noble Catalan blood, Bernard had been educated in law at Tarragona and perhaps Paris. But in 1214, after an illness which nearly cost him his life, he resolved to renounce the world. He entered Santes Creus in the full rigor of a Cistercian lent, and as if that were not enough to try his courage, various of his relatives, who had hoped to benefit from his successes as a lawyer, visited him there and tried to persuade him to change his mind and return to his worldly career.

Although they nearly succeeded, Bernard overcame the temptation and entered with great fervor upon the practice of Benedictine asceticism until in 1225 he was elected abbot of his monastery. Conditions everywhere in the twelfth and thirteenth centuries were of a kind to impose certain obligations on any Cistercian abbot that extended far beyond his own enclosure. In the Cistercian monastery was fulfilled the parable of the leaven which the woman took and hid in three measures of meal until the whole was leavened,[18] and if every monk was a reformer by his example, the abbot had to be one by precept also, preaching, traveling, rebuking the proud and avaricious, and fighting for the rights of the oppressed and for peace and for the unity of the Church.

If this was true of Europe as a whole, it was particularly so of Spain, more than half of which was still under Moslem rule. Bernard found himself preaching many missions in the diocese of Lerida, from which the Saracen armies had retired barely half a century before. Besides the Mohammedans that were left behind to be converted, there was also some danger from the Waldensians and the Albigensian heretics. True, these were not numerous yet, but Toulouse and Albi, the breeding ground of the heresy, were not far off, across the mountains, in Languedoc. That there was reason for fear is easily seen from the experience of the Church in Spain in our own century—particularly in Catalonia. The affinities, practically as well as ideologically speaking, between the Albigensians and the somewhat emotional and bloodthirsty brand of radicalism favored by the Catalans, are astonishingly great to anyone who does not realize that all the different enemies of the Church have always had the same hatred for the same aspects of Christianity and have always attacked it at the same points. First, denial of the Christian notions of good and evil and attack on the Christian moral code, particularly in matters affecting the sixth commandment. Then, denial of the Sacraments, beginning with that of the Holy Eucharist, and this is closely united with hatred for the priesthood and attacks upon priests and religious, the burning of churches, violence and cruelty towards Christians in general. The Albigensian notion of a double nature in man, one good and the

---

[18] Luke 13:21.

other evil, was adopted in a modified form by certain Protestant doctrines but has since become rather old fashioned; yet its consequent denial that there could be any such thing as a sin of impurity has a very modern and up-to-date ring about it.

The Church answered this heresy with the Inquisition, an institution which, to the modern mind, conjures up nothing but images of horror and wanton cruelty before which the poor heretics fell as martyrs. This is no place for a defense of the Inquisition or a palliation of its methods or an investigation into whether or not they were abused. But in any case, it effectively prevented the spread of these two heresies in thirteenth-century Spain, with much benefit, both spiritual and material, to the people of all the Christian kingdoms. Saint Bernard, who had been elected Bishop of Vich in 1233, was placed by Gregory IX in charge of the Inquisition in that diocese, where he carried out his duties with zeal and effect. As bishop he acquired a wide reputation for sanctity by reason of the simplicity and Cistercian austerity of his private life, as well as of the miracles he performed, and had already performed as abbot of Santes Creus. For there, in time of famine, he had miraculously filled the granaries of the monastery with wheat, and crushing one bunch of grapes in his hands over an empty barrel, he had instantly filled it and all the other barrels with good wine.

Once, too, when he was traveling on one of his missions in Lerida, some wanton women loitering at the roadside began to praise his handsomeness, and especially his white and even teeth. In an impulse of shame that he should be the occasion of such thoughts in other people, he picked up a great stone and dashed it repeatedly and violently against his mouth until he had knocked out his front teeth, which he flung at the feet of the women, and then went his way. If they liked his teeth so much, they could have them! This unexpected reaction had such an effect on the women that one of them entered a convent.

In 1238 the armies of James I of Aragon marched against the Saracens in southern Spain and laid siege to the city of Valencia. Together with Saint Raymond de Pennafort and Saint Peter Nolasco, Saint Bernard de Calvo also accompanied the Christian army, less as a soldier than as an adviser to the king, although he was, it is true, under arms. However, his most useful service to the army, in a military way, was when in a desperate engagement he knelt down on the battlefield and prayed until the tide turned in favor of the Christians. But it was when the Saracens sued for peace that Saint Bernard and his holy companions really began to play an important part.

The rank and file of the forces of Aragon were for storming the city, since this would give them the right to plunder the houses of the wealthy citizens—and massacre the inhabitants. Against their strong opposition, Saint Bernard and the others arranged a peace treaty which is a model of Christian prudence and charity in political affairs. The Moors were given twenty days to evacuate the city with all their possessions, under the safe conduct of the Christian army. Those, however, who wanted to stay, might do so, and their lives and property would be protected. Furthermore, James promised to refrain from any further fighting with these particular Saracens for the next seven years. And thus Valencia passed peacefully and without disorder into Christian hands.

The last important business of Bernard's life was the provincial Council of Tarragona, which imposed a severe reform upon the secular priesthood, especially upon the canons of cathedral chapters, who were generally drawn from the nobility. Absentee priests and canons were forced either to abandon their benefices altogether or live where they were supposed to work. Stern restrictions were imposed upon those who became too much involved in secular business and moneymaking, and the luxury of certain clerical households, as well as the finery affected by many priests in their dress, were all rigorously curtailed.

Saint Bernard died in 1243 with a great reputation for sanctity, and his death was followed by over one hundred forty well-authenticated miracles. His memory is still celebrated with veneration in Spain, and the Cistercians keep his feast on the twenty-fifth of October. He was beatified with the title of Saint in 1701.

October 29

Blessed Peter "Monoculus," Abbot of Igny, then of Clairvaux, France

(Sources: AASS, Oct. 13:53, including a life by his friend, Thomas of Reuil, and an account of his miracles and visions by a contemporary monk of Igny; EM 2.32.)

One of the most neglected saints in the Cistercian Order is this great abbot whose life was sanctified not only by the Rule and by ordinary sufferings but by two of the greatest tragedies in the early history of the Order. The portrait of this humble and courageous abbot, left to us by his biographer and friend, the monk Thomas of Reuil,[19] is one of the most attractive in the annals of Cîteaux. And if there be any doubt of the caliber of his sanctity, we may quote the words of a cardinal to Alexander III in submitting Peter's name with ten others as a good prospect for the cardinalate in 1177: "Since the Lord deigns to operate such frequent miracles through him, his sanctity is not to be doubted."[20]

It has not been our policy in this volume to examine the miracles of our saints so much as their virtues, and in the case of Blessed Peter as in most others, it is the virtues that are interesting rather than the miracles.

When this unprepossessing little man, small of stature, poor, silent, with one eye missing from its socket (hence the title *monoculus*—one-eyed), and without any of the social niceties that please others, was elected abbot of Clairvaux in 1179, to succeed Blessed Henry de Marcy (Menology, January 1), who had just become Cardinal Bishop of Albano, there was a certain amount of surprise and adverse criticism by those who did not know him and who judged merely by external appearances. But those who

---

[19] He was a Benedictine of the abbey of Reuil.
[20] AASS, Oct. 13:53.

had lived under his wise direction had learned to appreciate the depth of genuine humility in this man who really desired to appear as nothing in the eyes of all. Peter Monoculus did not concern himself with what others felt or thought about him. His was a simplicity so simple that it amounted to absolute plainness. But the monks who came to know and trust this quiet little man, sitting alone in the chapter room with his hands folded and his one good eye fixed on the ground, accessible to any one of his spiritual sons who might want to consult him, according to the custom, after chapter, soon began to love him in much the way as Saint Bernard and Saint Peter of Tarentaise and Saint Ælred and Saint Hugh of Bonnevaux had been loved by their spiritual sons.[21]

Peter was born in Italy, and it is thought that his parents were noble, but he never told anyone about that, so it is not known for certain. He was sent to France to study, which means that he must at least have been fairly well to do, and hearing of the Cistercians went to Igny to find out about their strict life. Confirmed in his desire to enter the Order by an interior grace, which showed him that this was truly the house of the Mother of God, he entered there.

His was a fervent and serious novitiate, and he seems to have advanced far in union with God even before the end of his period of probation. He once admitted, in order to show that the virtues someone had noticed in him were not to be credited to him:

> When I was a novice, a spirit entered into me, and now dominates and leads me. When my mind wanders off in external things, this spirit recalls me within myself. Even though I may want to do something else, it compels me to pray, and makes me impervious to whatever enters by my eyes and ears.[22]

---

[21] See Philippe Guignard, *Consuetudines* (Dijon: Imprimerie Darantiere, 1878), 172. Confessions were heard and spiritual direction given at that time in the chapter room. Bl. Peter Monoculus was remarkable for his accessibility to his monks and lay-brothers.

[22] Vita 1.8; AASS, 13:70.

An instance of his sensitiveness to the promptings of grace is given us by the story of a struggle he had in choir against a temptation to give in to a blinding headache and leave for awhile to rest and try to recover. But as the thought of leaving choir struck him, he heard an inward voice saying: "Praising, I will call upon the Lord, and shall be saved from my infirmities" (Ps 17:4). He decided to stay. Sometime later, however, the headache was so bad that he once again thought he really ought to leave and take care of himself and rest. But he heard the same voice again. The struggle continued all through the night office and throughout the other offices until the conventual Mass, where there was a general Communion. But all through it, Peter obeyed the voice and remained in choir. Then finally as he was going to receive the Sacred Host, and made the prescribed prostration on the knuckles *in plano* at the Epistle corner, it seemed to him as if a great stone rolled off his head and fell to the ground and his headache disappeared.

All his life he was tortured and, as it were, consumed by sicknesses, all of which he bore with admirable patience. Having been prior of Igny, then abbot of Val-Roi in the Ardennes, he fell ill at the latter house of a terrible disease, the nature of which is hard to judge from the account of Thomas de Reuil. At any rate, he got some infection in one of his eyes, which literally devoured the eye in its socket, and through it all he made no complaint. Perhaps it was at the time of this sickness that one of his miracles occurred. There was a secular who worked for the monks who had a dispute with the cellarer concerning his pay. Having demanded to see the abbot, he was not allowed access to him since he was too ill to see anybody. The secular, infuriated at the treatment given him, lost all reason and determined to be revenged. Accordingly, he went out to one of the "ranges and was just about to set fire to the building when Abbot Peter suddenly appeared at his side and said gravely: 'Do not commit this crime; tomorrow come and see me, and you shall have your pay, nor shall anyone keep you from coming to me.' " The man acquiesced and everything happened as he had been promised.

It was also when he was abbot of Val-Roi that Peter suffered from a fistula so serious and so dangerously placed that a monk of Clairvaux, who was an excellent surgeon and happened to stop at Val-Roi while on a journey, refused to operate and added, "If he lives until Easter, he will *never* die." But Peter recovered, nonetheless.

After his unanimous election as abbot of Igny in 1169 he showed some of the wisdom he had learned from so much suffering. A monk of Igny called Nicholas, who suffered from poor health and a weak constitution, was rather fearful about doing penance, lest it do him serious harm. But Peter told him: "Nicholas, you must never be afraid to do penance!" And this, as Thomas of Reuil points out, quoting Job, is very good advice to those who, because they are so afraid of the frost, shall be overwhelmed by snow.[23] But it does not mean that the good abbot was preaching an utter disregard of the needs of our bodies. We should never omit the care necessary to keep us fit for the regular life. We should not be like the imprudent souls Saint Teresa speaks of, who are led by the devil to practice furious and inordinate penances for three days and then finding them to be beyond their strength give up all penance, even the keeping of silence, and other such things that could never hurt our health.[24]

Although Peter Monoculus was very strict with himself, he never went to such a length as to destroy his own health—or what there was of health in him. And he was always solicitous for the needs of others, especially for the weaker members of the community, as Saint Benedict prescribes (RB 55.21).

At this time there was a soldier, one of those fierce, unprincipled knights who knew no law but their own cruelty, avarice and sensuality. His name was Baldwin de Guise and, says Thomas, if there was any crime he had not committed, it was because it was beyond his power to commit it. Yet when this knight fell sick and felt his death approaching, he called the holy abbot of Igny to his castle, made his confession, and was advised to take the religious habit at the last moment as a means of expiating at least some of his

---

[23] See Jb 6:16.

[24] Teresa of Jesus, *Way of Perfection* 10; trans. Benedictines of Stanbrook Abbey, rev. with notes and Intro. by Benedict Zimmerman (London: Thomas Baker, 1911), 60.

crimes. Accordingly, he was transported to Igny, where he received the habit and soon died amid the prayers of the monks.

Peter had several visions concerning his sorry state and urged all the priests to say thirty Masses for his soul, saying that he intended to keep such a tricenary himself. All through the thirty days, everywhere he went, poor Baldwin would appear before him in a mute and suppliant attitude, especially when one day, being on his way to a distant grange, Blessed Peter was unable to say Mass. Even after the tricenary, Baldwin continued to appear until, finally, on Good Friday, he was seen being led through the choir to the high altar by two figures, after which he appeared no more. Peter understood from this vision that he had been received into heaven.

The intensity of the prayers of the monks won heaven very quickly for this great sinner, as we may see by comparison with the long purgatory of a good and holy monk for whom the cantor asked absolution in chapter on the anniversary of his death. Such apparently was then the custom in the Order. It was revealed to Peter that he still needed the prayers of his brethren—in spite of his long years in religion as a good and regular monk and even in spite of his years of very painful sickness, which all had thought would serve as his purgatory.

Thomas of Reuil recommends this story as a topic for meditation to those who are in the habit of painting the mercy of God according to their own desires. But one may add, after a comparison of the two stories, that the principal moral to be drawn from them is that God's infinitely tender love desires to make us all the instruments of his mercy toward one another, and he has decreed that the length of our sufferings after death should depend largely upon the charity of the militant members of his mystical body. It would be idle to spend our time in beautiful speculations concerning the relations of God's mercy to his justice and omit to do the work of his love, that is, his mercy and justice all in one by praying for the dead. How many souls languish in purgatory because their friends, thinking they were too holy, have ceased to pray for them!

Peter himself, however, was to suffer trials so severe in this life that few abbots would like to face them. He had some foreboding of what was to come when Saint Bernard and Saint Malachy appeared to him and told him he was going to become abbot of Clairvaux. Even before this dreaded cross was laid upon his shoulders, the first of the trials struck Igny like a thunderbolt.

There had been a worthless and irregular monk in one of the filiations of Clairvaux, a nobleman of exalted station and equally exalted pride, who had found his way into the Order without any vocation. Not only did he disregard all monastic discipline, but he had spent much of his time out of the cloister and wandering about at will in the courts of princes and the castles of his friends. Such conduct was often excused in other Orders, and later on was to be tolerated in the Order of Cîteaux, after the White Monks entered upon the decline that lasted until Rancé's reform. But at this time, the Order was at the height of its fervor, and Abbot Gerard of Clairvaux had the monk apprehended and his horses taken away and committed him to the care of the abbot of Igny. This Hugh de Bazoches, as he was called, was accordingly living at Igny, and we can judge the enlightenment and good sense of Blessed Peter from the fact that he did not have the man chained up in a cell, as most medieval abbots would have done, but put him in the infirmary, for it was evident that he was mentally deranged.

In 1177 Blessed Gerard of Clairvaux came to make the annual visitation of Igny. Hugh de Bazoches was waiting for him. In the small hours of the morning, after the night office, Gerard retired from choir for a moment before returning to say his Mass and was passing through the dormitory. The criminal and demented monk leapt out of the dark at him, sank a knife deep into the abbot's entrails and vanished. The dying man staggered towards the steps and fell forward into a pool of his own blood. There he was found, still living but in intense agony; he did not die for three days. Meanwhile, of course, the murderer was apprehended and locked up. We can imagine the feelings of Peter Monoculus. Thomas does not tell us too much about them but merely relates how he ascended the altar to say the Requiem Mass with his face cheerful and peaceful for the benefit of his monks, but inwardly his heart was heavy with sorrow, for he could not but believe that this had happened to him as a punishment for his sins. However, during the Mass Saint Bernard appeared to him and told him not to lament, for Gerard was among the martyrs in heaven.

In fact, everybody was already calling him a martyr and a saint, and indeed he was a martyr, though in a broad rather than the strict sense of the word. His *cultus*, strong in the Order from the time of his murder, was confirmed by the Holy See in 1702 and so was his title as Blessed *per modum favoris*.[25]

Perhaps Blessed Peter thought that the prophecy of Saints Bernard and Malachy was now in danger of being fulfilled. But it was Blessed Henry de Marcy who became abbot of Clairvaux this time. Peter followed him, as Saint Bernard's eighth successor, in 1179.

At that time, summoned to the election, Peter not only failed to appear but went into hiding. The monks elected him as their abbot, however, and he was finally discovered at a distant grange, pitching hay with the lay-brothers. Only the orders of his higher superiors could move him from the grange and from Igny to Clairvaux.

The year after his election, and only three years after the martyrdom of Blessed Gerard, another blow fell to darken the history of the Order and to prove once more, in the furnace of tribulation, the soul of Peter Monoculus. While he, in his turn, was fulfilling one of his duties as abbot of Clairvaux and visiting the daughter-house of Trois Fontaines, an even more frightful crime was committed. This time it was the abbot of Trois Fontaines, Alard, who was attacked by one of his monks as he was going to say Mass. He was murdered in the church itself.

There is no need to go to great length to explain these crimes, and the fact that they were committed will only be astounding to those whose knowledge of history and of human nature has largely been gathered from fairy tales. However, they are simply another proof of the violence and barbarity of the medieval background, a background that only goes to show up in all the more startling

---

[25] *Cistercian Menology*, October 16. He was a holy and learned man, an Italian by birth, and had been abbot of Fossanova, Italy, before his election to Clairvaux. See EM 2.27–29.

relief the extreme gentleness and spirituality and simplicity and holiness of the medieval saints.

There is no religious order that has not had to contend with criminals or madmen, and it was the policy of the Cistercians not only not to close their doors to such men but to leave them wide open to all, no matter how brutal or violent or sensual, in the simple faith that God's grace would work miracles of conversion. We know what Saint Ælred thought on this subject—and what he had to suffer for his belief when one of his monks attacked him in his illness and threw him into the fire. The fact that God did not convert a few of these souls means only that he intended by their wickedness or madness to purify and sanctify the others all the more. Let us rather reflect on the patience and charity with which such men as Blessed Peter Monoculus weathered the storms caused by them, thinking not of retribution, revenge, and harsh punishment but only of their wretched souls.

What a contrast to the selfish pride, greed, and hatred of so many barbarians of his own day—and our own—is this incident in the life of Blessed Peter. There was a dispute between his abbey and a certain nobleman concerning a piece of property. A day was fixed for a meeting at which the affair was to be settled, if possible, out of court. The nobleman appeared at the appointed place with his armed retinue. Blessed Peter arrived with a single poor lay-brother, and quietly, without formulas of any kind, the abbot said: "You are a Christian. If you give me your word that this property really belongs to you, I will accept your word."

"I solemnly declare that the property is mine by right," said the nobleman.

"Then take what is yours. I will not try to keep it from you."

And with that, Blessed Peter quietly departed from the scene.

The nobleman went home to his castle in coarse and jocose exultation at the gullibility of a stupid little monk and boasted of his great piece of good fortune to his wife. She, however, was not of the same mind. On the contrary, filled with fear by what she heard, she cried out, "You have deceived a holy man of God! God will surely punish us." And she told him to go at once and make restitution, threatening separation if he did not. Thus the property went back to its rightful owners.

The reputation of Blessed Peter reached not only to the borders of France but even to Italy and the papal court. Even at Igny he had been considered for the cardinalate, and now so impressed was Lucius III by what he heard of this saintly abbot of Clairvaux that he sent for him to come and visit and advise him in spiritual matters at Verona. Blessed Peter made this journey in 1185 and was treated with the greatest respect by the pontiff, who confessed to him and received Holy Communion from his hand at Mass. It is even said that the Pope consulted him about the possibility of taking the Cistercian habit but was advised against any such thing by Blessed Peter.

His contact with the most important prelates in the Church's hierarchy did nothing to change his ways. There was a disputed election in a certain French episcopate, and the case had been given to a cardinal to settle. He was to choose one of the two candidates. He in turn put the matter up to Peter Monoculus, who considered it for a while and then said drily: "Between two bad pennies, there is no choice. They are both bad."

Yet we must not imagine him as a sarcastic man. He was always gentle, considerate, and kind. Thomas of Reuil was riding with him from Rheims, and the horses ahead of them on the road were raising great clouds of dust that blew back in their faces, blinding and choking them. Thomas, therefore, suggested that they ride ahead of the others and avoid their dust, but Blessed Peter said: "If we go ahead of them, then they will have to swallow our dust, and it is not charity to seek one's own comfort by causing others to suffer."

Finally, in 1188, after a long and fruitful career which had included the foundation of a daughterhouse as far afield as Hungary, he fell sick for the last time. As his death approached, several abbots from the filiations of Clairvaux came to bid him farewell. To these abbots and his own prior he confessed all the sins of his life, and afterwards the prior told Thomas of Reuil that a *Miserere* and a *Pater* were all the penance he needed to do. In other words, he had never committed a mortal sin or done anything that seriously offended God.

He died on October 29, 1185, and his death was followed by many miracles, which take up several columns in the *Acta Sanctorum.*

October 29

Blessed Ida of Leeuwen (of Leau), Belgium

(Source: AASS, Oct. 13:100. A contemporary life from two mss. of Brussels and Liege.)

In our times people do not know as much as they think they do about the Middle Ages. For example, it is a common opinion that in those days education was something difficult to come by, and nobody but a few clerics even knew how to read. Much less, then, were girls given any intellectual training. If it did happen that a woman knew how to read, she was probably the member of some noble family. But such an easy generalization is false. To be more precise, we must admit that conditions varied immensely in different parts of Europe and at different times.

It should not be surprising that thousands of children entrusted to monks and nuns in religious communities received at least the elements of an education. But it will come as a discovery to many that in thirteenth-century Flanders there were many schools conducted in towns and villages by clerics or Beguines for local children, both boys and girls, belonging to the artisan and bourgeois class or coming from neighboring farms. To such a school went little Ida of Leeuwen, the daughter of a farmer near the Flemish town of that name, and she derived such profit from the training she received that her insatiable taste for books made her rise from bed in the first grey light of dawn and apply herself to the study of spiritual things.

Ida was one of those simple and holy children who see God in everything and love to be with Him. Prayer and solitude attracted her more than the company of other children, and as often happens, a more worldly minded elder sister made poor Ida pay for this grace by petty persecution and mockery, all of which the child accepted with patient humility and forbearance.

She was fortunate, however, in having a father who encouraged her in her love of prayer and study, and it is interesting to read that he had his little seven-year-old-girl taught the rudiments of calligraphy, or the art of manuscript copying, in which she was later to excel in the scriptorium of the Cistercian nuns of La Ramee.

Another story of Ida's childhood: one day in the town she came upon a crowd of peasants and artisans and loiterers who had gathered around a group of strolling players and were shouting and guffawing with oafish and half-animal joy at the gross humor of the mountebanks. One is reminded of the scenes that were to be painted, not many centuries later, by Pieter Breughel. Ida did not join them or stay to watch the play. On the contrary, her deep spiritual insight was able to detect the underlying misery and sorrow and emptiness in these poor souls, and the sight so affected her that it brought tears of shame and pity to her eyes. It is a beautiful scene, this picture of the little Flemish girl with the soul of a mystic, this child who knew God, weeping over the false joys of those who could so easily forget Him.

She was thirteen years old, says her biographer, when she became a Cistercian nun at La Ramee, and while she was still a postulant, she had—so it seems—her first real taste of the mystical knowledge of God. It was then that she heard Christ truly speaking to her in the depths of her soul, not simply the voice of her own conscience or imagination, not a voice that she could hear whenever she attended to it in recollection and peace, but the voice of One Who was independent of her and far beyond the control of her will. The words He spoke came from the very substance of her soul, inflaming and transfiguring all its powers with love. Instantly she was filled with so great a desire to be with God forever, perfectly and without delay, that she begged (at any cost) to be allowed to suffer anything whatever in this life if only she might be so purified by these sufferings as to fly straight to God at her death. It would seem that her prayer was answered—probably in a way she did not quite expect. Instead of physical sufferings, she was assailed by a long and terrifying siege of interior trials. All kinds of temptations beat at the doors of her will. Night after night she was unable to sleep. But she suffered everything bravely, with great faith and love, seeking no other remedy than frequent Communion. Indeed, she had so deep and true an appreciation of the fact that these trials were a gift of God, that she preferred to suffer them than to be without them. And when they left her she wondered for a time if she had in some way offended God, that He should take away His precious graces from her.

But when this preliminary work of purification was done—Saint John of the Cross would have called it the "Dark Night of the Senses"[26]—she was rewarded with the delights and peace of uninterrupted and profound mystical contemplation. She had entered into a promised land, flowing with milk and honey: the peace, the "Sabbath," of mystical union which Saint Bernard and Saint Ælred had held out to their monks as the hundredfold promised on this earth to those who were truly generous in conquering themselves for the love of God. The characteristic of Ida's prayer was a deep and peaceful absorption in God. Here we must understand neither the natural recollection of the faculties in sustained, restful, though nonmystical contemplation nor on the other hand a trance-like or ecstatic state. It was not quite that, although she was, as we shall see, frequently in ecstasy. But especially after her Communions, and on Sundays, she would often remain the whole day completely absorbed in God, even though she was not altogether robbed of the use of her senses. If she could, then, she would simply sit apart somewhere, contemplating her Beloved. It seems that she had a favorite place, probably in the cloister, from which she could look into the church and see the ciborium. That is, she could see the little hanging container, usually in the form of a dove, that was suspended either from the ceiling of the sanctuary or from the hand of the statue of the Blessed Virgin, and in which the Blessed Sacrament was reserved in a pyx. Ida was perfectly content to sit and gaze in this manner at the Blessed Sacrament.

Yet this did not interfere with her charity to others. One day when she was thus occupied, and tasting the joys of mystical con-

---

[26] See John of the Cross, *Ascent of Mount Carmel* and *Dark Night of the Soul* (Bk. 1).

templation, another nun who did not share her gifts got excited at some trivial incident outside the window and called Ida over to behold the wonder. Ida came smiling to see what it was, although it cost her much, not only interiorly but even physically, to do so.

If her prayer had been no more complicated than this, it would certainly never have caused much remark in the community, and that would have made Ida very happy. But Our Lord had in store for her a considerable cross that came in the form of excessively strong mystical pleasures—too strong, in fact, for her weak human nature to stand. These experiences were generally connected with the Holy Eucharist and with Communion. It is interesting, however, that the reception of the Blessed Sacrament was not what caused these excesses, which threw her into ecstasy: to be more exact, her heart, in expectation of the joys of receiving her Spouse, would become so overwhelmed with joy that the delight became unbearable, and she was often helpless with ecstasy before she could even receive the Body and Blood of Christ. On such occasions, if she could still manage to get to Communion, the strength of the Sacrament worked rather to pacify this excessive sensible joy and give her grace to stand it.

Frequently, however, she received the Sacred Host from the hand of the priest and descended the altar steps in such a dazed and ecstatic condition that she wandered out of her place in line and could not find her way back. When the sisters had passed around the altar and paused on the other side to receive the Precious Blood, through a glass tube administered in a chalice by the deacon, Ida was already too far gone to be able to complete her Communion. In the end, she had to be supported and led back to her place in Choir. Now since there were two or three others who were affected in the same way in this community, the thing became rather a nuisance. The good order of the community was threatened, and it was a great distraction to those who had to struggle to keep recollected and make their Communion in the ordinary way, fighting dryness and lamenting their incapacities, to have to come back from the altar supporting a bevy of happy, irresponsible and completely intoxicated mystics. Consequently the superioress ordered that any nun who could not receive Communion more or less according to the Cistercian usages would have to do without it.

Thus it turned out that in more ways than one Ida's ecstasies were much more of a trial than a consolation. The superioress's ruling was to her a terrible chastisement for something she could not help, especially since it deprived her of her only remedy for the burning fire of love that caused her so much suffering by its excessive joy. Our Lord, however, did not leave her helpless. He deigned to produce in her the same effects by Spiritual Communion, and indeed, to increase the intimacy of His visit and the efficacy of its effects. So Ida wrote an epigram in Flemish to the effect that the Chalice administered by Jesus through His ministers was indeed full of delights, but that which He gave with His own hand was even more so.

On one occasion, after a Sacramental Communion, Ida went to the refectory with the other sisters. But though, since Mass, Sext had been sung, and some time had passed, she was still totally absorbed in mystical intimacy with her beloved: so much so that she suddenly startled all her companions and doubtless interrupted the reader with a passionate inarticulate shout in Flemish: *"Wi! Here, min harte!"* (What, Lord, my heart!) Another day, it is said, she was at dinner in the refectory (evidently not after one of her Communions) and suddenly went into ecstasy in the middle of the meal. She had to be left there all afternoon and did not come to herself until the evening. That gives us another somewhat unusual vignette of Cistercian life in the thirteenth century: a long, bare vaulted refectory with two or three nuns busy at the afternoon work, sweeping the floor, with robes trussed up, while Mother Ida, in full Choir dress, sits immobile at her place at one of the tables, lost in God, like a forgotten piece of expensive furniture that really belongs in some other room.

Ida was not always left alone like this in her ecstasies. At first, people showed a pardonable though excessive curiosity and concern about her in these states. They would push her and pull her around and shake her and maul her. What was worse, they would try to force food down her throat when she was manifestly completely unable to swallow anything. There are no miracles to her credit, but the mere fact that she survived all the delicate attentions of her sisters speaks volumes for some special supernatural intervention on her behalf. At least one is tempted to think so.

Blessed Ida also received great mystical lights and intuitions, and she was able to discourse with such wisdom about the Holy Trinity and the Incarnation and the great mysteries of our faith that she astonished learned men, and yet she always spoke with such simplicity that even the most ignorant could derive benefit from what she said.

Visions took a more or less secondary rank in her mystical life, but the most famous of those recorded in her life is also, without doubt, the most charming in all the annals of Cistercian mysticism. Ida was in choir at the night office on a big feast singing and rejoicing, as we are bidden to do, *in conspectu angelorum* (in the sight of the angels),[27] that is, with love and purity of intention and lively faith. Suddenly, the Mother of God appeared to her with the Child Jesus in her arms, and holding out the Divine Infant, placed Him in the arms of delighted Ida. The little sister was overjoyed; in fact, she was in very truth in heaven. But suddenly, in the midst of all her delight, she realized that it was her turn to sing a Versicle, which meant that she must stand up and face the altar, "in ceremony," that is, with her hands hanging down at her sides. There was not even time to hand the Holy Child back to His Mother: all she could do was exclaim, "Watch out for Yourself, Lord, I have to get up and sing!" But as she leaped to her feet and faced the altar and dropped her long sleeves, letting them fall almost to the ground, the Holy Child quickly clasped her firmly around the neck with his tiny arms and hung there, swinging, while Ida sang the responsory—and sang it better than she had ever sung in her whole life.

Another vision came later in her life in the infirmary. She was unable to go to choir for the beautiful festivities of that Holy Night: but in the infirmary the Mother of God came and again presented her with the Holy Child saying: "Here is my beloved Son. He is just now born. I have no dearer gift. I give Him to you and to all

[27] *Cogitetis de vobis, Domine, quia castans perfruar ordine*; Vita 4:38.

your sisters." After that, says Ida's biographer, she was so radiant with supernatural light that if she had been suspended from the ceiling she would have made a fine lamp to illuminate the whole house. The good monk was not the least original of thirteenth-century writers and seems to have a certain literary and spiritual kinship with the author of the Fioretti.

Ida was not without a delicate fancy of her own. One day she was considering her own name, Ida, which was evidently spelled with an "I." She thought to herself: "Now I is a sharp letter, and D stands for Deus, that is, God. A, on the other hand, stands for Amor, love." Her deduction from all this was that Ida should be sharp, that is, acute or proficient, in the love of God. That may have been a little unscientific even for medieval etymology, but anyway, the important thing is that she put it into practice.

All these delights gave place to another season of graver and more terrible trials. Ida had once known the dark night of the senses; now she entered upon that terrible desolation of spirit called the "Dark Night of the Soul," that deep mystical purification so mighty and so harrowing that it is reserved for only a bare handful of chosen souls. Her biographer does not give us a wealth of detail on the subject, other than that her interior trials were also accompanied by physical breakdown and dissolution: it was the final preparation for heaven. It all lasted three years, until her death in 1260.

Once as she lay on her bed in the infirmary, someone brought her a rosebud, and she reflected: "Just as this rosebud does not belong to me, so neither could I call my own all the good things God gave me heretofore." During the years in which she was slowly dying without consolation or refreshment of the spirit, she always obeyed her infirmarian to the letter, always took just what was given to her and never asked for anything at all. She never complained, but she offered up her whole being, body and soul, to God as a holocaust of love, not in fine and airy speeches and aspirations but in suffering and abnegation and pure faith.

Finally, having been granted as it seems an intimation of the exact time of her death, which came as she had long desired, on her favorite day, Sunday, she received the Holy Viaticum. Before receiving the host, she had asked the nun who would remain in the room with her to cover her face with the veil, but lifting the veil afterwards, the sister peeked out and saw Ida's face radiant with supernatural light. And thus she peacefully passed into the unveiled vision of God.

A "Chronicle of Brabant," compiled before the decrees of Urban VIII, lists Ida of Leeuwen as a canonized saint, but evidently in a very loose and inaccurate sense.[28] However, she is pictured with a halo, and there was a strong, lasting immemorial cult paid to her memory, which serves as the basis of her title of Blessed. Meanwhile, may this charming member of the saintly group of Cistercian mystics that perfumed thirteenth-century Flanders with the sweetness of their virtues and their prayers not forget us, her brothers and sisters, but pray for us to love God as she did and adore Him in spirit and truth, preferring, as she did, the Cross to consolations and always putting the love of our brethren before our own delights, no matter how holy and exalted those delights may be. For it is only thus that we can be true Cistercians.

[28] AASS, Oct. 13:105.

November

November 3

Saint Malachy, Bishop of Down, Ireland

(Sources: V Mal; AASS, Nov. 2:135; Ailbe J. Luddy, *Life of Saint Malachy*.)

This great Irish bishop, and the first Irish saint to have been formally canonized with all the legalities involved by a complete process (that was in the year 1190), is also one of the best-loved members of the Cistercian family, although he was never, in fact, a Cistercian. This was through no fault of his own: for it was only under obedience to Pope Innocent II that he sacrificed his heart's most cherished desire, which was to enter Clairvaux under Saint Bernard. But, at any rate, he died at Clairvaux in the arms of his friend and admirer and was buried there in the lady chapel and was revered and loved there as a father and friend to the Cistercian Order, for he, more than any other one man, was responsible for the establishment of the Order in Ireland—an event of tremendous importance in the history of that nation. For there, as well as everywhere else, the Cistercians, by occupying and reclaiming the worst lands and turning them into rich fields and throwing them open to secular workers, initiated a real economic revolution. But this revolution was all the more pronounced in Ireland, which had never, up to that time, been an agricultural but rather a pastoral nation. Yet this economic aspect of the arrival of the White Monks was nothing in comparison to the spiritual good done by their influence: for they were to serve as Malachy's most powerful weapon in ecclesiastical and moral reform.

Maelmhaedhoc Ua Morgair, which is reducible in English to Malachy O'More, was the son of Mugron Ua Morgair, a nobleman of great culture and learning who, far from being, as one would

392   *In the Valley of Wormwood*

expect in the France or England of the twelfth century, a soldier and a knight, was an intellectual, a lay-professor at the great school of Armagh: a fact which is surprising only to those who are unaware of what important traces of the great Irish civilization had survived the invasions of the Danes. And yet, of that amazingly brilliant culture, it is all too true to say that there remained little more than traces. It was to be the work of the son of Mugron Ua Morgair to lay the foundations for its reconstruction, not by fostering a merely cultural revival but by rekindling the fires of Christian faith and charity, the strong and purifying and vivifying flames of the Spirit of God, in the hearts of his countrymen. And the hearths on which these flames were to spring up most vigorously and with the most lasting effect were the great schools of charity, the Cistercian monasteries.

In his youth Malachy became the disciple of a holy recluse called Ivor O'Hagan and was soon joined by many of his young and noble friends: for like so many saints of our Order, Blessed Amadeus or Saint Bernard himself, Malachy was destined to draw with him, in the "odor of the ointments" of divine grace, many others who had been brought close to him by the bonds of a hitherto merely natural affection. Ivor O'Hagan taught his pupils not only the weapons and techniques of the spiritual combat against their own passions and the deceptions of the world and of the devil but also Gregorian chant, which was something new in Ireland, where the Ambrosian and Gallican chants, simpler and more primitive, were in common use. It was to be one of the most joyous tasks of Saint Malachy's life to fill the churches and cathedrals of his native Ireland with the strong and pure and sublime perfection of Gregorian chant in all the holy and passionate intensity of its many *neums*.

After his ordination as priest when he was twenty-five, about the year 1120, he was appointed Vicar General of Armagh by Archbishop Celsus with the specific charge of reforming the diocese from top to bottom. And indeed the Danish invaders had left the place in a sad condition. The people were in many places without priests and had fallen back into habits of vice and superstition: the Sacraments were forgotten, especially those of Confirmation, Penance, and Holy Matrimony—*a fortiori* the Eucharist, which is the Sacrament for which all the others exist. The Canonical Hours had long ceased to be sung in churches, but now once again they began to be heard, as we have said, with the Gregorian chant, and everywhere Malachy sought to introduce the Roman Rite.

Soon the once famous Abbey of Bangor, ruined by the Danes, came by a kind of natural and legal succession into the hands of one of Malachy's relatives, to whom it would have been no more than a piece of property of rather questionable value. Malachy assumed the abbatial charge and revived the religious life on this hallowed site where once not hundreds but even thousands of monks had congregated at the same time. The Rule kept there was that of Saint Comgall. But before long, another and great responsibility presented itself to him. He was only twenty-nine when he was elected Bishop of Down, and only under obedience to Ivor O'Hagan and Archbishop Celsus could he be persuaded to accept. And here, again, he was faced with the task of rebuilding a Christian society amid the ruins left by the Danes: he had become, in the words of Saint Bernard, "the pastor not of men but of beasts."[1]

The people would not come to the bishop, so the bishop went to the people, traveling about all day long on foot through the towns and villages of his diocese and preaching everywhere. But Malachy was more than a preacher; he was a saint and therefore he knew the one secret of making his ministry bear fruit. To him, the words of Our Savior, that whosoever remains in Him would bring forth much fruit,[2] were more than a dead letter. He made it the chief concern of his life and the vital center of his ministry to remain united with Jesus, the source of all life and vitality, by prayer. He spent entire nights in prayer for his people and did penance for them, and consequently, there was no need for him to worry over failures, like so many of our modern activists who talk themselves hoarse and never seem to do any good to souls and have to ask themselves why their ministry bears so little spiritual fruit. In the diocese of Down people once more became Christians, and fervent Christians.

At the time when Malachy had left the world to become the disciple of Ivor O'Hagan, his sister, scandalized by her brother's

---

[1] V Mal 3.10.
[2] Jn 15:5.

activities living as he was in the rags of a pauper and spending his days tending the poor and the sick and burying the dead, came to him with much worldly bitterness and upbraided him severely for so degrading a manner of life. She was one of those Christians whose Christianity has been completely perverted by worldliness, to the point that they consider their own social standards and ideals to be those of the Church of God. Such in our own day, for example, are those American Catholics who take it for granted that unless a priest owns a nice shiny automobile and lives up to the standard of a respectable businessman he is a dishonor to the Church. In any case, Saint Malachy's sister came to him quoting Scripture and telling him that he should let the dead bury the dead.

When Malachy was Bishop of Down this egregious exegete of a sister came to die, and Malachy with good reason set about praying fervently and saying Masses for her soul. In the course of time, however, as is natural, the intensity of his prayers and the frequency of the Masses diminished. Then one night he had a dream. And in his dream he heard a voice saying to him that his sister was outside in the court and had not tasted food for thirty days. On awakening he remembered that it was exactly thirty days since he had said Mass for her soul. And therefore he returned to his prayers and Masses. Presently he had another dream. This time he saw her standing in front of the church. She just stood there, unable to enter. She was dressed in black. Again he continued his Masses and prayers, and presently there was another of these strange, static, dream visions. He saw his sister again, inside the church this time, but unable to approach the altar, and she was dressed in grey. When he finally saw her dressed in white he knew that his prayers had all finally been answered.[3]

On the death of Archbishop Celsus, Malachy became Archbishop of Armagh and Primate of Ireland, but there was so much trouble caused by schismatics that he did not retain this position for more than three years. During this time, however, when certain noblemen had gathered together in a plot against Saint Malachy's life, a sudden thunderstorm burst over them, and all the conspirators were enveloped in a dense cloud from which came forth the

[3] V Mal 2.8.

most terrifying crashes of thunder. Then the brief cloudburst passed over, the charred bodies of the three ringleaders were seen dangling in the branches of a tree, and a dozen or so of the others were gravely injured.

In 1139 or 1140 Saint Malachy went on a pilgrimage to Rome, and it was on this journey that he stopped at Clairvaux and entered with Saint Bernard upon what is one of the most famous and fruitful friendships in the annals of the saints. And so impressed was the bishop with Clairvaux and all that he saw there, with the silence and recollection of the monks, their poverty and labor, their wonderful simplicity and devotion, and their perfection of peace and fraternal charity, that he wanted nothing more than to end his days in this earthly paradise—a paradise that was such because the souls that lived there, having died to themselves and to their self-will and love of creatures, were liberated, at least for the most part, from the tyranny of those passions which are the source of all our unhappiness and unrest on this earth. The first thing Saint Malachy asked Pope Innocent II on his arrival in Rome was permission to become a Cistercian, but we have seen that this was refused. Malachy was too important to his diocese and to his country. The next best thing was for him to leave four of his companions, monks from Bangor, including Blessed Christian O'Conarchy, at Clairvaux to become Cistercians that they might subsequently introduce the Order into Ireland.

So it was that a colony came from Clairvaux in 1142 to found Mellifont, near Drogheda, the most fervent of all Irish Cistercian Abbeys.[4] The greatness and spaciousness of this monastery is still visible—and well might it be spacious for it soon had to accommodate crowds of postulants. Six filiations were soon founded and from the flowering of this new and fruitful branch were to come many and rich fruits for the Irish Church and Irish society as a whole.

Malachy, however, was growing older and beginning to approach the end of his earthly pilgrimage. Seeing the end of it and looking forward eagerly to his reward, he answered a question of some of his monks at Bangor regarding the place and manner in

---

[4] Mellifont is today a Cistercian Abbey of the Strict Observance.

which he would like to die. His desire to die and be buried at Clairvaux expressed at that time was later taken to be in actual fact a prophecy, and he added that he would like most of all to pass from this earth on the Solemnity of All Souls.

So it was that Malachy set out on a second pilgrimage to Rome. His monks must have suspected that he would get no farther than Clairvaux and, as if to force him not to die, they extracted from him a promise to return to Ireland which he reluctantly gave. But Providence helped him to keep his promise in an unexpected manner: for the ship, only a few hours out of port, was driven back to shore by a storm but only for one night. Then the following morning Malachy was off for Scotland and thence to France with his conscience at rest and his promise fulfilled. He reached Clairvaux in good health but fell ill there suddenly on October 18, the Feast of Saint Luke. His sickness did not last very long. After barely two weeks he was anointed, coming down unaided from the room where he lay on the top floor of the monastery to receive Extreme Unction in the Church, and finally he expired, according to his wish, on All Souls' Day and in the arms of Saint Bernard. Such a death monks had traveled from the ends of Europe to obtain— indeed, the community of Clairvaux under Saint Bernard was *en bloc* venerated with an immorial cult by later generations for its mere contact with the great abbot. But there was never a more Cistercian death than that of Saint Malachy O'More.

November 6

Blessed Simon, Lay-brother of Aulne, Belgium

(Source: Nimal; closely follows the contemporary life, edited by Moschus, parish priest of Armentieres, in 1600.)

One of the most remarkable and famous of the great Cistercian mystics of the thirteenth century in the Low Countries was a humble lay-brother of Aulne, Simon, who had charge of the sheep.

So great was the fame of his prophetic gifts that he was even called to Rome by Pope Innocent III, in 1215, as the pontiff, and many of his cardinals desired to consult the holy man on matters of importance not only to their own souls but to the whole Church as well.

Simon was of noble birth, a son of the Count de Gueldre, whose name was illustrious in Holland and Flanders. But at sixteen the youth left all that his lineage and fortune could have led him to expect, in order to give himself to God and, under the guidance of his guardian angel, traveling he knew not whether, through an unfamiliar country, he eventually came to Aulne, where it was made known to him, in the depths of his conscience, that this was to be his home.

Concealing his noble birth, he entered the novitiate of the lay-brothers and became a shepherd. In the first years of his conversion, as is not unusual, his soul was inundated with great graces and consolations by the Holy Spirit, and so powerful were these consolations that like Blessed Arnulph, his contemporary at Villers, he was often unable to conceal his immense interior joy and exultation. He was frequently proclaimed and penanced for giving way to a sort of exultant spiritual mirth in the middle of Mass or the Office, for it is not always possible for all men to distinguish, from the exterior, between spiritual joy and animal dissipation in others. Besides, there are many who are unaware that an interior joy of a spiritual kind can, in some souls, seek an outlet in involuntary laughter. In any case, after three years, this "bonanza" of graces was followed by seven years of the most terrible interior trials and temptations, accompanied by severe illness. During these seven years he was sorely buffeted by a spirit of lust. But eventually these trials left him for good, and he was free of them. But that did not mean he was to be without temptations, for almost immediately came a worse affliction of the spirit. For now he was filled with disgust by all the good works, prayers and mortifications of the religious life that had once been so sweet to him. Not only that, but when he went to pray, his dark and arid soul seemed to fill with the blasphemies blowing through it, as it were, like a burning wind out of the deserts of hell. Until at last, one day he was assailed by these temptations in a wood called Viscou near his grange, and throwing himself on the ground he prayed in anguish while a real and yet seemingly preternatural tempest lashed the trees over his head. Finally the storm died down, and with it his temptations to blasphemy left him forever. Now he was sufficiently purified to receive the great graces which God had destined for him.

First he had a vision of a soul entering the glory of heaven and ascending in a progressive transformation from clarity to greater clarity as it grew nearer to God, as iron is more and more transformed into fire as the fire grows more intense, or the atmosphere into light as the sun comes out more brilliantly. But he was also terrified by a vision of hell in which he was abandoned in the middle of that horrible abode of demons and was about to be swallowed up in the abyss when he came to himself again. The soles of his feet were found to be so badly burned that he was unable to stand on them for forty days afterwards. This may sound like a joke, if we forget that just as the effects of a vision of glory pass through the soul and affect the body, giving it also a taste of glory, so too a vision of damnation may reach through the soul and even into the body.

Once in choir Simon beheld the soul of a brother who had at that moment died in the infirmary entering heaven. So rapt was he with this vision that he left his stall and followed it with his eyes fixed in midair until he was brought up short by bumping into the wall of the church.[5]

But the most important vision of his life was the one from which dated all his remarkable powers in the reading of consciences and the foretelling of future events and dangers facing souls. In one immense and absolutely simple intuition, which came as the answer to long years of prayer to see God, he was shown *all* souls, in all their depth, as plain as day, as they are seen in the ineffable clarity of the Divine Intellect itself. And thus, though he did not

---

[5] Simon's ancient biographer, like Goswin the Cantor, author of the life of Blessed Arnulph, was fond of these details of broad humor and was not afraid to make his heroes look ludicrous, for the sake of introducing them into his story. This fact should be remembered by those who might be perplexed at the notion that these holy brothers might have been harmless crazy men instead of saints.

see God, he was at least able to see Him mirrored in all souls through the Divine Intellect itself in a way that totally passes human comprehension. But the important thing about this was that he gained from it a permanent gift that was to be of immense value and service to souls.

We must not conceive that the poor lay-brother's mind had now become a huge card catalogue, a police file with the spiritual fingerprints and descriptions of all the men of his or any other time. But the effect of this infinitely simple vision remained with him, and he did, in fact, know by virtue of it what was in the souls of men. Consequently, he would often confront people, total strangers, and tell them to go to confession and hurry. And he told them in such a simple, assured and earnest way that they usually did just that. Once, on a road, he met a young girl who was going to the town with evident anticipation of an evening of pleasure— but with consequences which she could not foresee. Simon, who saw them, persuaded her to turn back.

A monk of Aulne yielded to the devil and after Compline secretly left the monastery with the intention of never coming back. Simon was at Maubouge, a town many leagues away: he set out at once and meeting the monk three leagues from Aulne, got him back into the monastery in time for the Night Office.

A woman had been many years without going to confession. Simon persuaded her to go, but she pleaded that it would take her a long time to remember all her sins. Simon said that, on the contrary, with God's help, no delay would be necessary, and he forthwith told her every sin, down to the smallest, she had committed.

When, in 1215, Simon was called to Rome by Innocent III, he had many conferences with the Holy Father and even procured from God that the latter should have a vision. He was shown the saints of the Cistercian Order gathered under the mantle of Mary in Heaven. But Simon's visit to Rome was of more importance than this: for he effected a reconciliation between that Pope and our Order in certain difficulties. Besides that, he predicted the hour of the Pope's death and made certain charitable observations which the Holy Father took in good part.

By now the fame of Simon's gift was well known, and so well known that many men thought they had reason to fear him, since they believed he was likely to be motivated by their own greed, envy or love of power. A senator of Rome had certain sins on his soul and became obsessed with the notion that Simon was going to reveal them publicly to the whole Lateran Council then in session. Those who are in hell think everybody else is a devil, but Simon had never gratuitously revealed anybody's sins in public. His gift was given him for the salvation of souls, not for political or civil motives. He was not a detective. But the obsessed senator decided that Simon would have to be put out of the way. So he invited him to visit his house.

Simon was ushered into his presence. The Senator led him through one room after another of his palace, to be sure they would be quite alone. Finally Simon said: "Well, what are you waiting for?"

Turning on him in a rage the Senator roared: "What do you know about me, tell me that!"

"I know, among other things," said Simon, "that yesterday you nearly stabbed yourself, and that today you nearly jumped out of a window. Also, you have brought me here to kill me."

This was said with such a peaceful and celestial calm that the Senator broke down and eventually went to confession.

When Simon went back to Belgium after all this, he sought nothing but to return to the obscurity of his grange and his sheep. More than ever he loved to be alone and unnoticed, out of the sight of men. He returned to his favorite austerities with great joy and fervor, like Arnulph Cornibout, the lay-brother of Villers, he lay on a bed of stones, *lectulus non floridus, sed horridus*, in an atrocious pun on a phrase from the Canticle of Canticles.[6] Obviously he could not take that with him to Rome. He made a forty days' fast, in imitation of our Lord, but there was still work for him to do among souls.

For example, there was a Beguine who was persecuted by a devil who threw dust in her face and first in her food and who insulted a priest who visited her. Simon delivered her from this demon.

Yet the devils sought revenge through sinners, their instruments. For a man working for the grange got angry when Simon reproved

[6] AASS, June 7:562. Vita 3.23.

him for selling all the clothes with which the monastery provided him. In a murderous desire for revenge, this miserable man crept into Simon's cell as he slept and was just about to split his head open with an axe when something stopped him. He could not move. And as he stood with the upraised axe over the brother's bed, Simon awoke and again said calmly: "Well, what are you waiting for?" The villain fled.

In spite of many attempts on his life, Simon lived to a great age. Finally during the meridian, when he was eighty-four years old, his couch was suddenly lifted up in the air, and he was told, to his immense elation, that he would soon die. And yet all the last days of his life were spent, not in a spirit of presumptuous reliance on himself or his gifts, which he well knew came to him from no merit of his own and did not make him in the least more pleasing, of themselves, to God but in humble and loving diffidence, which filled his eyes with tears for his many sins. It was hard for him to see how he could be saved, but he died on November 6, 1228, and was immediately seen, in a vision of a monk, in the glory of heaven. And there, let us hope, he looks down upon us with solicitude for the welfare of our souls. Let us ask him to guide us all our lives in the path of God, until we come at last to share his ineffable bliss with Jesus and Mary in Heaven. He was never canonized but enjoyed veneration as a saint for many centuries.

November 16

Saint Gertrude, Nun of Helfta, Germany

(Sources: *Le Héraut de L'Amour Divin* [French translation of *Insinuationes divinae pietatis* Benedictines of Solesmes (Paris, 1877)]; Ailbe J. Luddy, *Saint Gertrude the Great: Illustrious Cistercian Mystic* [Dublin: 1930].)

In the year 1563 the famous collection of Saint Gertrude's visions, the *Legatus divinae pietatis* or *Herald of Divine Love*, was rediscovered and reedited by the Carthusian writer and theologian, Lanspergius. It was an opportune time, for the spirituality of the great thirteenth-century Cistercian was very well attuned to the devotion of the modern age. In fact, it was she who had been, together with her spiritual mother Saint Mechtilde, the first really to penetrate the depths of the mystery of the Sacred Heart of Jesus and to preach the wonders of Christ's love for us all as Man as well as God under that symbol.

The love of the divine Heart for all is indeed the theme which dominates all others in the mysticism of Saint Gertrude of Helfta, and it is this above all that makes her teaching so popular and so useful for religious and laypersons alike. Father Ailbe Luddy, a monk of our time (Mount Melleray in Ireland), has rightly said of Saint Gertrude that "of all Christian seers since the apostolic times she is undoubtedly the most consoling."[7] And this is all the more true because the contemplation of the Divine Heart filled the heart of this saint with nothing but confidence and trust. Her visions are all supremely optimistic, and her teaching exalts the mercy of God by repeated reminders to souls that they must not allow themselves to become discouraged by their faults and imperfections. The infinite tenderness of Christ will swallow up all their mistakes if they will only abandon themselves to his Love and to his Mercy.

There is nothing harsh, nothing difficult, nothing exalted, nothing terrifying about the mysticism of Saint Gertrude, and her life is not marked by any of the fantastic and extraordinary mortifications which make the average person afraid of so many of the great saints—especially in the Middle Ages. Her visions are all easy to understand, and her life is not hard to imitate, at least for a religious with a normal amount of generosity.

That is undoubtedly why she has exercised so strong an appeal over generations of religious and why her books are among the most popular in many convent libraries. And there seems to be little reason to doubt that God in his mercy selected her especially for this kind of a mission in the Church. Christ told her many times in visions of his ardent desire for the love of men, and in instructing her to write down her visions he explicitly stated that he wanted her book to serve as a means to bring souls closer to Him in confidence and love—so much so that he promised her that her

---

[7] Luddy, 15.

volume would possess almost the character of a sacramental. "If anyone would read this book for his own spiritual progress," said Jesus to Saint Gertrude, "I will draw him to me in such a way that it will be just as if I were holding the book in my hands and associating myself with him in his action."[8]

When Saint Gertrude feared that her writing was only a delusion of pride and resolved to give it up, Christ appeared to her again and told her: "You may hold it as certain that you will not leave the prison of your flesh until you have paid your debt to the last farthing!" Her visions had not been for herself alone! Far from it; they had only laid upon her shoulders a heavy obligation of transmitting Christ's message to all. She was to be the Herald, the Legate, the Ambassadress of his Divine Love. And so Our Lord added: "I wish your writings to be an irrefutable testimonial of my Divine Love in these latter days in which I plan to do good to many souls!!"[9] It was Jesus himself who desired that the title of the book should be the *Herald of Divine Love,* and indeed he declared to the saint that the book was not hers but his. He was the author: "This book, which is mine, shall be called the *Herald of Divine Love* because souls will find in it a foretaste of the superabundance of my divine Love."[10]

Saint Gertrude was born in Saxony in 1256 and entered the convent at the early age of twelve. The little community of Cisterican nuns at Helfta had only recently moved to that site, although it had been founded in 1229 at Mansfeld, Saxony. It was however a convent of Cistercian nuns in the broad sense only. The sisters more or less followed the usages of Cîteaux, but they were not officially affiliated to the Order or subject to its visitations, nor were the nuns directed by Cistercian monks. This is the explanation of the long controversy about the filiation of the convent of Helfta, which is often described as "Benedictine." The spiritual direction of the nuns was probably in the hands of Benedictine priests, but nevertheless the convent was founded from a Cistercian community, Saint James of Halberstadt. In the donation of

[8] *Héraut,* Prologue.
[9] *Héraut,* 2.10.5.
[10] *Héraut,* Prologue.

land to the nuns, when they built at Mansfeld, the community is explicitly referred to as Cistercian.[11] Other official documents in the lifetime of Saint Gertrude refer to Helfta as a convent of Cistercian nuns.

The reason why they were not openly affiliated to the Order was that in 1228 the General Chapter at Cîteaux vetoed the admission of any more convents of nuns into the Order. The capitular fathers made no objection to independent houses following the Cistercian usages, but they refused to shoulder any responsibility for these communities since there had been a tremendous increase in the number of Cistercian abbeys all over Europe and the burden was already too great.

Saint Gertrude, then, entered the convent school of the nuns at the age of twelve. She was an intelligent child with a taste for secular literature. Unfortunately, however, this taste became too absorbing. Although in itself it was harmless, or even good, it grew to such proportions and came to occupy such an inordinate place in her life that it choked the development of grace in her soul. Unconsciously, and hardly knowing how or why, the young nun soon found herself in a condition in which nothing in the spiritual life made any appeal to her. She was completely devoured by this one passion for the pleasure she found in reading the literature of the world.

Psychologically speaking, what had happened was a completely unhealthy exteriorization of her whole self. She had developed a habit of pouring herself out, wasting her energies in the pursuit of her own satisfaction. True, the satisfaction in itself was good, like all other created satisfactions, but it had become altogether inordinate, and that was what was bad. And because of this disorder her studies were no longer of true profit for her soul. Instead of advancing her in the interior life they only hindered her progress.

---

[11] *Ad sustentationem sanctimonialium Cisterciensis ordinis quae in novella plantatione nostra juxta Mansfeld collocavimus.* See P. Emil Michael, "Die hl. Mechtilde und die hl. Gertrud die Grosse Benediktinerinnen?" ZKTh, 23 (1899): 548–52. See Luddy, 33.

Our Lord allowed the process to run its course until Gertrude found herself in what is commonly known as the state of "tepidity." In other words, she had come to the point when she frankly preferred her own will and her own satisfaction to the will of God in everything except deliberate mortal sin. She was living for herself, not for God. Therefore she felt nothing but disgust for the exercise and duties that were destined rather for the glory of God than for her own satisfaction. Yet at the same time, the inexorable law of her very nature, which made it impossible for her to find satisfaction in creatures apart from God, only communicated the same disgust to everything else around her. She was utterly miserable. Perhaps she still managed to find a little sweetness in a song, in a page of poetry, but at once it turned to bitterness.

What was the next step? Mortal sin? Apostasy? By the infinite mercy of God she was preserved from both. After this trial in its acute form had lain upon her soul with a crushing weight for several months, she suddenly had a vision of Christ. It was one night after Compline. She was on her way to her couch in the dormitory when she looked up and beheld a beautiful youth, about sixteen years of age, who spoke to her these words of the Scriptures and of the Advent Liturgy: "Thy salvation will come speedily: why art thou consumed with sadness? Hast thou none to give thee counsel, seeing that sorrow hath obtained such dominion over thee? But fear not, I will save thee and deliver thee." After that, he stretched out his hand and took her hand into his as a pledge of his sincerity and said: "Thou hast been licking the earth like mine enemies endeavoring to suck out some drops of honey from amongst the thorns. Come back to me and I will inebriate thee with the torrent of my divine pleasures." [12]

As he spoke to her, there seemed to grow up between them a high and thorny hedge, and Saint Gertrude was filled with an intense desire not to be separated from Him, and yet also with a great sense of her powerlessness to get over the barrier. But once again stretching out his hand, he lifted her easily over the hedge,

[12] *Héraut*, 2.1.

and then, looking down, she saw that those hands were pierced with wounds, and she recognized her interlocutor.

In a sense her whole mysticism is contained in embryo in this first vision: the renouncement of all things for Christ, an ardent desire for his love, the sense of her own immense helplessness balanced by an unbounded confidence in the merits of his sacred passion and in the love of his Sacred Heart—all is here. But one of the other chief characteristics of her mysticism is the great profusion of her visions; Christ and his Blessed Mother and his saints were to appear to her so often and speak with her so familiarly and fill her heart with the light of so many consoling revelations that we are astounded at the sheer quantity and variety and richness of them all.

This first vision was soon followed by others, and although for a time she could not see Christ distinctly—he was visible to her as one seen in the half-light before dawn—yet he encouraged her to desire a clearer vision and to pray and work for it, and within a short time her prayers were answered.

Thus in one bound, so to speak, Saint Gertrude had passed from tepidity to the closest mystical intimacy with the Sacred Heart. Her case is unusual in the annals of spirituality, but its suddenness only emphasizes the fact that it was utterly beyond her own powers and was a pure gift of God. Indeed, in spite of the great favors she received, Saint Gertrude does not seem to have abandoned the ordinary paths of prayer. She used vocal prayers, she meditated on the Scriptures and the Fathers of the Church, and she drew much profit from the liturgy and from the sacred chant. She seems to have prepared the way for many of her revelations by ordinary affective prayer.

Indeed, one of her greatest graces came to her in answer to the devout recitation of a vocal prayer she had found in a book. The prayer asked Christ to impress his wounds on her heart, and after she had made it and was at the evening collation,[13] she suddenly

---

[13] Collation was in the early days of the Order a public spiritual reading that took place in the cloister after Vespers; see *Consuetudines* 81. In spite of the explicit regulation that the community should leave and go to Compline

received the stigmata interiorly according to the terms of the prayer.

Her other devices to please the Heart of her Spouse were all of the kind that might occur to any simple soul in religion. She tried to make every note she sang in choir an act of love for Jesus. She even applied the most elementary form of attention, called "material attention," to that end considering the music "like one who did not know it by heart and had to look at the book."[14] It is an interesting aside on the convent life of the time and one which explains the small format of the old choir books. Neither monks nor nuns had to rely on antiphonaries and graduals as we do today [mid-1940s], but they spent many of their intervals in learning the responsories and antiphons by heart. Once then, when she was attending to this practice, Saint Gertrude saw in one of her symbolic visions how every note she sang flew like an arrow to the Heart of Jesus, giving Him great delight and bringing great accidental glory to the saint whose feast it was as well as many graces to the living and the souls in Purgatory.

We have said that the keynote of her spirituality was confidence: that means also abandonment. The two must go together. If they are separated, confidence might degenerate into presumption, and abandonment might turn into a kind of fatalism. The eyes of faith showed her the greatness of God's love for her and the infinity of his power. Therefore confidence impelled her to remove all limits to her trust in his divine will, his loving and merciful Providence. She sought the slightest manifestations of the desires of Christ and gathered them up as fragments of a treasure that she made her own by putting them into effect.

---

after the end of this reading, Vacandard, with some probability, believes that there was a custom of holding a period of recreational conversation at this time (see Vacandard, 1:58, especially n. 2). The French translation of the *Herald* mentions this incident in Saint Gertrude's life as taking place in the refectory. The same chapter of the *Consuetudines* that legislates for the collation gives the prescriptions for those who are late for *biberes* or the drink that was taken in the refectory in the evening in place of supper on fast days. It may be that the nuns of Helfta had their collation and *biberes* together in the refectory.

[14] *Héraut*, 2.4.

Therefore her divine Spouse praised Saint Gertrude, speaking of her to Saint Mechtilde in the following terms: "Walking at every instant in my presence, she seeks nothing but to know what will give pleasure to my Heart. And thus, as soon as she discovers that something is my will she applies herself with all her strength to carry it out in order to return thence to find out my other desires and satisfy them without delay: and it is in this way that her whole life is consecrated to my honor and my glory."[15]

It all sounds very simple and beautiful and easy. If one could always see one's religious life in this light, how consoling it would be! However, Gertrude, like practically everybody else who has ever tried to follow the path of monastic perfection to the heights of sanctity, was given sufficient opportunities to realize her own helplessness, her weakness and imperfection. It was not every day that she saw every note she sang in choir flying like an arrow to the Heart of her Beloved. But her distractions only served her as material with which to build up her edifice of confidence in God's merciful Love. Once when she had been struggling in vain to keep her attention on the psalms before her, Our Lord, "unable to bear the sight of her unhappiness, presented her as if with his own hands his Sacred Heart like a burning lamp. 'Rely in all confidence upon this Heart,' he said, 'It will make up for all that you cannot accomplish perfectly yourself.'" And when Saint Gertrude was astonished at such a gift, Christ gave her his explanation.

He placed before her mind the example of two singers: one of them an accomplished artist who could render anything with the greatest ease, and the other a person without ear or voice or talent. How would it be if the latter were always trying to push himself forward and take the place of the good singer, when the former was eager to fill his part for him, and fill it well? "And so my Divine Heart," said Jesus in conclusion, "knowing the weakness and inconstancy of men, desires with an immense ardor that you should invite it to replace you, and carry out in your stead the things that you are completely incapable of doing yourself."[16]

[15] *Héraut*, 1.2.
[16] *Héraut*, 3.25.

The *Herald of Divine Love* is a picturesque book, full of pleasant and attractive scenes that present the mysteries of Divine Love in terms that the simplest mind can understand and reduce to practice.

Jesus teaches Saint Gertrude abandonment by comparing it to a bride and her spouse walking in a garden plucking roses. The bride is entirely engrossed (of course) in her spouse and pays little attention to the roses. She takes every flower he plucks and adds it to her bouquet simply because it is the one her Beloved has given to her. "It is the same way with the soul that has faith," Jesus said to the saint. "My will is all her joy, and she takes her delight therein as in a flower garden. If I give her health, or take her out of this life, she accepts all as one and the same thing because, being full of confidence, she relies entirely upon my goodness." [17]

These quotations are amply sufficient to show how close Saint Gertrude is to the tradition of asceticism which was handed on by the writers of the French school, particularly Saint John Eudes, to modern devotion and is represented in the mysticism of abandonment as preached by Benigna Consolata or Saint Thérèse of Lisieux, to mention but two of the most important. Directly and indirectly Saint Gertrude has done a great deal to shape the course of spirituality in the modern Church.

All that has been said about her doctrine of confidence and love springs from the one big reality of her life, the Sacred Heart of Jesus. This mystery, reserved for the latter days of the Church, when faith had begun to grow cold in the world, is the impenetrable mystery of the love of God for us all—a love that became Incarnate, lived among us, died for us on the Cross, and returns to stay in our midst in the Blessed Sacrament. It was a love that positively haunted Saint Gertrude with the refrain, "My delights are to be with the children of men." [18]

It was this tenderness that most of all absorbed her attention when she considered the Heart of Jesus—this ineffable condescension that made God desire the company and happiness of ungrateful

---

[17] *Héraut*, 3.56.
[18] *Héraut*, Prologue 8.31.

men, in spite of all their coldness and inattentiveness to Him. The contemplation of the Heart of Jesus, that is, of his infinitely perfect love for us, cannot but set off in sharp relief the discouraging spectacle of sin, but Saint Gertrude's reaction was not so much Saint Margaret Mary's burning desire to make reparation to God's outraged justice and goodness. She could only sink deeper and deeper into the abyss of humility and repay Christ's love by confidence.

The fact is Saint Gertrude was never allowed to forget while she was on earth that the work of her sanctification was not yet complete. God humbled her by leaving her some defects of character that did not go unobserved in the convent in which she lived. She was a critical kind of person, and she occasionally gave outward expression to half-voluntary movements of pride and irritation. When this fact is quoted, it tends to comfort the hearts of religious who realize in their shame how close one can sometimes come to being a pharisee in the convent or the monastery. But heaven help the monk who allows himself to make a habit of uncharitableness and rash judgment on the ground that it is not only a purification of his soul but even a sign of possible sanctity since saints have been so tempted. We sometimes forget to compare the *resistance* with which the saints strove to overcome these movements of nature with our own self-complacent negligence.

Finally, and this is one thing that is not so modern about her, Saint Gertrude's mysticism is deeply liturgical. Her visions are not, to be sure, a logical sequence of commentaries on the feasts of the liturgical year, but many of her visions find their starting point, and sometimes the lines of their full development, in the liturgical *motif* of some feast.

The religious life of Saint Gertrude, unlike that of Saint Mechtilde, did not bring her into any of the important offices in the community. Her whole mission was to be an apostle of divine love, to preach the love of the Sacred Heart, and to inflame souls with a desire to reciprocate that love. And incidentally she frequently took up arms against that false humility that would keep souls from Holy Communion and fill their hearts with a kind of cold mistrust of Christ on account of our own inevitable human weaknesses.

The last fifteen years of her life were full of suffering caused by painful sicknesses, insomnia, and other interior trials. As the time of her death approached she developed the habit of retiring into solitude and reciting the prayers for the agonizing once a week, on Fridays, and on one of these occasions Our Lord deigned to make known to her what would be the manner of her death.

This revelation inflamed her with desire for the end of her exile. As the day of her liberation approached she faced it with an ever-more ardent love, using some of the spiritual exercises which she had herself composed and which she had left for our own use.

The date of her death is not certain. The new Cistercian Menology adopts the one that is usually accepted: November 17, 1302. Her name was inserted in the Roman Martyrology in 1678, after a feast and office in her honor had been approved in 1606. Her title to sanctity was finally ratified by what is known as "equivalent canonization" in 1739. At the request of the King of Spain, Saint Gertrude was named Patroness of the West Indies.

November 19

Saint Mechtilde, Nun of Helfta, Saxony

(Sources: *Revelations de Ste. Mechtilde*, trans. from the Latin ed., see the Benedictines of Solesmes; J. M. Besse, *Les mystiques bénédictins des origines au XIIIᵉ siècle* [Paris: P. Lethielleux, 1922].)

This great mystic is somewhat better known to secular scholars than many of our saints because of the fact that she figures in a controversy over the identity of Matilda, the guardian of the Earthly Paradise in the twenty-eighth and following cantos of Dante's *Purgatory*. This is a controversy which we are not capable of settling, but a few remarks on it would not be out of place. The three chief candidates for this distinction are our own Saint Mechtilde, Matelda the Grancontessa of Tuscany, and Mechtilde of Magdeburg, another Cistercian Nun of Helfta who is often confused with Saint Mechtilde. Of these three, it would seem that the most likely is Saint Mechtilde of Hackeborn, with whom we are concerned. The gay, singing maiden of Dante's poem has much in common with the spirituality of Mechtilde, the keynote of which is divine praise. Mechtilde herself was chantress of her convent, and indeed, an accomplished singer of plain chant. Then, while the beauty and pageantry of the earthly paradise reflects in some measure the beauty and color of Mechtilde's own visions, the most striking resemblance is to be found in Mechtilde's vision on Quinquagesima Sunday,[19] in which Lent, our annual liturgical Purgatory, was presented to her as a mountain, on the different degrees of whose ascent the seven deadly sins were purified from the soul, while at the top the angels and saints were gathered around the throne of God and four rivers proceeded from beneath the throne. Dante's mountain of Purgatory, with its "circles" and the Garden of Eden at the top and the two rivers there and the Apocalyptic pageant there presented to the poet's eyes, would all seem to have been influenced by Mechtilde's *Liber Specialis Gratiae.* While Matelda the Grancontessa has in her favor the fact that the oldest traditions identify her with the guardian of the earthly paradise, she was allied to Dante's enemies. Mechtilde of Magdeburg's mysticism has much less of the character of pageantry found in these cantos of Dante, although he may well have used her revelations on hell. We can only say that Saint Mechtilde of Hackeborn seems to have exercised a strong influence on Dante at this point, and we must not make the mistake of completely identifying her with the poet's figure, who presents some traits that are more appropriate to a muse on Parnassus than to a nun and mystic—for example, the comparison of her eyes to those of Venus.

Incidentally, however, we may say that the tradition which makes Matelda the symbol of the active life is not to be taken too seriously. There is nothing in the poet's cantos that makes this at all clear.

[19] Lib. Sp. Gr. 1.13.

Mechtilde was born in 1241, a daughter of the powerful Thuringian family of the barons of Hackeborn and Wippra. When she was seven years old she was received as a pupil by the nuns of Rodersdorf, where her elder sister Gertrude of Hackeborn[20] had already taken the habit. Later the community moved to Helfta, and Mechtilde became one of the most useful members of it, especially in her capacity as chantress and mistress of plainchant. It was she, too, who received the future saint Gertrude under her care and exercised a dominant influence in the formation of that great mystic. It was Gertrude who, with another nun, finally consigned the visions of Saint Mechtilde to writing, without the latter's knowledge. Indeed, when she found out about it, Saint Mechtilde was not a little disturbed, until Christ appeared to her Himself, assuring her that it was His will that these graces be made known and, indeed, that He Himself had directly inspired and assisted the two sisters who compiled the volume.[21]

The first thing that must inevitably strike the reader of these visions, even if he has no faith, is their singular beauty and attractiveness. The *Liber Specialis Gratiae* has all the charm and simplicity that we find in the greatest mystics and leads us to suspect that Saint Mechtilde must have had many traits in common with the great Saint Thérèsa of Avila. But above all, every page is alive with color and splendid with light and sound, without ever being lavish or over-decorated.

Mechtilde at Easter attends a celestial banquet. Christ presides in a green robe, decorated with golden roses. The light of glory that streams from His face fills all the goblets and is the wine of that feast. Delighted with the soul of His Mechtilde, Christ leans down and taking her soul, holds it in His hands, where it dances for the pleasure of the sainted guests.[22]

At Mass, at the little elevation (there was no major elevation of the Host at consecration), she beheld Christ offering up His heart like a dazzling lamp filled and overflowing with liquid light that

---

[20] Cistercian Menology (no date assigned in the new menology).
[21] Lib. Sp. Gr. 5.21.
[22] Lib. Sp. Gr. 1.19.

fell in drops of fire all about it. Earnestly desiring to have her own heart "poured out" into His, she prays for this favor and finds herself swimming in the divine Heart, as she says, "like a little fish."[23]

She also saw rays of burning light streaming from the Sacred Heart into the hearts of all the members of our Order. Again, retiring to bed at night, she saw herself sleeping on that same divine breast, like a rabbit, with open eyes—according to the traditional natural history of the time.

Even more than in the mysticism of her disciple Saint Gertrude, the Sacred Heart dominates the whole spirituality of the chantress of Helfta. Following the lines laid down by the great Cistercian mystics of the Low Countries in the early thirteenth century, Saint Mechtilde is the first to give full scope and development to the devotion to the love of the Man-God for us precisely as Man. It was for later generations to follow her lead and investigate the avenues leading to reparation and victimhood with and for the Sacred Heart, but all the essentials are present in Saint Mechtilde.

In fact, one might say that no one better than Saint Mechtilde has grasped the most fundamental thing in this devotion, which is admiration, adoration and love of the boundless love of Christ for us. The greatness of this saint will become evident when we realize that she is not surpassed by the most renowned mystics in the history of the Church in her appreciation and understanding of the love of the Sacred Heart for fallen man.

Take, for example, her Easter vision, already quoted in part. In this it was revealed to her how the glorification of the Sacred Heart consisted in three things: first in the omnipotent power to lavish, as man, the fullness of His divine generosity upon the souls of men; second in the ability to know, not only as God, but by means of His human senses, all the needs and desires in the depths of the souls of His creatures; and finally, the capacity to be everywhere, wherever He wills, in His divine Humanity, with His friends. Reflection on how much it means to a human heart to be able to pour out the infinite love of God, indeed, to be the Heart of God,

---

[23] Lib. Sp. Gr. 2.21.

will give us some idea of Mechtilde's penetration of this mystery. This same note constantly recurs: Christ's triumph and glory consist in receiving, as a reward for His sufferings, the infinite power to do, as man, everything He wants to do for those Whom he loves. How much follows from this central truth. It makes even darker the shadows of man's ingratitude, but Saint Mechtilde is inspired, above all, to unlimited confidence in this love. We find fully developed in her all the familiar ideas of Christ's love making up for our deficiencies, all the groundwork for the spirituality of abandonment which is so closely connected with devotion to the Sacred Heart. We need not dwell on these things here. Our limited space belongs, rather, to Saint Mechtilde's second great characteristic: her love for the Mother of God. Mary was, as she said, her spiritual directress, and all the relations of the saint with Our Blessed Lady are characterized with an even more charming and ingenuous simplicity, if possible, than her dealings with the Sacred Heart. To choose an example at random: Mechtilde goes to Our Lady to beg forgiveness for one of her little faults, and Mary takes the good nun's chin in her hand and makes her promise never to do it again.

Saint Mechtilde's devotion to the Mother of God, like all her spirituality, was strictly liturgical. Its center was the *Ave Maria* and the votive Mass *Salve Sancta Parens*. But it is above all interesting to observe how a medieval contemplative made use of the Gregorian Chant as an aid to her prayer. There was a responsory in which occurred the words *ostende te Maria* (show thyself, O Mary!),[24] and there was a long *neum* or *jubilus* on the second syllable of the word *ostende*. This *neum* divided into nine parts, and Mechtilde used to put her whole heart into singing it, while at each part earnestly praying for the nine choirs of angels, separately and in order, to join her in urging, or rather compelling, Mary to appear to her. And, says the "Book of Special Grace," she frequently won the victory and beheld, as she sang the end of the phrase, the Mother of God being swept into the church before her by the seraphim.[25]

[24] Lib. Sp. Gr. 2.19.
[25] Lib. Sp. Gr. i, 38.

Saint Mechtilde's mysticism was not limited to the comparatively low level of imaginary visions. It culminated in perfect union
of wills with the Divine Spouse, but this union is only, can only
be, consummated in suffering—suffering, that is, for the sensible
part of our nature. But always, no matter how much she suffered,
Saint Mechtilde continued to increase in joy in proportion as she
realized that suffering was bringing her into closer and closer
union with her Beloved: and again she uses the image of a fish
swimming in the joys of God or calls her soul a bird flying in God's
joy as in its atmosphere.

In her last sickness, Saint Mechtilde was so avid of suffering for
the love of her Divine Bridegroom that she would have liked to
refuse all alleviation of her pains. But she considered it still greater
charity to sacrifice even this desire, and so, in order to please those
who were nursing her, she accepted a so-called "soothing" potion
which, however, invariably made her suffer far more intensely, so
that the grace which she desired was not denied her after all.

As Mechtilde lay dying and received Extreme Unction, Saint
Gertrude, who was present, understood how, as each part of the
saint's body was anointed, she received strength from a corresponding part of the Divine Humanity, until after a complete
mystical transformation into Him, she died in ecstasy and was
absorbed, as it were, into the eternally burning love of His Sacred
Heart.

We have spoken of the beauty of the *Liber Specialis Gratiae*, but
that is only the beginning of its worth. Like Saint Gertrude, Saint
Mechtilde is above all valuable to us because, as mystics go, she
is easy to understand and is therefore most likely to inspire souls
who fear to penetrate into the realms of speculative mysticism
with a confident desire for intimate union with God by confidence
and love. Her visions are calculated to fill minds with a clear grasp
of the fundamental mysteries of our faith and to stir up hearts to
love God in His Incarnation and in His mercies to us through His
Blessed Mother and the saints. We should also treasure them as a
vast and varied commentary on the liturgical eye of her deep and
loving devotion. Finally, like Saint Gertrude, Saint Mechtilde never
offers even a suggestion of unorthodoxy, and therefore she can

safely be placed in the hands of the most simple without fear of misinterpretation.

The Catalogue of entries for the new Cistercian Menology registers her beatification but does not give the date. Her feast, together with that of Saint Gertrude, has been proposed to the General Chapter, but the decision awaits the pending reform of the Cistercian Breviary. [Her feast is now celebrated on November 19. —Ed.]

December

December 11

Blessed David, Monk of Himerrod, Germany

(Source: Le Nain, 6:355 [based on a contemporary life by the monk Hugh of Himmerod].)

While Blessed David, a native of Florence, was a young student in France, he was attracted by the fame of the great Saint Bernard, to the monastery of Clairvaux, where he sought to make profession as a Cistercian monk. During his novitiate, however, he suffered from very poor health, as indeed he did for his whole life: for his was a weak and frail constitution. On account of his weakness and youth, the monks rejected him when the time came to vote on him for profession.

David was inconsolable. It was as if he had been expelled from Paradise. He remained in front of the gate, and would not go away. So determined did he show himself in this that Saint Bernard was moved to compassion and admiration, and re-admitted him to the novitiate, where he showed that his courage and faith amply made up for any physical weakness he had. Indeed, after his profession, in 1131, his whole religious life was to be a heroic struggle against ill health.

The burning charity which made him so determined that his weakness would not keep him from observing the whole Rule was great enough for Saint Bernard to consider him a fit member of a pioneer group which he sent into Germany at the request of the Bishop of Trier to start a new monastery in the mountain forests between the borders of France and the Rhine. After trying a site called Winterbach, the Cistercians finally settled at Himmerod. David, by dint of ceaseless and fervent prayers for strength, was able to bear a fair share in the grueling labor of building and cultivating for the new monastery, so that eventually his body was actually strengthened and hardened until he could do as much as any of the others. Such was the reward of his courageous faith.

But his intense charity and desire to give himself entirely and without reserve to the service of God according to our penitential Rule obtained for him great spiritual graces, so that he was often totally absorbed in God for hours at a time, even at work. And in the refectory he frequently had to be reminded to eat by one of his neighbors. Joy shone always in his face—a serene and peaceful joy. He always smiled but never burst out laughing, for the *risum excussum* upon which Saint Benedict frowned is not a sign of spiritual peace and happiness but merely of a vain and stupid animality that disturbs one's own interior peace and attacks that of others. David's joy was not the laughter of a fool.[1]

He guarded his senses most carefully and never looked at seculars, not that there is anything wrong with seculars. We were all seculars once. But we have ceased to be, and they do not concern us except in our prayers. What need have we to look at them? We know they need our prayers, and we will not pray for them any better by letting ourselves be distracted through an idle and useless curiosity.

He did not waste his time in trying to perform a lot of works that have nothing to do with the Cistercian vocation, and he once said: "You will do more to instruct others by your patience than you could by any words you could possibly say to them."[2] He showed how deep was his understanding of the contemplative life when he said: "We should avoid not only all idleness, but also all activities which are pointless and useless."[3] For he realized that the anxious and distracting rush of activity which some souls

---

[1] RB 4.53–54.
[2] Lenain, 373.
[3] Lenain [page not cited. —Ed.].

imagine to be useful to the community is only a nuisance to themselves and to their brethren. The true activity of a contemplative is contemplation, and all the works imposed on one by obedience become contemplation when they are performed patiently and well in a spirit of prayer and recollection for the love of God and of the brethren.

He was also well known for his miracles by which he healed the sick and delivered the possessed from the fiends that had power over them. But his faith and fervent prayers also saved the monastery of Himmerod in a time of trouble. For the nineteenth and twentieth centuries were not the first to see persecution of the Church in Germany, nor was the reformation the first sign of such a thing. In 1170 Frederick Barbarossa, who had set up an anti-pope and was tearing Europe and the Church in half with schism for his own political advantage, announced that all priests and religious who would not swear allegiance to Callistus III would have to leave the Empire. Himmerod, like most other Cistercian abbeys, refused. For the whole Cistercian Order, led by Saint Peter of Tarentaise, was fighting for the true Pope. Accordingly, the monks of Himmerod began to make arrangements to leave. Blessed David had not heard what was going on, and when he was told he urged them to throw the whole thing into the arms of God and pray, pray when they sang the antiphon of the Magnificat, which was that for the last Sunday after Pentecost: *Amen dico vobis, non praeteribit generatio haec donec omnia fiant: coelum et terra transibunt, verba autem mea non transibunt, dicit Dominu* ("Amen I say to you, this generation shall not pass away until all things be accomplished: heaven and earth shall pass away, but My Word shall not pass away, saith the Lord"). These wonderful words should be often on our lips. And when they were sung that night by the monks of Himmerod, they obtained their answer, for almost immediately a message was received from the Emperor, telling them to stay where they were and pray for the Empire.

Towards the end of his life a terrible siege of dryness and darkness was added to the trial of his sickness. Blessed David lay in the infirmary, physically near death and spiritually in the very darkness of the abyss. For he was actually frozen with horror at his sins, and it seemed impossible to him to be saved. In the night of his immense temptation to despair, he clung blindly to a faith so obscure that he could not even see it himself, let alone see anything by it. And he earnestly begged the prayers of his brethren, of the abbot, and of the infirmarian. By their prayers and by the sacrament of Extreme Unction he received such miraculous physical and spiritual relief that the next day he was out of bed, and the day after that he joined the other monks at the common work, where almost single-handedly he disposed of a large oak tree that was being dug out by the roots to clear the ground for planting.

His death occurred in 1204 on December 11, and he was soon venerated as a saint. Rightly so. There is much we can learn in his fortitude and simplicity, and let us imitate him in our infirmities and trials. What point is there in our nursing and coddling ourselves and worrying about our pains and weaknesses? Will we be any the higher in heaven for our extravagant love of comfort on this earth? Quite the contrary. Let us welcome all our infirmities as opportunities, not to be reckless, certainly, but to prove our patience and submission and love of the Rule. And let our aim be always, as was Blessed David's and that of all the great Fathers of our Order: to keep the Rule without mitigation or relief, as long as possible, and to cling jealously to that privilege as long as obedience will permit.

December 12

Blessed Ida of Nivelles, Nun of Ramege, Belgium

(Source: Manrique, vol. 4, *passim* [based on a contemporary life from which long excerpts are given.])

When the Spanish Cistercian hagiographer, Chrysostomus Henriques, selected five of the great Flemish mystics of our Order to write a book that he called *The Five Prudent Virgins,* three of them were called Ida, and two of the Idas were from the same convent: Ramege. We have read of the great Eucharistic mystic, Ida of Louvain, or Roosendael, whose memory is kept by the Cistercian Menology in the spring of the year [April 13]. In October came the second Ida, who took her name from the village of Leeuwen, and who is distinguished for her simplicity in a group of most simple saints. Finally, there is Ida of Nivelles, whom we commemorate in December, for she died on the vigil of the great virgin martyr, Saint Lucy.

Born of poor parents in the province of Brabant, Ida of Nivelles was as a little child very little indeed. So small was she that in winter she could not cross the marshy fields to her favorite church because she got embedded in the quagmires and did not have the strength to get herself out of such a great morass of Flemish mud without assistance from the peasants attracted by her piteous cries.

In 1208, when she was only nine years old, she lost her father, and her relatives, wondering what was to be done with her, decided that it was perhaps not too early to marry her off, if that would provide her with a home and sustenance. The very thought so frightened the poor little girl that she escaped from the house under cover of night, leaving by the window of her room and taking nothing with her but her psalter. There were seven poor pious women living together in a little house under the wall of a church, and it was with these that Ida sought refuge. They kindly took her in and found no cause for regret in having done so, for this modest and loving little child brought joy to them all by her pleasing manners and quiet, modest behavior. There was nothing she liked better than to go out and beg for her new friends and to beg also for the sick in the hospitals, bringing them food and wine and clothing. Her relatives made no objection to her staying there, for after all, it was one solution to the problem of her board and lodging.

In 1214 she entered the newly founded Cistercian convent of La Ramee, or Ramege. Now as we may remember from Ida of Leeuwen's exclamations in Flemish, Ramege was not a French-speaking convent, and Ida of Nivelles did not know Flemish. Yet she was able by one of those mysterious graces of the Holy Spirit, which we find so often in many mystical nuns, to understand fully, by a sort of simple intuition, all that was being said in the Flemish sermons that were preached to the sisters. And these homilies filled her with light and sweetness more than they did many nuns who not only spoke Flemish but were also a great deal more learned than Ida in the bargain. Nor was there much need of human language in a silent order, and Ida was not overcome by any particular shyness because of this difference between her and her sisters. When she saw that one of the other nuns was sad or downcast, although she could say nothing, she would go and sit down beside her and smile in her simple way and make the nun happy. But above all she loved to talk to God, with whom there are no difficulties of language. She saw his words and his language all around her, for he spoke to her, in all living and inanimate creatures, innumerable silent and peaceful and loving words of an infinite depth of tenderness that filled her heart with tranquil and unspeakable joy. What a gift is that gift of knowledge which comes to us from the Holy Spirit and which attunes the ears of our intellect to catch the voice of God speaking to us in creatures, every creature being a living and intensely meaningful word, uttered from the depth of his perfection and speaking to us of his goodness and mercy! And all these words are but one Word, which is his Son, Jesus Christ, in whom all other created words were uttered. And the significance of that Word, a significance which the whole of eternity will not be enough for us to understand, is that God loves us.

That her poverty of spirit was so great as to amount to a very horror of anything to do with avarice may be seen from the scruple she had, lest the forty pounds' dowry left her by her father, who had been engaged in a very small way in commerce, might be the product of usury. She had to be reassured that ordinary business investments are not displeasing to God, which indeed they are not if they are honest and limited to economically productive and useful projects. It is a pity that some of our modern businessmen, whose endeavors lean more towards speculation than useful production, have not some such scruples.

While she was still a novice, one of her sisters who had fallen prey to hopeless darkness, asked her to help her with her prayers. Ida took the request so seriously that she prayed as earnestly to find out if this novice was saved as she might have prayed for herself. So ardent was the fire of her fraternal charity that her soul suddenly seemed to melt like wax in the intense fire of her desire for her poor sister's salvation and peace. Then Ida, transported out of herself in the liquefaction of her whole being, saw Jesus before her, who said: "Why do you worry so much about your sister's sins? They are forgiven!" And after this gentle and indirect rebuke, through Ida, of the poor nun's lack of confidence in him, Jesus showed Ida the place that had been prepared for that sister in heaven.

Another sister asked Ida's prayers for the soul of her father, and the charitable virgin responded just as ardently to this request. In due course, while the nuns were out harvesting, Ida sat down at the rest period next to a shock of wheat-sheaves and raised up her soul in prayer for the nun's father. Then she suddenly had a vision and saw that poor soul so horribly tormented in Purgatory that Ida cried out to the Lord to afflict her instead, so ardent was her desire to see such terrible tortures come to an end. Her prayer was heard, and she was instantly struck with a violent fever that kept her on the rack in almost intolerable pain for six weeks, but the soul was delivered. She also offered herself up as a victim to obtain grace for a fallen priest who had given way to a scandalous temptation, and she suffered six months with quartan fever until he was delivered.

Such great charity and gifts of prayer made Ida much respected and loved among her sisters so that there was general grief and consternation when her death was predicted in 1218. Immediately all the nuns began to besiege heaven with their prayers, and Jesus revealed to one of them that he would for their sake leave Ida among them for several more years.

During the thirteen remaining years of her life, she was not without attacks from the devils, who appeared to her in visible form, springing up in front of her, now as a dog, now as a monkey, or some other ludicrous animal. Once she caught the devil loitering about the dormitory in the form of a scraggy old dog. Taking him by the scruff of the neck, she gave him a sound thrashing and sent him packing with a few well-aimed kicks, nor was he permitted by God to retaliate in any way for this treatment. But she had a more terrible experience with the fiends one night when she was unable to sleep. For suddenly the door of the dormitory filled with flames, like the mouth of a furnace, and in these flames stood three huge devils of the most terrifying aspect. As she shuddered at this awful spectacle, what was Ida's horror to see a soul escape out of the flames and run to seek refuge in her cell, trying to hide from the devils under the covers of her bed. Calling upon the Holy Ghost and making the sign of the Cross, Ida got rid of the devils and then prayed earnestly for this soul, perhaps that of a dying sinner, which God then assured her was saved from hell by her prayers.

The loving soul of Blessed Ida was especially devoted to the Holy Spirit, who is the eternal and uncreated love of the Father and the Son. And one Pentecost, after receiving Communion at the High Mass, she had somewhat the same difficulties as her namesake Ida of Leeuwen about concealing her exceptional graces in the refectory, so soon afterwards! Indeed, her face began to blaze with light and she made an attempt to conceal it by hiding in the sleeves of her cowl, but the light escaped all around her anyway. And then the Child Jesus, who must have found in Ramege his second Bethany (or rather Nazareth, for he seems to have stayed there continuously rather than intermittently), appeared standing before her, glorious with light and arrayed in blue. He remained in front of her, filling her with the joy of his presence, sweeter than any earthly food or conversation, as long as the reading continued; and this was her physical and spiritual banquet on that day of Pentecost.

One Christmas eve, when she was sick in the infirmary and could not go to midnight Mass, she nevertheless was transported in spirit to the church where she saw the Christ Jesus appear on the altar at the consecration. She was down in the church for the Mass of the Aurora, and the same thing happened again. Finally, at the High Mass, at which she also assisted in church, no sooner had the sacred Host been consecrated than she saw the Holy Child, as a boy of about twelve, come running down to her from the altar. And when he reached her he flung his arms around her neck and gave her a kiss.

Nor was she without her visits from the Most Blessed Virgin, whose delights are to be with the children of men;[4] for Mary also came to her with her child, the embodiment of all joy and delight, and put Him in her arms to kiss and press to her heart.

After a seven month's illness Ida saw her last Pentecost, that of 1231. From that day to Trinity Sunday she was in an almost continual ecstasy, beholding the Holy Trinity dwelling within herself. This mystery, which is the most difficult to imagine, and therefore should never be imagined (for nothing we can imagine concerning it can ever be anything but ludicrous), must surely be something most pure and perfect: for there is no simplicity more simple than that of the Three Persons in One, Who are all Truth, Being, and Perfection, living and working in their infinite activity in the very center of a soul in the state of grace. And yet this, which is and must be in itself the simplest of all mysteries, can only appear in human language and reasoning as one of the most complex and incomprehensible. The only reason we can never hope to see it by ourselves is not that it is too hard for the human mind to see but too easy. It is so simple that it is, and always will be, totally incomprehensible to men. It is so obvious that only God can see it. Strengthened by a vision that gave her some understanding of this mystery, Ida continued to suffer bravely for sinners until the following December and then went to her reward.

On the day of her burial, a boy was miraculously cured of a toothache by her intercession, and a Dominican friar was also relieved of the same trouble some time later, with the consequence that Ida of Nivelles has ever since been invoked against toothache. However, her memory was made illustrious by the cure of many other diseases and ills, as well as by all kinds of favors obtained for her clients. Let us number ourselves, henceforth, among them,

---

[4] Pr. 3; Epistle for the Feast of the Immaculate Conception.

nor fail to pray that she may obtain for us the visitation of that Holy Spirit whom she so loved because he had so filled her with the gifts of his sevenfold love, springing up within her to life everlasting.

December 25

Blessed Foulques de Marseille, Abbot of Toronet, Bishop of Toulouse

(Sources: *Gallia Christiana*, vol. 13, col. 21; Peter of Vaux de Cernay; Mandonnet.)

It is fitting to bring this volume of saints' lives to a close with an article on a great Cistercian bishop who played a large part in the foundation of one of the most important of the Mendicant Orders. Foulques de Marseille, friend, adviser and patron of Saint Dominic, and one of the latter's strongest collaborators in the struggle against the Albigensian heresy, was the one who prepared the way for the foundation of the Preachers, presided over the first experimental steps in their distinctive form of the apostolic life of teaching and preaching, and gave them all the spiritual and material assistance essential for their first foundations, which were made in his diocese. Then, with the inception and growth of the new Order, Foulques himself sinks again into the background, eclipsed by the more striking sanctity of his friend and protégé. Today he is all but forgotten. Fr. Mandonnet has done something to rescue him from oblivion.[5]

Foulques de Marseille had not always been a priest or a Cistercian. Before entering the Abbey of Grandselve, north of Toulouse, he achieved a wide reputation as a poet, or more accurately, as a troubadour. As his name indicates, he was Provençal, and the fine

---

[5] Mandonnet.

strong music of the *trobadors* was in his blood. He was a compatriot and a contemporary of Arnaut Daniel and Bertrand de Born[6] and was in great favor with Richard the Lion-Hearted of England and Alphonso of Aragon. One of his most important works was a long poem, *Las Complanchas de Beral,* written for a friend on the occasion of the death of the latter's young wife.[7]

But the life of a troubadour was not a school of religious perfection, and when Dante met Arnaut Daniel in the fierce flames of the circle of the licentious in Purgatory he did not recognize him until the soul spoke to him in Provençal: *Ieu sui Arnaut, qui plor et eau cantan,*[8] "I am Arnaut [Arnold], who weep and sing as I go."

So Foulques de Marseille needed grace from God if he were to escape those same flames. That grace came to him with the thought of death and eternity. Realizing with sudden vividness the full meaning of these "last things," he entered deeply into himself and found a soul full of weakness and confusion, wandering in a strange country where it was impossible even to fill one's stomach with the husks of swine. So he turned to his Father's house and took the habit of a Cistercian. That was in the year 1199.

It was not long after his profession that he was sent back to the sunny coastal mountains of his native Provence to become abbot of Toronet among the olive groves of the Esterel, sweet with the scent of pine and mimosa and cool with the breezes of the Mediterranean Sea. He was not, however, destined to remain in this peaceful retreat for very long. In 1205 he received his cross, which was also to be his glory. The simoniac Raymond of Rabastens was deposed from the See of Toulouse after three years of brawling and fighting in which, neglecting entirely the remains of a Christian flock which the Albigensian heresy had left him, he had studiously attended to nothing but his own temporal interests. Foulques was elected to replace him and thus took upon his shoulders the government of the most turbulent and harassed diocese in the Christian world of his time.

---

[6] Mandonnet.
[7] "Beral's Lament," See. De Visch. He was praised by Dante.
[8] Dante, *Purgatorio,* Canto 26.142.

We need only refer the reader to the article on Saint Peter of Castelnau[9] for the details of the Albigensian heresy, of which Toulouse was in effect the capital. For though Albi gave its name, fortuitously, to the Cartharist movement, the mere fact that Count Raymond of Toulouse was not only sympathetic to the heretics but in many ways a practicing believer made Toulouse its most important point of diffusion, even though the heresiarchs themselves were more firmly entrenched in small towns like Lavaur Fanjeaux.

It was on the feast of Saint Agatha, 1205, that the new bishop entered upon the wasteland that was his diocese and surveyed what had fallen to his lot. The churches were empty. He had only a few handfuls of faithful Catholics. Many of his priests had deserted him. The bulk of the population was more or less in confusion, wavering between the strong influence of the "believers" and the striking example of the asceticism of the "cathari" on the one hand and the Catholic tradition on the other. And, after all, the inborn light of reason was still there to make men instinctively react against the Manichaeism of the heretics, with their contention that the whole created cosmos was evil and that the body and all its works were unutterably filthy, that marriage was a crime, that material creation was under the inexorable sway of the devil, and had in fact been created by him, while suicide was a legitimate way of liberating the spirit from the prison of the body. But heresy is an insidious thing, and when people forgot ultimate principles of reason and were dazzled by the fervor and energy of the ascetic "cathari" and, what is more, got a taste of the strong but spurious natural mysticism that went with all this fervor and mortification, they soon could see no truth anywhere except in this ancient importation from the East.

Of course, there was always a large number of people who took advantage of the chaos to indulge their own greed and sensuality. These, like Count Raymond, generally clung to the fringe of Albigensianism—as it were "fellow travelers"—without making too open a profession of their belief.

[9] March 5.

Peter of Castelnau, as we have seen, had failed to make any impression on the heresy as Papal Legate. Foulques began by seeking every possible kind of assistance from outside his diocese, appealing frequently to Rome, where Innocent III was forming his plan to induce the General Chapter of Cîteaux to send a force of abbots and monks to preach in Languedoc. But the year 1206 brought on to the scene the ones Divine Providence had selected for the work of overcoming the Catharist and Waldensian heresies. Diego, Bishop of Osma, and the young canon Dominic from his cathedral chapter arrived at Montpellier and began their apostolic journey through Languedoc.

Foulques probably met Dominic and Diego quite soon, but at any rate we know they were together at Pamiers in 1207, where they held so successful a debate against the Waldensians that the people of the town, especially the poor, were won over to their side, and the judge, an important man of the town, and hitherto in favor of the heretics, returned to the fold of the Church.[10]

Arguments were not enough. Mandonnet reports a conversation between Bishop Foulques and an interested member of the audience after one of those successful debates against heresy. The citizen had expressed his admiration of the Catholic arguments against the heretics and agreed that the case for the Cathari completely collapsed in the face of them.

"Why, then," asked the Bishop, "do you not expel them from your country?"

"We cannot," was the reply. "We are supported by them, and we see how they are living in perfection. Our own relatives are in their number."[11]

There was one answer to this: the foundation of a religious community in the heart of the Catharist territory, which would in the first place demonstrate that Catholics also led lives of prayer and penance, and in fact, of greater perfection than the "perfect" could hope to achieve without divine grace, and which in the second place would offer accommodation and training to children of the

[10] *Historia Albigensium*, cap. 6.
[11] *Historia Albigensium*, 368.

region in the way that the colleges of the *cathari* was doing. In such institutions, the heretics gladly took in children and bred them in the asceticism of their misguided creed in order to prepare them for initiation as *cathari*. The site selected was Prouille, near Fanjeaux, between Toulouse and the Pyrenees, and there a convent of nuns was established. Now Saint Dominic had not yet formed the plan of his own new Order. From the first, in the institution of his new enterprise, he looked to the Order of Cîteaux. There is a tradition that the nuns received the Cistercian habit,[12] and in any case, the rule of Prouille was full of Cistercian elements. In fact, Mandonnet believes that Saint Dominic intended to turn the convent over, as soon as it was on a sound footing, to the Cistercian Order as a house of Cistercian nuns, since it was "already following the Cistercian observance." To quote Mandonnet:

> When Dominic arrived in Languedoc he was neither prepared to be the founder of an order nor bent upon becoming so. It is quite natural to think that from the first he considered having his religious house incorporated with the Order of Cîteaux as an abbey of women. . . . Perhaps Dominic instituted some proceedings. The year 1213, on the other hand, marked the first show of resistance by the Order of Cîteaux to the new incorporations. It soon became invincible. Perhaps for this reason Prouille was not officially recognized as a Cistercian abbey, and was not confided to the administration of these religious.[13]

It is not for us to delay in speculation as to what would have happened had the house at Prouille become Cistercian. In actual fact, it saw the birth of the Dominican nuns. What we are concerned with is Foulques' part in the foundation, which was the all-important one of confirming it by his authority and providing land and maintenance for it by the gift of the Church of Our Lady of Prouille and other benefices.

---

[12] *Historia Albigensium*, 373, note.
[13] *Historia Albigensium*, 373.

The year 1213 saw another, and far more significant, step. Saint Dominic and his companions came to Toulouse at the request of Bishop Foulques and settled there in a house provided by him and went to work for him as official diocesan preachers, according to the legislation of the Second Council of the Lateran. Foulques was one of the few bishops in Christendom who had the initiative to carry out the vitally necessary prescriptions of the council in this matter which, at that time, amounted to an altogether new experiment. As a matter of fact, it was to bear fruit in the foundation of a new Order, or a type hitherto unknown in the Church.

In 1215, Dominic and Foulques traveled to Rome in order to arrive a little before the opening of the Fourth Lateran Council and acquaint Innocent III with the complete success of the body of preachers established at Toulouse. When the council opened some of its most important decrees revolved about the work that had been undertaken by Dominic and Foulques. The tenth canon, especially, bears the impress of Foulques' hand in reiterating the decree of the previous council that a permanent body of preachers be established in each diocese drawn, if possible, from secular canons. When this turned out to be impossible, the Friars Preachers solved the problem.

That Order, as yet, did not exist. But the time was coming for its birth. It was in the following year, 1216, that the first community of the new Order came into existence. Again, the site was Toulouse, the sponsor and adviser and patron was Bishop Foulques, who made Dominic a present of the ancient Church of Saint Roman. It remained for him, in 1220, to arrange for one-sixth of the revenues of his diocese to be devoted to the support of the Friars Preachers.

By that time, of course, Toulouse had been liberated from the hands of the heretics by victorious Christian arms. To retrace our steps to the early days of trial and sorrow: in Foulques' first years as bishop, when he was alone and struggling desperately against heavy odds, he wanted to ordain some badly needed priests in the Ember Week of Lent. Unfortunately Count Raymond was present in the city, and Raymond was excommunicated; Foulques sent him a polite request to leave town for a while, so that he might hold his ordinations. In reply, Raymond sent one of his soldiers to tell Foulques to get out of the city unless he wanted to lose his life. But the bishop was not to be intimidated:

> The Count of Toulouse did not make me Bishop, nor was I ordained here by him or for him. I was elected by the humility of the Church, not placed in my position by the violence of a prince, and I shall not leave it on his account. Let him come if he dares, I am ready for the sword and ready to go to glory by the chalice of this passion. Let the tyrant get his soldiers, arm himself and come: he shall find me unarmed and alone. I await my crown of victory. I am not afraid of anything men can do.

In his journeys to seek help against the enemies of the Church, Foulques went as far afield as Flanders, and there he found a powerful army of allies who were prepared to fight, not armed, with the word of the Gospel, like Saint Dominic, still less with the material arms of the Crusaders that were marching against the Albigensians, but with the arms of prayer and sacrifice in obscure Cistercian cloisters and hermitages and contemplative retreats. In 1213, Foulques was taken by his friend, the learned future Dominican, Jacques de Vitry, to visit Saint Lutgarde at Aywieres, and through him he also met Blessed Mary of Oignies. So profound was the impression made upon Foulques by these chosen souls, and so keen was his insight into the tremendous power of their sufferings and penances, in obscurity and desolation of the spirit, that he urged Jacques de Vitry to write the biography of Mary of Oignies, which is one of the masterpieces of thirteenth-century mystical literature.

Although history is almost completely silent concerning the deep interior life of Bishop Foulques, there is evidence that he also was favored with mystical graces from God, and the Holy Spirit was seen hovering over him in the form of a blazing dove, communicating some of its own visible radiance to Foulques himself.

This holy and courageous soldier of Christ went to his reward on Christmas day, 1231, and was buried in the abbey church of Grandselve, where he had made his profession as a Cistercian monk and where he was venerated as a saint.

Sources

Acta Sanctorum (Antwerp, Paris, Brussels, 1643–).

Bernard of Clairvaux, *Vita sancti Malachiae episcopi*.

Alban Butler, *Butler's Lives of the Saints*, ed. Herbert J. Thurston (New York: Kennedy, 1956).

Caesar of Heisterbach, *Dialogus Miracolorum*.

Joseph-Marie Canivez, *L'Ordre de Cîteaux en belgique des origines (1132) au XXme siècle: aperçu d'histoire monastique* (Forges lez-Chimay, Belgium: Scourmont, 1926).

Joseph-Marie Canivez, ed., *Statuta capitulorum generalium Ordinis Cisterciensis* (Louvain, 1933).

Claudii Chalemot, *Series sanctorum [et] beatorum ac illustri virorum sacri ord. Cisterciensis* (Paris, 1670).

M. F. Chuzel, *Histoire de l'Abbaye de Bonnevaux de l'Ordre de Cîteaux au diocese de Vienne* (Bourgoin, France: Paillet, 1932).

Compendium of the History of the Cistercian Order, by a monk of the Cistercian Order (Trappist, KY, 1944).

Conrad of Eberbach, *Exordium magnum cisterciense*.

John Dobres Dalgairns, *Life of Saint Stephen Harding, Abbot of Cîteaux and Founder of the Cistercian Order* (Westminster: Newman, 1898).

Anselme Dimier, *La Vita Hugonis*, Coll 6 (1939): 214–18.

Philippe Guignard, *Consuetudines* (Dijon: Imprimerie Darantiere, 1878).

Crisóstomo Henríquez [Henriques], *Fasciculus Sanctorum Cisterciensium*, (Brussels, 1623).

Crisóstomo Henríquez [Henriques], *Menologium Cisterciense* (Antwerp, 1630; Westmalle, 1952).

Hugues, *Annales De L'Abbaye D'Aiguebelle De L'Ordre De Citeaux* (1863).

Leopoldus Janauscheks, *Originum Cisterciensium*, vol 1 (Vindobonae: Hoelder, 1877).

Pierre Le Nain, *Essai de l'histoire de l'ordre de Cîteaux*, vol. 2 (Paris: Muguet, 1696–97).

Les Petitis Bollandistes [http://www.salve-regina.com/salve/Les_petits _Bollandistes,_vie_des_saints].

Ailbe J. Luddy, *Life and Teaching of Saint Bernard* (Dublin: Gill, 1950).

Ailbe J. Luddy, *Life of Saint Malachy* (Dublin: Gill, 1930).

Pierre Mandonnet, *St. Dominic and His Work,* trans. Mary Benedicta Larkin, O. (St. Louis, Mo., and London: Herder, 1944).

Ángel Manrique, *Cisterciensium seu verius Ecclesisticorum Annalium a condito Cistercio* (Lyon, 1642-1659), vols. 1 and 2 *passim*.

Edmond Martène, *Thesaurus novus anecdotorum* (Paris, 1717).

Éduard de Moreau, *L'Abbaye de Villers-en-Brabant aux XIIe et XIIIe siècles: etudes d'histoire religieuse et économique, suivie d'une notice archéologique pare R. Maere* (Brussels: Dewit, 1909).

Elphège Vacandard, *Vie de saint Bernard, abbé de Clairvaux* (Paris: Victor Lecoffre, 1895).

John Henry Newman, et al., *Lives of the English Saints,* 5 vols. (London, 1901).

H. Nimal, *Villers et Aulne* (Liege, 1896).

Peter of Vaux de Cernay: *Historia Albigensium;* PL 213:543–711.

Théophile Plogaerts, *L'Abbaye de Florival*, vol 3 of *Moniales cisterciennes dans l'ancien roman-pays du Brabant* (Brussels, 1925).

Laurentius Surius, in *De Probatis Sanctorum Historiis* (Coloniae: Agrippinae, 1570–1575).

William of Saint Thierry, *Sancti Bernardi vita prima*.